Work and Labor in Early America

Edited by Stephen Innes

Work and Labor in Early America

Published for the Institute of

Early American History and Culture

by the University of North Carolina Press,

Chapel Hill and London

The Institute of Early American History
and Culture is sponsored jointly by
The College of William and Mary
and The Colonial Williamsburg Foundation.
© 1988 The University of North Carolina Press
The paper in this book meets the guidelines for
permanence and durability of the Committee on
Production Guidelines for Book Longevity of the
Council on Library Resources.
Printed in the United States of America
92 91 90   5 4 3 2
Library of Congress Cataloging in Publication Data
Work and labor in early America.
Includes index.
1. Labor and laboring classes—United States—History.
2. United States—Economic conditions—To 1865.
3. United States—Social conditions—To 1865. I. Innes,
Stephen. II. Institute of Early American History and
Culture (Williamsburg, Va.)
HD8070.W67   1988   331'.0973   87-38088
ISBN 0-8078-1798-8
ISBN 0-8078-4236-2 (pbk.)

For Stan Katz, mentor and friend

Acknowledgments

The editor wishes to acknowledge his debt to the contributors to this volume and to the many other kind friends who commented on the introduction. Special thanks for particularly helpful readings go to W. W. Abbot, Joyce Appleby, Edward Ayers, Tico Braun, Janette Greenwood, James Henretta, Melvyn Leffler, Pauline Maier, Jackson Turner Main, Mary Beth Norton, Thomas Slaughter, Winifred Rothenberg, William Taylor, Mark Thomas, and Olivier Zunz. Much gratitude for their careful copy-editing of a very difficult manuscript goes to Gil Kelly and Charles Campbell. Deepest thanks to Kathleen Miller, Lottie McCauley, Bonnie Blackwell, and Ella Wood for their efficiency—and forbearance—in preparing the manuscript for publication. Finally, without the superb editorial efforts of Philip D. Morgan and the late Stephen Botein, Editors at the Institute, this collection would not have come to fruition.

Contents

Work and Labor in Early America

Stephen Innes

Fulfilling John Smith's Vision
Work and Labor in Early America

AFTER SURVEYING the breathtaking but untamed New World landscape in 1614, Captain John Smith remarked that it lacked but "the long labour and diligence of industrious people and Art." For Smith, the trilogy of work, industry, and enterprise promised to make British North America the equal of "any of those famous King-domes, in all commodities, pleasures, and conditions." In particular, he held out the hope that the New World would serve as a haven for the struggling laborers, tradesmen, and small producers of Stuart England. In his "note for men that have great spirits, and smal meanes," the captain declared his wish to "finde imployment for those that are idle, because they know not [where to find work]." Smith asked rhetorically: "Who can desire more content, that hath small meanes; or but only his merit to advance his fortune, then to tread, and plant that ground hee hath purchased by the hazard of his life? If he have but the taste of virtue, and magnanimitie, what to such a minde can bee more pleasant, then planting and building a foundation for his Posteritie, gotte from the rude earth, by Gods blessing and his owne industrie . . . ?" It was Smith's passionate belief that, in the New World, "every man may be master and owner of his owne labour and land; or the greatest part in a small time."[1]

Few questions were so compelling to Englishmen in the early modern era as the ownership of one's "owne labour." Christopher Hill has pointed to the growing disrepute of wage labor during the early seventeenth century. If, in an era of declining real wages, such work led only to poverty and dependency, then only men and women who controlled their own labor could be regarded as free. To lose control over one's labor, as Keith Thomas has shown, was "to surren-

---

1. John Smith, *A Description of New England* . . . (1616), in Philip L. Barbour, ed., *The Complete Works of Captain John Smith (1580–1631)*, 3 vols. (Chapel Hill, N.C., 1986), I, 332, 333, 343.

der one's independence, security, liberty, one's birthright." Not even the radical Leveller Gerrard Winstanley favored granting the franchise to wage laborers. The Fox in Edmund Spenser's *Mother Hubbard's Tale* rejected wage labor by asking, "Why should he that is at liberty Make himself bond?"[2]

But the prospects of controlling one's own labor, as a waged worker, craftsman, or husbandman, appeared to be growing more precarious in the early seventeenth century. The rich outpouring of scholarship on late Elizabethan and early Stuart England has left little doubt that the period from 1590 to 1650 witnessed a succession of some of the worst employment crises ever experienced by the British Isles. Earlier improvements in diet had spurred a dramatic growth in the laboring-age population, which by the 1590s had begun to outstrip the supply of both food and work. A series of bad harvests, together with textile depressions, enclosures, estate consolidations, rising prices, and falling wages, brought hardship to laborers and small producers alike. The rise in commercialized agriculture, with its resort to larger holdings and economies of scale, eventually produced sufficient long-term gains in efficiency by 1660 to enable England to feed most of its population; but in the short run it was devastating. Laborers, cottagers, and craftsmen whose wages had earlier allowed them to keep their families above the subsistence level could no longer do so. The result was the infamous era of Hugh Make-Shift, with its proliferation of masterless men, vagrants, beggars, drunkenness, and criminality.[3] By some estimates, unemploy-

2. Christopher Hill, "Pottage for Freeborn Englishmen: Attitudes to Wage-Labour," in Hill, *Change and Continuity in Seventeenth-Century England* (London, 1974), 219–238; Keith Thomas, "Work and Leisure in Pre-Industrial Society," *Past and Present*, no. 29 (Dec. 1964), 63. The quotation from Spenser is cited by Thomas.

3. See, especially, E. A. Wrigley and R. S. Schofield, *The Population History of England, 1541–1871: A Reconstruction* (Cambridge, Mass., 1981); Keith Wrightson, *English Society, 1580–1680* (New Brunswick, N.J., 1982), 121–148; William Hunt, *The Puritan Moment: The Coming of Revolution in an English County* (Cambridge, Mass., 1983), 3–84; Margaret Spufford, *Contrasting Communities: English Villagers in the Sixteenth and Seventeenth Centuries* (Cambridge, 1974), 3–167; B. E. Supple, *Commercial Crisis and Change in England, 1600–1642: A Study in the Instability of a Mercantile Economy* (Cambridge, 1959). In his analysis of the extraordinary rise in emigration to America from the British Isles on the eve of the Revolution, Bernard Bailyn makes an argument for the 18th century strikingly similar to the one offered here for the 17th. He points out that "not only was the demand for labor powerful in the expanding middle colonies and in the Chesapeake region, but the supply was potentially plentiful in the chronically underemployed population of London and in the many areas of the British provinces, north and south of the Scottish border, where 'declivities' in the upward slope of the British economy

ment and underemployment had brought nearly one-quarter of England's laboring population to the edge of starvation. Peter Bowden believes that the decades of extreme hardship from 1620 to 1650 "were probably among the most terrible years through which the country has ever passed." Margaret Spufford has found that in Cambridgeshire the real value of the wages of agricultural laborers stood at its lowest point by the second decade of the seventeenth century, only 44 percent of its fifteenth-century level. D. C. Coleman estimates that "in Stuart England between a quarter and a half of the entire population were chronically below what contemporaries regarded as the official poverty line." Skilled artisans and the yeomanry did not belong to this group, "but it undoubtedly included the majority of both unskilled and semiskilled working class[es]: cottagers and laborers, agricultural and industrial, the poor weaver as well as the poor husbandman." From the vantage point of the twentieth century, it may be possible to view this crisis as but the earliest cycle of the "creative destruction" Joseph Schumpeter found inherent in capitalism; but for those living through it, the very disintegration of the social order seemed at hand.[4]

Remedies for this crisis, as John Smith's vision makes clear, centered on the problem of unemployment. Such a focus was inevitable, given prevailing conceptions of political economy. Seventeenth-century economic theorists generally defined a healthy economy by the level of employment, not the level of productivity. The extent of "full" employment, not comparative advantage in the allocation of capital, served as the measure of productive efficiency. Prosperity was equated with the amount of spending necessary for full employment, not with capital accumulation and investment. For those concerned with public policy, if not for individual entrepreneurs, profit was calculated by net spending on labor, not by returns in productivity.[5] An employment crisis produced an economic crisis, not the

---

created the kind of misery and fear that impels people to search for radical solutions" (*Voyagers to the West: A Passage in the Peopling of America on the Eve of the Revolution* [New York, 1986], 296).

4. Peter Bowden, "Agricultural Prices, Farm Profits, and Rents," in Joan Thirsk, ed., *The Agrarian History of England and Wales*, IV, *1500–1640*, (London, 1967), 621; Spufford, *Contrasting Communities*, 48; D. C. Coleman, "Labour in the English Economy of the Seventeenth Century," *Economic History Review*, 2d Ser., VIII (1956), 283–284; Joseph A. Schumpeter, *The Theory of Economic Development: An Enquiry into Profits, Capital, Credit, Interest, and the Business Cycle*, trans. Redvers Opie (Cambridge, Mass., 1949), chap. 4.

5. J. E. Crowley, *This Sheba, Self: The Conceptualization of Economic Life in Eighteenth-Century America* (Baltimore, 1974), 37–38.

other way around. Work, in this mercantilist world—like bullion, like wealth generally—was still usually seen in zero-sum terms. It was not expandable; the more for some, the less for others. It is here that we find the logic for restrictions against bi-occupationalism and early entry of apprentices in the regulatory legislation of Tudor England.[6] Even those Englishmen who were beginning to embrace a more dynamic and expansionary interpretation of jobs-creation, the "projectors" described by Joan Thirsk, remained wedded to the equation of employment with prosperity. The risk-oriented merchant-entrepreneurs who were creating new industrial and business enterprises in Caroline England measured the success of their schemes "only by the amount of work they created."[7]

Unemployment, accordingly, served as one of the principal rationales for the colonial effort. Imperial propagandists (such as the Hakluyts) and Puritan advocates of colonization (such as John White) alike portrayed America as a haven for England's surplus laborers. A telling stanza from the Puritan epic poem, *Good News from New-England*, invited the distressed English wage laborers to seek their fortune in Massachusetts:

> New rais'd from sleepe, another cries,
> my earnings are but small,
> I'le venter to this new-found world,
> and make amends for all.[8]

James Horn has concluded from his examination of servant emigration: "One of the most common factors that uprooted people was lack of work. In town and countryside alike, lack of work forced the young especially to move from place to place in search of opportunity." Those emigrants to the Chesapeake, in particular, "were part of a general movement of people who migrated to cities and ports such as Bristol, London, and Liverpool in the expectation of finding work." Likewise, during the eighteenth century, as Bernard Bailyn has emphasized, "a large part of the British migration to America

6. Edmund S. Morgan, *American Slavery, American Freedom: The Ordeal of Colonial Virginia* (New York, 1975), 65–66.

7. Joan Thirsk, *Economic Policy and Projects: The Development of a Consumer Society in Early Modern England* (Oxford, 1978), 3, 18. The most trenchant discussion of the relationship between economic theory and public policy in 17th-century England is found in Joyce Oldham Appleby, *Economic Thought and Ideology in Seventeenth-Century England* (Princeton, N.J., 1978).

8. [William Wood?], *Good News from New-England* (1648), in Massachusetts Historical Society, *Collections*, 4th Ser., I (Boston, 1852), 197.

was the movement of a labor force, working people seeking some kind of economic security and a more promising way of life."[9]

These migrants, in both the seventeenth and eighteenth centuries, were overwhelmingly the men and women of "small meanes" for whom John Smith had singled out America as a haven. Not the most destitute poor from the back alleys of London and not the rural paupers living on public relief, and very rarely those at the gentry level or above, the migrants were instead struggling artisans, textile operatives, agricultural workers, day laborers, and domestics as well as displaced tenants and farm families from the provinces. During the seventeenth century, the flow of migration was cut in two main channels: a brief but substantial exodus of middling farming families, tradesmen, and textile workers from East Anglia, animated by Puritan ideals and bound for New England; and a much larger migration of generally youthful, unskilled males from the southeastern portions of England. Some 155,000 immigrants from England, Ireland, and Scotland arrived in the mainland colonies before 1700; the majority of these were indentured servants. Between 80 and 90 percent of the total white arrivals in the Chesapeake came as servants. Estimates suggest that, overall, some 350,000–375,000 white servants were imported into colonial British America between 1580 and 1775 —nearly two-thirds of all the whites who came to the colonies from Britain and Europe during this period.[10]

9. James Horn, "Servant Emigration to the Chesapeake in the Seventeenth Century," in Thad W. Tate and David L. Ammerman, eds., *The Chesapeake in the Seventeenth Century: Essays on Anglo-American Society* (Chapel Hill, N.C., 1979), 94–95; Bailyn, *Voyagers to the West*, 243. Even more than does Horn, Bailyn calls attention to the centrality of London in this "dual migration," asserting that throughout the colonial period, the city was "the main source of recruitment for the American work force." Bailyn goes on to point out that London "was not simply in itself an independent source of manpower for the colonies; it was also a selective conduit through which a particularly mobile part of the entire British and Irish work force was enabled to move westward to America." *Voyagers to the West*, 273–274, 276.

10. Bailyn, *Voyagers to the West*, 26; Bailyn, *The Peopling of British North America: An Introduction* (New York, 1986), 9, 16, 60–61; Henry A. Gemery, "Emigration from the British Isles to the New World, 1630–1700: Inferences from Colonial Populations," *Research in Economic History*, V (1980), 179–231; Gemery, "European Emigration to North America, 1700–1820: Numbers and Quasi-Numbers," *Perspectives in American History*, New Ser., I (1984), 283–342; Richard S. Dunn, "Servants and Slaves: The Recruitment and Employment of Labor," in Jack P. Greene and J. R. Pole, eds., *Colonial British America: Essays in the New History of the Early Modern Era* (Baltimore, 1984), 158; John J. McCusker and Russell R. Menard, *The Economy of British America, 1607–1789* (Chapel Hill, N.C., 1985), 242.

The eighteenth-century servants were drawn in much greater numbers from Scotland, Protestant Ireland, northern England, the Palatinate, and the Swiss principalities. Most of these were destined for the colonies between New York and North Carolina. Pennsylvania, in particular, became a magnet for German-speaking emigrants, who flocked to the colony by the tens of thousands. While most of the non-English tended to travel as families, substantial—and rising—numbers of young males from London and the home counties continued to pour into America. Bernard Bailyn's evaluation of English migration from 1760 until 1775 reveals that fully 83.8 percent of the English emigrants were males. Likewise, as many as nine of every ten English artisans arrived under bond of indenture.[11]

From the beginning of the colonial period, the prevailing labor market in the individual colonies was the central mechanism governing immigration patterns.[12] After the early dominance of the West Indies, the tobacco colonies of the Chesapeake absorbed most of the later-arriving white servants. By the eighteenth century, with the rise of plantation slavery in the West Indies and South Carolina and the continued high rate of natural population growth in New England forestalling significant servant migration to those regions, the central colonies absorbed most of the flow. Crop diversification, the expansion of iron-processing mills, and the continued boom in housing construction and shipbuilding resulted in especially acute demands for both skilled and unskilled labor in the colonies of Maryland, Pennsylvania, and Virginia. Bailyn's analysis of the British Treasury's emigration register for the months from December 1773 until March 1775 reveals that 87.8 percent of the indentured servants among the emigrants traveled to the three colonies of Maryland, Pennsylvania, and Virginia; somewhat startlingly, more than half of all the indentured servants went to the single colony of Maryland.[13]

Bailyn's study also reveals that the colonial period ended as it began—with a massive burst of immigration, most of which was composed of unfree laborers. During the fifteen years between the end of the Seven Years' War and the Revolution, some 125,000 people left the British Isles for America. These numbers included 55,000 Protestant Irish, 40,000 Scots, and some 30,000 Englishmen. In addition, some 12,000 immigrants from the German and Swiss principalities

11. Bailyn, *Voyagers to the West*, 112, 176; Bailyn, *Peopling of British North America*, 16.

12. David W. Galenson, *White Servitude in Colonial America: An Economic Analysis* (Cambridge, 1981), 174; Dunn, "Servants and Slaves," in Greene and Pole, eds., *Colonial British America*, 159.

13. Bailyn, *Voyagers to the West*, 210.

entered the port of Philadelphia during this period, and some 84,500 enslaved Africans arrived in the southern colonies. Some 15,000 new arrivals each year disembarked in ports from New York to Charles Town. As Bailyn points out, the grand total of 221,500 migrants constituted "almost 10% of the entire estimated population of British North America in 1775."[14]

In a pattern strikingly similar to John Smith's vision, Bailyn finds two distinct groups among the pre-Revolutionary migrants: a metropolitan pattern, consisting of impecunious and youthful artisans from London and the home counties, almost always arriving as indentured servants; and a provincial pattern, composed of families drawn from the Scottish Highlands, West Lowland textile centers, and northern agricultural areas such as Yorkshire, approximately 40 percent of whom arrived under bond of servitude. While the metropolitan migrants overwhelmingly concentrated in Maryland, Pennsylvania, and Virginia, the provincials headed instead for North Carolina and New York. Bailyn emphasizes that "the migration was not a general milling and thronging of people from Britain to America," but, rather, "discrete and patterned movements of people: a work force to the central colonies; a social movement of substantial families to New York, North Carolina, and Nova Scotia."[15]

As the distinction between metropolitan and provincial migrants suggests, while indentured servants ventured to America in search of work (and, eventually, land), small producers and lesser gentry came in search of a more fruitful vineyard. At the beginning, John Smith's linkage of control of both one's land and one's labor was an attempt to speak to the aspirations of these latter groups. And such appeals had their effect. Even a man so fired by religious zeal as was Massachusetts governor John Winthrop could cast his arguments for colonization in terms of the higher potential returns on labor effort. On the eve of his departure, Winthrop asked rhetorically, "Why then should we stand striving here for places of habitation etc. (many men spending as much labour and coste to recover or keepe sometimes an acre or twoe of Land, as would procure them many [hundred] as good or better in another Countrie [America]) and in the meane time suffer a whole Continent as fruitfull and convenient for the use of man to lie waste without any improvement?" In the same vein, Salem's Francis Higginson lamented to his former neighbors in Leicester, England, "Great pity it is to see so much good ground for corn and for grass as any is under the heavens, to lie altogether

14. *Ibid.*, 26.
15. *Ibid.*, 202–203, 228.

unoccupied, when so many honest men and their families in old England through the populousness thereof do make very hard shift to live one by the other."[16]

In economic terms, what both men were saying was that increasing population in England had produced diminished returns on both labor and capital investments. As labor-land ratios increased, both average and marginal returns to labor effort fell to progressively lower levels. In America, as John Smith had foreseen, these ratios would reverse themselves.

If colonization represented a search for work to some and for better working conditions to others, it represented a search for workers—particularly unfree ones—to still others. Such extremely labor-intensive crops as tobacco and sugar produced in the New World a voracious demand for bonded laborers throughout the colonial period. By some estimates, up to three-quarters of all the migrants to the British colonies performed a stint of unfree labor upon their arrival—most Africans, of course, for life. In addition to the white servants, there were growing numbers of convicts, vagrants, and war captives who were transported during the years 1607–1775, including rebellious Scots, royalists, Quakers, Monmouth Rebels, and Jacobites. Between the years 1718 and 1775, some 50,000 convicted felons were transported to America to serve out terms of service ranging from seven to fourteen years. But the most important source of unfree labor, by a considerable margin, was slavery. During the colonial period, as many as 1,800,000 slaves were brought to British America, concentrating overwhelmingly in the West Indies, the Chesapeake region, and the Carolina-Georgia lowcountry.[17] Their presence in America represented the most conspicuous denial of John Smith's vision of a world where all would receive the fruits of their labor.

THE *mentalité* of those migrants who came to America voluntarily has been a topic of longstanding and lively debate. A particular point at issue is the centrality of material incentives. Perhaps the most powerful school of thought, although never unchallenged, holds

16. Samuel Eliot Morison *et al.*, eds., *The Winthrop Papers, 1498–1649*, 5 vols. to date (Boston, 1929–), II, 138–139, hereafter cited as *Winthrop Papers*; "The Rev. Francis Higginson to His Friends at Leicester, September 1629," in Everett Emerson, ed., *Letters from New England: The Massachusetts Bay Colony, 1629–1638* (Amherst, Mass., 1976), 36–37.

17. Marcus Rediker, " 'Good Hands, Stout Hearts, and Fast Feet': The History and Culture of Working People in Early America," *Labour / Le travailleur*, X (1982), 129; Dunn, "Servants and Slaves," in Greene and Pole, eds., *Colonial British America*, 159; Bailyn, *Voyagers to the West*, 294.

up an ethic of antiacquisitiveness, mutuality, and reciprocity as the dominant value system of most early Americans.[18] One of the most influential of the many modern community studies refers to a "peasant ethic of mutual interdependence" in seventeenth-century Massachusetts and alludes to the "social realities of late seventeenth-century western culture—a culture in which a subsistence, peasant-based economy was being subverted by mercantile capitalism."[19]

But the subsistence-peasant portrayal of the first settlers departs noticeably from the conclusions of most earlier commentators, many of whom had little in common otherwise. John Smith, at the outset, had few doubts about the matter of incentives. Men and women could be induced to abandon home, hearth, and the familiar web of local connections only through the promise of material rewards. In his proposal for a commonwealth of farmers and fishermen in New England, Smith asserted: "I am not so simple, to thinke, that ever any other motive then wealth, will ever erect there a Commonweale; or draw companie from their ease and humours at home, to stay in New England to effect my purposes." In Smith's view, without sufficient material incentives, the entire colonial enterprise would fail. In *Advertisements for the Unexperienced Planters of New England* (1631), his last published work, Smith wrote that "hee is double mad that will leave his friends, meanes, and freedome in England, to be worse there [in America] than here."[20] In the most evocative expression of this view, Smith asked, What person with "judgement, courage, and any industrie or qualitie [of] understanding, [would] leave his Countrie, his hopes at home, his certaine estate, his friends, pleasures, libertie, and the preferment sweete England doth afford to all degrees [of people], were it not to advance his fortunes by injoying his deserts?"[21]

As an experienced seafaring man, John Smith knew that the dreaded ocean alone demanded strong incentives for undertaking its crossing. For Englishmen in the early modern era (not surprisingly for an island nation bounded in part by such dangerous waters

18. Still the most succinct and influential statement of this position is James A. Henretta, "Families and Farms: *Mentalité* in Pre-Industrial America," *William and Mary Quarterly*, 3d Ser., XXXV (1978), 3–32. One of the most penetrating critiques of Henretta's position is found in T. H. Breen, "Back to Sweat and Toil: Suggestions for the Study of Agricultural Work in Early America," *Pennsylvania History*, XLIX (1982), 241–258.

19. Paul Boyer and Stephen Nissenbaum, *Salem Possessed: The Social Origins of Witchcraft* (Cambridge, Mass., 1974), 178.

20. Barbour, ed., *Works of John Smith*, I, 346, III, 287.

21. *Ibid.*, I, 349.

as the Irish and North seas), the Atlantic voyage was a fearfully daunting enterprise. The popularity of Shakespeare's *Tempest* was no doubt partly attributable to a wide preoccupation with the perils of transatlantic travel. Peter Carroll finds that metaphors of the malevolence of the ocean flourished throughout Elizabethan literature. The Atlantic crossing was "extremely terrifying to men who had lived their lives entirely on land." A couplet from *Good News from New-England* declared flatly:

> Nine hundred leagues of roaring seas
> [will] dishearten feeble parts.

Those who crossed these "roaring seas," even the most devout New England Puritans, afterward recalled the passage as one of the most dramatic acts of their life. John Smith, like other promoters of colonization, held that the ocean crossing would act as a filter, drawing from the Old World its toughest, most resolute, most unillusioned, most risk-oriented inhabitants.[22]

Subsequent commentators as dissimilar as Adam Smith and Karl Marx have subscribed to John Smith's view. Both Smith and Marx placed heavy emphasis on the character and work habits of the early colonists. Both men regarded the economic growth of British America as extraordinary, and both found an explanation for it in the potent combination of an advanced people in an undeveloped land. On the eve of the American Revolution, Adam Smith wrote that the colony of a "civilized nation"—a nation of entrepreneurial inhabitants—"which takes possession, either of a waste country, or of one so thinly inhabited, that the natives easily give place to the new settlers, advances more rapidly to wealth and greatness than any other human society."[23] Marx, in *The German Ideology*, likewise characterized the colonists as the most avant-garde members of an avant-garde nation. Societies such as North America "begin in an already advanced historical epoch, [and] their development [accordingly] proceeds very rapidly. Such countries have no other natural premises than the individuals, who settled there and were led to do so because the forms of intercourse of the old countries did not corre-

22. Peter N. Carroll, *Puritanism and the Wilderness: The Intellectual Significance of the New England Frontier, 1629–1700* (London, 1969), 32–33; [Wood?], *Good News from New-England*, MHS, *Colls.*, 4th Ser., I (1852), 198; Patricia Caldwell, *The Puritan Conversion Narrative: The Beginnings of American Expression* (Cambridge, 1983), 119–134; Barbour, ed., *Works of John Smith*, I, 343.

23. Adam Smith, *An Inquiry into the Nature and Causes of the Wealth of Nations* (1776), ed. R. H. Campbell *et al.* (Oxford, 1976), II, 564, cited in McCusker and Menard, *The Economy of British America*, 5.

spond to their wants. Thus they begin with the most advanced individuals of the old countries, and therefore with the correspondingly most advanced form of intercourse, before this form of intercourse has been able to establish itself in the old countries."[24]

Several historians have entered objections to subsistence-oriented portrayals of the colonists in language strikingly reminiscent of that used by John Smith. In John J. McCusker's view, "men and women who chose to abandon home, family, and friends in England, to travel three thousand miles in appalling conditions, and to sell their lives for a period of indentured servitude seem [to be] easily characterized as interested in self-aggrandizement." For McCusker, "The planters of colonial Virginia were utility maximizers par excellence." Likewise, Bernard Bailyn characterizes the early migrants as "underemployed, frustrated, fearful, but still enterprising young artisans, journeymen and casually employed workers." He believes that they were "being lured, not driven overseas, by their own ambitions, plans, and expectations."[25] Making allowances for variations in the importance of material incentives among the British colonies, the essays in this collection lend support to these characterizations.

Rewards there had to be for those who took the risks of colonization, but—for John Smith, at least—these could only come "by labour." The captain had learned firsthand in Virginia the deadly price paid by following after the Spanish and Portuguese in choosing a public policy that emphasized raw exploitation over economic development. Not surprisingly for a Protestant Englishman, he reserved his greatest indignation for those who sought riches without effort, wealth without labor. Smith's description of the first (and fruitless) North American gold rush is one of the most memorable passages in his *Generall Historie*. "Golden promises," he laments, "made all men their slaves in hope of recompences." There was, reports the captain, "no talke, no hope, no worke, but dig gold, wash gold, refine gold, loade gold, such a bruit of gold, that one mad fellow desired to be buried in the sands [in order that the sand would] make gold of his bones."[26] Smith implored the Virginia Company to send only those willing and capable of working for their just "deserts." New World settlements, he declared, needed "neither more Masters, Gen-

24. Karl Marx, *The German Ideology*, in Eugene Kamenka, ed., *The Portable Karl Marx* (New York, 1983), 191.

25. John J. McCusker, review of Darrett B. Rutman and Anita H. Rutman, *A Place in Time: Middlesex County, Virginia, 1650–1750, Journal of American History,* LXXII (1985–1986), 129; Bailyn, *Voyagers to the West*, 196.

26. *The Generall Historie of Virginia, New-England, and the Summer Isles . . .* (1624), in Barbour, ed., *Works of John Smith*, II, 157.

tlemen, Gentlewomen, and children, than you have men to worke."
He told the company that "one hundred good labourers [would be]
better than a thousand such Gallants as were sent me, that could doe
nothing but complaine, curse, and despaire."[27]

Of course, while John Smith emphasized that "deserts" could only
come "by labour," less scrupulous promoters of colonial settlement
portrayed America in Edenic terms, as a veritable world without
work. Some of these writers, as Michael Zuckerman has shown,
went so far as to declare that, in the New World, "everything seemed
to come up by nature"; indeed, the land yielded "all things in abundance, as in the first creation, without toil or labor." Other pamphle-
teers limned images of food dropping into the settlers' mouths.
Some colonial promoters contended that American grains were so
fecund and easily planted that only forty-eight hours of labor were
required to provide a man's yearly supply of bread. Others argued
that two or three hours' work, three days a week, would suffice for a
comfortable subsistence.[28] Even in the so-called charnel house that
was Virginia during the days of the London Company, John Rolfe
could tell his London audience, "What happiness might [the mi-
grants] enjoy in Virginia . . . where they may have ground for nothing more than they can manure, reap more fruits and profits with
half the labour." In lamenting the social consequences of such exag-
gerations, Plymouth governor William Bradford reported that the
early settlers of his colony had fancied that "they would be great
men and rich all of a sudden."[29]

Some credulous souls may have believed such descriptions and
held out such false hopes, but the reports that quickly began filtering
back to England told of a more sober reality, a world that would
offer—and demand—more work than Englishmen had ever known.
A Virginia official in the 1620s wrote to his superiors in England: "I
assure yow the world goes hard with many even at this tyme. The
labor is infynite." Upon his arrival in Massachusetts Bay, Governor
John Winthrop affirmed that "only hard labour would transform the

27. Smith, *Advertisements for the Unexperienced Planters of New-England . . .* (1631),
ibid., III, 272.

28. Michael Zuckerman, "Identity in British America: Unease in Eden," in
Nicholas Canny and Anthony Pagden, eds., *Colonial Identity in the Atlantic World,
1500–1800* (Princeton, N.J., 1987), 123–125.

29. Great Britain, Historical Manuscript Commission, *Eighth Report of the Royal
Commission on Historical Manuscripts* (London, 1881), Appendix, part II, 31b, cited
also in Breen, "Sweat and Toil," *Penn. Hist.*, XLIX (1982), 245; William Bradford,
Of Plymouth Plantation, 1620–1647, ed. Samuel Eliot Morison (New York, 1952),
133.

wilderness into settled lands."[30] By mid-century, after the laborious transformation anticipated by his father had begun in earnest, John Winthrop, Jr., cataloged the daunting array of tasks the colonists faced. "Plantations in their beginnings have [more than] worke [e]nough, and find difficulties sufficient to settle a comfortable way of subsistence, there beinge buildings, fencings, clearinge, and breakinge up of ground, lands to be attended, orchards to be planted, highways and bridges and fortifications to be made, and all thinges to doe, as in the beginninge of the world."[31] To settlers confronted with the awesome charge of recreating in America the material basis of English civilization, Winthrop's allusions to the Creation must have seemed all too apt.

But the "infynite" labor demanded by the colonization effort is too often overlooked by historians. Forgetting, like the citizens admonished by Jefferson, that "our ancestors who migrated here, were laborers not lawyers," scholars have tended to slight the enormous exertions, both physical and psychological, that were required to establish European society in the New World. Such neglect is understandable. Settlers rarely wrote about the work that occupied most of their waking hours. And historians of the Anglo-American world have tended to be preoccupied with what Lawrence Stone describes as the "great political issues of sovereignty, authority, law, liberty, and religious liberty."[32] Somewhat more surprising is the lack of attention paid to work among modern scholars exploring such labor-related issues as demographic, community, family, ideological, and economic developments. It appears that, while our knowledge of some topics—especially with regard to New England—may indeed be approaching surfeit, we still know comparatively little about the organization of work in the fields, forests, households, gardens, shops, mills, fishing boats, and merchant ships of early America.

Richard S. Dunn has gone so far as to say that "in some respects the history of American colonial labor is almost untouched." Dunn's own scholarship, as well as the pathbreaking work done by Richard Morris, Gary Nash, Alfred Young, and their students, would appear

30. Susan Myra Kingsbury, ed., *The Records of the Virginia Company of London* . . . , 4 vols. (Washington, D.C., 1906–1935), III, *1607–1622,* 455; Carroll, Puritanism and the Wilderness, 56.

31. Richard S. Dunn, *Puritans and Yankees: The Winthrop Dynasty of New England, 1630–1717* (New York, 1971), 87.

32. Philip S. Foner, *History of the Labor Movement in the United States: From Colonial Times to the Founding of the American Federation of Labor* (New York, 1947), I, 13; Lawrence Stone, "The Century of Revolution," *New York Review of Books,* Feb. 26, 1987, 43.

to qualify this claim; but the general indictment stands. Still the standard secondary source on colonial work and labor is Morris's magisterial *Government and Labor in Early America*, first published in 1946.[33] The bill of particulars in Dunn's essay includes a wide array of neglected groups: female laborers, lumbermen, merchant seamen, fishermen, shipbuilders, fort builders, road builders, and rank-and-file soldiers. We are "generally ignorant about labor practices on small family farms," he writes, and are as yet in "no position to assess the *quality* of the labor performed in colonial America, to determine, for example, whether unskilled and semiskilled laborers worked any differently—harder, more purposefully, or more efficiently—than their counterparts in the Old World." Finally, we are not yet in a position to assess the myriad contributions made by Native Americans, in clearing the land, providing the furs and skins that served as the colonists' first staples, manning the Nantucket whaleboats, fighting the French, and potting colono.[34]

THE ESSAYS in this volume are an attempt to begin to address these questions. Most are derived from the new social history, rather than from a distinct field of colonial labor history; and both the shape and scope of the volume should be viewed with this consideration in mind. Many of the essays focus as much on labor arrangements or labor relationships as they do explicitly on work. Indeed, few of the

33. Dunn, "Servants and Slaves," in Greene and Pole, eds., *Colonial British America*, 158. Marcus Rediker likewise emphasizes that "only a handful" of historians "have studied the American working class before 1800" ("Working People," *Labour / Le travailleur*, X [1982], 124). In general, Rediker's essay makes many of the same points as Dunn's, although from a more theoretical perspective. For consideration of some of the larger questions that economic historians are beginning to ask for the colonial period, see McCusker and Menard, *The Economy of British America*, 236–257; Richard B. Sheridan, "The Domestic Economy," in Greene and Pole, eds., *Colonial British America*, 43–85.

The pathbreaking work: Gary B. Nash, "Up from the Bottom in Franklin's Philadelphia," *Past and Present*, no. 77 (Nov. 1977), 57–83; Nash, "The Failure of Female Factory Labor in Colonial Boston," *Labor History*, XX (1979), 165–188; Billy G. Smith, "The Material Lives of Laboring Philadelphians, 1750 to 1800," *WMQ*, 3d Ser., XXXVIII (1981), 163–202; Sharon V. Salinger, "Colonial Labor in Transition: The Decline of Indentured Servitude in Late Eighteenth-Century Philadelphia," *Labor History*, XXII (1981), 165–191; Alfred F. Young, "George Robert Twelves Hewes (1742–1840): A Boston Shoemaker and the Memory of the American Revolution," *WMQ*, 3d Ser., XXXVIII (1981), 561–623. Morris's *Government and Labor*, updated with a new preface, was reissued in a paperback edition by Northeastern University Press in 1981.

34. Dunn, "Servants and Slaves," in Greene and Pole, eds., *Colonial British America*, 158; William Cronon, *Changes in the Land: Indians, Colonists, and the Ecology of New England* (New York, 1983), 82–107.

authors began their investigations with the avowed intention of doing labor history. Most of the essays grew out of larger but related projects—the history of women, of slavery, of communities, or of economic diversification, for examples. All the authors, however, eventually found themselves confronted with the interrelated questions of work, labor, and production. Some attempt to combine these investigations into a single collection seemed desirable.

As the nature of its parturition suggests, this volume does not constitute a comprehensive survey of work and labor in early America. Readers will look in vain for extended treatments of some of the obvious groups that would be included in such a survey: urban and rural artisans; skilled journeymen and apprentices; domestic servants in the plantation South; soldiers, ironworkers, cod fishermen, and lumbermen in the mixed-economy North. Likewise, a number of obvious questions have not been addressed, the most notable ones being the role of merchant capital, public policy, artisanal corporations, wage and price controls, the rate of growth of labor productivity, and the relative place of work in comparative economic systems. Doubtless, each reader could supplement these two lists with additional omissions detected. In all respects, therefore, we view this collection as exploratory, not definitive. It is our hope to spark new debates and enliven existing ones, in regard to both those questions we do address and those we do not.

The subjects addressed and methodologies used in these essays reflect the diversity of the early American environment: an analysis of work relationships among male New Englanders during the seventeenth century by Daniel Vickers; a working biography of an eighteenth-century Maine midwife by Laurel Ulrich; an examination of the relationship between free laborers and the landed population of farmers and artisans in eighteenth-century Chester County, Pennsylvania, by Paul G. E. Clemens and Lucy Simler; an assessment of the impact of economic diversification on the work force of the Chesapeake from 1650 to 1820 by Lois Green Carr and Lorena S. Walsh; an examination of the patterns of task and gang labor among slaves in the Chesapeake, Deep South, and West Indies by Philip D. Morgan; a study of mobility among the laboring men of Philadelphia from 1750 to 1800 by Billy G. Smith; and a description of the working world of Anglo-American seamen from 1700 to 1750 by Marcus Rediker.

Although, as befits scholarship growing out of the new social history, most of the contributors employ both multiple-career and aggregative analysis, each relies heavily upon a particular kind of source: for Vickers, it is quarterly and probate court records; for

Ulrich, work diaries; for Clemens and Simler, account books; for Carr and Walsh, probate inventories and plantation ledgers; for Morgan, correspondence, travelers' accounts, and early histories; for Smith, tax and relief institution records; and for Rediker, High Court of Admiralty records. If there is an emergent trend in the use of sources by these authors, it is toward increased reliance on such subjective records as diaries and personal testimony. Such use results, it seems clear, from an effort to restore agency and human particularity to the past. The explicit biographical approach of one essay and the implicit biographical focus of several others also seem to reflect such a concern, although more familiar strategies from the new social history are found in the use of examples of individual families and plantations to illustrate larger general trends.

Equally important, these essays reflect divergent and in some cases contradictory intellectual and theoretical assumptions about work, opportunity, capital, consciousness, and the direction of historical change. For the most part, this diversity results from the fact that most of the contributors do not work within any of the established schools of labor historiography. With the exception of Marcus Rediker's, these essays do not emerge from either mainstream labor history, with its emphasis on systems and adversarial class relations, or from the newer cultural variety associated with E. P. Thompson and Herbert Gutman.[35] Most of the contributors find that the nature of landholding and social relations in early America makes it difficult to analyze the society primarily in terms of labor and capital. Despite recent attempts to document the emergence of a "labor consciousness" in the eighteeth-century Anglo-American world, it seems clear that the major social divisions in the colonies were not between labor and capital, but between the free and unfree.[36] And rather than

35. See, especially, E. P. Thompson, "Time, Work-Discipline, and Industrial Capitalism," *Past and Present*, no. 38 (Dec. 1967), 56–97; and Herbert G. Gutman, "Work, Culture, and Society in Industrializing America, 1815–1919," *American Historical Review*, LXXVIII (1973), 531–588. John Patrick Diggins has complained that the "values of ambition, enterprise, and opportunity are precisely the values that the new labor historians refuse to ascribe to the American working class" ("Comrades and Citizens: New Mythologies in American Historiography," *AHR*, XC [1985], 624). For a more theoretically oriented challenge to some of the longest-standing interpretations of labor history, see Aristide R. Zolberg, "How Many Exceptionalisms?" in Ira Katznelson and Zolberg, eds., *Working-Class Formation: Nineteenth-Century Patterns in Western Europe and the United States* (Princeton, N.J., 1986), 397–455.

36. Robert W. Malcolmson, *Life and Labour in England, 1700–1780* (New York, 1981); John Rule, *The Experience of Labour in Eighteenth-Century English Industry* (New York, 1981).

class, the boundaries to these categories largely were set by age in the northern colonies and race in the plantation South. For these reasons, a more flexible analysis of colonial labor systems seemed to offer the most fruitful possibilities—both for new advances and for building upon and refining existing scholarship. The major shared conviction of all the contributors is that only rigorous empirical investigations will enable us to test, modify, or ratify prevailing theoretical assumptions.[37]

Such empirical investigations of work and labor in the early modern era must first confront bedeviling definitional problems. Adoption of Marx's distinction between work and labor seems problematical for a society in which the majority of free whites owned or, as household members or tenants, had access to the means of production. Likewise, as the essays by Clemens and Simler and by Carr and Walsh make especially evident, such terms as "petty commodity production" are inappropriate for those northern and middle colony farmers who made innovation and diversification their watchwords while presiding over what Winifred Rothenberg describes as one of the most remarkable agricultural expansions in the eighteenth-century world. Jackson Turner Main's economic analysis of colonial Connecticut shows that, by the mid-eighteenth century—despite the handicaps of rocky soil, a short growing season, and the absence of a major staple crop—the colony had achieved some of the highest general standards of living in the early modern world.[38] As early as 1650,

37. A point of some consequence in this regard is that discussion of capitalism originally entered the literature in the form of a polemic, albeit a brilliant one. Such an adversarial stance, along with the neoclassical mirror opposite it spawned, helped give rise to what Frederick Crews refers to as theoreticism, or "a nascent impulse to ideologize knowledge." For Crews, "the major shift we have witnessed over the past generation is not a growing taste for big ideas but a growing apriorism—a willingness to settle issues by theoretical decree, without even a pretense of evidential appeal." In a classic *Zeitgeist* formulation, he argues that "the winning theory will be the one that better suits the emergent temper or interest of the hour." Crews's solution to this problem, one that the contributors to this volume have tried to endorse, is "not that we stop theorizing and expressing our sociopolitical views, but that we notice where our most substantial theories always originate: in concrete disciplinary engagement." Most important, such engagement must be rooted in "research traditions that generate well-focused debate [and] high standards of reasoning" within a shared scholarly community. Frederick Crews, *Skeptical Engagements* (New York, 1986), 163–164, 167, 174. Crews's provocative musings on contemporary intellectual life could be read with profit by all historians.

38. Winifred B. Rothenberg, "The Market and Massachusetts Farmers: Reply," *Journal of Economic History*, XLIII (1983), 479–480; Rothenberg, "Markets, Values, and Capitalism: A Discourse on Method," *JEH*, XLIV (1984), 174–178; Jackson

according to some economic historians, British North Americans had achieved a higher annual income than that of 53 percent of the world's population today. And income levels apparently continued to rise for free settlers during the eighteenth century. In *The Economic Rise of Early America*, Gary M. Walton and James F. Shepherd observe that, "shockingly enough, countries comprising almost two-thirds of today's world population [as of 1979] have *average per-capita incomes* at levels below that achieved by an average American two hundred years ago."[39] Without discounting the heavy price paid in the Indians' land and the Africans' labor, it seems clear that the vast productive energies of ordinary colonists played a central role in this prosperity.

If work is defined as "productive labor," then most of the colonial population must have worked. With the exception of children under the age of eight, the aged, and the infirm, everyone worked directly or indirectly to produce a profit. It may be that British America during its first century had one of the smallest leisure classes in the early modern Western world. America, in general, lacked distinct aristocratic, clerical, and courtly classes; and middling-level women and upper-class men performed tasks unthinkably vulgar by Old World standards. Gloria Main has shown that approximately half of the white women in early Maryland routinely worked in the tobacco fields. While traveling through Virginia, Jaspar Dankers marveled that some Virginia masters and their wives worked as hard as any slave.[40] Clemens and Simler show that, in the middle colonies, cot-

---

Turner Main, *Society and Economy in Colonial Connecticut* (Princeton, N.J., 1985); Main, personal communication, June 19, 1983. Throughout the discussion that follows, I am exceedingly indebted to Professor Main for his kindness in alerting me to the implications for questions of work and labor of his research on early Connecticut.

39. Douglass C. North *et al.*, *Growth and Welfare in the American Past: A New Economic History* (Englewood Cliffs, N.J., 1983), 7; Gary M. Walton and James F. Shepherd, *The Economic Rise of Early America* (Cambridge, 1979), 4. See also Alice Hanson Jones, *Wealth of a Nation to Be: The American Colonies on the Eve of the Revolution* (New York, 1980).

40. Gloria L. Main, *Tobacco Colony: Life in Early Maryland, 1650–1720* (Princeton, N.J., 1982), 108–109; Laurel Thatcher Ulrich, *Good Wives: Image and Reality In the Lives of Women in Northern New England, 1650–1750* (New York, 1982), chaps. 1 and 2; Bartlett Burleigh James and J. Franklin Jameson, eds., *Journal of Jasper Danckaerts, 1679–1680*, Original Narratives of Early American History (New York, 1913), 133. The age of 8 was chosen because this appears to have been the time when parents expected their children to begin in earnest the process of learning their life's work. With regard to such formal criteria as taxation policy, most colonies taxed young male polls at age 16, when they began to produce a product, surplus income. Some southern colonies such as Virginia taxed female slaves at

tagers' wives were regularly hired by landowners at harvest-time. In New England, early gentry leaders such as Governor Winthrop made a conspicuous example, perhaps for didactic purposes, of their willingness to work in the fields. As a settler informed a friend back in England, "So soon as Mr. Winthrop was landed, perceiving what misery was like to ensue through their idleness, he presently fell to work with his own hands and thereby so encouraged the rest that there was not an idle person then to be found in the whole planta-tion [so that the Indians] admired to see in what short time they had all housed themselves and planted corn for their subsistence." In *Wonder-Working Providence*, Edward Johnson emphasized that "even such men as scarce ever set hand to labour before, men of good birth and breeding," readily assumed the responsibilities of clearing, culti-vating, and building. Pamphleteer William Wood told his readers that "all New England[ers] must be workers in some kinde."[41]

To a greater or lesser degree, the same was true elsewhere in early America. Given the exigencies of farm formation and staple-crop ag-riculture, it could not have been otherwise. The one conspicuous exception to this rule, the settlers in Virginia between 1607 and 1623, paid for their refusal to work by suffering the highest mortality rate experienced by whites in the colonial period. Whatever else early America was, it was a world of work. As a result, in this collection we have defined work in the most inclusive terms possible—as any form of productive labor, whether performed for one's family, one's master, or one's employer.

IN HIS essay on field work in seventeenth-century Essex County, Massachusetts, Daniel Vickers stresses the heavy reliance the north-ern colonies placed on family labor, in sharp contrast to the southern tidewater colonists' dependence on bound labor. He points to how

the age of 12. Twelve was also the age at which the female domestic servants listed in the Pynchon account books in Springfield, Massachusetts, began their term of service. It may be possible, therefore, that the age of productive maturity for girls was seen as 12–14, in contrast to 16 for boys. Stephen Innes, *Labor in a New Land: Economy and Society in Seventeenth-Century Springfield* (Princeton, N.J., 1983), 117–122; Jackson T. Main, personal communication.

41. Winthrop in Emerson, ed., *Letters from New England*, 52; J. Franklin Jame-son, ed., Johnson's *Wonder-Working Providence, 1628–1651*, Original Narratives of Early American History (New York, 1910), 85; Wood, *New England's Prospect*, cited in Carroll, *Puritanism and the Wilderness*, 56. None of this discussion is meant to deny the importance of change over time. Later New England governors doubt-less were less likely to take up the hoe. But a leisured class on the continental model never emerged in Massachusetts—or elsewhere in colonial North America.

little we really know about work relationships that connected male New Englanders: fathers with sons, masters with servants, landlords with tenants, and employers with hired men—particularly in terms of the relative importance of each. Vickers's assessment of the degree to which New England households maintained or altered traditional English practices leads to some surprising findings. In his view, the migration to New England brought a significant enhancement of family labor. Vickers believes that both farm service and day labor withered in the smaller, less commercialized early New England towns, to be replaced by the labor of sons. Only by concentrating the efforts of two or even three generations within a single operation could families accumulate sufficient capital to provide for an English standard of living, with the normal complement of pewter plates, woolen cloth, printed Bibles, and flintlock muskets. Children, Vickers asserts, served the same economic function in New England as did indentured servants in the Chesapeake. At least in rural areas, adolescent boys were not sent out to service in other households, but remained at home to work for their fathers.

This reliance on the labor of sons for field work, contends Vickers, enhanced both parental authority and filial duty and prolonged a son's residence in the parental household, even beyond the age of marriage.[42] By keeping their sons at home, New England householders reversed the trend toward increased reliance on wage labor in late Elizabethan and early Stuart England. Depending so heavily on family labor, the New Englanders, Vickers avers, were turning away from the freer portion of the labor system on which the English rural economy had grown increasingly reliant.

Laurel Thatcher Ulrich's essay on work relationships among women in late-eighteenth-century Maine takes as its focus the richly revealing career of midwife Martha Moore Ballard. Ulrich, like Vickers, recognizes the centrality of family labor in early New England; but she emphasizes how much more radically deficient is our knowledge of work relationships among females than among males. She points out that, despite the considerable attention colonial historians have given to the intersection of economic history and family history, particularly regarding the passing of property from fathers to sons, little has been learned about mother-daughter, mistress-servant, and

42. For an earlier argument that New England fathers withheld land from their married sons, see Philip J. Greven, Jr., *Four Generations: Population, Land, and Family in Colonial Andover, Massachusetts* (Ithaca, N.Y., 1970); Greven, "Family Structure in Seventeenth-Century Andover, Massachusetts," *WMQ*, 3d Ser., XXIII (1966), 234–256. See also Christopher M. Jedrey, *The World of John Cleaveland: Family and Community in Eighteenth-Century New England* (New York, 1979).

neighbor-neighbor work relationships; nor have labor historians devoted much attention to the hired work of women in preindustrial New England. Studies that have directly addressed the issue of women's status in the colonial economy have usually examined such topics as the property rights of widows or the participation by wives in their husbands' work. The dominant issue has been whether the colonial family was more or was less confining than the later doctrine of separate spheres.

Ulrich, by contrast, seeks to avoid both the male-relational and teleological approaches by bringing female work patterns fully to center stage. In so doing, she finds that the levels of home production in late-eighteenth-century Maine "had as much to do with the availability of daughters as with the availability of flax," and she points to an unrecognized colonial elite: those housewives who had not only health and energy but also a sufficient number of daughters. The author draws on the diary of Martha Ballard to illustrate the concrete tasks of women's work and to document its variety and social complexity—attuned to men's work, but largely independent of it. She questions prevailing notions that early American women labored under the patriarchal control of men, showing that for northern New England one cannot assume a unified family system in which the work of wives and daughters was in some sense "owned" by their husbands and fathers. In the separate world of female exchange, work was given social value as well as economic valuation, was cooperatively performed and psychologically satisfying, and was carried on by a permeable group of mothers, daughters, and neighbors. Such goods as ashes, herbs, seedlings, and baby chicks may rarely have made it into male account books, but they served to strengthen neighborhood and community bonds. Moreover, as the career of Mrs. Ballard reveals so splendidly, women also participated in the larger commercial economy, exchanging goods and services, managing their own finances, and bringing in sufficient income to make a real difference in the family's standard of living. Mary Beth Norton, in a similar vein, has pointed to the importance of the manufacture and sale of cheese as a major female enterprise.[43] Finally, the textiles and similar import-replacing and female-directed operations such as Mrs. Ballard's weaving played an increasingly vital role in moving Maine's economy beyond the frontier stage.

One of the paradoxes to emerge from a comparison of Ulrich's findings with those of Daniel Vickers's (which may be attributable to

43. Mary Beth Norton, "The Evolution of White Women's Experience in Early America," *AHR*, LXXXIX (1984), 593–619; Norton, personal communication.

the time difference between the two essays) is the relative independence of Maine's adolescent women in contrast to the relative dependence of early Essex sons. Frontier Maine women were free to leave the family household at a considerably younger age, either to become servants in another's household or to marry, than were the men in Massachusetts. While additional comparative work is clearly needed in this area, the relationship between mobility and independence is among the most promising themes developed in Ulrich's essay.

The essay by Paul G. E. Clemens and Lucy Simler focuses on the system of mixed wage-cottager labor found in Chester County, Pennsylvania, between 1750 and 1820. By the mid-eighteenth century, this section of southeastern Pennsylvania had witnessed the fruitful union of agriculture and rural industry, with a remarkably productive balance between agriculture and industry, self-sufficiency and market activity, and family labor and hired workers, all characteristics that helped distinguish the Middle Atlantic rural economy from New England's and the South's. In addition to prospering farms, the typical Chester County township contained a wide array of gristmills, sawmills, and tanyards along with numerous joiners, wheelwrights, smiths, masons, and tailors.

The three most distinctive characteristics of Chester County identified by Clemens and Simler were the prominence of market production, the high proportion of artisans within the rural work force, and the growing reliance of landowners on landless wage laborers and artisans during the late eighteenth century. With regard to this last group, the authors call attention to the as yet unrecognized importance of such live-in workers as inmates and freemen. Occupying a midway position between a servant in husbandry and the usual wage worker, the inmates (married or widowed men living on the property of someone else) and freemen (unmarried men living in someone else's household) functioned as part-time workers, who could hire themselves out to others or engage on their own in gardening, animal husbandry, or handicraft manufacture while not in service. This mixture of informal and formal work relationships has been identified by some scholars as a key point in the transition from implicit to explicit contractual relations. Clemens and Simler also emphasize, as does Vickers, that landowners, particularly in the pre-Revolutionary period, preferred to have surplus lands developed by tenants rather than by day laborers.[44] The tendency after 1750 was for live-in help

44. On mixture of work relationships, see George R. Boyer, "An Economic

such as inmates and freemen to move out of the owner's house into separate cottages located elsewhere on his property. All told, small-holding tenants, along with cottagers and freemen, provided a large and—most important—flexible pool of laborers available to young farmers without grown children, to farmer-artisans, and to large commercial wheat farmers.

Clemens and Simler find that Chester County's labor system generally offered farmers the opportunity to hire help according to the seasonal and market dictates of commercial agriculture as well as their own life cycle. It afforded cottagers a greater measure of comfort and security than they otherwise would have obtained; and at least until the early nineteenth century, it enabled the landless to remain in market areas and acquire capital for upward mobility.

During the late eighteenth century, as the authors show, intensification of commercial agriculture provoked significant changes in the labor system. Farms with an increasingly higher concentration of crops and livestock per acre and the spread of industry throughout the countryside were the principal features of this intensification. Increases in land prices, rents, market activity, wage differentials by skill, and the numbers of landless laborers undermined the old mixture of family, dependent, and free labor. By the 1750s, prospective leaseholders now found entry costs high, and farmers and artisan-owners found it cheaper and more convenient to house their workers. Out of all this emerged a cottager class. By the early nineteenth century, inmates and freemen, along with indentured servants and slaves, had effectively disappeared from the countryside, to be replaced by growing numbers of landless workers.

Diversification of the rural economy is also a major theme in Lois Green Carr and Lorena S. Walsh's analysis of changes in Chesapeake labor practices from 1650 to 1820. Carr and Walsh illustrate general colonywide trends at the level of individual plantations and neighborhoods. In a departure from usual approaches, the authors analyze white and black work patterns within the confines of a single essay. They examine such themes as male-female divisions of labor, specialization, gang and task labor, unit size, seasonality, local exchange, and artisanal work. Their essay charts a number of major transformations experienced by the Chesapeake world in the eighteenth century as the region shifted from tobacco to mixed farming,

---

Model of the English Poor Law, circa 1780–1834," *Explorations in Economic History*, XXII (1985), 129–146. For a discussion of the general practice of land speculators' using tenancy to develop their lands, see Bailyn, *Peopling of British North America*, 82–83.

from servant to slave labor, from farm formation to farm maintenance, and from hoe to plow cultivation.

Carr and Walsh show that, in the seventeenth-century Chesapeake,
the bulk of labor time was devoted to three activities: clearing land,
growing tobacco for export, and raising corn and livestock for both
subsistence and sale. The Chesapeake economy lacked mills, major
concentrations of artisans, and significant household manufacture;
and so virtually all cloth, tools, metalwares, and luxury goods had to
be imported. Money to pay for imports came from the main cash
crop, tobacco, and from salable surpluses of livestock, hides, meat,
tallow, and (if women were present in the household) dairy products
and cider. Masters and servants shared work routines and generally
were housed and clothed alike.

The 1690s witnessed the beginning of three major shifts in the
Chesapeake economy, all of which brought parallel changes in the
world of work: the diversification of agriculture into wheat and corn,
raised for export; the growing specialization of the labor system
through the increase of artisanal and household manufacturing; and
the conversion of the bonded labor force from servants to slaves. The
authors' analysis of probate data enables them to confirm that the
general economic diversification and shift to slave labor began first
in households of the wealthy. But both processes eventually were
adopted by those lower on the social scale. Settlers turned to diversification as a way of reducing cash outlays for imported goods, and
the prolonged period of depressed tobacco prices from 1680 until
1716 prevented a return to a sole reliance on the staple crop to sustain the economy.

Carr and Walsh demonstrate that in the Chesapeake region, as in
Chester County, diversification brought an increase in both the pace
and complexity of work. The conversion to wheat and the greater
corn production helped fill in the few gaps of leisure in the tobacco-
based agricultural year, and the new density of craftsmen and craft-
related activities spurred increased specialization. The need to plow
the land and mill the harvested wheat brought new demands for
carpenters, millers, millwrights, carters, wheelwrights, and related
craftsmen. For the first time, genuine craft specialization emerged in
the Chesapeake. Likewise, as in the rural economy of late-eighteenth-
century Maine, a growing level of female-produced goods such as
yarn and stockings, butter and eggs, and cider and honey brought
both greater levels of productivity and a more rigorous work regimen
for women and young girls.

Carr and Walsh contend that by the 1720s the work roles of masters and servants and of servants and slaves increasingly diverged.

Moreover, the conversion to slavery threatened both to debase all manual labor and to create a distinct master class. The biggest losers in this transformation, as Walsh shows vividly from her work in plantation account books and journals, were black women. Female slaves were now relegated to the most monotonous, dispiriting, and unrelenting field work. While many male slaves took up the plow or became smiths or carpenters, slave women were left to hoe tobacco, clear brush, dig ditches, and drain swamps. As whites moved into a new world of prosperity and consumption—wearing India cottons, drinking Brazilian coffee, eating off English china, living in solid brick homes or in a few cases palatial estates—not only were all blacks excluded, but black women experienced further degradation.

Based on her extensive study of plantation account books elsewhere, Lorena Walsh also links gender to the gang system of slave labor. The period from 1720 until the American Revolution was the heyday of the gang; but after approximately 1750—as Philip Morgan shows in greater detail in his essay—crop diversification began to help effect a shift from gang to task labor. For Walsh, more than for Morgan, gender is an emergent issue in analyses of task and gang systems. In her view, the archetypal slave gangs of the late-colonial and early national period were increasingly composed of females. Through the use of plantation work diaries, she shows that this sexual division was most pronounced on the estates of agricultural innovators such as George Washington.

In his essay, Philip Morgan, like Carr and Walsh and Clemens and Simler, charts some of the ramifying effects of economic diversification; but here the focus is exclusively on the systems of task and gang labor. Within the space of a generation after 1690, the earlier small-scale, decentralized labor units—whether servant or slave—were transformed into large gangs of slave workers under the direction of an overseer. Gang labor—in which the slaves toiled from dawn to dusk in large, depersonalized groups, controlling neither their work nor their time—was favored whenever supervision and social control were overriding concerns. Staples requiring a carefully calibrated and quasi-industrial production cycle (such as sugar) or those crops that were delicate and easily damaged (such as tobacco) gave rise to gang systems. Gang labor predominated on the large sugar islands in the West Indies and in the tobacco-growing regions of the Chesapeake and South America. In addition, plantations in North and South America that grew short-staple cotton and coffee usually adopted a gang system.

Morgan's survey of the labor systems of New World plantations, however, suggests that gang labor was neither so widespread nor so long-lived as historians have thought. Tasking, it appears, was common in a significant proportion of slave societies. Major crops organized around the task system included rice and Sea Island cotton in the South Carolina–Georgia lowcountry, long-staple cotton in the West Indies, naval stores, and some coffee. Lesser crops grown by task labor included pimento, hemp, and arrowroot. And on all plantations, male slave artisans—whose numbers swelled during the eighteenth century—performed their labor on a piecework basis. Moreover, by the early nineteenth century, most of the gang-organized plantations were introducing elements of individual tasking into their operations or even adopting the system outright. On the mainland, the increased use of the plow as well as slaves' new responsibilities in handicraft and manufacturing enterprises helped bring about the shift to tasking. By the mid-1830s, it appears, a majority of slaves in the Anglo-American world were working by the task.

Morgan emphasizes that in terms of the domestic economy, patterns of resource use, consumption, accumulation, and independence of spirit, slaves were generally better off under a task system. Tasking left bondspeople with more time to devote to their own crops and livestock, and by the end of slavery a significant internal slave economy had been created, especially in the lowcountry and West Indies. Morgan suggests, in an appropriately tentative fashion, that it may be possible to postulate a modal type of slave culture under various regimes: more autonomous and self-assured under coffee than under sugar production, more acquisitive and outward-looking in the regions where slaves were protopeasants rather than gardeners, and the like. Equally tentatively, he raises the possibility that—in contrast to routine depictions of the Deep South as the most oppressive slave regime—work conditions for the tasked slaves of the lowcountry may have been easing while things improved less for the ganged Chesapeake slaves and in fact worsened for women. The emergence of a significant provision economy in both the lowcountry and the larger West Indian islands likewise points to better social conditions for these slaves resulting from greater marketing opportunities.

In the final two essays in the volume, by Billy G. Smith and Marcus Rediker, respectively, the focus shifts from plantation and domestic labor to urban and maritime work. Smith's analysis of the laboring men of Philadelphia from 1750 to 1800 charts the emergence of what is often regarded as the first genuine working class in America, composed of men owning few of the means of production, often unskilled, and constrained to sell their labor in an international economy.

In his wealth profile of Philadelphia, Smith emphasizes the strait-ened circumstances and limited prospects for upward mobility of many of the city's laboring men. He focuses on two groups of les-ser craftsmen, cordwainers and tailors, and two groups of manual workers, mariners and laborers. Members of these four occupational groups composed no less than one-third to one-half of all of Philadel-phia's free males. Smith's research design enables him to avoid the confusion resulting from historians' use of the term "mechanic" to describe urban workers whose ranks differed dramatically with re-gard to property, wealth, and economic interests.

Smith's findings lead him to question what he regards as some of the excessively optimistic mobility studies of eighteenth-century ur-ban dwellers. Measuring absolute rather than relative mobility, he concludes from the evidence of six tax lists that, for most laboring Philadelphians, growing older did not mean growing wealthier. The close correlation between age and wealth that historians have found in rural areas apparently was not duplicated in the cities. Indeed, especially when compared with the preceding essays, Smith's find-ings suggest the existence of a real rural-urban split in the nature of work and community—a dichotomy that doubtless will be the focus of future research. In the city of Philadelphia, Smith discovers that a majority, and sometimes a substantial majority, of members of the four occupational groups and of Philadelphia's lower sort in general were propertyless during the second half of the eighteenth century. Possibly as many as three-quarters of the propertyless who remained in the city failed to acquire any taxable property within a decade, although those men who did manage to obtain a modicum of prop-erty usually managed to hold on to it. While cordwainers and tailors experienced higher occupational than economic mobility, seamen and the unskilled tended to make little progress on either count. Smith finds that laboring men generally fared best during the late 1750s, the early 1760s, and the 1790s, when the smallest proportion of them were propertyless and the greatest opportunities for ad-vancement existed. Like Marcus Rediker, Smith calls attention to the dangerous nature of the lives of the working poor, particularly the seamen. Maritime work left disabled sailors by the hundreds to spend their declining years on poor relief or in charity hospitals. Smith also underscores Rediker's finding that during the eighteenth century mariners were becoming one of the first groups of perma-nent, fully waged, self-conscious workers.

Indeed, in his analysis of eighteenth-century Anglo-American sea-men, Rediker views mariners as key transitional figures in the move-ment from paternalistic forms of labor to the contested negotiations of waged work. The seamen symbolized what he regards as the "dominant, overarching tendency, particularly in Britain and America . . . toward ever greater employment of waged labor." Prominent among these laborers were merchant seamen, whose work routines Rediker chronicles in vivid detail. Mariners helped transport the burgeoning quantities of sugar, tobacco, wheat, corn, rice, lumber, and livestock produced by the other laborers discussed in this volume; and, of course, they also carried the swelling numbers of slaves to the New World, in voyages that could last as long as eleven months.

Drawing on Eric Hobsbawm, Rediker examines the links between an expanding market economy and a growing free labor force. He explores the ways in which labor processes, markets, and work experiences were shaped by the drive of mercantile capitalist development. Rediker analyzes what Marx described as the law of the concentration and centralization of capital and the law of the socialization of labor. He contends that maritime workers, by linking producers and consumers in an international market, signaled the emergence of new relations between merchant capitalists and laborers. Of first importance for Rediker is the fact that these seamen worked in a labor market that was international. Mariners came from England, America, the Caribbean, France, Holland, Spain, even from Africa and Asia. The seaman's identity, in a mirror opposite of the Puritan villagers with whom we began this volume, came from the workplace, not the community.

Viewing the ship as similar in many ways to the factory, Rediker analyzes the activities and consciousness of eighteenth-century seamen. Forged by what he describes as the "massive confrontation between the seaman and his work," this consciousness enabled the sailors to reduce the dangers of harsh conditions, excessive work, and oppressive authority—to resist the master's attempt to curtail their customary rights, push the crew too hard, or take the ship into unmanageable waters. Displaying a solidarity they viewed as necessary for survival, sailors responded to such threats with verbal taunts, literal-mindedness, work stoppages, desertion, mutiny, or piracy (the ultimate expropriation of the workplace). Rediker suggests that the pirate ship, with its more egalitarian form of labor organization, higher pay, and shorter hours, represented a kind of lower-class utopia, reminiscent of similar collectivistic tendencies among medieval peasants or seventeenth-century radicals such as the Diggers and Levellers.

The mariners' world, with its round-the-clock hours, complicated machinery, carefully calibrated division of labor, and fully contractual relations between owners and workers, adumbrated the coming industrial age. And, when London mariners decided in 1768 to "strike" their sails to protest wage rates and working conditions, they helped inaugurate a very different world of labor relations. Their actions mark a fitting point of transition from the quilt-patterned labor relations of colonial America to the increasingly homogeneous—and more adversarial—ones of the nineteenth century.

FOUR MAJOR THEMES emerge from these essays. First is the surprising importance of family labor in early America. Family labor was dominant throughout New England, in more than half of the settlements in the middle colonies, in the southern backcountry, and in substantial portions of the tidewater. In the colonial Chesapeake, no more than half of all householders owned any slaves. Even among slaveowners, the proportion who owned enough slaves to exempt white family members from labor was comparatively small. In the northern colonies, family labor declined in importance in ocean ports, major commercial towns, and those areas where large landowners employed tenants or white workers to develop their property or cultivate their crops. Such areas included the Connecticut, Hudson, and Delaware river valleys and the hinterlands of major urban areas. An eclectic mixture of family-servant-free labor prevailed in the wheat- and livestock-producing regions of Pennsylvania, New Jersey, and Maryland. Bonded labor, at first servants, then slaves, was more prominent in the Chesapeake, lowcountry, and West Indies wherever tobacco, wheat, rice, or sugar were grown as staple crops.

Bonded labor has, of course, received considerable historical scrutiny; but the same has not been true for family and mixed family-servant-free labor systems. This situation, however, may be about to change. Corroboration for many of the findings of Daniel Vickers and Laurel Ulrich is found in Jackson Turner Main's study of the social and occupational structure of colonial Connecticut—the first such longitudinal analysis to be made for the entire colonial period for a New England colony. As with Vickers's account, Main finds that more than half of the laborers in eighteenth-century Connecticut were local boys living at home with their parents or working for a neighbor. Fewer than two in ten were young migrants, the same number were older men, and fewer than two in twenty were in servitude.[45] Moreover, as with the Essex County sons studied by Vickers or the frontier daughters and domestics examined by Ulrich, these Connecticut laborers did not constitute a permanent rural proletariat. Main discovers that, among those who began as laborers, ap-

45. J. Main, *Colonial Connecticut*, 174–199, 367–382.

proximately three in five eventually became independent farmers or craftsmen. Both Vickers and Ulrich find that most of the young men and women who labored in New England households eventually established independent households of their own. As Fred Anderson likewise discovered from his study of Massachusetts soldiers during the Seven Years' War, laboring was a stage, not a condition, for most New Englanders. This was a society with laborers, but without a distinct laboring class. Powerfully buttressed by a religious ideology built around family government, New England's labor system rested primarily on the household.[46]

The importance of family labor in New England and elsewhere in early America raises a number of suggestive questions regarding family formation. Such issues as age at marriage, birth rates, child exchange, economic strategies, and life cycles might all be approached anew with the prominence of family labor in mind. To what degree, for example, were northern householders conscious of the fact that they needed to produce their own workers? Did families with a preponderance of either girls or boys attempt to achieve sexual parity through apprenticeship or domestic service agreements with their neighbors? Vickers's essay, at least, suggests the contrary for New England; but things may have been different elsewhere in early America. Mary Beth Norton, for one, has wondered whether families with a skewed sex ratio among the children, as well as families with relatively fewer offspring, tended to be less economically successful than more balanced or more fecund ones. In her essay, Laurel Ulrich speculates that the fact that Stephen Barton's wife bore six daughters before the first son was born "may account for the difficulty [Barton] had in establishing a foothold in Maine." In their essay, Clemens and Simler show that farm families with very young children were one of the three groups most likely to hire wage workers, especially at harvest-time. The fluidity of such a system, with the same individuals functioning as family workers one day and short-term wage workers the next—as these essays show clearly—was one of the keys to its success. This feature of the family system, too, seems to invite future investigation.[47]

46. Fred Anderson, *A People's Army: Massachusetts Soldiers and Society in the Seven Years' War* (Chapel Hill, N.C., 1984), 28. The best discussion of the Puritans' social ethic is found in Stephen Foster, *Their Solitary Way: The Puritan Social Ethic in the First Century of Settlement in New England* (New Haven, Conn., 1971), a book deserving far more attention than it has received.

47. Mary Beth Norton formulated many of these questions in an evaluation of this collection. I am also indebted to Professor Norton for a number of exchanges on issues of work and gender that helped crystallize my thinking on these issues.

Indeed, the general relationship between gender and work roles promises to be one of the most fruitful areas of future inquiry. Laurel Ulrich's essay as well as the current research of Mary Beth Norton raises the intriguing possibility that men and women conceptualized work in quite distinct, even contradictory ways.[48] To a surprising degree, we are not even certain that colonial women regarded the manifold activities they did all day long as "work" in the ways that men clearly did. While men tended to work alone, at commercialized tasks, in openly demarcated periods of work and rest, in fairly evident cost-benefit terms, women appear to have conducted their labors in groups, at noncommercialized tasks, in continually interrupted activity patterns, in fairly evident *non*-cost-benefit terms. Men appear to have focused more on producing a surplus, women more on strengthening neighborhood and kinship ties. Such an interpretation seems to be supported by the high levels of social instability and pathology in women-short societies such as the early Chesapeake and West Indies. It is conceivable, as Laurel Ulrich finds from her analysis of bookkeeping patterns in male and female ledgers, that men and women saw the purposes of their labors differently. Men may have focused more on exchange and profit, women on use and neighborliness. Such a division may account for the fact that, as both Ulrich's essay and Gloria Main's *Tobacco Colony* suggest, women could perform field work for their father or husband but not for an employer.[49] The same tasks, in different contexts, could be construed as either "helping" or "working." Perhaps the most telling divisions in the colonies, therefore, between "commercialists" and "communalists," were more a feature of gender than of geography (Virginia versus New England, for example) or chronology ("Puritans" into "Yankees," and the like).

But, in a paradox that may be more apparent than real, the less commercialized women may have played a growing role in the eighteenth-century "consumer revolution." As Robert A. Gross has wryly observed: "To hear many writers of the eighteenth and nineteenth centuries tell it, the demands and desires of women were the basic cause of the new consumerism on the farm. . . . From Benjamin Franklin's charming account of the sudden appearance of a china

48. Norton reports such a finding, based on her current research on sexual roles in 17th-century America.

49. G. Main, *Tobacco Colony*, 175–185. As Patricia U. Bonomi has pointed out, the "feminization" of church congregations during the 18th century may have been part of this widening process of demarcating values along the lines of sex (*Under the Cope of Heaven: Religion, Society, and Politics in Colonial America* [New York, 1986], 111–115).

bowl and silver spoon on his breakfast table to Henry David Thoreau's denunciation of the false 'economy' of his times, the complaint is invariably the same: status-conscious women first introduce the corruption of luxury into the home."[50] If one substitutes the more probable concern with comfort, utility, and refinement for the more invidious "status-consciousness" (and abandons the conceit that luxury equals corruption), then such a formulation makes considerable sense. It also accords with what we now know about the relatively new autonomy eighteenth-century women enjoyed in making household purchases.[51] The growing numbers of domestic furnishings found in probate inventories by the mid-eighteenth century suggest more female input in decisions about purchases. Possibly there was some connection between women's roles as consumers and as account keepers. As females took greater responsibility in purchasing decisions, it would be logical for them to gain greater familiarity with accounting procedures. But, for the moment, all this remains conjectural. Perhaps the best we can say now is that, by the mid-eighteenth century, both men and women found acquisition of some of the accoutrements of gentility desirable, sometimes for similar, sometimes for contrasting reasons. Future studies of domestic purchases, accounting procedures, and prescriptive literature should begin to provide answers for some of these questions. The sources for investigating such queries are likely to be exceedingly difficult; but the forays of Ulrich, Norton, and Gloria Main suggest that such efforts may well be worth pursuing.[52]

THE SECOND major theme emerging from these essays, as much of the foregoing has implied, is that work patterns were governed by production for the market. On family farms, farmer-artisanal households, and staple crop plantations, work routines and labor discipline were geared toward surplus production. Men and women, young and old, servant and free, black and white, all found—for

50. Robert A. Gross, "America's Agricultural Revolution, 1750–1850," comment on papers at the 77th Annual Meeting of the Organization of American Historians, Los Angeles, Apr. 4–7, 1984.

51. Research in progress by Lois Green Carr and Lorena S. Walsh; Ulrich, Good Wives; Gloria L. Main, "The Standard of Living in Colonial Massachusetts," JEH, XLIII (1983), 101–108.

52. For an evaluation of the related, and increasingly vibrant, field of material culture, see Richard L. Bushman, "American High-Style and Vernacular Cultures," in Greene and Pole, eds., Colonial British America, 345–383. See also the illuminating catalog for the Boston Museum of Fine Arts' exhibition on the material culture of 17th-century New England, New England Begins: The Seventeenth Century, 3 vols. (Boston, 1982).

good or for ill—that their work lives were tethered to the market. People worked longer and harder, and imposed greater restrictions on themselves and on others, in order to produce for domestic and foreign markets. A market-oriented interpretation may be applied with varying degrees of cogency to the mixed cereal-lumber-fishing economy of New England, the commercial wheat townships of Pennsylvania, the tobacco plantations of the Chesapeake, and the rice- and indigo-producing counties of the Georgia-Carolina lowcountry. And, as Philip Morgan's essay reveals, even within the domestic economy of the slaves, marketing opportunities played a key role in shaping the quality of a bondsman's life. Morgan contends that not only is it incontestable that incentives spurred slaves to greater work efforts but that what "clearly demarcated all Caribbean slaves . . . from their North American counterparts . . . were radically different marketing opportunities." Throughout early America, even in the most unlikely work environments, the material incentives so important to John Smith's vision helped shape productive activities.

Indeed, as Captain Smith had prophesied, and the eighteenth-century consumer revolution ratified, a middling level of material comfort became the goal of most white settlers. While such terms as "utility maximizers" should not be used to describe a world still deeply imbued with religious and neighborly sensibilities, comfort— not rude sufficiency—was the level toward which work routines were geared. (Indeed, it is possible to believe that visions of "rude sufficiency" are more appealing to twentieth-century historians than they were to eighteenth-century colonists.) Although some scholars have misconstrued the meaning of the word "competency" for early modern Englishmen, it did not connote frontierlike simplicity. The term came much closer to implying the accoutrements of a middling-level household. In those regions where manifest conditions of rude sufficiency did prevail, as in the seventeenth-century Chesapeake, it was because most of the settlers' energies were going toward accumulating the capital goods necessary for a middling standard of living—land, livestock, and sometimes bound labor.[53]

53. Lois Green Carr and Lorena S. Walsh, "The Standard of Living in the Colonial Chesapeake," paper delivered at the 80th Annual Meeting of the Organization of American Historians, Philadelphia, Apr. 3, 1987; Lorena S. Walsh, "Urban Amenities and Rural Sufficiency: Living Standards and Consumer Behavior in the Colonial Chesapeake, 1643–1777," *JEH*, XLIII (1983), 109–117; G. Main, *Tobacco Colony*, 140–266; James Horn, "Adapting to a New World: A Comparative Study of Local Society in England and Maryland, 1650–1700," in Lois Green Carr, Philip D. Morgan, and Jean B. Russo, eds., *Colonial Chesapeake Society* (Chapel Hill, N.C., 1988).

Likewise, in the remote, godly villages of Puritan Massachusetts, Daniel Vickers finds a strong determination to achieve an "English" standard of living—a goal that could not be achieved without commercialized production. As early as the 1640s, Edward Johnson's town-by-town canvass found that in Dedham, the locus classicus of the closed corporate peasant village, the inhabitants carted their surplus corn and livestock to Boston regularly. In Andover, according to Johnson, despite "the remoteness of the place from Towns of trade, [which] bringeth some inconveniencies upon the planters," the townsmen continued to "carry their corn far to market." In Hingham, our observer reports that "the people have much profited themselves by transporting Timber, Planke and Mast for Shipping to the Town of Boston, as also Ceder and Pine-board to supply the wants of other Townes, and also to remote parts, even as far as Barbadoes. They [lack] not for Fish for themselves and others also." It was by such means, repeated in every village and town throughout early New England, that "this Wilderness should turn a mart for Merchants in so short a space, Holland, France, Spain, and Portugal coming hither for trade."[54]

Throughout early America, it seems increasingly evident, a similar market orientation prevailed. Laurel Ulrich's essay documents not only growing levels of spinning and weaving for the market but also a vibrant and diverse "female economy" based on local production and exchange among both married and unmarried women. Even at the modest annual wage of six pounds, a domestic servant worked to "accumulate something toward her future." Clemens and Simler make reference to the "prominence of market agriculture in the lives of most residents" of southeastern Pennsylvania, an observation that, of course, applies with much greater force to the staple-producing areas of the Chesapeake, lowcountry, and West Indies. Moreover, the diversification of the rural economy of the Middle Atlantic and Chesapeake colonies during the eighteenth century merely accelerated the pace of market activity. Diversification, as Carr and Walsh point out, "did not imply greatly increased self-sufficiency on plantations; rather, diversification encouraged local exchange and created a more complex network of local interdependence."

In regard to work patterns, therefore, there was no inherent conflict between the household economy and the market economy in early America, between the economics of self-sufficiency and the economics of profit and accumulation. Indeed, these essays suggest

54. Jameson, ed., *Johnson's Wonder-Working Providence*, 116, 179, 247 (quotation), 249, 250.

that any dichotomization between subsistence and commercialized agriculture is likely to be somewhat artificial. As the work of James T. Lemon and of Bettye Hobbs Pruitt has shown for eighteenth-century Pennsylvania and Massachusetts, home consumption used up no more than one-half to two-thirds of the total produce of most northern farms.[55] The only thing to be done with this surplus was to exchange it with one's neighbors or local traders. Hence, there was no obvious line of demarcation between local and external trade, or between self-sufficiency and commercialization. In a telling depiction of Pennsylvania households, Pruitt points out that these farms were "*both* more self-sufficient *and* more commercialized" than Massachusetts farms, "because they were, quite simply, more prosperous in every respect."[56] By the same token, household self-sufficiency— given the economic interdependence of early America—*depended* on market exchange.

Throughout the colonial population, lively networks of local exchange—within the compass of an international market economy— produced both individual prosperity and mutual reliance. While much research will be needed to sort out the relationships between local, regional, interregional, and international commerce, the general importance of market production for the work lives of early Americans seems beyond question. As Daniel Vickers has observed elsewhere, "If the *idealization* of the hardy, self-sufficient farmer of past centuries has any reality, it is as a sentimental invention of the industrial world." In a similar vein, John J. McCusker and Russell M. Menard have concluded from their survey of the economy of early America: "The fully self-sufficient yeoman farmer of colonial America is largely mythical: almost all colonists were tied to overseas trade."[57]

It is important, however, not to replace one stereotype with another. Market orientation did not connote a fully competitive, maximizing ethic. Free men and women in early America did "accumu-

55. James T. Lemon, "Household Consumption in Eighteenth-Century America and Its Relationship to Production and Trade: The Situation among Farmers in Southeastern Pennsylvania," *Agricultural History*, XLI (1967), 59–70; Lemon, *The Best Poor Man's Country: A Geographical Study of Early Southeastern Pennsylvania* (Baltimore, 1972); Bettye Hobbs Pruitt, "Self-Sufficiency and the Agricultural Economy of Eighteenth-Century Massachusetts," *WMQ*, 3d Ser., XLI (1984), 333–364.

56. Pruitt, letter, *WMQ*, 3d Ser., XLII (1985), 559.

57. Vickers, " 'Cherries . . . Are Ready Cash': A Case Study in Early American Economic Values," MS, 14; McCusker and Menard, *The Economy of British America*, 10.

late," but they did not "maximize," particularly at the expense of their neighbors. Far from being Weberian "rational calculators," most colonists, especially in New England, worked in part to "entertain each other in brotherly affection."[58] Perhaps the best term to describe such activity, one that may permit us to get beyond the sterility of the "maximization" versus "sufficiency" debate, is Herbert Simon's "satisficing." Such a term has the virtue of both allowing for future elevations of expectations and accepting the necessity of communal obligation.[59] Early Americans, it is clear, understood that work and its products benefited the community as well as the individual household. Laurel Ulrich's essay (as well as the Clemens-Simler and Carr-Walsh pieces) shows vividly that crops and goods were used both as commodities and as means to foster neighborly ties among households. A number of reigning dichotomies—use versus exchange, sufficiency versus commercialization, petty commodity production versus plantation mode of production, moral economy versus market economy—distort this complex social reality and need to be used with greater caution.

Indeed, as the earlier comments regarding definitions of work and labor have suggested, the entire problem of nomenclature demands additional refinement. What do we call a market-oriented society in an era without a reliable currency, banks, and general incorporation laws, and with relative scarcities of both capital and wage labor? One fruitful approach may involve a return to the distinction made some years ago by Karl Polanyi between a "market society," which early America surely was not, and a "society with markets," which it surely was. Fred Block and Margaret R. Somers have pointed out in a provocative discussion of this question that, for Polanyi, "the distinction between the existence of markets in society and the existence of a market society is fundamental." In Polanyi's view, a market society came into being only in the nineteenth century when regulatory restrictions were eliminated and land, labor, and money were fully commoditized. And in an observation that could be applied without

58. For a compelling discussion of the Puritan psychology of work, see Charles Lloyd Cohen, God's Caress: The Psychology of Puritan Religious Experience (New York, 1986), 111–133.

59. Herbert A. Simon, "A Behavioral Model of Rational Choice," Quarterly Journal of Economics, LXIX (1955), 99–118. Simon's essay was called to my attention by Albert O. Hirschman, Rival Views of Market Society and Other Recent Essays (New York, 1986), 13–14. On the relationship between "vaulting ambitions" and economic growth, see Joyce Appleby "Ideology and Theory: The Tension between Political and Economic Liberalism in Seventeenth-Century England," AHR, LXXXI (1976), 500–505.

distortion to colonial British America, Polanyi believed, "The issue is not the existence of markets, but the way in which markets are inserted into the social whole." Moreover, following Émile Durkheim's emphasis on the noncontractual underpinnings of contract, Polanyi contended that market transactions rested on such general collective social goods as trust and regulation that needed to be drawn from moral and civil agencies ancillary to the market system.[60] All of these observations, it seems possible, could be investigated with profit in future studies of the economy of colonial British America. Indeed, as the fluid and ever-changing labor systems revealed by the essays in this volume suggest, analyses of the relationship between markets and society in early America deserve a prominent place in future research agenda.[61]

60. Fred Block and Margaret R. Somers, "Beyond the Economistic Fallacy: The Holistic Social Science of Karl Polanyi," in Theda Skocpol, ed., *Vision and Method in Historical Sociology* (Cambridge, 1984), 64–65.

61. Capitalism, it needs to be stated, requires cooperation even while it invites competition. As Thomas Haskell has pointed out, "After nearly two centuries of criticism of market society, it is easy to forget how brutal life could be before the profit motive ruled supreme and how moderate, in the long perspective of human history, the capitalist's license for aggression really is." In particular, Haskell emphasizes: "Contrary to romantic folklore, the marketplace is not a Hobbesian war of all against all. Many holds are barred. Success ordinarily requires not only pugnacity and shrewdness but also restraint." And, in a formulation that seems to apply with especial force to a society composed primarily of dissenting Protestants, he avers that market participation helped teach people both "to keep their promises" and "to attend to the remote consequences of their actions." For Haskell, "in the long history of human morality there is no landmark more significant than the appearance of the man who can be trusted to keep his promises." He believes that it was not until the 18th century "that societies first appeared whose economic systems depended on the expectation that most people, most of the time, were sufficiently conscience-ridden (and certain of retribution) that they could be trusted to keep their promises." At this juncture, all that we can say with confidence is that there was no *inherent* conflict between commerce and community. As studies of Gloucester, Marblehead, and Springfield, Massachusetts, have attempted to show, market relationships could play an integrative as well as a disintegrative role in early America, often fostering social harmony more than undermining it. Likewise, both the Clemens-Simler and the Carr-Walsh essays show that diversification of the rural economy—with the progressive specialization of labor it engendered—increased rather than attenuated mutual reliance. It also generated increased opportunities for those far down on the social scale, such as day laborers. Haskell, "Capitalism and the Origins of the Humanitarian Sensibility," parts 1 and 2, *AHR*, XC (1985), 339–361, 547–566 (quotations, 549–553); Christine L. Heyrman, *Commerce and Culture: The Maritime Communities of Colonial Massachusetts, 1690–1750* (New York, 1984); Innes, *Labor in a New Land*. For an example of a sociologist who has been converted by contemporary events to the view that working people fare better under capitalism—with all

In this regard, it is also worth noting that the eighteenth century produced what Albert O. Hirschman describes as the first "political arguments for capitalism before its triumph." As early as 1704, political economists like Samuel Ricard were asserting that "commerce attaches [people] one to another through mutual utility." In *The Rights of Man*, Tom Paine declared that commerce is "a pacific system, operating to cordialise mankind," by making individuals as well as nations "useful to each other." The "invention of commerce," for Paine, was "the greatest approach towards universal civilization that has yet been made by any means not immediately flowing from moral principles." It was during the eighteenth century, in the persons of James Steuart, Montesquieu, Hume, and Condorcet, that the *doux commerce* thesis came into prominence. According to this formulation, not only would material "interests" check the more dangerous "passions," but commerce would promote personal civility and rectitude. The classic expression of this thesis was provided by Montesquieu in *De l'esprit des lois*: "It is almost a general rule that wherever the ways of man are gentle [*moeurs douces*] there is commerce; and wherever there is commerce, there the ways of man are gentle."[62] While the rise of industrial capitalism during the nineteenth century would make such confidence problematical, its ascendancy during the colonial period warrants more attention than historians have given it. This seems particularly true for those concerned with labor and its products in an era when hard work and market orientation apparently were conjoined for the first time in a systematic fashion.[63]

The reference to hard work, of course, demands engagement with one of the most venerable questions pertaining to New World labor—the impact of the Protestant ethic. Despite the vast literature dealing with this topic, and despite the centrality of Calvinism in the lives of most white colonists, there has been to date no study assess-

---

its uncertainties and inequalities—than competing economic systems, see Peter L. Berger, *The Capitalist Revolution: Fifty Propositions about Prosperity, Equality, and Liberty* (New York, 1986), esp. 32–49. For a theoretically grounded critique of Marx's analysis of capitalism, see Leszek Kolakowski, *Main Currents of Marxism: Its Rise, Growth, and Dissolution* (Oxford, 1978), I, 262–420.

62. Ricard (*Traité général du commerce* [Amsterdam, 1781]), Paine, and Montesquieu cited in Hirschman, *Rival Views of Market Society*, 107–108. See also Hirschman, *The Passions and the Interests: Political Arguments for Capitalism before Its Triumph* (Princeton, N.J., 1977), 56–66.

63. A more detailed consideration of the general argument being pursued here will be found in Stephen Innes, "The Puritan Productive Ethic: Work, Religion, and Development in Colonial New England" (forthcoming). See also Joyce Appleby, *Capitalism and a New Social Order: The Republican Vision of the 1790s* (New York, 1984), 25–50.

ing the impact of dissenting Protestantism on both the work calendar and work habits of colonial British Americans. There is reason to believe, for example, that the elimination of both the old Catholic holidays and Saint Monday was more complete in the colonies than in the mother country, and this presumably led to higher levels of productivity. In calling our attention to "how much was lost" in the way of holidays, recreations, and rituals in the transit to the New World, Richard L. Bushman has asked: "Where were the morris dancers, the wassailing, the annual wakes, the craft holidays, the maypoles?" Where, too, were the alehouses, stool-ball matches, revel feasts, church-ales, and annual perambulations of the bounds? Apparently, the combination of the heavy work needs of colonization and the religious sensibilities of the white settler population left little room for such rituals and recreations in early America.

All of this suggests the possibility that, in a number of important ways, the colonial work culture was distinct from that of Britain. We see from the Carr-Walsh essay that English metal miners arriving to work in Virginia mines in the 1730s were incensed to discover that they would not receive as a customary right some 130 of the old holidays. In New England, Puritans took especial measures to purge the calendar of most red letter days, and selectmen were enjoined to monitor the population to keep potential idlers at their labors. Likewise, in regard to the intensity and purposefulness of labor patterns during the workday, it seems reasonable to suppose that the Protestant dignification of labor played some role in increasing efficiency. Comparisons with the Catholic colonies of Spanish and Portuguese America, where the Thomistic emphasis on the penal nature of work was more prominent and notions of the calling were less pronounced, may prove especially fruitful.[64]

THE THIRD major theme of this collection is that work patterns became more intensified during the eighteenth century. Throughout the British colonies, there appears to have been a clear movement from semiseasonal to continuous work patterns. The timing of the movement from seasonal labor to incessant labor appears to have been roughly the same in both the wheat-livestock and the tobacco-corn-wheat regions. Fed by economic diversification, the conversion

64. Bushman, "High-Style and Vernacular Cultures," in Greene and Pole, eds., *Colonial British America*, 371; Charles H. George and Katherine George, *The Protestant Mind of the English Reformation, 1570–1640* (Princeton, N.J., 1961), 131; Christopher Hill, "Protestantism and the Rise of Capitalism," in F. J. Fisher, ed., *Essays in the Economic and Social History of Tudor and Stuart England* (Cambridge, 1961), 15–39; A. J. Gurevich, *Categories of Medieval Culture* (New York, 1984).

to slavery, new war- and famine-related demand in Europe and the West Indies, and possibly the consumer revolution, such a transition had been achieved in most portions of early America by the mid-eighteenth century. Multiple cropping helped fill out the agricultural year, and the rise in both household manufacturing and craft activities gave free men and women more tasks to occupy previously slack periods. Slaves—those bearing the greatest brunt of the change—now worked longer days, had fewer slow periods, and found themselves increasingly called out for night work. Wage earners in the rural countryside found a more nearly constant demand for their services, particularly during the post-Revolutionary era.[65] While in the New England colonies the shift from farm formation to farm maintenance may have partially abated the intensification of work regimes, everywhere else the overriding trend appears to have been toward more continuous patterns of work.

The possibility also exists that, with the passage of the eighteenth century, work habits became increasingly linked to consumption. That is, people may have worked harder out of a conscious design to augment their store of material possessions rather than concentrating, as before, on capital accumulation. In the larger scheme, we know that most of the fruits of harder work continued to go into savings or capital investment.[66] The productivity gains in the American economy are inexplicable otherwise. In addition, the increasingly compelling notion of America as a Christian Sparta, peopled by hardworking and frugal republicans, served to check excessive enthusiasm for acquisition of luxury goods. And, from a sheerly economic perspective, the fact that consumer goods were becoming cheaper by mid-century meant that families could improve their standard of living without working harder. All this said, there are still powerful indications that, after 1750, free men and women began to work more often with a view toward purchasing the newly available housewares and wearing apparel earlier deemed to be luxuries. In what has come to be a familiar story for Americans, one luxury after another came to be redefined as a necessity. T. H. Breen, who has gone so far as to describe Staffordshire ceramics as the "Coca-Cola" of eighteenth-century British North America, contends that the desire to purchase such luxury imports proved "overwhelm-

65. Ester Boserup, *The Conditions of Agricultural Growth: The Economics of Agrarian Change under Population Pressure* (London, 1965).

66. Lois G. Carr and Lorena S. Walsh, "Consumer Behavior in the Colonial Chesapeake," in Cary Carson, Ronald Hoffman, and Peter J. Albert, eds., *Of Consuming Interests: The Style of Life in the Eighteenth Century* (Charlottesville, Va., forthcoming).

ing." As a result of this continual upgrading of the notions of comfort, freeholders may have driven themselves, their servants, their waged workers, and especially their slaves harder and more continuously.[67] Many of the larger implications of this issue as well as those pertaining to the overall question of work intensification still await systematic investigation.

THE FOURTH major theme to emerge from these essays relates to the direction of historical change. To begin, it seems evident that, excepting the rise of slavery, there was no manifestly visible transition from one form of labor relations to another in early America—from custom to contract, from subsistence to commercial society, or from paternal to impersonal labor relationships. While Marcus Rediker and Billy Smith find a marked shift from patriarchal to contractual labor relationships among deep-sea mariners and Philadelphia's lesser artisans and laborers, Daniel Vickers finds an increased resort to patriarchalism, at least for several generations, in seventeenth-century New England. By the same token, Clemens and Simler document the emergence of *both* cottager and wage-laboring classes in late-eighteenth-century Pennsylvania. And Laurel Ulrich finds during the same period a continuation of the old permeable system of mixed family–domestic servant labor. Even on slave plantations, as the essay by Carr and Walsh helps document, the movement from gang to task labor was at least in part a return to the smaller, more decentralized work units that had prevailed before 1690. In addition, as Philip Morgan forcefully reminds us, even at its height from 1720 to 1750, the gang system was never so dominant and widespread as some have assumed. We also have the paradox that, while some white workers, such as mariners, were moving toward more collective work, male slaves were moving toward more individualistic task labor.

Changes doubtless there were in the early American labor system, both from gang to task work and from implicit to explicit contractualism. Of these, there can be no doubt. But these shifts should be seen as variations on existing themes or amplifications of existing tenden-

67. Breen, "Creative Adaptations: Peoples and Cultures," in Greene and Pole, eds., *Colonial British America*, 222–223. Jack P. Greene has quoted the possibly apocryphal comments of a Barbadian slave regarding the English productive ethic: "The Devel was in the English-man, that he makes every thing work; he makes the *Negro* work, the Horse work, the Ass work, the Wood work, the Water work, and the Winde work" ("Changing Identity in the British Caribbean: Barbados as a Case Study," in Canny and Pagden, eds., *Colonial Identity in the Atlantic World*, 222).

cies rather than as replacements of one form of labor relations by another. The hallmarks of the early American labor system were its flexibility and fluidity in combining—in highly diverse work environments—customary and contractual, free and bonded labor for the purpose of producing for the market.

The evolution of household manufacturing of fibers, as a case in point, was quite the reverse of the oft-posited transition from "personal self-sufficiency" to "production for the market." The age of homespun came at the end of the colonial period, not at the beginning. The vast majority of textiles used by colonists during the seventeenth century were imported, paid for with the profits from tobacco, grain, lumber, or livestock husbandry. In the Chesapeake, as Carr and Walsh show, it was not until the 1680s that sheep, flax, and weaving began to become common. Spinning wheels, rare in the seventeenth-century Chesapeake, by the mid-eighteenth century were becoming omnipresent. By century's end, as Carr and Walsh report, the probate inventories of fully 90 percent of married tenants owning property worth fifty pounds or less indicated the presence of spinning wheels. As white women became increasingly active in household manufacturing, the authors conclude that "opportunities for such income were not being overlooked." In their essay on southeastern Pennsylvania, Clemens and Simler find a transformation parallel to the one identified for the Chesapeake by Carr and Walsh. And similarly in frontier Maine, Laurel Ulrich finds that "the late eighteenth century was an era of burgeoning household production," and she too uses probate records to document the expansion and dispersion of spinning and weaving, finding that in the post-Revolutionary era "all of the weaving in Hallowell was done by women and girls." The expansion of household manufacture during this period, therefore, did not represent the rise and expansion of market relations—these had existed at the outset—but, rather, the rise of import-replacement activities. It was now more economical for American households to manufacture coarse cloth for use or sale and still buy finer textiles. It is also possible that, in those regions where women had worked in the fields, their employment in household manufactures reflected the presence of substitute field hands, most notably, of course, slaves. And the rising desires among farm women for more, and more refined, household amenities also may have spurred greater efforts to produce a larger surplus product for exchange purposes.[68]

68. Carole Shammas, "How Self-sufficient Was Early America?" *Journal of Interdisciplinary History*, XIII (1982–1983), 247–272.

Finally, for historians studying work and labor in early America, there is the question of the psychological relationship between work and landownership. Simply stated, did the prospect of owning land spur men and women to greater work efforts? When John Smith made ownership of one's "owne labour and land" the core of his vision for the New World, he became one of the first in a long line of commentators who would link the psychology of work effort to the prospect of landownership. In both Virginia and Plymouth, as contemporaries quickly discovered, the period of collective ownership produced lassitude and inefficiency, which the conversion to private property eventually reversed. As Plymouth Colony Governor William Bradford described his reluctant decision to abandon communal ownership: The settlers "began to think how they might raise as much corn as they could, and obtain a better crop than they had done [under the communal system], that they might not still thus languish in misery. At length, after much debate of things, the Governor (with the advice of the chiefest among them) gave way that they should set corn every man for his own particular [household], and in that regard trust to themselves." And so the leaders "assigned to every family a parcel of land, according to the proportion of their number, for that end." "This had," reports Bradford, "very good success, for it made all hands very industrious, so as much more corn was planted than otherwise would have been. . . . The women now went willingly into the field, and took their little ones with them to set corn; which before would allege weakness and inability; whom to have compelled would have been thought great tyranny and oppression." In the governor's political economy, barring families from private ownership of land had been "found to breed much confusion and discontent and retard much employment that would have been to their benefit and comfort."[69] Not surprisingly for migrants from a land-short society, English colonists apparently worked harder when the prospects of becoming yeomen beckoned.

The larger productive gains achieved through anticipation of landownership, while in many respects beyond historical recall, continue to demand scrutiny. We will never know how many extra hours were spent in the field or shop or at the wheel or loom in the anticipation of obtaining either some land or more land. But it is likely to have been considerable. Then, as now, the most onerous tasks could be palatable when undertaken voluntarily. Reporting to the Board of Trade near the end of the colonial period, New York Governor Sir

69. Bradford, *Of Plymouth Plantation*, ed. Morison, 120–121.

Henry Moore penned an especially acute commentary on what he regarded as this peculiar American characteristic:

> The genius of the People in a Country where every one can have Land to work upon leads them so naturally into Agriculture, that it prevails over every other occupation. There can be no stronger Instances of this [phenomenon], than in the servants Imported from Europe of different Trades; as soon as the Time stipulated in their Indentures is expired, they immediately quit their Masters, and get a small tract of Land, in settling which for the first three or four years they lead miserable lives, and in the most abject Poverty; but all this is patiently bourne and submitted to with the greatest cheerfulness, the Satisfaction of being Land holders smooths every difficulty.[70]

In the century and a half between the time when John Smith first stepped ashore in Virginia and when these words were written, America had seen its share—some believe more than its share—of misery and even abject poverty. The most conspicuous, and most tragic, disfigurement of Smith's vision of smallholding prosperity, of course, was the growing institution of slavery. As Lincoln, whose labor theory of value closely paralleled Smith's, pointed out during his debates with Stephen A. Douglas, blacks were doubly cursed in being denied both the fruits of their labor and the expectation of eventual betterment. Until such time as the institution became condemned as a moral abomination, it would mock what was best about Smith's vision. In addition to the slaves' uniquely burdensome hardships, there were the privations and overwork experienced by white servants in the early Chesapeake, many of whom never survived their seasoning time. White women in both the plantation South and in the cereal grain colonies apparently experienced fewer comforts, greater dangers, and a more rigorous work regimen than did their Old World sisters. The daily lives of urban laborers and deep-sea sailors were often a litany of hardship, privation, and uncertainty. From the vantage point of the twentieth-century observer, colonial America indeed was a hard, even a brutal world.

But it also had its compensations. After the initial settlement years, few people starved in America—a fact that European visitors from John Josslyn through Tocqueville and Dickens felt compelled to comment upon.[71] In the often uncertain early modern era, a full pot was

---

70. In Richard B. Morris, ed., *A History of the American Worker* (Princeton, N.J., 1983), 19.

71. In 1769 South Carolina's Christopher Gadsden observed that what differen-

a basic consideration, not to be discounted.[72] In a direct echo of John Smith's vision sounded on the eve of the Revolution, the Quaker labor entrepreneur and reformer Thomas Clifford instructed his recruiting agents to "acquaint the poor labouring people with the genuine state of this country, and the opportunitie industrious honest poor men have of supporting themselves by their labour here." In contrast to the Old World, Clifford emphasized, in America wages were high, work was plentiful, and provisions were cheap.[73] The fact that the colonial period ended as it began—with a great burst of migration to North America—suggests that such appeals were being heard and heeded by the working men and women of late-eighteenth-century Britain. Equally important, as the recurrent waves of immigrants also attested, was the "Satisfaction of being Land holders." The growing difficulty of attaining this goal in America during the late eighteenth century and the tragedy of plantation slavery were the principal disfigurements of John Smith's vision. But the essays in this volume suggest that this vision in all other ways came remarkably close to fulfillment. Although at a higher price in labor and suffering than Smith had anticipated, British North America had indeed given many men and women of "small meanes" a chance they otherwise would not have had.

---

tiated the American poor from the European poor was the unlikelihood that the former would ever face starvation. See Pauline Maier, *The Old Revolutionaries: Political Lives in the Age of Samuel Adams* (New York, 1980), 76.

72. Gloria Main has pointed out that "for the poorer planters of the Chesapeake, a full belly and a good smoke could be mighty satisfying" (*Tobacco Colony*, 205).

73. Bailyn, *Voyagers to the West*, 264.

Daniel Vickers

Working the Fields in a Developing Economy
Essex County, Massachusetts, 1630–1675

IN THE MIDDLE of the seventeenth century, an unknown English-man observed: "Virginia thrives by keeping many servants and these in strict obedience. New England conceit they and their Children can doe enough, and soe have rarely above one Servant."[1] Here, stated for the first time, was a basic truth about early America: that free families were to the northern colonies what bound servants were to the South—the human foundation of the dominant mode of production. That planters in the Chesapeake exporting tobacco for profit adopted indentured servitude while New Englanders producing for home consumption and local markets did not made perfect sense: one economy required such help, and the other could not afford it. New Englanders lacked a bonanza crop that would generate both the rapid growth of capital and a pressing need for large amounts of labor. These contrasts, however, tell only half of the story, for settlers in both regions did share one basic challenge—developing a new country. If the Massachusetts colony never experienced the acute scarcities of capital and labor that prevailed in Virginia and Mary-land, it was still a growing settlement; and relative to the abundance of unexploited land and the work required to bring it under the plow, productive equipment and manpower were in short supply. The difficulty that these northerners faced was a milder though similar version of what troubled the first settlers to the Chesapeake: how did one go about accumulating capital in a labor-scarce environment?

Although New Englanders had intended to construct a society

This essay benefited greatly from criticism by Stephen Innes, Edward Ayres, Philip Morgan, Lewis Fischer, and Laurel Ulrich.
    1. As quoted in Abbot Emerson Smith, *Colonists in Bondage: White Servitude and Convict Labor in America, 1607–1776* (Chapel Hill, N.C., 1947), 29.

out of households transplanted intact and unchanged from the Old Country, the exigencies of farming the wilderness would not permit this. The division of labor by gender, which in the English rural tradition meant that women worked in and around the house and yard while men toiled in the fields beyond, was preserved in Massachusetts. Several historians have portrayed the female domain within the family economy with considerable sensitivity. But what about the work relationships that connected male New Englanders: fathers with sons, masters with servants, landlords with tenants, and employers with casual help? Historians have studied most of these separately in some detail but rarely together and with little attempt to assess the relative importance of each.[2] And this last is an important omission, for Massachusetts farmers and their sons had to adjust the rural traditions of Old England when they encountered the American frontier.

But what exactly did the English inheritance amount to? Although it is difficult to do justice to the amazing variety, both by region and class, of seventeenth-century English farm work experiences, some broad truths stand out. First, we know that agricultural labor was generally carried out in household units. Farmers usually worked the land that they occupied with the consistent help only of their children and servants. Times of special activity, such as harvest (mowing, reaping, carting, threshing, and a variety of other tasks), might necessitate the employment of some outside hands, but few farms depended on such individuals the year round. True, over the course of the early modern period, rising numbers of men and women, displaced by enclosures or by the pressure of population growth upon the land, did attempt to make a living from different forms of short-term employment, especially in the southern and eastern portions of the country which produced most of the Puritan migration. Some of these dispossessed individuals rented cottages on the fringes of the large consolidated farms that offered them daily work; others dwelt on small holdings in the forest and migrated seasonally to regions where help was in demand; still others simply drifted up and down the countryside, selling their services on a casual basis. Yet, even if contemporary Englishmen voiced growing alarm at the

2. Laurel Thatcher Ulrich, *Good Wives: Image and Reality in the Lives of Women in Northern New England, 1650–1750* (New York, 1982), 11–86, and her essay in this volume. The most comprehensive works that deal with the working lives of white male New Englanders are Eric Guest Nellis, "Communities of Workers: Free Labor in Provincial Massachusetts, 1690–1765" (Ph.D. diss., University of British Columbia, 1979); and Stephen Innes, *Labor in a New Land: Economy and Society in Seventeenth-Century Springfield* (Princeton, N.J., 1983).

rising number of masterless men, it would still be a mistake to make too much of day labor in this period, for its advance was gradual and intermittent. In the years when the Puritan emigrants were departing for America, the bulk of England's agricultural output was still the product of household endeavor, even in the regions they had left behind.[3]

Second, we know that the exchange of goods and services between households was given its primary shape by the division of property. Rural Englishmen everywhere understood that the position each occupied in the hierarchy of wealth implied power over some and submission to others. "There is nothing more plain nor certain," as one writer put it, "than that God Almighty hath ordained and appointed different degrees of Authority and Subjection."[4] In the world of everyday work, subjection meant harking to the commands of others, and freedom from such commands stemmed only from control over land and capital. The more that one owned, the fewer days in the year that one spent in the employ of one's neighbors. Through the long procession of working days that constituted life for ordinary people, the only sure source of independence—and status—was the possession of property.[5]

Another major factor that gave shape to the organization of work in early modern England was age. From the time when they first began to help out with minor chores until, at marriage, they established households of their own, farm boys toiled under the direction of their elders. Through their early teens, they served mainly as agents of their fathers' will, learning the arts of husbandry under continual supervision. Then, about the age of thirteen or fourteen, almost two-thirds of them departed from their parents' quarters to enter the homes of other families short of help. Thenceforth, on a series of yearly contracts, they labored as servants in husbandry and saved what they could toward launching households of their own. Even after marriage, the majority of young Englishmen continued, for a few years at least, to seek daily employment at the farms of

3. Peter Laslett, *The World We Have Lost: England before the Industrial Age*, 2d ed. (New York, 1971), 1–22; Alan Everitt, "Farm Labourers," in Joan Thirsk, ed., *The Agrarian History of England and Wales*, vol. IV, *1500–1640* (London, 1967), 396–465; David G. Hey, *An English Rural Community: Myddle under the Tudors and Stuarts* (Leicester, 1974), 169–175; Keith Wrightson and David Levine, *Poverty and Piety in an English Village: Terling, 1525–1700* (New York, 1979), 33, 35–36.

4. As quoted in Robert W. Malcolmson, *Life and Labour in England, 1700–1780* (New York, 1981), 14.

5. C. W. Chalklin, *Seventeenth-Century Kent: A Social and Economic History* (London, 1965), 242; Everitt, "Farm Labourers," in Thirsk, ed., *Agrarian History*, IV, 416, 430–435.

older and wealthier neighbors. There was a dimension to economic power, therefore, that was generational.[6]

Finally, as E. L. Jones put it, "farming proper was something done by tenants."[7] Although the dauntingly complicated history of tenancy and other forms of dual ownership is only beginning to attract the attention it deserves, we do know that most of England's land area was held, not by outright owners, but by occupiers who paid for its use in a variety of ways. Some tenants satisfied their landlords with rents in cash or kind; most were also liable for tithes, heriot, or entry fines; others owed labor services. With growing frequency, the obligation to repair property also fell onto the shoulders of the occupier, who might even be expected to make improvements, although, in other instances, the landlord still assumed this responsibility himself. Nowhere was tenancy simple, nor did it escape enormous regional variation, but for most English farmers of the period it framed the work experience.[8] A hierarchy of tenant householders, therefore, assisted by sons, servants, and an increasing array of hired hands, operated the greatest part of the English rural economy in the seventeenth century.

Those families who left in the 1630s to colonize Massachusetts Bay intended to build there a "New England"—a purified re-creation in the New World of that to which they were accustomed in the Old. In their letters home, they stressed time and again the ways in which Massachusetts seemed to resemble or even improve upon their relinquished homeland. Francis Higginson believed that the countryside around Salem contained as "much good ground for corn and for grass as any is under the heavens." Thomas Graves celebrated the "goodly woods," the "open lands" where "grass and weeds grow up to a man's face," and the meadows "without any tree or shrub to hinder the scythe." Furthermore, New England was good for one. Wrote Higginson: "There is hardly a more hea[l]thful place to be found in the world that agreeth better with our English bodies." Those writers emphasized, moreover, that in New England there were enough lands, rivers, and forests for everyone to partake of

6. Laslett, *World We Have Lost*, 15, 16; Ann Kussmaul, *Servants in Husbandry in Early Modern England* (Cambridge, 1981), 34–84.

7. E. L. Jones, Introduction, in Jones, ed., *Agriculture and Economic Growth in England, 1650–1815* (London, 1967), 14.

8. See L. A. Clarkson, *The Pre-Industrial Economy in England, 1500–1750* (New York, 1972), 61–68; F.M.L. Thompson, "The Social Distribution of Landed Property in England since the Sixteenth Century," *Economic History Review*, 2d Ser., XIX (1966), 505–517; Peter Bowden, "Agricultural Prices, Farm Profits, and Rents," in Thirsk, ed., *Agrarian History*, IV, 674–694.

these advantages. With hard work, any settler could procure, if not riches, at least a fair share of this natural bounty—in brief, a comfortable and independent subsistence. Those who planned to enrich themselves were mistaken, observed Thomas Dudley in 1630, but those who had removed for spiritual ends would find ample building materials, fuel, soil, seas and rivers full of fish, pure air, and "good water to drink till wine or beer can be made." "Howsoever they are accounted poore," concluded William Wood in *New England's Prospect*, "they are well contented, and looke not so much at abundance as a competencie."⁹

One can distinguish here two separate aspirations. First, the settlers hoped to reproduce the level of material comfort which people of their condition had known at home; and, second, they intended to go about it in an English manner. At first glance, given the natural abundance that surrounded them in the new land, the reconciliation of these two purposes might seem to be a simple affair. But between them, as events were to prove, there existed a fundamental tension. It was difficult to build farms on New England's first frontier that could guarantee their owners the level of prosperity and civilization to which, in the Old World, they had been accustomed. Land had to be cleared, barns erected, fences built, and mills constructed—all from scratch and demanding more manpower, equipment, and skill on each piece of land than most early settlers could readily obtain. So "much labour and servise was to be done aboute building and planting," complained William Bradford in 1642, that "such as wanted help in that respecte, when they could not have such as they would, were glad to take such as they could." In a thinly settled country, where most family heads could acquire an independent freehold, the means to avoid working for others, help was simply too scarce and too expensive. Servants whose times were out, declared John Winthrop with obvious annoyance in 1645, "could not be hired . . . but upon unreasonable terms."¹⁰ This, indeed, was a problem: how

9. In Everett Emerson, ed., *Letters from New England: The Massachusetts Bay Colony, 1629–1638* (Amherst, Mass., 1976): Francis Higginson to his friends at Leicester, Sept. 1629, pp. 36–37; Thomas Graves to ———, Sept. 1629, p. 39; Francis Higginson to his friends at Leicester, Sept. 1629, p. 34; Thomas Dudley to the Lady Bridget, countess of Lincoln, Mar. 12, 28, 1630/31, p. 74; William Wood, *New England's Prospect*, as quoted in Peter N. Carroll, *Puritanism and the Wilderness: The Intellectual Significance of the New England Frontier, 1692–1700* (New York, 1969), 56.

10. William Bradford, *Bradford's History of Plymouth Plantation, 1606–1646*, ed. William T. Davis, Original Narratives of Early American History (New York, 1908), 367; John Winthrop, *Winthrop's Journal: "History of New England," 1630–*

could the rural economy of old England be reestablished in an environment where workmen were so difficult to procure? How, in other words, were the twin scarcities of capital and labor to be overcome? Such a dilemma, in truth, could not be resolved within the customary rules of labor organization familiar to the resident of a seventeenth-century English village. Paradoxically, the very urge to re-create what was familiar led the Bay colonists to order their working lives in a manner that was decidedly new.

Most free colonists in the Great Migration belonged to households prosperous enough to keep servants. Indeed, the surviving passenger lists from the 1630s indicate that servants were almost half again as common among the arriving settlers as in the towns and villages left behind. Nor should this surprise us, since the poorest English households—the only ones certain not to keep servants—were scarcely represented in the planting process. Those families who departed in the 1630s to establish themselves on the far side of the Atlantic were not a wealthy group, but their landholdings in the Old Country had normally been extensive enough to support some live-in help. And since they harbored no illusions about the task ahead of them, they took their servants along. Founding new settlements, warned Edward Johnson, required "every one that can lift a hawe."[11]

The Puritan migrants expected, therefore, that service in husbandry could be reestablished in New England; and, indeed, there were individual towns where the institution took root. In Springfield, Massachusetts, for example, John Pynchon employed servants to raise wheat, cattle, and timber for shipment abroad; and in Bristol, Rhode Island, a commerical town whose gentry bred horses and sheep for the market, such live-in help clearly was as important as in the villages of the Old Country.[12] In Essex County, however, the

1649, ed. James K. Hosmer, Original Narratives of Early American History (New York, 1908), 228.

11. T. H. Breen and Stephen Foster, "Moving to the New World: The Character of Early Massachusetts Immigration," *William and Mary Quarterly*, 3d Ser., XXX (1973), 194. For example, of 271 emigrants on board three ships that left Sandwich and Great Yarmouth in 1637, 54, or 21%, were servants. This compares to the average of 13% in early modern England reported by Peter Laslett, "Mean Household Size in England since the Sixteenth Century," in Laslett and Richard Wall, eds., *Household and Family in Past Time* (Cambridge, 1972), 152. Edward Johnson, *Johnson's Wonder-Working Providence, 1628–1651*, ed. J. Franklin Jameson, Original Narratives of Early American History (New York, 1910), 114 (quotation).

12. Stephen Innes, *Labor in a New Land*, 6–9, 106–117; John Demos, "Families in Colonial Bristol, Rhode Island: An Exercise in Historical Demography," *WMQ*, 3d Ser., XXV (1968), 43; Wilfred H. Munro, *The History of Bristol, Rhode Island* (Providence, R.I., 1880), esp. 111–112, 367.

English pattern did not persist. Once those servants accompanying the original migrants of the 1630s had dispersed, the system of service in husbandry swiftly collapsed. Male servants had accounted for at least 8 percent of the population of most English villages back home, and the rate was even greater if one included farming households alone. It was certainly so among those families as prosperous as those who joined in the Puritan migration. Indeed, it has been calculated that in early modern England 72 percent of yeomen, 47 percent of husbandmen, and 23 percent of tradesmen, the dominant occupational groups among New England's settlers, customarily kept at least one servant (male or female) under their roofs at any given time, and more frequently men than maids. In Essex County during the first half-century, by comparison, we can be confident that the proportion of male farm servants to the farming population as a whole did not exceed 4 percent.[13] The owners of the large estates—the Bradstreets, Appletons, Gardners, and others—who generally scorned physical labor themselves, did employ menservants on some of their property, but rarely more than two or three. Samuel Symonds, for example, one of the wealthiest landholders in

13. Kussmaul, *Servants in Husbandry*, 12, 52, 58, 146; Laslett, *World We Have Lost*, 66, 71–72; Peter Laslett and John Harrison, "Clayworth and Cogenhoe," in H. E. Bell and R. L. Ollard, eds., *Historical Essays, 1600–1750: Presented to David Ogg* (London, 1963), 169, 178. Where no breakdown by gender is given, I have assumed that 55% of servants were male, following Kussmaul, *Servants in Husbandry*, 4. The maximum figure of 4% for Essex County was derived as follows. First, in the agricultural work experiences described in the records of the county court involving masters in the top wealth decile of the population and their servants, the ratio of servants to masters was 1.4: 1. Second, the ratio of servants belonging to masters in the top wealth decile to the servants belonging to masters in the other nine deciles was (coincidentally) also 1.4: 1. Third, it was assumed that all householders in the top decile owned at least one servant. It follows that in a hypothetical community of 100 householders and a total population of 600 (assuming a 6: 1 ratio of total population to householders), the 10 wealthiest householders would have kept 14 servants, and the remaining 90 would have employed together only 10. A total of 24 servants constitutes, therefore, 4% of the population. Even 4%, however, must be regarded as a maximum, since the multiplier for population / householders of 6: 1 is probably low and since it is possible that some of the householders in the top decile did not own any servants. The work experiences were drawn from George Francis Dow and Mary G. Thresher, eds., *Records and Files of the Quarterly Courts of Essex County*, 9 vols. (Salem, Mass., 1911–1975), I–VI (hereafter cited as *Essex Courts*). The wealth status of masters was estimated from probate records, tax lists, town histories, and some secondary modern works (too numerous to be listed individually here). In Dedham, Mass., it has been calculated that 5% of the inhabitants during the 17th century were male and female servants. See Kenneth A. Lockridge, *A New England Town, the First Hundred Years: Dedham, Massachusetts, 1636–1736* (New York, 1970), 72.

the colony, who died in possession of seventeen hundred acres, told the Essex County court in 1661 that he kept only two such men in his home. Indeed, four-fifths or more of the county farmers kept no male servants at all. By comparison to rural households of equal estate in England, about half of which included menservants, Essex families did largely without.[14]

Furthermore, the limited system of servitude which did exist on county farms before 1675 bore little resemblance to English practice. Not only were farm servants seldom the sons of neighbors, but they rarely possessed kin anywhere in the county. Some were Scots and Irishmen, stolen from their beds by Cromwell's soldiers, clapped into prison ships, and transported across the Atlantic "by order of the State of England" to be sold. Others, on the pattern of migrants to the plantation colonies, were Englishmen who had formally indentured themselves or had been indentured by their parents for several years' bound labor on Massachusetts farms in return for the cost of their passage. Still others were single and unattached residents of the colony, perhaps at one time indentured immigrants themselves, who now sold their labor by the month or year and lived with the masters for whom they worked.[15] It is true that certain characteristics of farm servitude did not change when it crossed the Atlantic. In age, these young men ranged, for the most part, between fifteen and

14. *Essex Courts,* II, 295. On Samuel Symonds, see Edward Spaulding Perzel, "The First Generation of Settlement in Colonial Ipswich, Massachusetts, 1633–1660" (Ph.D. diss., Rutgers University, 1967), 184. Following the same data and assumptions as in n. 13, we can set the maximum number of householders with male servants at 20% of all householders in the county. Lawrence Towner, in "A Good Master Well Served: A Social History of Servitude in Massachusetts, 1620–1750" (Ph.D. diss., Northwestern University, 1955), 10, 160, estimates that in all of Massachusetts, three-quarters or more of the colonists kept no servants of either gender. In Bristol, R.I., the number of households containing male or female servants in 1689 amounted to 31% of the town's total; Bristol, however, did lie in a region of commercial farming on a scale unknown in Essex County. See George T. Paine, "Census of Bristol in Plymouth County, Now in Rhode Island, 1689," *New England Historical and Genealogical Register,* XXXIV (1880), 404–405. For proportion of English households containing servants broken down into occupational categories, see Laslett, *World We Have Lost,* 72.

15. Of those servants who could be identified from the court records, only 22% ($N = 40$) possessed kin in Essex County; and very few more (although identification becomes more difficult over the wider area) appear to have had relatives anywhere in New England: *Essex Courts,* I–VI; James Savage, *A Genealogical Dictionary of the First Settlers of New England . . . ,* 4 vols., (Boston, 1860–1862). For some specific examples of these servant types, see *Essex Courts,* I, 381–382, II, 294–296, 357–358, III, 371–372, 457, VI, 156, 159–160. See also Towner, "Good Master Well Served," 51–74, 127–129.

twenty-five years, and in aspiration they hoped to establish a means of marrying and settling down, much as they had in the mother country.[16] And like English farm servants, they found that the path to real prosperity and independence was difficult to negotiate. In fact, almost half of them had given up the attempt, at least in Essex County, within ten years of their appearance in the record and had left the region.[17] There, however, the similarity ends; for although it is possible to identify from the seventeenth-century records a smattering of live-in help, male (and probably female) service in husbandry was not as important in this part of the New World as it had been in the Old. Rural householders were not averse on occasion to apprenticing their sons into skilled trades. But simple farm service for native New England men and boys—contrary to the assertion of Edmund Morgan in *The Puritan Family*—was never common.[18]

Given the scarcity of servants, could the yeomen and husbandmen of Essex County turn easily to the employment of neighbors by the day? English farmers, especially in the southern and eastern portions of the country, had been dipping into regional labor markets with growing frequency for a century or more; but was the same choice open to their cousins in the Bay Colony? The quantitative importance of day labor in the rural economy of Essex County is difficult to measure, for the simple reason that almost every man at one time or another worked for somebody else. The majority of these workmen were in their twenties and thirties, but then so were most of the county's adult population. Indeed, it was only the very wealthy and the very old who spared themselves employment on these terms.[19]

16. Of the farm servants in Essex County between 1630 and 1675 whose ages could be determined, 60% ($N = 37$) were between 15 and 25 years old at the time when the court records identified them as working for their masters (*Essex Courts*, I–VI). Their ages were calculated from internal evidence in the court records, town histories, and genealogies (esp. Savage, *Genealogical Dictionary*).

17. About 47% ($N = 43$) of farm servants in this period had disappeared from the records, either by death or by leaving the county, within ten years of their being identified as servants working for masters (*Essex Courts*, I–IX). Probate, tax, town, and vital records were also checked for evidence of residency in the county. For a few surviving records of probate relating to ex-servants, see Essex County Probate Files, nos. 370, 576, 1336, 8232, 19222, 25057, 29645, Registry of Probate, Essex County Courthouse, Salem, Mass.; *Essex Courts*, III, 94–95. They range from insolvency to the £736 left by John Bailey of Rowley (unusual for being the son of an early settler and therefore the heir to an estate), "deceased in the voyage to Cannada" in 1691.

18. Edmund S. Morgan, *The Puritan Family: Religion and Domestic Relations in Seventeenth-Century New England* (New York, 1966), 66–78, 109.

19. Those termed "day laborers" in this essay were men who hired themselves out by the day and did not live with their employers. Of such individuals whose

Thus, day laborers cannot, as with servants, be dismissed as an insignificant portion of the population. Nor, on the other hand, since hiring oneself out may have occurred only a few times a year, can we be certain of its importance. The question would seem to rest upon the issue, not of how many residents of the county were laborers, but of how many days the average villager spent in the employ of his farming neighbors. We know that, in the latter half of the eighteenth century and in the more commercialized economy of rural Pennsylvania, labor was exchanged with some frequency and that there was a similar, if less commercial, interdependency among the women of late-eighteenth-century Maine. For the seventeenth century, however, without detailed diaries or account books to guide us, equivalent precision is impossible.[20]

Yet, significantly, the first New Englanders, fresh from their experience with the mature economy of the mother country, had few doubts on the matter. Daily help, they complained, was both expensive and difficult to find. Ecclesiastical synods, sessions of court, town meetings, and private individuals alike took account of labor's cost, though they viewed it as a product less of market forces than of moral failings. "Extortion" and "Oppression" were the terms they preferred, echoing one another repeatedly through the end of the seventeenth century. And on one level they were right: the twenty to thirty pence per day (if one converts local currency into sterling) that common agricultural labor obtained in Essex County before 1675 was an unusually healthy wage. By the English standard of twelve to fifteen pence per day, such earnings quite understandably provoked attention, and they bespoke the favorable bargaining position that scarce labor commanded.[21] For a while, the General Court attempted

---

ages could be estimated, 64% ($N = 17$) were between the ages of 20 and 30, while none was over 70. Only 2 of the 65 day laborers who could be identified from the court records belonged to families that were clearly in the top wealth decile of the town in which they lived (*Essex Courts*, I–IX; Savage, *Genealogical Dictionary*; as well as tax lists, probate records, town histories, vital records, and genealogies).

20. See, below, the essay by Paul Clemens and Lucy Simler on 18th-century Pennsylvania as well as Laurel Ulrich's portrait of women in 18th-century Maine. As for the 17th century, Stephen Innes has calculated that more than half of the population of Springfield, Mass.—a town where the demand for labor was usually large—in any given year worked a month or more for John Pynchon, the community's only major employer. For less than 20% of Springfield's inhabitants, however, was he the primary source of income (*Labor in a New Land*, 38, 72).

21. Richard B. Morris, *Government and Labor in Early America* (New York, 1946), 55–78. Examples of daily wages in Essex County during this period can be found in *Essex Courts*, II, 328, 363–364, IV, 107, VI, 87, VII, 208, VIII, 64, IX, 80; Winthrop, *Journal*, ed. Hosmer, I, 112. These values were converted into British cur-

to regulate these wages, but by 1641 it had given up. Workmen, explained John Winthrop, "for being restrained . . . would either remove to other places where they might have more, or else being able to live by planting and other employments of their own, they would not be hired at all." So irregular, indeed, was the employment of hired help in this land of economic independence that the occupational designation of "labourer" almost disappeared.[22] Of course, there were artisans—house carpenters, blacksmiths, and millers, for example—whom farmers might employ periodically to perform some specialized work, particularly in the early years of farm building.[23] And no farm, of course, was entirely free of the need to ask neighbors for occasional assistance. Still, in the regular round of field chores and property maintenance, it was the rare husbandman who placed much reliance on neighbors or strangers employed by the day.

If free labor was not critical to the raising of livestock and crops, it still possessed characteristics that are important to understand. First, we know that it commonly involved men with less land and fewer draft animals, supplementing their income by selling their labor to those with more. Indeed, usually a great deal more, for 52 percent of the employers who surfaced in the court records were within the top wealth decile of the towns in which they lived and were clearly engaged in production for the market.[24] Thus, in 1660, we find John Fuller of Ipswich, a middle-aged husbandman of moderate means, working on the land of John Lee, one of the most prosperous farmers in the village. Similarly, Edmund Batter, a merchant in Salem with considerable property, employed a wide variety of poorer neighbors on his estate cutting thatch and carting hay. Second, it was usual for younger married men who had yet to accumulate much property

---

rency, using John J. McCusker, *Money and Exchange in Europe and America, 1600–1775: A Handbook* (Chapel Hill, N.C., 1978), 138–139. The English wage of 12d.–15d. was obtained from Innes, *Labor in a New Land*, 75 n.

22. Winthrop, *Journal*, ed. Hosmer, II, 24. Notice, for example, the infrequent references to "laborers" under the "tradesmen" heading of the indices to *Essex Courts*, I–VIII.

23. Innes, *Labor in a New Land*, 82–106.

24. Of 37 instances where the approximate relative wealth of both employer and employee could be determined (that is, whether they belonged to different wealth quartiles in the town in which they lived), 26 involved employers who were wealthier than their employees. In 6 cases, the parties involved were from the same quartile; and in 5, the employee was actually wealthier. *Essex Courts*, I–VI. Wealth estimates were based on evidence from probate records, tax lists, and town histories.

to find work from the older and more established farmers in their community. Nathaniel Felton, for example, as a young householder clearly on the rise though only recently married, cut timber in the 1650s for the Bay Colony's venerable first governor, John Endecott —twenty-five years his senior.[25] In forty-four cases of hired labor where the ages of both parties could be determined, only nine employees were older than the men who gave them work.[26]

The labor that was exchanged between households, therefore, was exchanged much as it had been in England, along the lines of economic power that were determined in turn by age and wealth. To suggest, as some historians do, that the sale of goods and services between members of the same community was structured in a cooperative manner by considerations of use and need is to obscure a simpler and more fundamental truth.[27] These early New Englanders hired themselves out on occasion to their older, wealthier, and more market-oriented neighbors because they could not satisfy all of their families' wants from their own holdings alone.

Still, those occasions, at least by English standards, were never very frequent. On the Essex County stretch of New England's first frontier, day labor, like farm service, withered. The two forms of help which husbandmen in the mother country had employed to supplement the efforts of their own offspring could not be recreated on this side of the Atlantic in quantities or at prices that made economic sense. There were parts of New England, such as the Connecticut Valley, where the fertility of the soil and ease of transportation could justify the expense of taking in outside help on an English scale; but, in Essex County, that was not the case.[28] Even more than historians have realized, therefore, it must have been the family— not the English household of parents, children, and servants with the occasional hired hand, but the nuclear family alone—that dominated the rural economy of the region.

A farm boy was first likely to appear in depositions taken before the county court, working under his father's eye, about the age of ten. At the beginning, though he might be expected to help on occasion at any of the classic field chores, most of his hours were spent

25. *Essex Courts*, II, 199, III, 276, 445, VII, 15. Biographical information on these individuals was gathered from *Essex Courts* and the sources listed in nn. 13, 16.

26. *Essex Courts*, I–VI. Ages were determined as in n. 16.

27. See, for example, James A. Henretta, "Families and Farms: *Mentalité* in Pre-Industrial America," *WMQ*, 3d Ser., XXXV (1978), 3–32, esp. 13.

28. The most convincing case for the *importance* of free labor and farm service in rural New England can be found in Innes, *Labor in a New Land*, xv–xxi, 72–122.

caring for livestock. By his thirteenth birthday, young Stephen Cross of Ipswich already had been helping his older brother for several years, tending their father's sheep; and Abraham Adams of Newbury knew the family cattle well enough at eleven years that he could describe a missing steer to the court down to its hastily cut earmark. As his teens advanced, the young New England male gradually took on a wider variety of tasks, such as fencing, carting, mowing, and breaking sod—shouldering in every respect a man's workload. Always, however, he toiled under his father's orders. William Story, aged seventeen, like most others at his age of whom we have record, went off to mow in his family's meadows, we learn from court testimony, because he had been ordered to.[29]

Once the age of majority had been passed, the instances of direct parental supervision began to ebb. Sons continued to work on the father's lands. But less often, in their testimony before the courts, did they remember being "ordered" or "sent" to their tasks or laboring by his side.[30] Yet, significantly enough, no real evidence of true independence normally surfaced in the economic endeavors of these young colonists until the age of twenty-five or thirty. Neither in the ownership of land and livestock nor in dealings in farm produce did men in their twenties play a part even remotely approximating their importance in the population.[31] True, the maturing son exercised considerable control over his daily routine. Having learned what farming was about, he could be trusted, as his father discovered, to work by himself, to assume direction of the property in his parents'

29. *Essex Courts*, I–VI. The court records contain no instances of boys less than 10 years of age performing any farm labor. For Adams and Cross, see *Essex Courts*, I, 212, III, 396 (biographical information gathered as in n. 25); for incident involving Story, see IV, 47.

30. See, for example, *Essex Courts*, II, 279, V, 415, VIII, 171.

31. Young men, aged 20–29, composed between 30% and 40% of the adult male population in 17th-century Massachusetts: Springfield (1668), 32%; Rowley (1645–1685), 37%; and Newbury (1678), 41%. For Springfield, see Gloria L. Main, "The Correction of Biases in Colonial American Probate Records," *Historical Methods Newsletter*, VIII (1974), 14. For Rowley, I have used my own computations, based on taking age profiles of the town at 10-year intervals from George Blodgett and Amos Jewett, *The Early Settlement of Rowley, Massachusetts* (Rowley, 1933). For Newbury, I have used my own computations based on the oaths of allegiance for 1678 in *Essex Courts*, VII, 156–157. Young men in their 20s accounted for only 10% of those mentioned in the court records between 1630 and 1660 as owning livestock (*N* = 39). Similarly, they numbered only 16% of the farm produce suppliers listed in the account book of the Salem merchant, George Corwin, between 1653 and 1655 (*N* = 79). See *Essex Courts*, I, II; George Corwin Account Book, 1653–1655, Essex Institute, Salem, Mass.; the ages of these young farmers were determined as in n. 16.

absence, and even to contribute his own ideas to the running of the farm. A neighbor of Peter Tappen testified in 1673 that, since the age of nineteen, young Tappen had "bin vary dutiful too his father and vary carfull of his bisnis when the old man was in Ingland . . . and late willing to Improv all sesons for his fathers good."[32] At marriage, moreover, when the new householder first erected a dwelling elsewhere on family land and began working fields apart from his father, he came to manage even more of his own affairs.

Nevertheless, it was not until, either by deed or inheritance, he had assumed full legal control over his portion of the parental estate that a son became an independent man in his own right. And although this might happen when he formed a household of his own, it might also be delayed by years or even decades until his father's death. He was not encouraged, therefore, as in England to strike out on his own. In the new colony, where there was work to be done and few alternative sources of labor, parents preferred that their sons spend their young adulthood, even beyond the age of marriage, developing the family estate. These young householders may no longer have been living under daily parental direction, and they surely understood that they were contributing to the improvement of land that could one day be theirs. But, in the degree of their commitment to property that was still under their fathers' authority, at a time in life when they were beginning to raise children of their own, they were still accepting, albeit hesitantly, limitations on their freedom of action that were foreign to English tradition.[33]

It was, therefore, at a measured pace, even a tardy one by the standards of the Old Country, that the male offspring of Essex County moved out from under parental control. Several centuries later, this tale possesses a familiar ring, for it is the story of the American family farm. To these English emigrants of the seventeenth century, however, it was new; the exigencies of farming in the New World had forced them to alter their habits of household production.

Emphasizing the nuclear family at the expense of larger working units that took in outside help, however, is not to argue for economic equality. Early New Englanders had grown up in a class society, and their leaders took pains to recreate those different "Condicion[s] of mankinde" with which they were familiar, especially through

32. *Essex Courts*, V, 176–177. Biographical information gathered as in n. 16.
33. Philip J. Greven, Jr., *Four Generations: Population, Land, and Family in Colonial Andover, Massachusetts* (Ithaca, N.Y., 1970), 79–99; Laslett, *World We Have Lost*, 15; Kussmaul, *Servants in Husbandry*, 78–85.

their distribution of land.[34] At the foundation of most Essex County towns, close to half of the apportioned property was assigned to the wealthiest 10 percent of the population who controlled community affairs.[35] These were the county elite: personages, like the Endecotts and the Downings, who could devote their time to public service, since the extent of their granted lands had freed them from the mundane rounds of daily work. They served as magistrates or militia captains, involved themselves in international commerce, and represented their towns at the General Court, but rarely did they ever handle livestock or wield a sickle.[36] Virgin land, however, did not translate itself into income automatically. Owners of such estates, who considered manual labor demeaning, had to arrange for others to do the work of development. Rejecting the direct operation of their farms through the employment of servants and hired help, most of them turned, instead, to the granting of leaseholds.

Tenancy was one feature of the English countryside that Americans successfully carried with them into those portions of the new continent—notably Maryland, Pennsylvania, New Jersey, and the valleys of the Hudson and Connecticut rivers—where mixed husbandry aimed at the market was important. Estate owners discovered that their lands were most profitably managed when they rented them out to single farming families. Often obliged by their agreements to make capital improvements, in addition to rental payments, these tenant families proved to be the most effective agents for the transfer of English agricultural custom to the larger landholdings of the northern colonies.[37]

34. Samuel Eliot Morison *et al.*, eds., *Winthrop Papers*, 5 vols. to date (Boston, 1929–), II, 282.

35. David Grayson Allen, *In English Ways: The Movement of Societies and the Transferal of English Local Law and Custom to Massachusetts Bay in the Seventeenth Century* (Chapel Hill, N.C., 1981), 32, 111; Greven, *Four Generations*, 46; Richard P. Gildrie, *Salem, Massachusetts, 1626–1683: A Covenant Community* (Charlottesville, Va., 1975), 57.

36. From a sample of 83 work experiences from Ipswich recorded in court depositions, only one involved a member of the town's elite performing any manual labor (*Essex Courts*, I–IX; Perzel, "First Generation in Ipswich," 171–172).

37. Gregory A. Stiverson, *Poverty in a Land of Plenty: Tenancy in Eighteenth-Century Maryland* (Baltimore, 1977); James T. Lemon, *The Best Poor Man's Country: A Geographical Study of Early Southeastern Pennsylvania* (Baltimore, 1972), 94–96; Lucy Simler, "Tenancy in Colonial Pennsylvania: The Case of Chester County," *WMQ*, 3d Ser., XLIII (1986), 542–569; Sung Bok Kim, *Landlord and Tenant in Colonial New York: Manorial Society, 1664–1775* (Chapel Hill, N.C., 1978); Innes, *Labor in a New Land*, chap. 3.

Leaseholding flourished in those parts of Essex County where adequate land that was close to the sea made commercial agriculture possible. Portions of several towns met those conditions, but none so much as Newbury, Ipswich, and Rowley, at the northern end of the county where the Merrimack River emptied into the Atlantic. Ipswich, in particular, oriented itself toward the provisioning of seaport towns with its surplus produce from the very beginning. Many well-to-do immigrants settled there in the 1630s, and, for the duration of the century, it remained a community of large properties with a concentration of wealth that was, by Massachusetts standards, extreme. Edward Johnson noted the "faire built" houses with gardens and orchards and the "very good Land for Husbandry" to be found there. "They have many hundred quarters [of meat] to spare yearly," he told his readers, "and feed, at the latter end of Summer, the towne of Boston with good beefe."[38] Strikingly, this single town, which accounted for only about 20 percent of the county's population, included a full 44 percent of its tenants; and in Newbury and Rowley, where there dwelt a mere 15 percent of Essex residents, one found a further 24 percent of its leaseholders.[39] The appropriate natural conditions, therefore, could attract men of sufficient wealth and status to acquire land and engineer its development by parceling it out to those with little property, but willing backs.

The form assumed by leaseholding in Essex County reflected the most modern of English practice. The actual agreements, for one thing, aimed foremost at a simple specificity. Copyhold, tithing, labor services on the demesne, and all the other myriad complications of the English manorial tradition were replaced, for the most part, by written agreements that spelled out the obligations of both parties in specific contractual terms. Thomas Rowell and Robert Collins in Ipswich, for example, agreed in 1656 to rent from Alexander Knight the major part of his farm with its oxen and implements for seven years, in return for corn and hay sufficient for the wintering of three cows, two acres of plowing twice a year, firewood, clay, and sixteen pounds in currency. Similarly, Peter Palfrey leased a farm on the Ipswich-Wenham line to Richard Coy in 1658 for eight years at five pounds

38. Johnson, *Wonder-Working Providence*, ed. Jameson, 96; Allen, *In English Ways*, 131–136.

39. *Essex Courts*, I–VI. The population estimates for these towns were calculated from Nathaniel B. Shurtleff, ed., *Records of the Governor and Company of the Massachusetts Bay in New England*, 5 vols. (Boston, 1853–1854), I, 192; Evarts B. Greene and Virginia D. Harrington, *American Population before the Federal Census of 1790* (New York, 1932), 20.

per year, payable "half in wheat and half in Indian corn. . . . To be delivered within one quarter mile of the Salem meeting house."[40] Furthermore, Essex County leases, like those in other colonial regions, were often developmental. Some induced tenants to undertake capital improvements by offering them credit for work accomplished; thus the above-mentioned Richard Coy was to be allowed for "whatever building or fencing" that he added to the property. Other agreements, assumedly in return for a reduction in rent, required the leaseholder to develop the property in a specified way. One tenant from Salem named George Norton, for example, agreed in addition to his annual payment of eighteen pounds "to build upon the farm a strong and sufficient house . . . and . . . to leave the house tenantable at the end of the term." Such contractualism was characteristic of leaseholding in most portions of early America.[41]

Farm tenants in Essex County were more likely than their neighbors to be recent immigrants, part of that minority of settlers whose families had come to America after the Great Migration. Almost three-quarters of those leasing housing *and* land who made their way into the court records arrived in Essex County after 1640, when a system of land apportionment had already been decided upon and a distinct group of proprietors established.[42] Some had come originally as servants, and others moved into tenancy directly, but all had presumably failed to obtain an outright grant of land from any of the towns they approached, and none possessed the necessary capital or credit to purchase property and set himself up on his own. From the larger estate owners in the county, they rented farms on relatively short terms—usually less than ten years—with the intent of eventually establishing themselves on an independent freehold. Few of them ever achieved real prosperity, but most found a living sufficient to maintain them in the county for several decades, often until the end of their lives.[43]

40. *Essex Courts*, II, 177, III, 207–208.

41. *Ibid.*, III, 208, 286. For contractualism, see Innes, *Labor in a New Land*, 49–71; Kim, *Landlord and Tenant*, 162–234; Stiverson, *Poverty in a Land of Plenty*, xii, 10–13.

42. Of the 36 farm tenants who could be identified from the court records, only 10 came from families that arrived in Massachusetts before 1641 (*Essex Courts*, I–VI; Savage, *Genealogical Dictionary*; and various town histories).

43. In 73% of farm leasing arrangements (*N* = 37) drawn from the court records, the landlord could clearly be placed in the top wealth decile of the town in which he lived. Of 30 farm tenants, only 3 had disappeared from the county within a decade of their being identified as leaseholders in the court records (*Essex Courts*, I–VI; sources listed in nn. 13, 19). For a few surviving inventories of

It was chiefly by dint of the tenants' labor and the labor of their families that the greater landholdings of Essex County were first brought into production. Estate owners in the seventeenth century preferred to hand over the direct operation of their farms to tenant households, rather than seek out the servants and hired help needed to conduct it themselves. Of course, potential leaseholders might also prove difficult to find; both the Winthrops and the Downings complained of this problem.[44] But the shortage of tenants and the feebleness of rents never sparked the same degree of comment as did other labor problems of the Bay Colony. And whereas it is certain that male servants numbered less than 4 percent of those who actually farmed the soil of Essex County before 1675, tenants and their families may have accounted for as much as 25 percent.[45] Householders who rented undoubtedly were less numerous than those who owned their farms outright, but, throughout the period in question, tenancy was the active force in the development of large estates.

Tenants, however, shared this with landowning farmers: they followed their annual round of toil free from direct supervision. Fathers and sons, therefore, on rented farms as on those that were owned, performed the field work that generated the raw materials of agriculture. Even in those regions where commercial agriculture and inequality held sway, the dominant unit of production in which daily

---

their estates at death, see *Essex Courts*, I, 148–149, III, 77–78, 338, VI, 343, VIII, 420–421, IX, 129; Essex County Probate Files, nos. 8609, 13782, 17355, 24820. Of these 12, 7 had estates valued at less than £100 sterling (using McCusker, *Money and Exchange*, 138–140, for conversion).

44. Morison *et al.*, eds., *Winthrop Papers*, V, 261, 340; Shurtleff, ed., *Records of Massachusetts*, I, 114; Winthrop, *Journal*, ed. Hosmer, I, 144.

45. The maximum figure of 25% was obtained as follows. First, in the rental agreements described in the court records involving landlords in the top decile of the population and their tenants, the ratio of tenants to landlords was 1.6: 1. Second, the ratio of tenants to landlords in the top wealth decile to tenants of landlords in the remaining nine wealth deciles was 2.2: 1. Third, it was assumed that all landowners in the top decile hired at least one tenant. It follows that, in a hypothetical community of 100 householders, the 10 wealthiest would have had 16 tenants, while the remaining 90 would have hired together only 7. A total of 23 tenants represents slightly less than one-quarter of the total number of householders. This has to be regarded as a maximum estimate for the importance of tenant labor in the rural economy of the county. First, it seems likely that tenant families were smaller than those of freeholders; accordingly, a tenancy rate of 23% for householders would not imply that 23% of the population belonged to tenant families. Second, it may be that not all of the householders in the top wealth decile were landlords, thus further reducing our percentage. See *Essex Courts*, I–VI, and the sources listed in n. 13.

tasks actually were organized was the nuclear family operating without help. Despite all their intentions to recreate the Old Country in which they had grown up, these emigrants ended up scuttling the freer portion of the labor system on which the English rural economy had relied. On this particular segment of the early American frontier, and at least among men, work relationships collapsed in upon the family.

To show that, by contemporary standards, these New England households were singularly dedicated to the management of their own economies is not to argue for their economic autonomy. The web of local exchange was a part of life in New England from its foundation. Most of what rural householders exchanged, however—and this was true of the entire colonial period as even a cursory examination of contemporary account books will show—was not labor, but produce, and rented capital equipment. It was through a local trade in cider, barley malt, footwear, and oxen by the day rather than by "changing works" that New Englanders made good most specific shortcomings on their individual farms.[46]

This brings us to a further question: whether the picture sketched here for the male portion of these families has any relevance for the female half. It has been argued, in reaction to the older and inaccurate understanding of colonial women as isolated home producers, that seventeenth-century housewives traded commodities *and* labor equally within a highly integrated community economy. Granting that the social context of female work did extend far beyond the household, it would still be interesting to know whether women, like men, saw the labor system with which they had grown up in England reorganized in the Great Migration. I suspect that it was, and in the same direction (toward family production) and for the same basic reason—because the task of farm-building in this empty land was as demanding on wives and daughters as on husbands and sons. All this remains conjectural, of course, but the issue of transatlantic comparison is clearly one that matters as much for women as for men.[47]

46. Bettye Hobbs Pruitt, "Self-Sufficiency and the Agricultural Economy of Eighteenth-Century Massachusetts," *WMQ*, 3d Ser., XLI (1984), 333–364, although she disagrees with my specific point regarding labor exchanges, at least for 1771 (p. 349), as does Susan Geib, " 'Changing Works': Agriculture and Society in Brookfield, Massachusetts, 1785–1820" (Ph.D. diss., Boston University, 1981).

47. See Ulrich, *Good Wives*, 51–52, her essay in this volume, and "Housewife and Gadder: Themes of Self-Sufficiency and Community in Eighteenth-Century New England," in Carol Groneman and Mary Beth Norton, eds., *"To Toil the Livelong Day": America's Women at Work, 1780–1980* (Ithaca, N.Y., 1987). By demol-

Farm labor in Essex County assumed its new configuration in response to two problems common to frontier life everywhere: the dual and interrelated scarcities of capital and labor relative to land. Where there was work to be done, as there had to be in unusual quantity during a period of farm formation, and where the alternative sources of help were few, rural landowners were loath to part with the labor of their sons. So long as there was country to be cleared, farms and fences to be built, and the hungry mouths of numerous younger children to be fed, the inexpensive labor of offspring was essential to family welfare. Furthermore, in a rural economy with few large and well-equipped estates that could have generated employment opportunities, farm boys had little choice but to remain at home. Unless they sought out maritime work in the booming fisheries or in the carrying trade (both dirty and demeaning, even ungodly, businesses for the sons of Puritan yeomen freeholders), labor for young men meant toiling for their fathers.[48] Both generations were committed to the provision of economic independence for themselves and their descendants that never could be achieved if the family scattered its scarce labor resources in pursuit of scarce capital across the county map. This exaggeration in parental authority and filial duty—beyond anything that had been known in England—stemmed primarily from the problem of developing the wilderness. Our unknown observer, with whose intuitive remarks this essay began, was absolutely right: children served the same economic function in New England that indentured servants did in the Chesapeake.

If restrictions on the mobility of labor were so important to the accumulation of capital in this frontier society, then why did the northern colonists not follow the lead of their countrymen to the south and import bound servants themselves? Could not the process of economic development have been, in that way, accelerated? The seasonality of northern agriculture might provide one answer; for if winter was, in fact, a period of severely slackened farm activity, it certainly would make little sense to employ servants the year round. Yet it is not entirely clear exactly how seasonal this mixed rural economy, during its period of farm formation, really was. With land to clear, fences to build, animals to be tended, and a small export

---

ishing the female counterpart to the "rugged individualist yeoman" myth, she does our understanding of colonial society a singular service.

48. Daniel F. Vickers, "Maritime Labor in Colonial Massachusetts: A Case Study of the Essex County Cod Fishery and the Whaling Industry of Nantucket, 1630–1775" (Ph.D. diss., Princeton University, 1981), 57–58, 65–66, 104–108, 117–131, 142 n. 120.

trade in timber products, there was work to occupy these settlers between the end of harvest in the autumn and the preparation of soil in the spring. And New Englanders, it should be remembered, were not opting for day laborers who could be dismissed when they were not needed; the family help upon which they relied was year-round—no different from servants in this regard. New England farmers were reluctant to purchase imported servants, not from any preference for free labor, but because the marginal productivity of their lands was not high enough to justify the cost. They relied on their sons for the task of farm development, because offspring provided an inexpensive, efficient, and available version of the bound labor that prevailed everywhere in early America where manpower was scarce.

Never was the market incentive to expand production and take on additional help entirely absent, for all of these householders sold something in the way of an agricultural surplus. Every year in a commercial town like Ipswich, for example, most of the middling and wealthier inhabitants sent some cattle, wheat, or Indian corn down the coast to Salem for provisioning the maritime trades or for export. By comparison to the staple colonies of the Chesapeake, however, this was a relatively limited business.[49] It is true that in a few peculiarly well situated portions of New England, farming did afford sufficient returns to interest some larger producers in the direct operation of their property. Those individuals could make use of and did, in fact, recruit indentured servants from abroad. But even they preferred to draw their income from tenancies rather than from the direct personal management of agriculture. They too relied on householders and their sons to organize production.

Agricultural development on the northern frontier of seventeenth-century America demanded restrictions on the mobility of labor that the family could provide, but never did the lure of bonanza profits prompt the widespread recourse to the harsher forms of coercion that were typical of the Chesapeake. As matters stood, the family farm, with its heightened interdependency of father and son, furnished sanctions on the organization of work that were entirely appropriate to the frontier economy of early New England.

49. George Corwin Account Book, 1653–1655, Essex Institute, Salem, Mass.

Laurel Thatcher Ulrich

Martha Ballard and Her Girls

Women's Work in Eighteenth-Century Maine

NEAR MIDNIGHT on November 26, 1795, a sixty-year-old Maine woman named Martha Ballard sat writing in her diary. She had stayed up late waiting for Sarah Neal, her hired girl, to come home from watching with a sick neighbor. "I have been doing my housework and Nursing my cow. Her bag is amazingly sweld," she wrote. "Sarah went to watch with Mary Densmore . . . shee returnd and Sarah Densmore with her at 11 hour Evening. I have been picking wool till then. A womans work is never Done as the Song says and happy shee whose strength holds out to the end of the rais [race]." Then she added, "It is now the middle of the night and Mr Densmore calls me to his house."[1]

Because Martha Ballard was a midwife as well as a housewife, her regimen was somewhat unusual, yet her attitude toward women's work was not. The song she quoted was probably an American version of a seventeenth-century English ballad that begins, "There's

I would like to thank Stephen Innes, Alan Taylor, Jack Larkin, Nancy Grey Osterud, Elaine Crane, Lorena Walsh, Daniel Vickers, James Henretta, Mary Beth Norton, and Alfred Young for helpful comments on an earlier version of this article. I also wish to acknowledge research support from the Central University Research Fund of the University of New Hampshire and the National Endowment for the Humanities.

1. Diary of Martha Moore Ballard, 1785–1812, MS, Maine State Library, Augusta, hereafter cited as MMB. Charles Elventon Nash included extensive excerpts from the Ballard diary in *The History of Augusta: First Settlements and Early Days as a Town* (a book printed in Augusta, 1904, but not published until 1961, when Edith Hary assembled the unbound signatures). The Nash abridgment, heavily biased toward genealogy, includes only about a third of the original, though it does suggest the range of material in it. Except for brief references in Nancy F. Cott, *The Bonds of Womanhood: "Woman's Sphere" in New England, 1780–1835* (New Haven, Conn., 1977), 19, 29; and in Richard W. Wertz and Dorothy C. Wertz, *Lying-In: A History of Childbirth in America* (New York, 1977), 9–12, 18, 20, the diary has been unused by scholars. I am writing a book-length study of the MS diary.

never a day, from morn to night, / But I with work am tired quite." Each verse of this old song discusses some aspect of a housewife's duties, from textile production to feeding crying babies in the night, ending with the familiar proverb, "A woman's work is never done." Laments of overburdened housewives continued in the American folk repertoire well into the twentieth century.[2]

In his study of nineteenth-century farm families in the midwest, John Mack Faragher argued that the burdens described in such sources were genuine; rural women actually performed more than their share of subsistence labor, freeing men to participate in the public sphere.[3] Mary Beth Norton, in her survey of the Revolutionary period, came to similar conclusions about the difficulties of women's work, though she did see differences in attitude over time. Before the Revolution, women who left letters and diaries "generally wrote of their household work without joy or satisfaction. . . . Their tasks, with rare exceptions, were 'duties,' not pleasures." During and after the war, some women developed a more positive sense of their roles, paving the way for the sentimentalized domesticity of the nineteenth century. These are illuminating and provocative studies. As yet, however, few historians have given serious attention to the actual structure of women's domestic burdens in early America or attempted to discover the particular conditions that may have given rise to their complaints. Nor has anyone considered working relations among women in the preindustrial female economy.

Martha Ballard's diary is a remarkably valuable source for such a study. Detailed daily entries for more than twenty-seven years not only document the full range of one woman's economic activities from maturity to old age but tell much about the lives of the young women who assisted her. These "girls" (she used the same collective term for them all) included her daughters Hannah and Dolly; her nieces Pamela, Parthena, and Clarissa Barton; and a succession of hired helpers like Sarah Neal. Although Martha Ballard's diary shows the gender division of labor that Faragher has commented upon, and though it provides ample evidence of a dutiful rather than

2. William Chappell, ed., *The Roxburghe Ballads* (Hertford, 1875), III, 301; Alan Lomax, *The Folk Songs of North America in the English Language* (Garden City, N.Y., 1975), 124, 133; Vance Randolph, ed., *Ozark Folksongs*, 4 vols. (Columbia, Mo., 1980), III, 69–70.

3. John Mack Faragher, "History from the Inside-Out: Writing the History of Women in Rural America," *American Quarterly*, XXXIII (1981), 537–557, and *Women and Men on the Overland Trail* (New Haven, Conn., 1979), chap. 2; Mary Beth Norton, *Liberty's Daughters: The Revolutionary Experience of American Women, 1750–1800* (Boston, 1980), 38–39.

a joyful attitude toward work, it also documents the genuine satisfactions that one woman derived from mastering her domestic environment. It shows both the variety and the social complexity of household labor, highlights the interdependence of mature women and young women within the family economy, and modifies earlier conceptions of patriarchy.

Although Martha Ballard lived almost to the era of industrialization, in education and in sensibility she belonged to the colonial period. Born in Oxford, Massachusetts, in 1735, she emigrated to the Kennebec River country of Maine in 1777 with her husband, Ephraim, and five children. Three other children had died in the diphtheria epidemic of 1769.[4] For the rest of their lives, the Ballards lived in that section of Hallowell, Maine, that separated in 1798 to become the town of Augusta. The extant diary opens in 1785, the year Mrs. Ballard turned fifty. It closes in May of 1812, about a month before her death. This essay will focus on the first fifteen years of the diary, 1785–1800, the period in which her two youngest daughters came of age and married.

The importance of such a document for our understanding of women's work in early America is clear. Martha Ballard's diary is the intact delft platter that allows us to identify and interpret the shattered fragments that are all that remain for so much of New England. The diary confirms, for example, the existence of a separate female economy existing beneath the level of traditional documentation. In Hallowell, as in other New England towns, male names predominate in surviving merchant accounts, while tax lists and town records give little, if any, evidence of female enterprise. Yet the diary makes quite clear not only that women were managing a rich and varied array of tasks within their own households but that they were trading with each other (and sometimes with men) independent of their husbands.

Martha Ballard's diary shifts our attention from the by now rather tired question of whether women shared men's work to far more interesting issues about how they interacted with each other within the female economy. To John Faragher's query about the relationship of female labor to male public service, we can now add detailed questions about the interaction of mothers and daughters, and mistresses

4. *Vital Records of Oxford, Massachusetts* (Worcester, Mass., 1905), 13, 14, 268; MMB, Feb. 20, Mar. 30, 1785, June 26, 1788, Oct. 7, 1789; Ernest Caulfield, "Some Common Diseases of Colonial Children," Colonial Society of Massachusetts, *Publications*, XXXV (1951), 23–24.

and servants within the household. We can also begin to discuss the changes in female consciousness that Mary Beth Norton described, not as evidence of the emergence of women from patriarchal dominion, but as evidence of changing values within an already cohesive female realm.

Close study of such a document also shows the complexity of the family labor system (as discussed in Daniel Vickers's essay in this volume). New Englanders may have preferred their own offspring to hired laborers, but no family gave birth to full-grown workers, nor could even the most powerful patriarch ensure an optimal balance of sons and daughters. By its very nature, a family labor system demanded a web of connections beyond the household. Households self-sufficient in land, livestock, and tools (and they were few) could never be perennially self-sufficient in labor. Furthermore, because mothers invested more heavily in childbearing and rearing than fathers, and because daughters married earlier than sons (and perhaps moved further away than their brothers), the transitions within the household were sharper for women and potentially more disruptive. This was particularly so in young towns where the sex ratio limited the number of single women available for household work.

Martha Ballard's diary is a record of a particular time and place, a Maine river town in the years just after the Revolution, but it is also a record of a particular kind of economy: one characterized by a clear gender division of labor, by reliance on family members and neighbors rather than bound servants, and by mixed enterprises (men engaged in lumbering and fishing as well as farming, women in small-scale textile production, poultry raising, and dairying). Exportable products were nonagricultural, and they were in the male domain. These conditions were not characteristic of every town in New England, but they were certainly typical of many from the seventeenth century forward.

Ephraim Ballard was one of the middling sort of Maine pioneers who opened up the river valleys in the years after the Revolution. According to the Hallowell tax list for 1784, he had three acres of tillage, eighty acres of "unimproved" and ten acres of "unimprovable" land. In addition, he had three cows and a pair of oxen, the latter as useful for lumbering as for farming. From 1779 to 1791, he and his sons operated saw- and gristmills, just as he and his father had done in Oxford and as his grandfather and great-grandfather had done a hundred years before in Andover, Massachusetts. Ephraim was also a surveyor. Into his eighties he continued to run lines for the Commonwealth of Massachusetts and for the wealthy Kennebec

Proprietors, who were attempting to assert control over squatter lands in the newly settled Maine interior.[5]

Equally important to an understanding of patterns of work in the diary is an appreciation for the composition of the Ballard family. When Martha Ballard began her diary in 1785, she was already a grandmother; her oldest daughter, Lucy Towne, lived upriver at Winslow. Yet, at the age of fifty, she still had five children living at home: Cyrus, twenty-nine (a quiet and dutiful son who alternately worked with his father and for other men and who never married); Jonathan, twenty-three; Hannah, fifteen; Dolly, twelve; and Ephraim, six.[6] Martha Ballard's comment ten years later that "womans work is never Done," though formulaic, was grounded in the particular circumstances of her own life. She stayed up late picking wool on November 26, 1795, in an effort to sustain a system of household production established seven years before when her two youngest daughters were in their teens. Now both daughters were married. For a time, Martha Ballard had belonged to an unrecognized colonial elite, that corps of housewives who had not only health and energy but daughters. That she now sat alone waiting for her hired girl, Sarah Neal, marked a change in status. Close analysis of the diary not only reveals the variety, the social complexity, and the necessary autonomy of a mature woman's work; it shows, in striking detail, her close dependence on her girls.

AT THE MOST general level, Martha Ballard's diary simply confirms what we already know about the division of labor in northern New England and in other rural societies in the Western world: men worked "abroad," farming, surveying, lumbering, shipping, and milling; women worked in houses, gardens, and yards.[7] Yet to see fif-

5. Charles Frederic Farlow, *Ballard Genealogy* (Boston, 1911), 82; James W. North, *The History of Augusta, Maine* (Somersworth, N.H., 1981 [orig. publ. 1870]), 185–189; MMB, Oct. 30, 1786, Aug. 23, 1790, Nov. 9, 1791, Dec. 14, 1795, Mar. 30, 1802; Nash, *History of Augusta*, 235, 301; North, *History of Augusta*, 819; Vincent York, *The Sandy River and Its Valley* (Farmington, Maine, 1976), 66; Ephraim Ballard Depositions, Kennebec County Deeds, book 8, 461–463, book 9, 400–401, Kennebec County Court House, Augusta; Invoice of the Rateable Property in Possession of the Middle Parish in Hallowell, 1794, MS, Maine State Library.

6. Although there is no source to confirm this, one wonders whether Cyrus was of below-average intelligence; certainly, he was markedly less ambitious than were the other Ballards, seeming never to have accumulated any property or to have established a family of his own.

7. This is not to say that women never did field work—when needed. I have described the general division of labor and variants within it in *Good Wives: Image and Reality in the Lives of Women in Northern New England, 1650–1750* (New York,

teen years of one woman's work pieced out through the pages of her diary is to understand more fully both the variety and the complexity of this work. Consider the vocabulary of textile production. The Ballard men sowed, turned, and broke flax; the women weeded, pulled, combed, spun, reeled, boiled, spooled, warped, quilled, wove, bucked, and bleached it. Slaughtering meant more than cutting, weighing, and salting meat; it also meant caring for the "orful" (offal) of the animal—cleaning ox tripe, dressing a calf's head or pig's feet, preparing sausage casings, or cooking the organ meats (or "harslet") of a veal. Candle and soapmaking meant trying tallow as well as spinning wicks and leaching wood ashes for lye.[8]

Even such an ordinary activity as knitting had multiple applications. Mrs. Ballard produced woolen "leggins" and "buskins" as well as stockings for her husband and sons; she knitted tow, linen, and cotton hose and even "footed" some pairs with "twine." Though the Ballards employed a tailor to make men's coats and breeches and called in a dressmaker to cut out women's gowns, Mrs. Ballard and her daughters made shifts, skirts, aprons, petticoats, night caps, trousers, jackets, and even a pair of "staise" (stays). They also hemmed sheets, stitched and filled mattresses, pieced quilts, and turned "raggs" into woven "coverlids."[9] Outdoor work was just as insistent. Martha Ballard milked cows, fed swine, set hens, and more than once trudged "up the Crik" looking for a wandering calf. When a sheep came in from the pasture wounded on the neck, she "drest it with Tarr." When a lamb was born with its "entrails hanging out," she sewed it up.[10]

Gardening chores stretched from the end of April, when Mr. Ballard plowed the various plots near the house, until late October, when the cabbages were brought into the cellar. Martha Ballard

---

1982), chaps. 1 and 2. See also Louise A. Tilly and Joan W. Scott, *Women, Work, and Family* (New York, 1978), 32–37, 44–47; Olwen Hufton, "Women and the Family Economy in Eighteenth-Century France," *French Historical Studies*, IX (1975), 1–22; Priscilla Waggoner, "Producers and Participants: Women in the Rural German Culture of Eighteenth-Century Pennsylvania" (paper delivered at conference, "The Lives of Early Americans: Anthropological Perspectives on Colonial Society," Millersville State College, Apr. 30–May 2, 1981); G. E. Fussell, "Countrywomen in Old England," *Agricultural History*, L (1976), 175–178, and the essay by Lois Green Carr and Lorena S. Walsh in this volume.

8. MMB, Apr. 1, July 27, Nov. 28, 1785, Oct. 29, 1787, Nov. 1, 1788, Nov. 15, 1791.

9. MMB, Mar. 26, Apr. 15, May 19, Aug. 6, 1785, Mar. 28, Nov. 4, Dec. 6, Dec. 25, 1786, Dec. 25, 1789, Jan. 8, 30, 1790, July 9, Sept. 15, Nov. 19, 1791, Dec. 23, 1800.

10. MMB, June 5, 1785, July 12, 1788, Dec. 13, 1791, May 4, 1792, June 4, 1800.

transplanted hundreds of seedlings every spring in addition to the usual sowing and weeding. In late summer and early autumn, she gathered seed for next year's garden as well as fresh vegetables for the table. She grew culinary herbs like sage, saffron, coriander, anise, mustard, and parsley as well as beans (in several varieties), cabbages, parsnips, turnips, beets, cucumbers, radishes, onions, garlic, peppers, carrots, "French turnips," lettuce, peppergrass, and melons.[11] She obviously was proud of being able to gather a milk pan full of "Poland King" beans as early as July 11, of having parsley "fresh and green from my gardin for to put in my gravy" on December 27, of bringing fresh cabbage from her cellar on March 13, and of cutting a "fine mess of greens from our cabbage stumps" on May 19.[12]

Martha Ballard was not given to lyrical effusions. Such pleasure as she experienced in her work was expressed in her careful account of it. In this respect, it is interesting to compare her diary with the diaries of her younger contemporaries, Mary Yeaton and Ann Bryant Smith. Although Yeaton did some of the same work as the Ballard women on her father's coastal farm in Eastport, Maine, the diary that she left for the year 1800 is filled with sentiments like, "How pleasing [it is] to do for those who are bound to us by the ties of nature and affection," or, "Who would envy the splendors of the great when little folk can enjoy so many tranquil hours?"[13] Smith, the wife of a Portland shopkeeper, also was tuned to the charms of domesticity, as in this entry for June 8, 1807: "I was up this Morn before the (Lazy) Sun, baked a Large loaf of bread in a Duch oven (our usual mode of baking in Summer) which I mixed and sit to rising last night) put on the tea kittle—while I was thus imployed our boy Ben harnessed the horse, and put him to the Chaise—My husband and self steped in, and had a charming ride and returned at Seven o'clock and took our breakfast."[14]

Both Yeaton and Smith had been educated in sophisticated coastal communities; Mary Yeaton's father had been a merchant in Portsmouth, New Hampshire, before moving to Maine. Although both were more likely than Martha Ballard to enlarge upon the pleasures

11. MMB, May 25, 1785, May 5, 1787, May 13–14, 25–27, 1790, June 25–26, 1790, Apr. 14, June 17–18, July 28, Aug. 20, Oct. 14, 1791, Apr. 28, 1800.
12. MMB, Mar. 13, 1791, May 19, 1796, July 11, 1800, Dec. 27, 1800.
13. Mary Yeaton's Journal, 1801, typescript, Maine State Library, Augusta, entries for June 20, July 29.
14. Diary of Mrs. Ann Smith, 1806–1807, MS, Maine Historical Society, Portland.

of their lives, it would be difficult to argue from their diaries that either had a more positive self-perception than she. They wrote of melancholy and dullness as well as of joy. Expecting more of life, they were less disposed to perceive it as a "rais" in which the winner was "shee whose strength holds out to the end."

Both Yeaton and Smith gave some attention to beautifying or ornamenting the houses in which they lived. Martha Ballard did not. The three houses the Ballards inhabited during the years of the diary probably differed little in floor plan or space—each had two rooms on the first floor and two "chambers" above. All three houses, like many in Hallowell, were in some stage of incompleteness or disrepair. The upstairs rooms in the first could not be used in winter, though the kitchen had something that many lacked—an oven. Mrs. Forbes, Mrs. Savage, Mrs. Williams, and Mrs. Voce all baked in the Ballard's oven from time to time.[15] The second house had a "store" as well as the two rooms below and above, and it may have been more tightly built than the first, though the Ballards laid a hearth in the kitchen two years after they moved in and put new sashes in the chamber windows four years after that. The third house was new, but unfinished. The family moved in on October 27, 1799. On January 1, the men completed the clapboarding; on January 3, they put in partitions and built the cellar stairs. A year later, they were still caulking rooms, finishing doors, and building window sashes.[16] On April 7, 1802, Ephraim put the lower casements into three windows and a "light" (or window) in the privy.

In such a setting, there was small occasion for housekeeping in the modern sense, though Martha Ballard was concerned about cleanliness. When the girls washed, they usually reused the water to scrub floors; on August 24, 1798, Mrs. Ballard spun yarn for a mop. Though the women occasionally "scoured pewter," there is no mention in the diary of window washing. "Housework" for Martha Ballard might just as well mean chopping wood, building fires, hauling water, pitching snow out of unsealed chambers, or chipping away ice from the platform around the well.[17] In the fall of 1800, she banked her new house with dirt, shoveling it away in the spring. On Bowman's Brook, where the family ran the mills, water was a continual

15. MMB, Mar. 15, 21, Apr. 27, 1785, Apr. 17, Oct. 21, Dec. 2, 1786, June 8, July 2, Oct. 15, Nov. 6, Dec. 19, 22, 1787, May 2, 1788, Jan. 11–12, July 19, 20, 24, Aug. 12, Oct. 13, 18, 1797, June 2, 1799, Jan. 3, Dec. 20, 1800; William Allen, "Now and Then," Maine Historical Society, *Collections*, 1st Ser., VII (1876), 275–276.

16. MMB, Nov. 27, 1793, May 18, 1797, Dec. 20, 1800, Jan. 6, 1801.

17. MMB, Jan. 12, 1790, Feb. 28, 1791, May 11, July 24, 1797, Nov. 22, 1798.

problem. On one July day, after a heavy rainstorm, she carried no fewer than fifty pails of water from the cellar.[18]

Through all this, Martha Ballard pursued her own specialties—midwifery and healing. She delivered 797 babies in the twenty-seven years of the diary and practiced folk medicine as well. Like most female practitioners, she concentrated on diseases of women and children, though she was also adept at treating burns, rashes, or frozen toes and ears. She did not set bones, nor did she let blood—human blood, that is. On October 13, 1786, when Mr. Davis came to her house suffering from shingles, she noted, "We bled a cat and applied the blood which gave him relief." She occasionally opened an abscessed breast, though usually applied to doctors for anything approaching a surgical procedure.[19]

Mrs. Ballard's patients came to her house seeking salves, pills, syrups, ointments, or, more often, simply advice. Forty to seventy times a year, she went to them, spending a few hours or several days administering clysters, dressing burns, or bathing inflamed throats, this in addition to the thirty to fifty deliveries she performed annually. Although she bought imported medicines like camphor or spermaceta and compounds like "elixir proprietas" from Dr. Samuel Colman, she grew or processed most of the medicines she used, sowing and harvesting herbs like chamomile, hyssop, and feverfew; gathering wild plants like burdock, Solomon's seal, or cold-water root; and transforming household staples like onions, tow, or soap into remedies for coughs, sore nipples, or the colic.[20]

Martha Ballard's obstetrical and medical specialties added to an already varied array of domestic tasks that shifted with the weather and the seasons, drawing upon a number of large- and small-muscle skills. To comprehend more fully both the variety and the social complexity of her work, it is helpful to compare her diary with a similar one by a New England male, Matthew Patten. Like Ephraim Ballard, Patten was a surveyor. He was also a carpenter, a farmer, and a public official in the town he had helped to pioneer, Bedford, New Hampshire. Bedford was laid out along the west bank of the Merri-

18. MMB, July 27, 1788, Apr. 7, Oct. 27, 1789.

19. I discuss this side of Martha Ballard's work in detail in "Martha Moore Ballard and the Medical Challenge to Midwifery," in James Lemon and Charles E. Clark, eds., *From Revolution to Statehood: Maine in the Early Republic* (forthcoming, 1988).

20. For imported medicine, see MMB, Feb. 5, 1791, Oct. 5, 1793, Nov. 3, 1795; homegrown herbs, Sept. 30, 1788, Apr. 5, 1790, Oct. 4, 1792, Sept. 16, 1793; wild plants, July 28, 1787, July 12, 1792, June 5, 1794; and household staples, Mar. 4, 1789, Jan. 17, 1792, Mar. 29, 1797.

mack River and had a population of 495 by 1775. Patten's diary, like Martha Ballard's, serves as an account book in the broader sense, not only as a record of specific economic transactions but as a record of daily work, social exchanges with neighbors, and important family events. The tone and scope of the two diaries is similar, and they overlap chronologically, though Patten was fifteen years older than Ballard and began his diary in the 1750s, when he was in his early thirties. For comparison, I have selected passages from the two works that fall at roughly the same point in the authors' life cycles.[21]

In July 1780, Matthew Patten was sixty-one years old; his wife, Elizabeth, was fifty-two. The Pattens had at least five unmarried children, three sons and two daughters. In July 1786, Martha Ballard was fifty-one years old; her husband, Ephraim, was sixty-one. The Ballards also had five unmarried children, three sons and two daughters. The Patten's sons were twenty-three, nineteen, and fifteen; their daughters, twenty-one and seventeen. The Ballard's sons were thirty, twenty-three, and seven; their daughters, seventeen and thirteen. From July 20 to 31, 1780, Matthew Patten spent most of his time haying, an activity that also engaged Ephraim Ballard in late July and early August 1786. Both men were also involved in public affairs. As a justice of the peace, Patten spent part of one day taking evidence in a case and most of another attending quarterly court. In July 1786, Ephraim Ballard also attended court as a grand juryman from Hallowell. They are, then, two diarists from the same social class, from the same time period, and from roughly the same geographic area.

From July 20 to 31, 1780 and 1786, Matthew Patten and Martha Ballard were both involved in several different kinds of work; both had contacts with neighbors; both used the labor of their children; both engaged in barter and trade. Yet Martha Ballard's work, at least as recorded in her diary, was not only more varied but more socially complex. Patten mentioned six specific tasks—mowing, hauling hay, sowing ("I sowed our Turnip seed in the Cow yards that we yarded Last summer"), taking depositions, attending court, and trading. Martha Ballard was herself involved in nine—carding, spinning, boiling warp, baking, cleaning cellar, gathering herbs, treating the sick, making fence ("I Cutt Alders and maid a Sort of a fence part round the yard by the mill Pond"), and trading. (There were no deliveries in this period.) In addition, she mentioned three other female tasks that her daughters performed independently—washing clothes, berrying, and brewing beer.

21. *The Diary of Matthew Patten of Bedford, N.H.* (Concord, N.H., 1903), 3, 416–417; *History of Bedford, N.H., 1737–1971* (Bedford, 1972), 7–8.

Matthew Patten had economic exchanges with six other persons, Martha Ballard with thirteen. There is a striking difference, however, in the way the two diarists recorded these transactions. In every case, Patten spelled out exactly what was given or expected on each side. On July 25, 1780, for example, he wrote, "I got a bushell of Salt from john Wallace on acct of the Stuff he had from us last Spring and I paid Zechariah Chandler the ½ bushell of salt I borrowed from him the 30th of last Decbr and I got 14 jills of Rum from Lieut Orr for which I paid him 28 Dollars."[25] The reader who cares to do so can easily trace Patten's arrangement with Zechariah Chandler back to the original entry for December 30: "I borrowed ½ a bushell of salt from Zechariah Chandler it weighed 39 £ and 5 ounces I am to pay it by weight and if it is dirtyer than what I got I am to make him such allowance as he thinks will be right."[22] That sort of precision was characteristic of Patten.

By comparison, Martha Ballard's accounts are indirect and vague. Although she includes some entries of the sort typical of Patten ("received a pair of shoes and 2/ from Mr Beeman for attending his wife and for medisen"), she has more entries like that for July 29, 1786: "I went afternoon to Mr Edsons Carried 32 skeins of Linning warp for her to weave 11½ skeins of Tow yarn and 8 of Cottne the girls went to Mr Savages for green Peas I let them have 1 lb of Butter."[23] While it is quite clear from other entries in the diary that Martha Ballard had a long-standing economic relation with Mrs. Edson, only with great effort can the credits and debits in that account be extracted and arranged. Even more difficult to define is the apparent trade of green peas for butter. Informal food exchanges were an integral part of life in rural New England, and they frequently appear in the Ballard diary, yet, in this case, it is entirely possible that a social event was implied. The girls may have been going to the Savages' to eat green peas, the butter being their contribution to the dinner.[24]

22. *Diary of Patten*, 410, 417.
23. Martha Ballard gave or received payments from five persons, performed medical services for four others (without specifying payment), and carried wool for weaving to another; the remaining three entries may represent borrowing, gift giving, or trade.
24. There is a growing literature on rural interdependence in the 18th century. Richard L. Bushman, "Family Security in the Transition from Farm to City, 1750–1850," *Journal of Family History*, VI (1981), 238–256; Carole Shammas, "How Self-Sufficient Was Early America?" *Journal of Interdisciplinary History*, XIII (1982–1983), 247–272; Joyce Appleby, "Commercial Farming and the 'Agrarian Myth' in the Early Republic," *Journal of American History*, LXVIII (1981–1982), 833–849; Michael Merrill, "Cash Is Good to Eat: Self-Sufficiency and Exchange in the Rural Econo-

There is an even stronger contrast between entries in the two diaries involving other family members. Matthew Patten clearly had help with the haying, since he wrote in the plural, "We began to mow," but only once in the ten days did he specifically mention another person, on July 31, recording that "David and I mowed in the meadow." In contrast, Martha Ballard included fifteen references to other workers. Two mention Mr. Ballard, six record specific activities of the girls (though only one mentions a daughter's name), two note the activities of a neighbor, and five acknowledge the arrival or departure of a male worker.

Male diarists, like Matthew Patten, are notorious for ignoring their wives. Not only are there no references to Elizabeth Patten in this section, I can find only two references to her in the entire year, the first on May 12, when she fell and "Strained" her ankle, and the second the next day when Patten went to Goffstown to get some rum to bathe it. In contrast, there are few weeks in Martha Ballard's diary when the reader does not know, at least in a general way, what Ephraim Ballard was doing. She also regularly noted the activities of her sons. Although Patten does give more attention in other parts of his diary to his sons, in 1780 he made only one reference to a daughter, that on November 30 when "Polly set out for Chester . . . to stay and help her Uncle Majr Tolfords folks to Spin Wool."[25]

The differences in the two diaries cannot be explained simply in terms of personality. In her study of a commercial dairying region of New York in the late nineteenth century, Nancy Grey Osterud found a similar, though even more pronounced, contrast between the recording practices of men and women. Although both sexes were involved outside the market in labor exchanges of the sort common to the Ballard and Patten diaries, men tended to assign such transactions a monetary value even when no money was exchanged, while women "generally recorded their cooperative work as a direct, personal relationship, unmediated by market values." The blurring between sociability and trade that we have noted in the Ballard diary was even more pronounced in the records of the New York women.

---

my of the United States," *Radical History Review*, III (1977), 42–71; and Bettye Hobbs Pruitt, "Self-Sufficiency and the Agricultural Economy of Eighteenth-Century Massachusetts," *William and Mary Quarterly*, 3d Ser., XLI (1984), 333–364. Although none of these authors explicitly considers commodity exchanges among women, the Ballard evidence fits well with Merrill's description of the rural economy. Pruitt's reference to surpluses in widow's portions is also suggestive.

25. *Diary of Patten*, 414, 423.

The contrasts between Patten and Ballard may reflect, then, larger gender differences within the northern rural economy.[26]

The comparison between the two diaries also suggests that the old adage that "woman's work is never done" derived not only from the large number of tasks for which women were responsible but from the complexity of the social relationships that structured their work. That a woman might more frequently note the activities of male workers than vice versa is hardly surprising, since (as Nancy Cott expressed it) women stood in "an adjunct and service relationship to men in economic activity." Matthew Patten's diary suggests that, unless his wife were absent or disabled, her activities really had little effect on his daily work. He simply took for granted that his meals would be ready and his clothes washed and mended. His wife, however, had to tune her work to his. But the point is larger than that. Martha Ballard's attentiveness to the work of the men in her household suggests that, even when their work did not directly affect her, as, for example, when the addition of another worker meant more food to prepare, she felt somehow connected to it. Some part of her duty was to be aware of the activities of others. In this respect, her behavior corroborates the importance of affiliation in the psychology of women.[27]

26. On rural New York (and for the quotation), see Nancy Grey Osterud, "Sharing and Exchanging Work: Cooperative Relationships among Women and among Men in an Upstate New York Dairying Community during the Late Nineteenth Century" (paper, based on "Strategies of Mutuality: Relations among Women and Men in an Agricultural Community" [Ph.D. diss., Brown University, 1984]). For sharply differing interpretations of the use of cash values in 18th-century account books, see Merrill, "Cash Is Good to Eat," *Rad. Hist. Rev.*, III (1977), 42–71; and Winifred B. Rothenberg, "The Market and Massachusetts Farmers, 1750–1855," *Journal of Economic History*, XLI (1981), 283–314. For our purposes, it really does not matter whether the differences between Patten and Ballard reflected "market" versus "use" exchanges or two modes of reporting the latter. The differences are nevertheless there. Accounts like Patten's and Ballard's developed in a broad middle space between sophisticated mercantile ledgers and purely oral transactions. Men clearly dominated in the former; perhaps women gradually came to predominate in the latter. Although few historians have explicitly considered gender differences, there is a growing literature on the early 19th-century rural economy. Useful studies include Christopher Clark, "Household Economy, Market Exchange, and the Rise of Capitalism in the Connecticut Valley, 1800–1860," *Journal of Social History*, XIII (1979), 169–189; Robert A. Gross, "Culture and Cultivation: Agriculture and Society in Thoreau's Concord," *Journal of American History*, LXIX (1982–1983), 46; and Jack Larkin, "The World of the Account Book: Some Perspectives on Economic Life in Rural New England in the Early 19th Century" (paper presented at the T.A.R.S. Symposium on Social History, Keene State College, October 1984).

27. Cott, *Bonds of Womanhood*, 23. For the importance of affiliation to women,

Martha Ballard's affiliations, however, extended to other women as well as to men. Certainly, she was a supportive wife, a "meet help" as a seventeenth-century housewife would have put it. She baked biscuit for sea journeys, fed and found beds for rafting crews, constructed packs for surveying trips, and washed the heavily soiled bedding and clothing when the men returned. Once in a while, she also took a direct part in the men's work, going into the field to rake hay or keeping account of mill transactions when Mr. Ballard was away. Her daughters also occasionally "rode horse to plough" or helped "drop corn."[28] Because their work was defined as supportive, women could more easily step across role boundaries to perform male work than vice versa. What is most striking about Martha Ballard's work in its totality, however, is not its relation to the work of the men, but its independence from it.

Some historians have assumed that the domestic labor of women was somehow subsumed in a patriarchal family economy. Martha Ballard's diary, however, supports scattered evidence from earlier sources arguing that housewives managed the products of their own labor. "I medle not with the geese nor turke's," said one seventeenth-century New Englander, "for thay are hurs for she hath bene and is a good wife to me."[29] A domineering husband could, of course, "medle" in his wife's affairs, but a division of responsibility was encouraged not only by tradition but by the practical difficulties of minding his wife's business while sustaining his own. Ironically, the very dearth of evidence for women's work in male diaries and ledgers may in itself be presumptive evidence for a separate female economy. Ebenezer Parkman's indifference to his wife's activities may be a consequence of "male chauvinism" (as Richard Dunn has suggested). It may also mean that Mrs. Parkman was managing quite well on her own.[30] Martha and Ephraim Ballard cooperated in providing for their family—he plowed her garden, she mended his packs—but, in large part, they worked independently, and they kept separate accounts; significantly, she paid her workers, he his.

What is equally apparent is that other Hallowell women did the

see, especially, Jean Baker Miller, *Toward a New Psychology of Women* (Boston, 1976).

28. MMB, July 26, Aug. 1, 1785, Apr. 25, 28, May 12, July 14, 1776, May 11, 19, 1787, May 11, June 8, 9, Oct. 14, 1789.

29. George Francis Dow and Mary G. Thresher, eds., *Records and Files of the Quarterly Courts of Essex County, Massachusetts*, 9 vols. (Salem, Mass., 1911–1975).

30. See Richard S. Dunn, "Servants and Slaves: The Recruitment and Employment of Labor," in Jack P. Greene and J. R. Pole, eds., *Colonial British America: Essays in the New History of the Early Modern Era* (Baltimore, 1984), 187.

same. The diary mentions male shoemakers, tailors, and carpenters as well as a pewterer, a printer, a tinker, and a clothier. But female dairywomen, nurses, spinners, weavers, dressmakers, a bonnet maker, a chair caner, and seven midwives other than Martha Ballard are noted also. Although the diary never mentions teachers, the town treasurer's accounts for the fall of 1787 record payments to three women for "keeping school."[31] Martha Ballard traded textiles and farm products with her female neighbors as well as physic and obstetrical services. She gave Mrs. Densmore three pounds of flax for cutting and fitting a gown, she traded Mrs. Porter tow yarn for blue-dyed yarn, and when Polly Savage helped with the washing, she paid her in flax and ashes.[32]

Martha Ballard's diary fills in blanks in women's lives left by traditional sources. Hallowell women did not just trade commodities that required visible tools, like spinning wheels or churns, objects that might be traced through probate inventories; they exchanged products that have left little trace in written records, things like ashes, herbs, seedlings, and baby chicks. On June 17, 1786, for example, Martha Ballard paid Mrs. Bolton one-half pound of tea for four hundred plants she had received a few days before. Nor was their manufacturing confined to obvious products such as textiles or cheese. Mrs. Ballard herself, for a time, baked biscuit for Brook's store. In this lumbering and shipping town, some of her neighbors also kept boarders.[33]

The diary helps us to recognize the selective nature of the evidence in male account books. In the handful of Hallowell records that survive, as in account books from other towns and from earlier periods, male names predominate. Even when female products appear, they are usually listed under men's names. One might assume that the sixteen and a half pounds of butter credited to Ebenezer Farwell in a ledger kept by Samuel and William Howard was produced by his wife, or that the four pounds of spun yarn on James Burns's page came from the women of his family, but there is no way of knowing from the record whether the women personally profited from the

31. MMB, Feb. 15, Dec. 23, 29, 1785, Mar. 10, June 6, Aug. 10, Sept. 28, Nov. 15, 28, Dec. 6, 1786, Oct. 21, Nov. 23, 1787, Mar. 14, 1788, Feb. 25, June 27, 1789, Mar. 6, 1790, Jan. 5, June 27, 1791, Dec. 9–11, 1801; Nash, History of Augusta, 525.

32. MMB, July 10, 1787, separate entry after Dec. 31, 1787, Mar. 6, 1788.

33. MMB, June 7, 1786: "Daniel Breakfasted here means to Bord at Boltons from this time." Martha Ballard may have been charging travelers and logging crews for the meals they ate with the family. There are 148 entries regarding persons sleeping or eating at the Ballard house; though there is no mention of payment, this seems in excess of ordinary sociability.

transaction. Once in a while, the Howards mention a female worker, as in accounts with the shoemaker Samuel Welch which include references to "your wife's weaving"; but, in the Howard accounts as in all the others, most of the women of Hallowell are invisible.[34] Indeed, without the diary we would have no way of knowing anything about Martha Ballard's enterprises, including midwifery; the few references to the Ballards in extant account books are all listed under Ephraim's name.[35]

In a letter to an associate regarding the establishment of a potash works in Thomaston, Maine, during this same period, Thomas Vose wrote, "Ashes in general being the women's perquisite certain articles of goods must be kept on hand for payment which will induce them to save as many as they can and often to send them to the works."[36] Vose recognized that the success of his industrial experiment depended upon the willingness of women to divert their ashes from household use and from neighborhood trade toward his store. He also recognized that women had "perquisites," that there were certain products they could sell or barter on their own.

The Ballard diary gives ample evidence that the family economic system was based not only upon cooperation but upon just such a division of responsibility. Mrs. Ballard paid Mr. Savage, the blacksmith, for a spindle and for making irons for her loom, but she reckoned directly with Mrs. Savage, who offered not only her own labor in spinning but also a woolen wheel. Mr. Ballard negotiated with Mr. Densmore, the tailor; Mrs. Ballard dealt directly with Mrs. Densmore, the dressmaker. Mr. Ballard settled accounts for lumber with Mr. Weston, the merchant; Mrs. Ballard traded cabbages with Mrs. Weston for brandy and spices from their store.[37] Such evidence helps us to see the range of activity that may have lain behind the occasional entries in male ledgers, such as those of Thomas Chute of Marblehead, Massachusetts, who, in the 1730s, balanced an account "By you[r] wives accoumpt with mine."[38]

34. Samuel and William Howard Account Book, 1773–1793, MS, Maine Historical Society, 126a, 141b, 116b.

35. *Ibid.*, 117ab (mostly timber transactions) and Anonymous Account Book, Augusta, 1809, MS, Maine State Library, which lists mostly garden seeds in a period when Martha Ballard clearly was doing the gardening. Internal evidence suggests that the book was kept by Joseph North.

36. Thomas Vose to Henry Knox, Dec. 14, 1789, Henry Knox Papers, MS, Maine Historical Society. I am indebted to Alan Taylor for this reference.

37. MMB, Mar. 11, 13, 1786, Jan. 16, 1787, Apr. 15, 1788, Sept. 1, 1789, Sept. 14, 1791.

38. Account Book of Thomas Chute, Maine Historical Society, 6.

Thus, Martha Ballard's diary points to a world of women unrecorded in standard sources. That males dominated written records should not be taken as conclusive evidence that men dominated women. This is not to say, however, that women competed in the public economy on the same terms as men. Although it is difficult to develop precise comparisons because the two sexes not only performed different work but traded different products (how shall we measure the relative values of ashes and dung?), it is possible to derive rough wage differentials from the diary and other contemporary sources. Although men were, in general, paid more than women, the discrepancy varies considerably according to age and skill. In the 1790s, the Howards paid male laborers three shillings per day whether they were planting potatoes, reaping rye, or unloading the sloop. During the same period, Mrs. Ballard paid her household workers from one to two shillings. A weaver working full-time at her loom could earn four shillings a day, about the same as a skilled worker at the Howard mills. Yet few weavers could work full-time at their looms, women's work being subject to interruptions for cooking the meals and washing the clothes that millworkers and farmhands required.[39]

Martha Ballard could earn roughly six shillings per day as a midwife, about the same amount as her husband could claim for writing plans or for appraising an estate, though of course the time involved in a delivery was more variable and the hours less appealing (see table 1). In all, Martha Ballard's earning capacity was probably considerably less than her husband's. In 1790, when her total cash income was twenty pounds, he earned thirty-eight pounds in three months' work for the Kennebec Proprietors.[40] Of course, such a comparison takes no account of the diversity of Ephraim Ballard's work or of the importance of barter transactions to the family economy. Nor does it consider the greater financial obligations of men. That Ephraim Ballard had cash to pay his taxes and buy meat and flour for the family strengthened Martha Ballard's ability to concentrate on her own enterprises.

The complexity of her economy is suggested in a matter-of-fact

39. Howard Accounts, 11b, 82b, 93b, 94b, 116b, 160b; MMB, Jan. 8, June 15–25, July 8, 1791, Oct. 15, 1792, Dec. 11, 1801. I arrived at daily rates for female workers by comparing piece rates with typical daily outputs.

40. Ephraim and William Richardson Accounts with Luke Barton Estate, 1787–1790, in Towne Papers, 3:9, MS, Maine State Museum; Kennebec Purchase Company, Waste Book, 1754–1800, MS, Maine Historical Society, 169 (see also 185, 187, 467). Mr. Ballard received £31 in 1794, $145 in 1796, and $67 in 1798.

TABLE 1
Daily Wages, Hallowell, Maine, 1785–1790

Work	Wages (approximate)
Surveying	9s.
Writing plans	7
Midwifery	6
Appraising an estate	6
Labor of a man and ox	5
Millwork	4
Splitting staves	4
Weaving	3–4
Planting, reaping, unloading sloop, etc.	3
Washing	2
General work (young male)	2
General work (young female)	1

Sources: Martha Moore Ballard Diary, Maine State Library; Luke Barton Accounts, Maine State Museum; Lincoln County Court Records, Suffolk County Court House; Samuel and William Howard Account Books, Maine Historical Society; Kennebec Purchase Company Papers, Maine Historical Society.

entry for July 2, 1791: "I went to Mr Weston Bot 3 lb pott ash at /6; went to Mr Burtuns Left four Dollars and an order on Mr Cogsill of Boston for 3,000 of shingles left by Hains Larned in Oct 88, which he is to purchase articles with for me in Boston." The next day, the six pennies' worth of potash she had purchased at Weston's store helped her complete a process begun almost a year before when her girls had spent four days harvesting flax. Parthena had recently finished the weaving, and now the cloth was ready to wash and "putt in ley." Thus, the cash transaction at Weston's store was a small link in a complex home production system.[41]

The exchange at Burton's store was also linked to the larger female economy. The four silver dollars plus the timber credit earned through unspecified services to the Learned family three years earlier brought eight yards of chintz home from Boston in September. Dolly picked up the cloth on September 14. On September 16, Mrs. Ballard

41. MMB, Aug. 4–7, 1790, June 17, 1791.

went to the Densmores, to bring Lydia Densmore and her three children "home with me [to] cutt out my gown." On September 22, she closed accounts with Mrs. Densmore by delivering her of a daughter.

These July transactions suggest two quite different economic objectives. Martha Ballard labored not only to provide essentials for her family but to secure small pleasures for herself. Chintz from Boston was as much a part of her economic system as was homespun linen.[42] Her ability to buy a new dress in the summer of 1791 is particularly interesting, given the disruption in the men's work that year. Mr. Ballard's relinquishment of the sawmills in March had no effect on Mrs. Ballard's ability to purchase a new dress in September. Martha Ballard was as independent as an eighteenth-century housewife could be.

MRS. BALLARD'S economy was built upon the deft management of many resources, including the labor of the young women who worked with her. Early Americanists have given a great deal of attention to the intersection of economic history and family history, particularly to the passing of property from fathers to sons. There has been little, if anything, written about the relationship of mothers and daughters; nor have labor historians given much attention to the hired work of women in preindustrial New England.[43] To explore these themes better, we must consider the chronological development of Martha Ballard's work.

Midwifery, like other female specialties, had to be integrated into a life span that typically included marriage in the early twenties and alternating periods of pregnancy and lactation for the next two decades. Martha Ballard performed her first delivery in July 1778, about a year after her migration to Maine.[44] She was then forty-one years old, near the end of childbearing. When she gave birth to her last child in 1779, her next oldest child was already six. Unfortunately, there is no detailed account of her midwifery practice between 1778 and 1785. The surviving diary makes quite clear, however, that the sort of obstetrical practice she sustained after 1785 would have been difficult for a woman who was herself giving birth every other year. This does not mean that young women were entirely excluded from

42. These transactions support the conclusion of Shammas, in "How Self-Sufficient," *Jour. Interdisc. Hist.*, XIII (1982–1983), 247–272.

43. For an exception, see Gary B. Nash, "The Failure of Female Factory Labor in Colonial Boston," *Labor History*, XX (1979), 165–188.

44. MMB, Jan. 15, 1796: "This is the 612 birth I have attended at since the year 1777 the first I assisted was the wife of Pelton Warrin in July 1778."

the sort of experience that ultimately might lead to such a practice. Mothers—including nursing mothers—assisted at births. At the Abiel Herrington house in June 1796, for example, "there are 22 in number slept under that roof the night."[45] Yet occasionally assisting at a birth was something less than routinely officiating as a midwife.

Midwifery was both time-consuming and unpredictable. Babies arrived in snowstorms, during harvest, and in the middle of the night. Labors could be frighteningly intense or annoyingly lackadaisical. After Mrs. Ballard had spent four days at James Caton's house in the spring of 1796, and then only after Mrs. Caton had consumed eleven glasses of wine in one day and "bisquit and wine at evening 3 times" were her twins finally born. (Even then, although Mrs. Ballard had been without sleep for three days, she "could not sleep for fleas.") A midwife sometimes spent two or three days at a delivery and sometimes did not make it at all. For Martha Ballard, the average time between "call" and delivery was ten hours. She usually spent another three to four hours in postpartum care, remaining through the night if the baby were born after dark. A pregnant woman might have managed such a schedule, but not a nursing mother. To carry an infant through stormy weather in the middle of the night on horseback or in a canoe would have been foolhardy.[46]

Freedom from childbearing, therefore, was one prerequisite for a midwife's work. A secure supply of household help was the other. If midwifery was dramatically episodic, housewifery was relentlessly regular. At home, day after day, there were meals to cook, cows to milk, fires to build, dishes and clothes to wash. The diary suggests a strong taboo against male involvement in such chores; if Martha Ballard was not at home to get her husband's breakfast, some other female had to be. After 1788, Martha Ballard consistently used a marginal notation "AH" to mark days spent entirely "at home." They were surprisingly few. Between 1790 and 1799, she left home, for some period of time, more than half of the days of the year. Midwifery doesn't account for all these excursions, of course, but it was responsible for a good many.

From 1785 until 1796, Martha Ballard relied upon her own daughters as well as upon a number of young women who lived temporarily in her house. "Girls washed" is a typical entry for these years. Martha Ballard was not the sort of woman to turn her growing

45. MMB, June 15, 1796, and see Nov. 26, 1790, July 25, 1798, Mar. 5, 1801.
46. MMB, Apr. 7–12, 1796. I have discussed the importance of lactation in determining a woman's ability to travel in *Good Wives*, 138–145. In a densely settled town, of course, a midwife's travel would be less arduous.

daughters into household drudges, however, even if she could afford to. Hannah and Dolly needed skills to sustain their future families as well as to contribute to their own livelihood in the present. This, no doubt, explains why textile production accelerated in the Ballard household at exactly the same time as midwifery (see figure 1).

We have long known that the late eighteenth century was an era of burgeoning household production. The Revolution and the nonimportation movements that preceded it gave new importance to textile skills. As James Henretta has pointed out, the expansion of cloth production led, not to proto-industrialization, the consolidation of spinning and weaving in centralized factories or through a putting-out system under the control of a merchant capitalist, but to dispersed and petty household production.[47] Both the expansion and the dispersion of home production can be glimpsed in probate inventories from northern New England. In the 1730s, in York County (which then included all of the settled parts of Maine), 40 percent of household inventories listed spinning wheels, but only 3 percent had looms. (The corresponding figures for Essex County, Massachusetts, in the same decade are 38 percent and 13 percent.) In this period, weaving often was done by professional male weavers. In the Kennebec Valley in the late eighteenth century, more than 60 percent of probate inventories included wheels (sometimes several per household), and more than 25 percent had looms.[48] Judging from the Ballard diary, all of the weaving in Hallowell was done by women and girls.

In 1785 and 1786, the Ballard girls were already spinning home-grown flax, which they carried to Mrs. Edson, Mrs. Chamberlain, or Susanna Cowen to weave. In May 1787, the Ballards acquired a loom. Hannah Cool, who lived with the Ballards all summer, knew how to weave. Hannah Ballard, who was eighteen, and Dolly, fifteen, soon learned. Between 1787 and 1792, the girls wove check, diaper, hucka-back, worsted, dimity, woolen "shurting," towels, blankets, "rag coverlids," and lawn handkerchiefs as well as "plain cloth." But they still relied on skilled neighbors for help. Mrs. Pollard came to "instruct Dolly about her weaving," while Mrs. Welch frequently came to the

47. James A. Henretta, "The War for Independence and American Proto-Industrialization" (paper presented at 1984 conference, U.S. Capitol Historical Society).

48. *Good Wives*, 16. No long-range study of inventories exists, though a small sample of Kennebec Valley inventories is included in Edwin A. Churchill, "Textile Tools in Early Maine Homes—Chronological Samples," research notes, Maine State Museum. Of the 10 Hallowell inventories taken in the 1790s, 8 had wheels, and 5 had looms.

FIGURE 1. Martha Ballard's Obstetrical Practice, 1785–1812

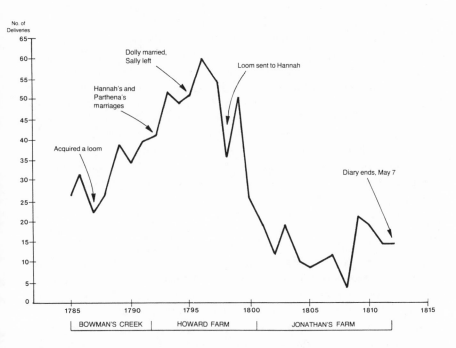

house to "warp a web."[49] Warping is the most difficult part of the weaving process. Once the threads were properly attached to the loom, an inexperienced girl could weave.

Dolly learned her craft well, however, for in October 1792, when she was living at the Densmore house learning dressmaking, she came home to instruct her sister and cousin "how to draw their piece of Dimmity."[50] Although most of the cloth seems to have been intended for household consumption, the girls also wove for several of their neighbors, relying on others to help them with skills and supplies. The intricacy of this textile network is suggested in a diary entry for April 20, 1790: "Cyrus borrowed a 40 sleigh of the widdow Coburn for Dolly to weav a piece for Benjamin Porter."

By expanding textile production, Martha Ballard provided household help for herself and an occupation for her girls. An entry for

49. MMB, Dec. 15–19, 1787, May 1, Sept. 12, 13, 1788, Jan. 9, Apr. 7, 1790, Jan. 3, 7, July 4, 15, 1791, Oct. 15–17, 1792.
50. MMB, Oct. 10, 1792.

October 26, 1789, puts it succinctly: "My girls spun 23 double skeins and wove 27½ yds last weak and did the houswork besides." Another solution would have been to keep the mother at home and send the daughters out. This was what Martha Ballard's younger sister, Dorothy Barton, was forced to do. Perhaps "forced" is too strong a word. Working for a while outside one's own family seems to have been part of a young woman's education in this period. Still, economic necessity doubtless played a part in Dorothy Barton's case. By 1784, she had six growing daughters and only one son, a fact that may account for the difficulty Stephen Barton had in establishing a foothold in Maine.[51] Pamela and Clarissa Barton each spent time with the Ballards, and, in 1788, when her parents returned temporarily to Oxford, Parthena came to live in Hallowell. Except for short periods, Parthena remained with the Ballards until her marriage in 1792.

Parthena's presence may have allowed Hannah to spend eight months in 1789 with another aunt in Oxford and probably had something to do with Dolly's availability to apprentice for a year with Lydia Densmore.[52] By the time of Parthena's and Hannah's marriages in 1792, Dolly had finished her training and was able to live and work at home, going for short periods to neighbors' houses to cut and fit their gowns. In April 1793, Sally Cox began a service of almost three years. She and Dolly, like Hannah and Parthena before them, were an effective team. Not only did Martha Ballard's obstetrical practice grow, but her domestic economy did as well.

There is not space here to detail Mrs. Ballard's various enterprises, though it seems clear that she concentrated on one activity at a time. When that was mastered, she moved on. Not surprisingly, 1788, the year after the Ballards acquired their loom, was an important year for weaving entries in the diary; but once textile production was securely in the hands of the girls, Mrs. Ballard reduced her entries, simply noting yardages from time to time or acknowledging the introduction of a new slay, or reed, for the loom. In 1790 she focused on gardening, carefully noting dates of planting and harvest and, for some crops, including yields. The year 1792 was remarkable for turkeys. On April 17, she found a hen on its nest "5 eggs therein." From the end of April until the end of May, she was busy "setting" tur-

51. George F. Daniels, *History of the Town of Oxford, Massachusetts* (Oxford, Mass., 1892), 390–391; Stephen Barton Account Book, MS, Maine State Library. Elijah Barton, born in 1784, became a leader of a settler rebellion in the town of Malta (North, *History of Augusta*, 374).

52. MMB, Oct. 23, 1788, July 13, 1789, Nov. 15, 1791, Nov. 15, 1792.

keys, usually seventeen eggs to a bird. On May 26, the black turkey brought out fourteen chicks. On June 2, there were forty-three fledglings in the yard. Another fourteen hatched in mid-August, not long before the first of the spring brood was ready for the table. The Ballards dined on roast turkey for the first time on September 7. They ate turkey at least ten other times between the middle of October and the middle of December, including November 29, Thanksgiving Day. Mysteriously, turkeys disappear from the diary soon after. Whether they also disappeared from the Ballard table we cannot know.

The years between 1785 and 1795 were vintage ones for Martha Ballard. Her loom and wheels were busy, her garden flourishing, and even her poultry yard was booming. With the girls assuming routine household chores as well as the spinning and weaving, she was free to develop her own specialties. The system also seems to have worked well for the girls. There were quiltings, huskings, dances, and frequent visits to and from neighbors. By 1794 there was also a singing school that Sally Cox attended. Unfortunately, Mrs. Ballard was not systematic in recording wages. Her final reckoning with Pamela Barton and a fragment of an account with Parthena show that the base pay for the Barton girls was six pounds a year. In addition, of course, they received board and room and perhaps some basic clothing; Mrs. Ballard did not charge Pamela for the stockings she knitted for her in February 1787, but she did debit the apron "patren" she bought her in July.[53]

By tradition, a servant received her wages at the end of her service; in reality, most of the girls probably spent their income as they earned it, accumulating debits as well as credits on their mistress's accounts. A fragmentary account for Parthena Barton shows that her three-pound wage for six months' labor barely covered the "sundry articles" she had purchased in December 1792 and "a hatt made and fitt to wear." In 1789 Mrs. Ballard paid Polly Wall, a short-term worker, directly in clothes; a hat, a shift, and a petticoat equaled six weeks' work. Most accounts are less explicit. When Sally Cox finally left Martha Ballard's employ, her mistress simply wrote, "I reckoned with Sally Cocks and paid her all I owd her." Even without detail, such references are conclusive evidence that these young women, rather than their parents, received the rewards of their labor.[54]

53. MMB, Feb. 6, May 5, July 5, 1787.
54. MMB, July 11, 1789, Nov. 21, 1795. Although the work of a very young girl might be credited to her mother, as in Mrs. Ballard's account with Mrs. Weston,

Even at the low rate of six pounds per annum, a young woman could, over the period of six or eight years that she worked, accumulate something toward her future. Parthena Barton and Sally Cox took not only quilts and bedding from their service with Mrs. Ballard but the skills to make more, having, for several years, shared both the equipment and the instruction Martha Ballard provided her daughters.[55] Although there is no reference in the diary to marriage "settlements" or "portions," some part of Mrs. Ballard's own income clearly went toward providing household goods for Hannah and Dolly. On June 3, 1795, as Dolly was preparing to set up housekeeping, her mother bought her a bureau, table, and bedstead as well as porringers, candlesticks, and canisters. Two weeks later, she added two sets of teacups and a teapot. Meanwhile, Dolly was herself purchasing crockery and furniture, and she and Sally were quilting.[56]

For the girls as well as for Martha Ballard, there was strength in cooperation. Such a system, however, carried the source of its own destruction. Preparing her helpers for marriage, Mrs. Ballard helped speed up their departure. The girls went by twos, Hannah and Parthena in 1792, Dolly and Sally in 1795. That is why, on November 26, 1795, we found her sitting, waiting for a hired girl, Sarah Neal, to come home. Sarah was gone within the month.

Not surprisingly, 1796 turned out to be a distressing year for Martha Ballard. So long as she had daughters at home, she had been able to count on at least one worker who would not quit, and for many years she had also been able to rely on her niece Parthena and Dolly's friend Sally Cox. Now she was at the mercy of her helpers. Her obstetrical practice was at its height, the work at home was as insistent as ever, and much of the time there was no one to help. In 1796 eight girls entered and left the Ballard house. In such a situation, a woman's work truly was "never done." On January 6, 1796, Mrs. Ballard began her washing, laying it aside when company came, then finishing it "except for rinsing" after they left. Such an interruption might have been a minor irritation had she not been called away early the next morning to a woman in labor. Not until three days later would she be able to write, "I finisht my washing." On June 4, 1796, she was busy cleaning the head and feet of a newly

---

Jan. 16, 1787 (which included a credit for two days of 14-year-old Dolly's work), this was rare.

55. MMB, Oct. 30, Nov. 20, Nov. 26, Nov. 27, 1792; Mrs. Ballard and Dolly helped Sally Cox quilt, Nov. 11, 1795.

56. MMB, Nov. 14, 1792, June 6, 17, Nov. 11, 1794, Mar. 21, June 4, 1795.

FIGURE 2. Diary Entries, 1786–1802

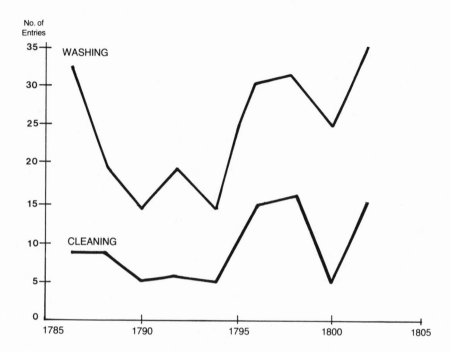

slaughtered calf, when Joseph Young called to say his wife was in labor. From Mrs. Young, she went to Mrs. Carter and then to Mrs. Staton. Having delivered three babies in twenty-four hours, she was ready for a rest. "I came home at Evening and do feel much fatgud," she wrote, "but was oblidged to sett up and cook the orful of my veal."[57]

Laundering and cleaning, acknowledged earlier in the diary, if at all, by the simple notation "girls washd" or "girls scourd rooms," now became serious matters (see figure 2). What are we to make of a record that lists thirty-three washdays in one year and only fourteen in another? Do we assume that the Ballards had clean clothing four times in June 1796 but only once between the beginning of April and the end of June in 1792? Clearly, Martha Ballard was less likely to note washday when it was someone else's responsibility.

57. MMB, Jan. 6–9, June 4–5, 1796. This theme continues through the next five years: Jan. 15, 26, 1796, Jan. 18, 1797, Apr. 27, 1798, and May 13, 1800.

FIGURE 3. Full-time, Live-in Labor, 1786–1802.
Includes Martha Ballard's daughters

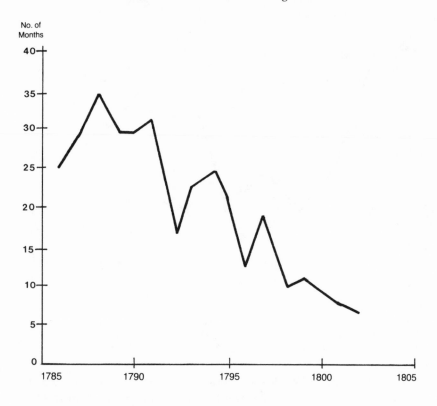

The problem was not just in securing helpers, but in keeping them (see figures 3 and 4). Although the number of labor months available to Mrs. Ballard declined each year after Hannah's and Parthena's marriages, the crucial issue was how many workers she had to recruit and train in a year. One Sally Cox settling into the family was worth half a dozen short-term helpers. The persistence problem developed in 1796, and though it improved slightly in 1800, Martha Ballard's household never was quite the same (figure 4). Between 1785 and 1795, eleven girls had lived and worked, for some period, in the Ballard house; in the six years from 1796 to 1802, there were twenty-nine. Diary entries for the spring and summer of 1798 are typical. On May 8, Mrs. Ballard sent her husband to Winthrop to see whether he could get Hepsy Brown to come and work for her. He was unsuccessful. Polly Barbareck came on May 10, but left again the next week. On May 30, Mr. Ballard went to Sidney to "seek a girl"

FIGURE 4. Length of Worker Residency, 1786–1800.
Excludes Martha Ballard's daughters

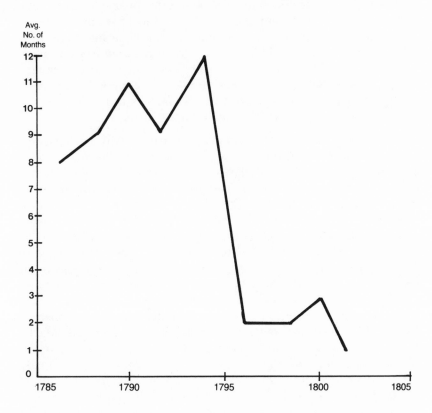

but couldn't find one. Nabby Smith came on June 1 and stayed about six weeks. On July 12, the diary notes, Nabby tried to get Nelly Coogin to come but "did not suckseed." On July 17, there was another crisis—"Nabby left me."

The effect on her morale—and on her diary—was marked. For the first time, Martha Ballard began to use her journal to plumb her frustrations. Crisp and confident entries gave way to long laments, and, in a few places, she even penned vignettes of women's oppression. The day after Polly Barbareck left, Martha Ballard scrubbed the bedroom and kitchen, even though she had a funeral to attend that day. During the next few days she was ill. Her sense of abandonment may account for the length of the diary entry for May 22 and 23, 1798, and for its tone:

I have been very unwell. I Eat a little cold puding and Cold milk twice in the coars of the day and perform part of my washing. I Laid myself on the bed in the bedroom, was not able to rise from there. My Husband went to bed and not come to see me so I lay there in my Cloaths till 5 hours morn when I made shift to rise. I got the men Breakfast but was not able to Eat a morsel my self till after 3 pm but I finisht my washing. How many times I have been necasatated to rest my selfe on the bed I am not able to say. God grant me patience to go thro the fatages of this life with fortitude looking forward to a more happy state.

Captured by self-pity, Martha Ballard quarreled with her husband and with the girls on whom she depended. She dismissed Patty Easty for theft and Elizabeth Taylor for "ill manners." Sally Fletcher walked out on her own, returning to collect her "duds" and threatening to "sue us in a weak from this time if we did not pai her what was her due."[58] In May 1798, Mrs. Ballard sent her loom to her daughter Hannah. She seems to have recognized that she could no longer maintain the home production that had been so effective in the past. Fewer girls would now be needed, but, ironically, without the weaving, there may have been less reason for them to come and fewer yards of cloth with which to pay them.

It is too simple to conclude that Martha Ballard had grown irascible in her old age or the young women of the town less dependable. Surely some part of Mrs. Ballard's troubles can be attributed to the unusual demands she placed on the girls. It cannot have been easy for a sixteen-year-old to have taken total responsibility for a household when its mistress disappeared in the night, especially for one that contained no young persons at all, simply an old man and an aging bachelor. Yet Martha Ballard's troubles have wider significance. The problems she faced were both demographic and social, and they affected other women.

Laments over a shortage of servants have a long tradition in northern New England. In 1689, in one of the earliest extant letters from a mother to a daughter, Elizabeth Saltonstall of Haverhill, Massachusetts, wrote, "You may be sencible by your own experience how unsteady servants are, ther fore little incouragement to keep a great dairy." Such problems continued into the eighteenth century and still formed a persistent theme in women's diaries in the early Republic.[59]

---

58. MMB, Dec. 19, 1795, Oct. 15, 1796, July 2, 1799, Oct. 1, 1801.
59. Robert E. Moody, ed., *The Saltonstall Papers, 1607–1815* (Massachusetts Historical Society, *Collections*, LXXX–LXXXI [Boston, 1972–1974]), I, 189 (quotation). See also Cott, *Bonds of Womanhood*, 29–30.

The problem was both geographic and demographic. In frontier towns like Haverhill in the 1680s or Hallowell in the 1790s, there were more males than females in the age groups from which servants came. Although the overall ratio in Augusta-Hallowell had evened out by 1800, as in many country towns, the earlier age at marriage of women than men still ensured that there would be fewer available female workers in the same age bracket. Only in coastal towns, where women strongly outnumbered men, was a supply of girls assured. Contemporaries recognized this geographic distinction. One of the liveliest pieces of satire from eighteenth-century New Hampshire is a poem composed sometime before 1782, presumably by Ruth Belknap, the wife of the Dover minister. Entitled "The Pleasures of a Country Life," it was written when Mrs. Belknap had "a true taste of them by having no *maid*."[60]

Martha Ballard was experiencing, then, the "peculiar pleasures" of a country life. She was also facing the realities of a sex-gender system that grounded women's work in the family and gave it less market value than men's. When the full record of employment in the Ballard house is examined, what is surprising is, not the instability of the hired help after 1795, but the persistence of Sally Cox. The most reliable servants were relatives, Mrs. Ballard's daughters and her niece Parthena. Even Sally eventually acted like a member of the family. After Parthena died in 1794, Sally married Shubael Pitts, Parthena's former husband. From 1785 to 1795, Martha Ballard periodically employed short-term helpers to supplement the labor of her daughters. The girls who came to the house for short periods between 1795 and 1802 stayed about as long as did their predecessors, though now the helpers with deep personal commitments to the family were gone. There was no longer anyone who could be

---

60. Elaine Crane is studying women's work in Philadelphia, Boston, Newport, Salem, and Portsmouth during the 18th century. She tells me that Elizabeth Drinker, the Philadelphia diarist, was much less concerned about the comings and goings of maids, a fact that undoubtedly had something to do with the availability of indentured servants. See Sharon V. Salinger, " 'Send No More Women': Female Servants in Eighteenth-Century Philadelphia," *Pennsylvania Magazine of History and Biography*, CVII (1983), 29–48. Mary Holyoke of Salem seems to have been equally indifferent, unless complaints have been edited out of her journals published in George Francis Dow, ed., *The Holyoke Diaries, 1709–1856* (Salem, Mass., 1937). A woman of Portsmouth, New Hampshire, glibly told her daughter, in the 1760s: "Betty Tripe has Left me. I've got a better Maid." Mary Cochrane Rogers, *Glimpses of an Old Social Capital (Portsmouth, New Hampshire) as Illustrated by the Life of the Reverend Arthur Browne and His Circle* (Boston, 1923), 47. For the poem, see [Ruth Belknap?], "The Pleasures of a Country Life," Mass. Hist. Soc., *Colls.*, 6th Ser., IV (Boston, 1891), 228–229.

counted on to initiate short-term workers or to sustain the system on her own when needed.

The limited information available suggests that single women not only were in high demand in Hallowell because of the limited supply of workers but that most of them, like the Ballard girls, also had commitments and opportunities at home. Because the earliest federal censuses name only heads of households and vital records for the area are limited, firm identification of the Nabbys and Pollys and Hittys in the diary is difficult, but such evidence as there is suggests that most had family connections in Hallowell or Augusta (if not fathers and mothers, then brothers, sisters, or cousins). The surnames of twenty-two of the twenty-nine girls who worked for Mrs. Ballard between 1795 and 1802 appear on tax lists or the censuses for 1800.[61] Four of the seven remaining girls also seem to have had local ties. Thankful Godfrey was engaged to Augustus Ballard (Ephraim's nephew), Polly Butterfield and Polly Hodges probably were daughters of men who had recently moved to newer settlements, while Nabby Jewell may have been a sister of Joanna Jewell (who had married a local man in 1794).[62]

Why might a girl leave home to work? Like Parthena Barton, some of them had too many sisters at home. If Polly Butterfield was the Mary born to Ephraim and Mary Butterfield in 1776, she had good reason to stay in Hallowell to look for household employment. There were seven daughters in her family, at least three of whom, probably, were unmarried in 1796. Poverty is, of course, another explanation. Two of Martha Ballard's helpers were daughters of Jane Welch, a propertyless widow and sometime ward of the town, who had given birth to at least one illegitimate child and who herself sometimes did washing for Martha Ballard.[63] It may also be significant that the surnames of three of Mrs. Ballard's helpers match up with those of families warned out of the town in the 1790s. At least two of these three families remained, however, the fathers having accumulated enough property to be on the tax list for 1800.[64]

61. 1800 Tax Valuation Lists, Augusta and Hallowell, microfilm no. 959907 (filmed by the Church of Jesus Christ of Latter-Day Saints, Genealogical Dept.), Massachusetts State Library.

62. Mabel Goodwin Hall, ed., *Vital Records of Hallowell* (Portland, Maine, 1923), III, 64, IV, 16; North, *History of Augusta*, 92; W. B. Lapham, ed., "Births from Hallowell Records," Maine Historical Society, *Collections and Proceedings*, 2d Ser., III (1892), 331, 441; Hallowell Tax Valuation, 1794, Maine State Library.

63. Maine Hist. Soc., *Colls. and Procs.*, 2d Ser., III (1892), 331; Nash, *History of Augusta*, 531; *Augusta Vital Records*, I, 150, II, 187, 463; MMB, Sept. 10, 1801.

64. Nash, *History of Augusta*, 533.

Where genealogical information is unavailable, census data on family composition allow a conjecture of family affiliation for twenty-one of the twenty-nine girls. Most of the girls appear not to have been poor at all. The majority came from families whose assessed property fell just below Ephraim Ballard's $685. Like the New Hampshire girls who entered Lowell textile mills a generation later, Martha Ballard's helpers were from the middling ranks of property owners (see table 2). Their work, like that of the millworkers, was also episodic. Although the persistence of Martha Ballard's workers can be more easily measured in weeks than in months, the pattern is strikingly similar.[65] Nineteenth-century workers probably followed patterns long established in the countryside from which they came.

We have already seen that much of women's work was in support of male workers and that women's wage labor was less lucrative than men's. This disparity, combined with a lower age at marriage, tended to concentrate the labor of women in the family. While a man of twenty-three might be rafting boards or splitting staves for Samuel Howard, a woman of the same age would probably be married, doing much the same work for her husband that she had earlier done for her father and brothers. Unless a family had an unusual number of daughters, it also made sense to let boys work outside the family while girls remained at home. The boys could earn more, and the girls could do some of the work they left behind, being able to perform tasks within the family setting that would have seemed inappropriate beyond it. Even Mary Yeaton, the sentimental diarist of Eastport, helped with the harvest on her father's farm, though she never would have hired herself out to do similar work.[66]

To say that women's work was concentrated in the family, however, is not to say that it was confined there. As we have seen, the female economy was characterized by both commodity and labor exchanges. A girl might help in the haying at home, then go out for a few weeks or months to work in another family, coming home again to help with the spinning, go out again when sought by another household, then move on to help a sister in childbed. Such a pattern is confirmed repeatedly in the diary.[67] Though Martha Ballard sometimes negotiated with mothers ("Mrs. Cypher says she may come again"), most of the time she appealed to and reckoned with the

65. Thomas Dublin, *Women at Work: The Transformation of Work and Community in Lowell, Massachusetts, 1826–1860* (New York, 1979), 184–185.

66. Yeaton Journal, Sept. 3–4, 1801.

67. This was true even of the Ballard daughters and of Parthena and Sally; see Feb. 15, 1790, June 23, 1786.

girls themselves.[68] The mobility of her helpers assured their independence.

European visitors commented frequently on the lack of deference shown by American servants. An English immigrant, Charles William Janson, observed: "The arrogance of domestics in the land of republican liberty and equality, is particularly calculated to excite the astonishment of strangers. To call persons of this description *servants* or to speak of their *master* or *mistress* is a grievous affront." He told of approaching the house of an American gentleman and asking the young woman who answered the door whether her master was home. "I have no master," she replied. "Don't you live here?" he responded. "I *stay* here," she answered.[69] The young woman understood that the source of her freedom was her ability to leave. Ironically, then, the very system that assured women's secondary status in the market economy allowed them a certain independence of it. Ruth Belknap put it this way in a letter to her daughter: "As to maid affairs they remain as you left them But I hourly Expect alterations as Madam says she is to Nurse Mrs. Kenny."[70] Ruth Belknap's sarcastic reference to "Madam" marked the limits of her own authority as a mistress.

The female labor supply was both fluid and, like the textile production system it sustained, widely dispersed. Both factors help explain why roughly 6 percent of the servant-age population of Hallowell passed through Martha Ballard's kitchen between 1795 and 1802. Although such conditions affected all women—the ceiling on home production being set by the availability of hands to spin, reel, weave, churn, or sew—the nature of Martha Ballard's occupation exaggerated the problem. Dressmakers or chair caners could schedule their excursions to other women's houses; weavers and dairywomen could do all their work at home. Furthermore, the low age at marriage, a condition that increased the burdens of housewifery, improved the market for midwifery. For a time in the 1790s, Martha Ballard was caught in a demographic squeeze.

In retrospect, what is surprising about this period is, not the

68. MMB, July 31, 1801.

69. Charles William Janson, "Stranger in America," in Gordon S. Wood, ed., *The Rising Glory of America, 1760–1820* (New York, 1971), 123. Although some 17th-century householders also complained about the impertinence of helpers, the independence of servants may have grown in the 18th century. Certainly, there is evidence for a larger breakdown in family government apparent in such things as rising premarital pregnancy rates.

70. Ruth Belknap to Sally Belknap, Aug. 28, 1786, MS, New Hampshire Historical Society, Concord.

TABLE 2
Economic Status of Ballard Servants

Estate Value	All Taxpayers	Servant Families
$ 0– 99	36%	24%
100– 599	40	62
600–1299	19	14
1300 +	5	0

Sources: 1800 Tax Valuation, Augusta and Hallowell, Maine, Microfilm, Massachusetts State Library, Hallowell and Augusta Vital Records, and speculative linkages for servants based on surnames and household age distributions in 1800 census.

stress, but the remarkable productivity. Martha Ballard delivered more babies in each of the two years after Dolly's marriage than in any other year in her career. Although deliveries declined in 1798 (the year she sent the loom to Hannah), they rose again in 1799. Commitment to her patients only partly accounts for her struggle to keep moving. In the fifteen years since her fiftieth birthday, she had built a rewarding career and had established a flourishing household system. She had no wish to retire.

IN DECEMBER 1799, Martha and Ephraim Ballard moved to a new house built on their son Jonathan's land. During construction, Mrs. Ballard always referred to it as "Mr. Ballard's house" or "his house," suggesting that she may not have entirely approved. The year 1800 indeed marked the end of an era for Martha Ballard. Although she never entirely gave up midwifery, her practice rapidly declined. Her illnesses during the next two years were undoubtedly organic, yet one cannot but wonder what role exhaustion and even periodic discouragement may have played. Still, illness brought minor triumphs. On November 28, 1800, when his wife was doubled over with a fit of "colic," Ephraim Ballard got out of bed, made her some tea, and warmed a brick for her stomach. In July 1802, during another bout of illness, Cyrus did the brewing, though she strained the wort and cooked him his supper.[71]

Eventually, determination conquered despair. "I have sufered much

71. MMB, July 20, 1802.

with my malladies in the coars of this weak," she wrote on October 30, 1802, "but God has held me up to perform for others." The story of Martha Ballard's last ten years belongs in another place, but it is appropriate to note here that in 1809, at the age of seventy-four, she delivered almost as many babies as she had in the year in which the diary began. She performed her last delivery on April 19, 1812, a month before her death at the age of seventy-seven. Her strength had held out to the end of the "rais."

The diary of Martha Moore Ballard is, above all else, a compelling record of a remarkable life; but, in telling her own story, Martha Ballard also recorded part of the larger history of early American women. Her diary documents the variety, the social complexity, and the considerable independence of women's work in late-eighteenth-century Maine, demonstrating the existence of a female economy that encompassed the activities of mothers, daughters, and neighbors. It shows how one group of women cooperated to build resources and to increase their own productivity. It suggests that the level of home production in individual households had as much to do with the availability of daughters as with the availability of flax. It demonstrates the importance of understanding the female life cycle in studying the family economy and of carefully delineating the sometimes very different obligations of women as wives, housewives, and village specialists. Finally, it vividly portrays the personal, and, to twentieth-century women, all too familiar complications of working "abroad" while continuing to work "at home."

Martha Ballard's diary demonstrates the existence of a richly nuanced world beneath the level of documentation available in standard sources. At the same time, it invites historians to make more creative use of such sources. As we learn to read the blanks in men's diaries and account books, to see tax lists and deeds for the partial records that they are, and to reformulate the questions we ask of our materials, we will discover the lives of women. Men's and women's lives were inextricably bound together in the family labor system of early New England, but the experiences of the two sexes were not identical. Nor can we make sense of the dramatic changes in the northern rural economy in the early nineteenth century if we fail to differentiate the experiences of young women, childbearing women, and "old wives" like Martha Ballard.

We need to recognize the ways in which small-scale home manufacturing and traditional specialties like midwifery sustained the female economy in early New England, tying women of various ages together through the exchange of goods and services, providing independent sources of income for wives, and giving mothers primary responsibility for the education and employment of daughters. Such an appreciation almost certainly will help us to ask better and more sophisticated questions about the nineteenth century. Obviously, the transition to factory production involved more than a move of young women from the household. It, potentially at least, disrupted a multitude of connections within the female economy.

Tracing that story is a task for another time—or person. History, like women's work, is never done.

Paul G. E. Clemens and Lucy Simler

Rural Labor and the Farm Household in Chester County, Pennsylvania, 1750–1820

IN MARCH 1781, to secure labor for the coming year, Caleb Brinton, a prosperous Chester County farmer with more than four hundred acres of land in the fertile Brandywine Valley, drafted a number of work agreements—among them a joint agreement with James Greenway and John Cuff (laborers) and one with George Henthorn (weaver). The arrangements he offered the three men were typical of those between householders and laborers in late-eighteenth-century Chester County. Caleb agreed to lease to Greenway and Cuff, for £4 per year, the same west end of the house and garden as Greenway had the last year and to give them apples to break and dry for their own use, such firewood as Caleb directed, and the privilege of running two pigs in the lane. In return, they were to help with all the hay and wheat harvest and other work as he wanted, the "whole to go towards [Brinton's] book account until the whole is paid." Further, if Greenway and Cuff should neglect or refuse to work, Caleb had the right to hire other workers, with Greenway and Cuff liable for the costs. The terms offered Henthorn were not as harsh. He was to have "the Mill House and Garden," enough wood for one fireplace (and additional wood when Caleb allowed him to cut it), the crop of the six apple trees "nearest to the house," and the privilege of keeping one cow and pig, all for the sum of £4 15s. per year. In return,

The authors wish to thank the staffs of the Chester County Archives and the Chester County Historical Society (both in West Chester) for their assistance. Lois Green Carr, Kathleen W. Jones, Allan Kulikoff, Jackson Turner Main, Richard L. McCormick, Thomas Slaughter, Jean R. Soderlund, Frank Thistlethwaite, and Daniel Vickers helped us with comments on various drafts. Research was supported with grants from the American Association of State and Local History, the National Endowment for the Humanities, the Philadelphia Center for Early American Studies, and the Rutgers University Research Council.

Southeastern Pennsylvania and Chester County in the 1780s and 1790s. After U.S. Bureau of the Census, *Heads of Families at the First Census of the United States Taken in the Year 1790: Pennsylvania* (Washington, D.C., 1908); and Gilbert Cope, comp., *Genealogy of the Smedley Family, Descended from George and Sarah Smedley, Settlers in Chester County, Penna. . . .* (Lancaster, Pa., 1901) (courtesy of the Historical Society of Pennsylvania, Philadelphia)

Henthorn was to help with the hay and wheat harvest and do all the Brintons' weaving at the previous year's rate.[1]

The agreements drawn up by Brinton describe a little-studied but quite common arrangement through which Pennsylvania farmers secured the workers they needed for commercial agriculture, and landless laborers and artisans not only avoided poverty but procured a modest subsistence. These contracts had four characteristics, explicit or implicit: cottage tenancy, wage labor, customary obligations, and a definition of power. For their part, Greenway, Cuff, and Henthorn received lodging and fuel, the opportunity to raise part of their own food, and, customarily, for a small sum, the chance to keep a cow and to sow a half-acre or so of flax. They were also promised wages as harvest hands and work by the day (Greenway and Cuff) or piecework (Henthorn). Essentially, they became Brinton's cottagers, with enough land to subsist on and time to earn additional income on the side, but without the means to farm for a living. For Brinton, the reward was more specific: he was assured help during the crucial harvest season. His ability to produce a marketable surplus and turn a profit depended on having laborers on hand at specific times, but he was not obligated to pay them at other times when there was less to do. James Greenway and John Cuff would be there when Caleb Brinton needed them and were not his responsibility otherwise.

As cut and dried as the contract seemed, there was much left unstated. The arrangement implied an ordered society in which reciprocal responsibilities existed which no contract could fully specify. Wage rates were established for various tasks by custom: common work was paid at a lower rate than harvest work, and there was a deduction from wages whenever liquor was included. The cottager

1. Copies of the agreements Caleb Brinton offered Greenway in 1780; offered Greenway, Cuff, and Henthorn in 1781; and offered Samuel Scott in 1783 are in the Caleb Brinton Files, 1727–1826, Murtagh Collection, Chester County Historical Society (hereafter CCHS). These agreements make it clear that Greenway had been Brinton's cottager in 1779 as well as 1780 and 1781. For other examples of work arrangements, see the agreement between Joshua Marshall and John Cooper in 1790, MS 632a, CCHS; and the Appenticeship Indenture between Caleb Brinton and John Morrison, 1787, Murtagh Collection, CCHS. Information on landholding was taken from the State Assessments for Thornbury and Birmingham Townships, S-6a, Chester County Archives (hereafter CCA). Through 1800, most of the provincial, county, and state tax records for Chester County have been microfilmed. Hereafter, references to these records will include the year, the jurisdiction to which the tax was paid (province, county, state), a description of the record (assessment, rate, return), and the identification number assigned by the CCA. Originals of most records are at the CCA; microfilm copies are at the Pennsylvania State Archives, Harrisburg, as well.

expected the use of a plow and horses in the spring and a wagon and team to haul his wood or, on moving day, his family's goods, and he realized that he would be charged customary rent for these privileges. He knew that his wife and older children would probably be able to earn additional money by helping with the harvest or spinning flax.[2] Who was in control is clear: Cottagers (like Greenway, Cuff, and Henthorn) served at the discretion of landowners (like Brinton). On a day-to-day basis the owner regulated the work of his cottagers, and he could terminate the arrangement; his needs took precedence over those of his workers and their families.

But this is not a complete picture, because some workers were more independent of landowners than the contracts indicate. Spring negotiations allowed some laborers an element of choice in the bargains they made. George Henthorn, for example, turned down Brinton's offer for, presumably, a preferable arrangement in Westtown. In 1799 he purchased a six-acre property there for £165. His moderate success shows what level of comfort an initially landless artisan and his family could achieve in the farm economy of southeastern Pennsylvania (see table 1).[3] But not all workers were as successful as Henthorn. John Cuff, a free black laborer without a trade, left goods valued at only $42 (one-tenth of Henthorn's estate) when he died in 1807, which was not even enough to cover the expenses of his illness, burial, and estate sale.[4] The lot of most Chester County laborers probably fell somewhere between the modest accomplishments of George Henthorn, a skilled worker, and the virtual destitution of John Cuff, his unskilled counterpart.

The pervasiveness of cottagers (like Greenway, Cuff, and Henthorn) and the dependence of landowners on wage laborers were essential parts of the economy of rural Chester County from 1750 to 1820. As such, this essay is not primarily about the use of servants and slaves, the renting of land to household tenants, or the distribution of responsibility for production within the family (although each subject is touched on here as part of the story of labor relationships). It is, rather, about the place of contractual or wage labor in a thriving and diversified rural household economy. By examining the background of Chester County and, in detail, the lives of Samuel Swayne

2. The list of customary services provided by householders is based on information found in 18th- and early 19th-century account books in the CCHS. These books are being cataloged.

3. Henthorn's moves were traced in the Chester County Tax Record, CCA; and the Chester County Deed Book, S-2, pp. 93–94, County Courthouse, West Chester.

4. Chester County Wills and Administrations, 1413, 5417, CCA.

TABLE 1

Inventory of George Henthorn, 1815

Wearing apparel	$18.00	Two cows	$ 44.00
Copper kettle	9.00	Mare	50.00
Stove in the house	20.00	Ewe and two lambs	4.00
Bed and bedstead	30.00	Four hogs	35.00
Three beds	30.00	Wheelbarrow	3.00
Corner cupboard	6.00	Plow and harrow	5.00
Walnut box, looking glass	2.00	Cart and gears	37.00
Old chairs	2.00	Shovel, maul, wedges, ax	3.00
Doughtrough and table	2.00	Three looms, two wheels	48.00
Steelyards, flat irons	2.00	Spinning wheel	3.00
Hackle	1.00	Big wheel	1.00
Copper tea kettle	1.00	Gun	5.00
Shovel, tongs, andiron	2.00	Two scythes	2.00
Old chest	.50	Two saddles	8.00
Warming pan	2.50	Meat tubs and pails	4.00
Eight tablecloths	8.00	Pots and sundries	12.00
Chest and table	5.00	Rakes and pitchforks	.75
Old casks	5.00	Stove in the shop	15.00
		Saw and drawing knife	.50
		Total	$426.25

Source: Chester County Wills and Administrations, 6175, CCA.

(a middling farmer of the colonial period), William and Elizabeth Smedley (a carpenter-farmer family also of the colonial period), and George Brinton (a prosperous farmer of the post-Revolutionary era), one can get a sense of how the county's rural labor system operated.

CHESTER COUNTY's location (convenient to both Philadelphia and Wilmington), rich farmland, and moderate climate as well as the high proportion of artisans in its settler population help explain the three most distinctive features of its economy. The first was the prominence of market agriculture in the lives of most residents. Wheat, corn, and flaxseed were the primary export crops, but most other farm produce, when not consumed by the family, entered a thriving regional market. Rye, barley (for malting), oats, hay (and other fodder crops), wool, meat, and hides all figured in local sales or went to the expanding urban market. Farm wives added to the market surplus by making cheese and butter, and their daughters spun wool and flax. For most families, such farming required a significant investment in land, equipment, livestock, and buildings. But the greater their capacity to produce, the greater was their ability to provide simultaneously their own food and engage in market agriculture. The security and profit such a livelihood brought were measured in the gradual accumulation (and subsequent transmission to heirs) of land, the acquisition of consumer goods that redefined the notion of modest comfort, and the periodic purchase of bonds at interest, Revolutionary-era loan certificates, and, in the early nineteenth century, bank holdings and turnpike stock.[5]

The second distinctive feature of the county's economy, arising from the artisanal component of its rural work force, was the significance of rural industry. The more prosperous artisans found that the county's swift streams and creeks facilitated the erection of mills. In 1765, for example, the township of East Caln had three sawmills, three gristmills, three fulling mills, a tanyard, and a distillery. In 1820 the township (now smaller in extent) had five sawmills, three tanyards, two gristmills, a distillery, and a rolling mill and nail factory. A pottery employed four men, five women, and six boys and girls. But even these figures do little justice to the full complexity of the economy (see table 2). At the turn of the century, well over half the landowners made their living from more than farming. Rural industry provided profit-making opportunities for a significant number of entrepreneurially inclined farmers, and farming allowed many skilled artisans to maintain themselves in considerable comfort. A

5. This paragraph rests primarily on our continuing study of account books and probate records in the CCA and CCHS. We also consulted the standard treatment of Chester County, James T. Lemon, *The Best Poor Man's Country: A Geographic Study of Early Southeastern Pennsylvania* (Baltimore, 1972); and Jack Michel, *"In a Manner and Fashion Suitable to Their Degree": A Preliminary Investigation of the Material Culture of Early Rural Pennsylvania, Working Papers from the Regional Economic History Research Center*, V, no. 1 (1981). See also Robert B. Case, *Prosperity and Progress: Concord Township, Pennsylvania, 1683–1983*, vol. I, *The Colonial Legacy* (Chester, Pa., 1983); Katharine Hewitt Cummin, *A Rare and Pleasing Thing: Radnor Demography (1798) and Development* (Philadelphia, 1977); Mary McKinney Schweitzer, "Contracts and Custom: Economic Policy in Colonial Pennsylvania, 1717–1755" (Ph.D. diss., Johns Hopkins University, 1984); Jean R. Soderlund, *Quakers and Slavery: A Divided Spirit* (Princeton, N.J., 1985); Joan M. Jensen, *Loosening the Bonds: Mid-Atlantic Farm Women, 1750–1850* (New Haven, Conn., 1986); Lisa Wilson Waciega, "A 'Man of Business': The Widow of Means in Southeastern Pennsylvania, 1750–1850," *William and Mary Quarterly*, 3d Ser., XLIV (1987), 40–64; and the lengthy (and still quite useful) 19th-century account, J. Smith Futhey and Gilbert Cope, *History of Chester County, Pennsylvania, with Genealogical and Biographical Sketches*, 2 vols., (Philadelphia, 1881).

similar mix of agriculture and industry can be found in other Chester County townships, such as Charlestown (a virtual copy of East Caln) and West Marlborough. The latter was one of the centers for the county's iron industry, with two slitting mills, two coal houses, a smith shop and forge, as well as a dozen iron workers. Artisanal products, of course, entered the regional as well as local market, thus providing both profit for specific individuals and a significant measure of self-sufficiency for the community as a whole.[6]

The third distinctive feature of the economy, one related to Chester County's mix of market agriculture and rural industry, was the increasing dependence of landowners on landless wage laborers and artisans. These workers were the laborers Chester County tax collectors called "inmates," if they were married or widowed, and "freemen," if they were single. Together with slaves, indentured servants, and apprentices, they made up the dependent labor force. Before the 1740s, most inmates and freemen were live-in servants or lodgers. Servants were hired by the week, month, or year and usually received room and board as well as some additional payment, usually in cash or credit. Lodgers paid room and board and often worked not only for the householder with whom they lived but for others as well. Because the householder with whom they lived was responsible for their tax, few dependent laborers were listed in the early tax records.

In the mid-eighteenth century, the labor system changed markedly. Previously, most workers had delayed marriage until they could set themselves up in a home of their own, and, with land inexpensive and labor in short supply, most were successful. As rents rose, market activity intensified, and the number of landless laborers increased, householders found it more difficult to house their workers in their own homes, and workers found it more difficult to rent or purchase smallholdings. From this conjunction of circumstances came the cottager class. Cottagers (like Henthorn, Cuff, and Greenway) were housed in a cottage on the farm, paid a small rent, received certain privileges, and were paid by the day or by piecework. They were not tenants (as tenants rented farms, were generally taxed

6. For East Caln, see the 1765, 1766, and 1767 Provincial Assessments, P-8, 9, and 10; and the 1799 County Assessment C-49a, CCA. (See also the Pennsylvania Septennial State Census of Taxable Inhabitants, 1793, 1807–1842, and 1856, CCHS.) Censuses for 1779, 1786, and 1800 are in the Pennsylvania State Archives. Starting in 1807, each inhabitant's principal occupation was listed. Additional manufacturing data came from the Record of the 1820 Census of Manufacturing, microfilm, reel 14, National Archives. The data on Charlestown and West Marlborough were obtained from the 1799 County Assessment.

TABLE 2

Summary of Occupations, East Caln, 1799

Occupation	Type of Resident			Avg. Acres per Landed Resident
	Landed	Inmates	Freemen	
Farmers	19	1	10	195
Farmers with extra income[a]	7			204
Artisans	8	19	15	77
Artisans with extra income[b]	9			91
Storekeepers / merchants	4	1	2	120
Innkeepers	2	1		39
Laborers, wagon drivers, drovers, gatekeepers	1	7	14	12
Professionals	1		4	500
Others	1		3	50
Overall	52	29	48	148

Source: 1799 County Tax Assessments, C-49a, CCA.
Notes: Some artisans had more than one shop or mill. Landed artisans were also farmers; artisan-inmates and artisan-freemen might also be agricultural laborers. [a]Three sawmills, two smith shops, hatter shop, tan house. [b]Three gristmills, two sawmills, malthouse, fulling mill, distillery, oil mill, carpenter shop, saddler shop, pothouse.

as householders, and were not bound by labor arrangements). By the end of the colonial period, most inmates were probably cottagers; some single men were cottagers, but most continued to live either with their parents or in the household of their employers, often sleeping in a garret or loft. Most single female workers were live-in servants rather than cottagers.[7] The number of landless laborers grew steadily (see table 3). In 1760 there were approximately fifty-six

7. Most (but not all) freemen and inmates were landless wage earners. For example, in 1792, after the death of his first wife, Caleb Brinton rented his farm to William West and moved into lodgings. West, his tenant, was taxed as a householder, and Caleb was taxed as an inmate. West was in control of the property he occupied; Caleb was the lodger in another's household (perhaps West's). In 1796, soon after he remarried, Caleb resumed control of his farm. To avoid confusion and clarify the distinction between tenants and cottagers, the term "tenant" in this essay is reserved for tenant-householders. For a more general discussion of

taxable workers (inmates, freemen, bound servants, and slaves) for every one hundred householders; in the 1770s and 1780s, there were more than sixty laborers for every one hundred householders; and, by 1820, the ratio had risen to eighty-one to one hundred.[8]

There was, of course, no entirely typical Chester County farmer, but there is a well-developed image of colonial Pennsylvania's yeoman farmer guiding his plow across neatly furrowed, fertile fields in order to provide a comfortable living for his growing family. Samuel Swayne comes as close to mirroring the mythical family farmer as the reality of mid-eighteenth-century Chester County provides. Swayne lived his entire life in East Marlborough, a typical Chester County township. East Marlborough had the standard assortment of gristmills, sawmills, and tanyards and a significant complement of wheelwrights, masons, and tailors and even a scrivener and a doctor. Twenty-seven of the fifty persons with whom Swayne maintained accounts between 1767 and 1781 can be identified readily with a trade (other than or in addition to farming). In essence, an extensive web of sales of goods and services among these shoemakers, joiners, shopkeepers, and the like bound Swayne and his neighbors together and created an interdependent community. Just as clearly, the produce of East Marlborough farms and goods fashioned in township shops made their way to Philadelphia and Wilmington and from there into the export trade.[9]

Swayne farmed much like his neighbors: he devoted more acres to wheat (the principal export staple) than to any other crop, and he also raised rye, oats, hay, corn, and barley. But the family's economic position within the township depended not simply on grain sales but also on Samuel's skill as a saddletree maker, on the renown of his nursery with its special varieties of apple and peach trees, and on the butter and cheese making of his wife, Hannah. The family's economic links to their neighbors and the local market are spelled out in the account book. In 1768, for example, Swayne debited 19s. 1d. cash

land and labor relationships, see Lucy Simler, "Tenancy in Colonial Pennsylvania: The Case of Chester County," *WMQ*, 3d Ser., XLIII (1986), 542–569.

8. *Ibid.*, 549. See also the following documents in the CCA: 1783 State Assessments, S-12b; 1789 State Quota Tax, Returns and Assessments, S-18a, S-18b; 1799 County Tax Assessments, C-49a, and the 1820 County Tax Assessments.

9. The following discussion of the Swayne family relies (unless otherwise noted) on three sources: Samuel Swayne Account Book, CCHS; Chester County Tax Records, CCA; and Samuel Swayne's Probate Record, Wills and Administrations, 5480, CCA. Specific tax record citations will not be given unless the text makes the source of information ambiguous (see n. 3, above, for further information).

TABLE 3
Chester County's Taxable Population, 1760–1820

Year	Total Taxables	House-holders	Nonhouseholders			
			Inmates	Freemen	Slaves	Servants
1750	3,950	3,166	183	601	—	—
1760	5,676	3,646	883	665	293	189
1766	6,085	3,760	734	1,027	280	284
1774	6,098	3,662	863	929	208	436
1783	6,772	4,011	1,386	1,065	255	55
1789	6,653	4,059	1,222	1,151	144	77
1799	8,243	5,000	1,557	1,649	37	—
1820	13,265	7,336	3,030	2,899	—	—

Sources: For 1750, 1760, 1766, and 1774, see Lucy Simler, "Tenancy in Colonial Pennsylvania: The Case of Chester County," *WMQ*, 3d Ser., XLIII (1986), 549. See also the 1783 State Assessments, S-12b; the 1789 State Quota Tax, Returns and Assessments, S-18a, S-18b; 1799 County Tax Assessments, C-49a; and the 1820 County Tax Assessments. The originals are in the CCA. Because of the division of southeastern Chester County into Delaware County in 1789, Delaware County assessments were added to the Chester County figures in 1799 and 1820. The best available figures came from 1801 and 1822. The 1822 Delaware Assessment, however, did not include inmates and freemen; these were estimated from assessments in 1807, 1810, and 1828. No slaves or servants were listed on the 1750 county returns; the sources would not allow meaningful estimates of the number of servants and slaves in 1820. The Delaware County assessments are at the Neumann College Library.

and £12 5s. 8d. in goods, produce, and services: of this, 13 percent can be accounted for from dairy products, 21 percent from grain, 14 percent from meat, 32 percent from making saddletrees, and the remaining 20 percent from miscellaneous sales and services. He received £4 4s. 6d. in cash, £6 4s. 2d. in labor, and £10 5s. 2d. in goods, food, and services.

Diversified market farming and saddletree making allowed Swayne to improve his position in East Marlborough gradually. At the time of his marriage in 1756, Swayne, age twenty-five, received a ninety-one-acre farm from his brother William, the administrator of their parents' estate. When he and Hannah set up the farm, they were taxed in the bottom quarter of East Marlborough householders; by the early 1770s, they ranked just above the bottom third. But, after the purchase in 1772 of an additional thirty-five acres (with a house that could be rented), their relative position jumped to the upper third of the taxable householders, and, by the turn of the century, only 16 of the 110 householders in East Marlborough paid more taxes than they did. Samuel's inventory, taken in 1808, reflected years of comfortable accumulation: a desk and corner cupboard (presumably the products of local artisans), decanter and wineglasses, an armchair, queensware and pewter plates, a clock, a library of Quaker readings, and other items. He left his heirs some sixteen hundred dollars in credits and more land valued at a substantially higher price than when he and Hannah had begun the farm.

Swayne's account book, then, is that of a comfortably situated, middling farmer. Its principal value is in letting us explore the relationship between family labor and hired help over the life cycle of a fairly representative farm family. In their early years, before they had adolescent sons to help with field work and daughters to spin and milk, the Swaynes relied on intermittent wage labor. Samuel's account book, which begins in 1767, provides some sense of how he used paid laborers during the harvest and for assorted routine tasks, such as ditching and dunging his fields and collecting firewood (see table 4). In 1768, at the peak of the harvest season, Swayne hired four youths and paid them 12s. 6d. for a total of six days work. In addition, he hired, as needed, six day laborers (at least one of whom was a cottager on his farm and two of whom probably were single workers lodging with the family). The six men were paid by the day or task at the rate of 18d. to 2s. per day for common work and 2s. 6d. per day (with liquor) for harvest work. In the twelve-month period they worked, in all, about 105 days and received a total of £12 11s. 5d. Over the year, they averaged about three weeks of work each; counting the youths, Swayne paid £13 3s. 11d. in wages.

Swayne's labor expenses were moderate relative to his return. Based on prices from his account book, the wheat and barley threshed by the wage laborers had a gross value of forty-five pounds. Furthermore, Swayne's records show that he paid about one-third the amount due his workers in debits for goods (potatoes, wheat, bacon) and services (the use of carts and horses). The balance was paid in cash and in goods not produced on the farm, but the outlay was covered by the income he earned through local exchanges and from making three saddletrees. While Swayne's earnings allowed him to hire landless workers, wage rates were high enough (given the seasonal nature of his demand for labor) to discourage the full-time employment of dependent laborers.

Swayne needed men at harvest-time and for specific tasks; he and his wife could handle the day-to-day routine of an established farm of ninety-one acres. After 1770, Swayne's children gradually assumed many of the tasks previously performed by hired laborers. For the remaining ten years or so covered by the account book (1771–1781), one cottager was sufficient to meet his needs for supplemental farm labor. His demand for hired workers was not apt to rise again, given the size of his family: eleven children (eight of whom survived him), two children of a deceased sister, and his father-in-law (who did the family shoemaking and mending in exchange for lodging).[10] When Swayne's youngest son came of age, married, and left, Swayne was already sixty-nine and approaching retirement.

Swayne's workers were obviously not as comfortably situated as he was. In 1768 a fully employed farm laborer, paid at the going rates, could earn about thirty pounds a year (including harvest-time) if he worked twenty-six days a month every month. In the 1760s, this was probably an unrealistic goal.[11] The demand for farm labor was not only seasonal but also restricted, as in Swayne's case, by the life cycles of the farmers. Only a limited number of householders were interested in hiring by the year; for them, slaves or indentured servants may well have been less costly investments. For the more typical farmer, dependent on wage laborers, it was essential that cottage holdings be created to provide these landless workers with lodgings, a garden plot, and an opportunity to engage in domestic industries.

Daniel Burk's position as one of Swayne's workers and cottagers provides some sense of what such employment meant to the laboring population. Burk was a married man, probably with children. Between February 1768 and February 1769, he worked for Swayne for twelve days and earned 23s. 1d. When, at the end of the year, Swayne balanced his credits against his debits (24s. 9d.), Burk owed Swayne 1s. 8d. Given the number of landless workers and the seasonality of demand for labor, Burk could reasonably hope to earn no more than an additional £5 by working for neighboring householders. He stayed with Swayne for two years; Swayne provided him with a cottage and sufficient land to plant a garden, sow a crop of flax, keep a cow, and run a pig or two. Burk had access to a plow and mares and to a cart to draw his wood. The tax assessments indicate that, in 1768 and 1769, he paid neither the provincial nor county

---

10. In Dec. 1767, Swayne recorded his father-in-law's arrival: "William Hayes came to live with Samuel Swayne and did agree to give one year the sum of 10 £ and make and mend all the shoes for the family."

11. Wage rates and economic opportunity will be dealt with more systematically in a subsequent publication.

TABLE 4

Samuel Swayne's Payments to Farm Laborers, 1768–1769

Date	Task	£	s.	d.	Worker
			Payment		
Mar.	Drawing dirt and digging dung in the nursery (1 day)		1	6	Burk
	Breaking flax (1 day)		1	6	Garner
	Digging in the nursery (½ day)		1		Garner
	Scutching flax (3 days)		4	6	Burk
Apr.	Plowing and drawing dung (1 day)		2		Garner
	Plowing (1½ days)		3		Garner
	Cutting and splitting rails (2½ days)		6		Woodward
	Drawing rails (1 day)		2		Garner
	Plowing at Preston's (1 day)		2		Garner
	Plowing, digging at dam, and planting potatoes (2½ days)		5		Garner
May	Drawing rails and digging (1 day)		2		Garner
	Fencing (½ day)		1		Garner
	Splitting rails and fencing (1 day)		1		Garner
June	Work (5 days)		10		Woodward
	Work		1	5	Woodward
	Reaping barley (1 day)		1	6	Burk
July	Binding barley, plowing corn, and mowing (2 days)		4	6	Garner
	Mowing (2 days)		5		Garner
	Hoeing in nursery (1 day)		1	6	Burk
	Hoeing corn (1 day)		2		Garner
	Reaping (6 days)		12	6	Youths
	Reaping (1 day)		2	6	Garner
	Reaping wheat (2½ days)		6	3	Burk
	Reaping (2 days)		5		Garner
Aug.	Mowing (3 days)		7	6	Garner
Sept.	At hay (½ day)			9	Burk
	Threshing 48 bus. wheat		16		Glasco
	Threshing 29 bus. wheat		7	3	Glasco
	Threshing flaxseed (2 days)		4		Glasco
Oct.	Making cider (1½ days)		2		Glasco

Table 4. Continued

Date	Task	Payment			Worker
		£	s.	d.	
Jan.	Scutching 27½ lbs. of flax		4	7	Cavenaugh
	Ditching and drawing dung (2½ days)		4		Garner
	Threshing 56 bus. barley		14		McLoughlin
	Threshing 67 bus. wheat		16	9	McLoughlin
Feb.	Scutching 24½ lbs. of flax		4	1	Burk
	Breaking and scutching 80 lbs. flax	1			Cavenaugh
	Digging in nursery (½ day)		1		McLoughlin
	Work (6 days)		12		McLoughlin
	Breaking 38 bus. of flax		3	2	McLoughlin
	Scutching 5 lbs. of flax			10	McLoughlin

Source: Samuel Swayne Account Book, CCHS.

taxes (suggesting that Swayne paid them for him or that he was too poor to be taxed). Furthermore, after meeting the obligations of his cottage tenancy, he had the time to follow a trade, engage in artisanal work, or market the produce from his garden. That he was taxed in 1770 as an inmate at more than the minimum rate suggests some improvement in income.

From the tax records and the account book, it is possible to piece together a little about Swayne's other workers. William Garner, who was the only laborer to be kept on after 1769, was an inmate in East Marlborough from 1753 through 1762, a resident of West Marlborough in 1765, and in Swayne's employ from 1768 to, at least, 1779. In 1774 he became Swayne's cottager, paying thirty shillings in rent, and, in later years, he paid additional rent for pasturing a cow. A second worker, Richard Woodward, was probably the son of a neighboring householder. Another, Edward McLoughlin, appears on the 1767–1770 tax lists as a freeman; he and James Glasco (a free black) may have lived in a garret or loft in one of Swayne's outbuildings. From 1770 to 1774, Thomas Preston, a weaver, had the cottage and garden that had been occupied by Burk and was later held by Garner; in return, he did the weaving for the family at customary rates.

Timothy Cavenaugh, however, left a fuller record behind. Cavenaugh, hired by Swayne in 1769, was born about 1730 and was thus Swayne's contemporary. In 1753 he and his wife lived in East Marlborough as cottagers; in 1756 he rose to householder status as a tenant; and, in 1758, the Guardians of the Poor of Philadelphia bound Thomas Young, age fifteen, to him. In 1760 the Cavenaughs leased a property in New Garden township, but six years later they were living in yet another township, London Grove, and again as inmates. In April 1767, Cavenaugh, still described as "laborer," purchased 12 acres in East Marlborough for thirty-seven pounds. In 1774 he and his wife, Catherine, sold the 12 acres, now with a tenement, to Joel Baily for sixty pounds. In 1778 and 1780, the family was taxed in Goshen Township as inmates, but, by 1781, Cavenaugh had rented a 23-acre property in East Bradford and was once more a householder. Perhaps, by 1785, he reached his goal, for, in that year, a Timothy Cavenaugh purchased 554 acres in western Pennsylvania (perhaps a grant for Revolutionary war service).[12]

These short glimpses at the individual lives of Swayne's workers provide a first impression of the situation of free laborers in late colonial Chester County. Laboring families moved frequently, although apparently within a restricted radius of townships; at the same time, many remained in Chester County over a long period. Their economic well-being was measured on a scale that spanned a range from unmarried freeman, to cottager, to tenant, and (perhaps) to landowner. Having both livestock and skills must have mattered significantly when farm work was slack and not even the most fortunate worker found steady employment. With the exception of Timothy Cavenaugh, all were dependent on Swayne for housing, and most bought part of their food from the family. Seen from Swayne's perspective, his cottagers were only one, and not even the principal, source of goods and services for his family. Neighboring householders were more likely than his own inmates to meet his demand for skilled labor, and his children, as soon as they reached adolescence, assumed most of the responsibilties for planting and harvesting the crops and tending livestock.

12. The land records for Cavenaugh can be found in Original Deeds, Cloud to Cavenaugh, 1767, and Cavenaugh to Bailey, 1774, East Marlborough Lands, vault, CCHS; and in *Warrantees of Land in the Several Counties of the State of Pennsylvania, 1730–1898, Pennsylvania Archives*, 3d Ser., XXVI (1899), 52, 53, 409. His changing tax status was traced in the 1753, 1756, 1758, 1760 County Rates, C-20, 22, 23, 24; 1767, 1768 Provincial Assessments, P-10, 11; and 1778, 1780, 1781 State Assessments, S-4, 6a.

FARMERS SUCH AS Swayne, consequently, provided limited employment opportunities for Chester County laborers, but not everyone was primarily a farmer. William Smedley was a carpenter; he also managed a farm. But, by training and choice, his economic life revolved around his trade, and, although he was not particularly wealthy, he made significantly greater use of cottagers than did Swayne. Smedley's importance is thus twofold: by occupation, farmer-artisans, like Smedley, gave Chester's rural economy its distinctive industrial character and provided the principal source of demand for wage laborers in the colonial period.

William and Elizabeth Smedley lived in Middletown, in the older part of Chester that, in 1789, would become Delaware County. At mid-century, Middletown was a well-established, prosperous agricultural settlement of some fifty farms and numerous multigenerational families, with both a Presbyterian church and a Quaker meetinghouse. By Chester County standards, Middletown farms were typical in size, averaging about 158 acres in 1760 (excluding the six properties under 20 acres). Because the creeks used for powering mills bordered rather than transversed the township, the town, at first glance, might have seemed a quite pastoral village; but the presence of rural industry was as substantial in Middletown as in East Caln or East Marlborough. In 1760 there were four mills in the township and several others on the opposite banks of the bordering creeks; in addition, Middletown boasted two taverns and a tanyard as well as at least fourteen householders with more than 20 acres of land and a craft occupation that complemented their farming. Twelve slaves, four bound servants, and twenty-nine free but landless taxables did the work not done by family members.[13]

William Smedley began his account book in 1751, within weeks of his completed apprenticeship to John Taylor, a local carpenter. He entered the trade at a propitious time. In 1748, shortly before he left his apprenticeship, the end of war between England and Spain had brought new vigor to Atlantic trade and offered increased profits to those farmers who grew wheat for the export market. Moreover, as Smedley was still unmarried and owned no land, he presumably lived with his parents and, as a single man, had minimal living expenses and responsibilities. The trade boom meant that farmers had

13. 1760 County Assessment, C-24, CCA. Many freemen and inmates did not appear on the tax lists; thus, the count of 29 landless workers is probably low. Likewise, the 1760 tax list does not provide information on trades and occupations; the 14 craftworkers noted in the text are only those who could be easily identified. There were undoubtedly more.

money with which to build new homes and barns, and this, in turn, meant work for carpenters. Between 1751 and 1757, Smedley and his workers built or enlarged more than twenty-six houses, barns, shops, stables, and springhouses. In 1752 Smedley earned £17 16s. 8d., and, in 1753, his trade brought him £18 13s. 2d. At the established daily wage for carpenters, 3s., this meant he was employed at least 119 days in 1752 and 124 days in 1753. In addition, as was customary, he left his craft during the harvest season and worked in the field. In 1753, for example, he worked for 11 days at the harvest wage of 2s. 3d. and earned 24s. 9d. When Smedley's work for his parents is added to his labor for himself, his early years were busy and profitable.[14]

In April 1753, some earnings in hand, William married Elizabeth Taylor, the daughter of a Quaker family from Upper Providence, and, in October, the couple received from William's father a sixty-eight-acre farm in Middletown on which to start a household. They began modestly. The house was small, and their tract was less than half the size of the farms of many of their older and wealthier neighbors. The couple started with some livestock, a good set of joiner's tools, a few farm implements, and, probably, the simplest of household furnishings; William bought, on credit, additional farm tools from Thomas Calvert (a local blacksmith) and a new plow from Joseph Edwards. In January 1754, their first child, Peter, was born, and Thomas Green began his apprenticeship with William. In March, with spring plowing to do, Smedley hired Felix Miller, a local smallholder, for a day's work and then hired him again at harvest-time for two additional days. In August, Miller finished clearing a new piece of ground for Smedley (a job on which he had probably worked for two or three months) and then put in an additional day and a half, probably sowing winter wheat. Smedley balanced his debt to Edwards over the summer by reaping and carpentry. He paid his debt to Calvert in two cash installments, one in November and one in December.

14. Unless otherwise noted, all the material on the Smedley family comes from the William and Elizabeth Smedley Account Book, MS 77049, CCHS; Tax Records, CCA; Futhey and Cope, *History of Chester County*, 725–726; Gilbert Cope, comp., *Genealogy of the Smedley Family, Descended from George and Sarah Smedley, Settlers in Chester County, Penna.* . . . (Lancaster, Pa., 1901), 104–106. For economic trends in the 1740s and 1750s, see Anne Bezanson et al., *Prices in Colonial Philadelphia* (Philadelphia, 1935); and, more generally, Thomas M. Doerflinger, *A Vigorous Spirit of Enterprise: Merchants and Economic Development in Revolutionary Philadelphia* (Chapel Hill, N.C., 1986).

The pattern in Smedley's early life is commonplace but significant: an apprenticeship, support from comfortably established parents, a good marriage, the exchange of labor with neighbors, and enough income (and credit) from carpentry to hire workers and stock his farm. Elizabeth and William lived much like Hannah and Samuel Swayne; both couples, as was common for householders, began marriage with small farms and little income. If there was a difference, it was the money William made at carpentry, money that gave the young Smedleys choices that their neighbors without artisanal skills presumably did not have.

By the mid-1750s, the farm had begun to take hold, and it became increasingly evident that Elizabeth and William were in a relatively good financial position. Elizabeth hired domestic laborers and contracted for services in managing the household. She settled the account with William McMinn for fulling with 19½ pounds of butter and paid Elizabeth Claypoole twelve shillings for three weeks' spinning. In September 1755, before their daughter Mary was born, Eleanor Moore "came to stay" for sixteen weeks at three shillings per week. Elizabeth's role, both in contracting for the services of nearby artisans and in bringing female domestic laborers into the home, was similar to that of farm wives in many Chester County households (although, in contrast, Swayne's account book, from a household of slightly more moderate means, records little use of domestic labor).

The great majority of the Smedleys' account-book entries were of three types: with dependent laborers (with whom they presumably had daily contact), with their neighbors in Middletown and the surrounding townships, and with members of their own families at customary rates. In reflecting the day-to-day activities of the family, these entries yield considerable information on how things got done. Elizabeth and William sent their leather to be tanned and then paid Frederic Engle and Isaac Moore for making shoes. They sold farm surplus (a pound of butter, a bushel of apples, or a peck of flaxseed) to their neighbors. William continued to work in the fields during harvest and was paid the customary wages by his neighbors, William Malin and Peter Taylor, and by his father, George.

As early as 1756, Smedley began adding substantially to his income through more general market activity. When, late in 1756, the economy slumped and Smedley's carpentry business stagnated, he invested in brickmaking and sold some eight thousand bricks for £37 5s. From 1759 through 1762, with a trade boom on, he and his workmen manufactured more than fifty-eight thousand barrel staves, some of which were sold to a local flour dealer and some of which went to Philadelphia. The purchase, in 1759, of 148 additional acres at about £2 10s. per acre confirmed the family's improved position.[15]

The expansion of nonagricultural production and the increase in acreage in 1759 (and again in 1766) paralleled an increase in the number of laborers in the household, in the total number of days worked by these laborers, and in the use of nonhousehold labor; at the same time, the Smedleys began to get rental income. In the 1750s, small-holding still seemed to offer landless laborers the possibility of own-ing their own farm, while renting provided landowners an opportu-nity to retain laborers and make a profit on landholdings. Although cottagers were increasing in number as the economy expanded, there was also an increase in the number of smallholding tenants among the householders. In 1757 Smedley leased a shop to Thomas Taylor, a weaver. Taylor, a smallholder (rather than a cottager), re-tained control over his own time and labor; he was not bound to Smedley, as a cottager would have been, by a labor contract. By renting to Taylor, Smedley added an artisan to the community labor force and a potential harvest hand. The importance of such small-holders within the labor force is indicated by Smedley's numerous payments to them for farm work, cottage manufacturing, and minor services. Taylor, for example, remained a tenant for more than twenty years and wove much of the yarn spun by Elizabeth and her helpers.

The Smedleys also increased the number of laborers within the household. In 1760 William hired William Taylor for a year at £17 10s. Taylor continued to work for Smedley in 1761, and Robert Woolley, a freeman, came to stay for eight months. Richard Noblitt (a carpenter) and his wife became cottagers in 1761 and remained until 1763, when they leased a forty-acre farm from Smedley; John Greentree then moved into the cottage at an annual rent of £3 10s. (including garden and cow pasture). Smedley got the guarantee of harvest help in July and August, periodic work in the fields at other times, and assis-tance with his carpentry (see table 5). Greentree cleared considerably more than the cost of his rental property. The balance owed Green-tree was made up by periodic debits for food, rum, seeding his flax, and paying his cash debts to local farm owners. Smedley balanced

15. Names in the account book were identified in the Tax Records, CCA. The account book provides detailed information on local exchanges and the sale of carpentry products, but, as seems to be the rule in Chester County account books, usually no mention is made of substantial wheat sales. The deed for the land purchase has not been found; the price is an estimate from the sale of comparable tracts.

TABLE 5
John Greentree's Work Schedule, 1764–1765

Month	Task	Days Worked	
		1764	1765
Jan.	Making staves	6	0
Feb.	Cleaning flax	8[a]	2
Mar.	Hauling hay, gardening, in meadow	9	3
Apr.	Mending fences, making staves	5	9[a]
May	Making staves, fencing	0	8
June	Clearing fields	10.5	2.5
July	Reaping, mowing, making staves	7[b]	7.5
Aug.	Making staves, mowing, seeding, making cider, cleaning wheat	20	10
Sept.		0	0
Oct.	General work, loading wheat	0	17
Nov.		0	0
Dec.	Fencing, crosscut sawing	9	6
	Total	74.5	65

Source: William and Elizabeth Smedley Account Book, CCHS.
Notes: His earnings were £9 6s. 3d. (1764) and £8 2s. 6d. (1765), based upon an average rate of 2s. 6d. per day.   [a]Additional amounts were paid by the task (in 1764) for cleaning flax and (in 1765) for splitting rails.   [b]Includes one day of reaping by his wife.

his account with Greentree annually, and usually little more than a pound changed hands.

In all, from about 1757 to William Smedley's death in 1766, the household included at least one domestic servant, an apprentice, a single laborer, a bound servant, and a family living in the cottage. In addition, there were probably three regularly leased smallholdings. While the number of workers in the Smedley household may have been unusual relative to other rural households in the middle and northern colonies, the mix of family, dependent, and free workers was typical of agricultural life in much of the eighteenth-century Anglo-American world. Agricultural production on specific farms increased modestly, and manufacturing was still, for the most part, custom work. Entrepreneurial enterprises, such as Smedley's, obtained sufficient labor by remaining flexible in what was produced; by making use of the alternative labor sources in the family, household, and community; and by providing opportunities for landless laborers and artisans.

The importance of free wage labor to the economy of Chester County becomes obvious by the end of the century, when slaves and indentured servants had all but disappeared. The ability of householders to retain substantial numbers of free laborers in the 1750s and 1760s, by renting smallholdings to some and by hiring others as cottagers and servants, was critical to the buildup of the labor force required to meet current demands and further expansion. In the 1750s, smallholding still offered the nonlandowner the possibility of upward mobility. As the economy became more closely tied to external markets in the decade before the Revolution, however, the position of the smallholder became less viable and more precarious. While smallholders might survive a year or two of unseasonable weather, they lacked the capital necessary to ride out a combination of natural disasters and contracting markets. In the end, it was largely the landless free worker who provided the labor necessary to the continued economic development of the Philadelphia region.

Smedley's records provide useful insight into the reasons for the eventual rise of the cottager class. The picture they present of days worked and income earned as well as of the continuing seasonality of labor demand indicates that lines between landless laborers, artisans, and tenant-smallholders were not yet clearly drawn. Cottager status represented an improvement in living conditions for inmates and freemen over former living-in arrangements; cottagers fell somewhere in between the servants who had traditionally eaten with the family and the independent, upwardly mobile individual who started small. Although he was the primary hired hand for the Smedleys in 1764 and 1765, John Greentree still had considerable control over his time. For him, Chester County probably was still a "best poor man's country." But it no longer promised independence.

None of William Smedley's smallholding tenants or cottagers became independent landowning farmers. Most of them still rented property through the years of Elizabeth Smedley's widowhood. In spite of all the time Greentree had as his own, he was still living as a cottager on the Smedley farm in 1782 (when Elizabeth died). Thomas Taylor was, it appears, still living in the shop. George Razor was renting pasture for his cow. Richard Noblitt, the possible exception, died in 1764, soon after renting the forty-acre farm from Smedley.

His assets were not sufficient to cover his debts, and his widow claimed poverty.[16]

The careers of William and Elizabeth Smedley suggest how the late-eighteenth-century economy of southeastern Pennsylvania supported an increasing number of landless (or nearly landless) laborers. In contrast to Samuel Swayne, the Smedleys had a year-round (but seasonably variable) need for labor, both for craftwork and to allow them to manage a farm while William pursued carpentry. They expanded their household by hiring a mix of free and dependent male and female workers; by providing a cottage for a family; and by leasing a forty-acre smallholding to a carpenter who then worked for William by the day. The improvement in the grain market made possible the gradual acquisition of a comfortable reserve of land, just as it fueled demand for better homes and barns and more barrels and casks for shipping Atlantic cargoes. But the lives of the individuals employed by the Smedleys suggest that getting ahead in this economic environment if one were a laborer meant having a skill in addition to the strength to do field work; at best, the economy promised the laborer regular employment and a living, but little more.

WHEN, IN 1781, James Greenway and John Cuff contracted with Caleb Brinton, they went to work for a member of a well-established Chester County family. William and Ann Brinton had come to Pennsylvania in 1684 with the first Quaker settlers. They had settled on a 450-acre tract in Chester County in a log house twenty-five miles from the Delaware River. When William died in 1700, he owned more than 1,000 acres, land that secured the position of both his children and grandchildren. At the end of the American Revolution, third- and fourth-generation members of the family were prosperous householders in the contiguous townships of Birmingham and Thornbury in central Chester County. In 1783 Caleb Brinton was farming two tracts (one of 268 acres in Birmingham and one of 190 acres in Thornbury), moving his cattle back and forth, and rotating his crops. In the mid-nineteenth century, Caleb's descendants remembered him as an ambitious moneylender:

> His bonds and mortgages, spread over the county, and his large tracts of land, together with his great age [he died in 1826, age 98], made him a noted character. Whomever he met he asked, "Does thee owe me any interest?" One day while jogging along

16. Chester County Estate Papers, 2124, CCA.

the road, he spied a copper cent in the dust. Being too old to dismount, he trotted to a neighboring field, brought a boy from his work to pick up the cent for him, put it into his pocket, and rode away.

His 1826 probate inventory, which listed a remarkable $303,015 in cash, bank balances, mortgages, and bonds at interest, more than confirms these reminiscences. Caleb's brother, George, owned some 547 acres in Thornbury, occupied by eleven people (the largest land-holding and household in the township), and six other members of the Brinton family owned a total of some 730 acres in either Thornbury or Birmingham.[17]

The Brintons were archetypal agricultural entrepreneurs; they owed their wealth to market farming, milling, financial investment, and land accumulation as well as to the head start one generation gave the next. Judged by the standards of the great slaveowners of the Chesapeake or the merchants of Philadelphia, these were people of modest means. Their significance lies, then, not so much in their wealth as in their number. By the late eighteenth century, there were brothers and sisters, uncles and aunts, and nieces and nephews, all of whom shared an inherited advantage, handed down, generation by generation, from the time Ann and William Brinton spent their first winter in a log hut along the Brandywine. Each township in Chester County had its equivalent landed gentry. Because farming families, such as the Brintons, took the lead in responding to market incentives, their practices defined the contours of entrepreneurial agriculture and shaped the labor market in the region.

Caleb and his wife had only one child, George, presumably named after his uncle and known to his neighbors and the township tax collector as George Junior. In 1787 George Junior married Elizabeth Yeatman, the sixteen-year-old daughter of a Delaware farmer, and the two established themselves on a 282-acre property provided by George's father. For the next three decades, George Brinton kept a detailed account book of his farming activity and jotted intermittently in an agricultural diary. With these sources, it is possible to reconstruct much of his economic world and to study the place of

17. The Brinton family is chronicled in Daniel Garrison Brinton, *The Brinton Family* (Media, Pa., 1878); and Janetta Wright Schoonover, comp. and ed., *The Brinton Genealogy: A History of William Brinton, Who Came from England to Chester County, Pennsylvania in 1684, and of His Descendants, with Some Records of the English Brintons* (Trenton, N.J., 1925), 167 (quotation). The probate record comes from the Estate Papers, 7870, CCA.

landless workers in Chester County as the rural economy expanded and the demand for labor increased.[18]

Following George Brinton through a typical year (March 1792–February 1793) provides some sense of farming routines in Chester County and of the role of hired labor in the households of prosperous farmers in the post-Revolutionary era. By March 1792, the family had two small children, and, before the year was out, Elizabeth (just turned twenty) would be carrying a third. In January, George hired Phebe Cooper to help in the house at 3s. per week and paid Rebecca Cammel 7d. per day for additional house labor. In March, when Rebecca left, Brinton renegotiated with Phebe, and she agreed "to make her home here to give a week's work"—presumably a direct exchange of room and board for housework. Brinton also hired Margaret, the stepdaughter of one of his field hands, from mid-March through September at 7s. 6d. per month. Late in the year, after Phebe Cooper left, Polly Worrillow was hired at 3s. 6d. per week for four weeks; Mary Moore completed the year (at the same rate). Over the course of the year, then, the Brintons usually had one full-time and one part-time female worker in the household; in addition, the wives of the cottagers were paid for some forty-five days of "work in the house." The arrangements were flexible: they were short-term, and pay could be by the day, the week, or the month. Whether these women cared for the Brinton children, did the cooking, worked in the dairy, or spun flax and wool is unknown, but clearly the sum of their work was too much for Elizabeth alone and important enough to the household's well-being to require extra help.

In the spring of 1792, after assessing his own labor needs for the coming year, George took on two laborers, Caesar Evans and John Rock. Each agreed to pay £4 rent for a cottage (as in the case of the Greenway and Cuff arrangements with Caleb), and each agreed to be paid 2s. for common work and 2s. 6d. for mowing. Cradling was paid at 5s. per day, because, in the hands of a skilled worker, the cradle was at least twice as efficient as the sickle. The dramatic increase in days worked per laborer per year can be seen by comparing the days worked by Swayne's six laborers in 1768, Smedley's cottager John Greentree in 1764, and John Rock in 1792 (see tables 4, 5, and 6). During the summer and early fall, Brinton also hired Julius Richardson (Margaret's stepfather), who had been a dependable part-time worker since 1789, for help with the mowing, and both Rock's

18. The sources for the following discussion of George Brinton, unless otherwise noted, are his account book, cattle book, and agricultural diary, CCHS.

and Evans's wives for field work (at one-half the male rate). He contracted with a third woman, Caety Robeson, at 18d. per day for occasional help with the hay and wheat.

For Elizabeth and George Brinton, farming was a fully diversified enterprise (table 6). George began the spring plowing his fields; sowing clover, parsnip, and radish seeds; and planting turnips and cabbages. Rock carted dung and lime to the newly plowed fields. In April, Brinton turned his cattle to pasture and cut and cropped his lambs; "sowed 2 bu[shels] of flax seed and 6½ bu[shels] of spring wheat"; took his winter grain to the local gristmill and had "22 barrels in all: 20 of superfine and 2 of common flour"; and finished his vegetable garden. In May, his attention turned to corn and to weeding the wheat and vegetables that had been planted earlier. Brinton wrote in his diary in June: "Took our 6 calves from the cows and took 3 steers to fatten, put them in the field next to Thatchers [where the winter wheat had just been harvested]." The somewhat relaxed pace of farm life ended abruptly on June 14, when Brinton and Rock began mowing hay; they finished three days later (with the help of a cottager's wife) and then immediately started sowing buckwheat. July and August were, perhaps, the busiest months of the year. In the field, Rock was reaping, cradling, and binding virtually every day, first at the Beehive (Brinton's residence) and then at the Old Thornbury Place nearby (where he and Evans lived). Brinton sorted out fifteen of his three dozen sheep for fattening and slaughter, pulled flax (Rock's wife and Sarah, Evans's wife, helped with this), and carted cheese (presumably made by Elizabeth or her helpers) to the Wilmington market (there would be a second trip in mid-August, and, by year's end, Brinton had sold almost seven hundred pounds).

On September 19, Brinton noted in his diary the first frost of the year. Several days earlier, he had written: "Henderson had done my cider works, 2 hands at work 23½ days. Paid 9-5-0." Brinton was ready for fall. On September 22, he began making cider, and the rest of the month was spent at the cider mill or in seeding winter wheat. After the wheat was sown, in early October, Brinton, Rock, and Evans turned to harvesting apples, buckwheat, and potatoes (work that kept them occupied for much of the fall). Because field work now proceeded at a somewhat more relaxed pace, Brinton could dispatch Rock and Evans to cut and haul firewood, erect fencing, and gather winter fodder for the cows. In November he settled with Levi Pyle for weaving ninety-four yards of cloth for the family. Brinton harvested 145½ bushels of spring wheat, and, on February 21, he reserved 26 for next year's seed, held back 18½ for the family, and sent 101 to the mill to be ground, packed, and sold. Even as winter forced people into the shelter of home and barn, there was work to be done—foddering the cattle, butchering livestock, breaking and dressing flax, and spinning yarn—before the March sun and spring rain began again the ritual of plowing and planting.

Clearly, the workings of a late-eighteenth-century Chester County farm were complex. If wheat was the staple crop of Middle Atlantic agriculture, it was by no means the only market crop, for urban demand now rivaled the export market in importance to Chester County farmers. Brinton needed wage laborers not just at harvest-time but, in varying degrees, throughout the year. He sold cheese in Wilmington and Philadelphia, purchased cattle from western Pennsylvania and Ohio (and fattened them for resale to butchers in Germantown), and had his wheat milled and then sold for shipment at "the Hook." He raised flax and sheep and hired laborers and spinners to process the flax and wool. Butter, hides, meat, hay, and livestock were traded locally, and he sold some of virtually everything he raised (except vegetables) to his hired hands. Brinton had surely made a choice in pursuing a diversified agricultural regime; he could have specialized in wheat and produced a surplus for the market, limited production of most other crops to what was needed for home consumption, and hired laborers only for harvesting his cash crop. Rather, because diversified farming was profitable, he added laborers and provided them some assurance of regular employment. The routine nature of John Rock's farm work downplays the multiplying market opportunities that the rural economy offered farmers like Brinton in the late eighteenth century.

Over the three decades spanned by the account books and diary, the Brintons managed their farm basically the same way from year to year. Of immediate interest are the practices they followed in order to ensure the right mix of labor at the lowest cost throughout the year. One persistent characteristic of their husbandry was the use of a great number of short-term workers. In the first ten years of the nineteenth century, they hired approximately seventy workers (one-quarter of them women). None was hired full-time for more than four continuous years, and many were paid for a few days of harvest help or for a few months as needed and then not heard of again. A few of these short-term workers were transients passing through the area, but many more were sons, daughters, and wives of local householders and cottagers.

In a typical year, the Brintons managed with one or two steady (but part-time) field hands, two cottagers with yearlong labor obligations and their wives (who helped with housework and harvesting), and several women who worked in the house regularly. For example,

TABLE 6
Work Record of John Rock and His Wife, 1792–1793

Month	Task	Days Worked	Rate per day	
			s.	d.
Mar.	Loading dung	6	2	
Apr.	Plowing, spreading dung, harrowing	17	2	
May	At corn, washing sheep, trimming meadow, weeding wheat	9.5	2	
June	At hay	8.37	3	
	At hay (Rock's Wife)	1.75	1	6
	In house (Rock's Wife)	1		7
	At corn	2	2	
	Total	13.12		
July	Cradling	6.25	5	
	Raking and binding wheat	3	3	
	Reaping and binding wheat (Rock's Wife)	1.75	1	6
	In house (Rock's Wife)	9		7
	At potatoes, trimming	3	2	
	Tending masonry, reaping, fencing	5.25	2	6
	Total	28.25		
Aug.	Mowing hay	11	3	
	In house (Rock's Wife)	10.5		7
	Plowing, drawing wood for cider mill, beating flax, at potatoes	10	2	
	Total	31.5		
Sept.	At hay (no mowing), loading dirt, plowing, other work	21.25	2	
	Threshing 25 bus. wheat for seed		5	(per bu.)

Table 6. Continued

Month	Task	Days Worked	Rate per day	
			s.	d.
Oct.	Plowing, at buckwheat, potatoes, apples and cider	20	2	
	At potatoes (Rock's Wife)	1	1	6
	Total	21		
Nov.	At cider, corn, cutting wood, fencing, killing bull, plowing orchard	14	2	
Dec.	Drawing logs, thrashing clover seeds, killing pigs	5.75	2	
	Cleaning 18.5 bus. wheat			6 (per bu.)
Jan.	Drawing logs, sawing	2.5	2	
Feb.	Thrashing 33.5 bus. wheat			6 (per bu.)

Source: George Brinton Account Book, CCHS.

Brinton employed Julius Richardson each summer from 1789 to 1794; but even in 1789, the year Richardson worked the most, he accumulated no more than sixty days of agricultural labor. Richardson disappeared from the record until 1799, when he agreed to "make his home here for good and all," and his wife, Jane, came to work at four shillings per week. She stayed only fourteen weeks, and he left in November. He reappeared in 1806 and worked approximately two weeks at summer mowing and occasionally did a day or two of mowing for Brinton in the years that followed. In contrast, there were hands (such as John Rock) who rented cottages and stayed on for several years.

Of the cottage laborers, George Waggoner probably had the longest relationship with the Brintons. On February 4, 1794, Waggoner rented a house on the Old Thornbury Place (Brinton lived at his other property, the Beehive) for £3, bought a cow from Brinton, rented pasture, and began a contractual labor relationship with his employer that would last for at least a decade and a half. By the end of the year, he had worked 208 days and his wife, Caty, an additional 8 days; they earned £24 7d. (including piecework spinning tow yarn). On March 28, 1795, he rented again, working 178 days; he and Caty earned £26 8s. 3d. In 1796 they accumulated 181 days and grossed £23 9s. 9d. When the year ended, Waggoner left, presumably to take up a cottage with another of the area's landowners. But, in the fall of 1798, Brinton noted in his ledger: "George Waggoner came back to the Old Thornbury House again and is to have the same part of the house as he had before and to come under the Old Article again." This time they stayed through February 1800, and, over seventeen months, earned £38 16s. 6d. On average, Waggoner earned 2s. a day and his wife 18d.

From February 1803 through September 1804, Waggoner worked for Brinton from time to time but apparently was not his cottager. In mid-October, he signed a contract to work for £3 a month; and, in December, he moved back into the "old stone house" at a higher rent (£6 for the year). In March, they agreed for day labor, and Waggoner worked 162 days for £25 11s. 1d. Waggoner spent from March 1806 to March 1807 renting from Joseph Hanns and working for someone other than Brinton; then, on March 18, he and his family returned, agreeing to work that year for £30 and renting a cottage for £6. By spinning tow yarn and through Caty's work on the hay harvest, the family's earnings for the year came to £34 17s. 3d. George and Caty remained through 1808 under similar terms, but moved out in April 1809. In 1812 Waggoner again worked for Brinton, but if he again moved into a cottage, it was after 1817 (the year the account book ends).

What is apparent about the Brinton-Waggoner relationship is how readily Waggoner moved from landlord to landlord and from job to job. Waggoner remained in the area for at least eighteen years, spent seven years as Brinton's cottager, and worked part-time for Brinton during four other years. It is not clear whether he moved by choice or necessity. As Brinton was willing to rehire Waggoner, perhaps Waggoner left by choice; but, on at least two occasions, Brinton requested that Waggoner leave by a specific date. Probably, on different occasions, each negotiated with an eye to bettering himself.[19]

19. Brinton's request that Waggoner leave was probably not merely a routine step in renegotiating his contract; only one other such letter to a cottager is among Brinton's papers, and, in that case, the cottager also left.

A second characteristic of Brinton's husbandry was the way he negotiated with female laborers for their time and skills. As in the mid-eighteenth century, the occasional work by the wives of cottagers was often included in the accounts of their husbands (see table 6). Brinton's account books make no mention of milking and dairying (women's work), even though the sale of cheese and butter makes it clear that such work was being done. But, unlike Swayne and Smedley, Brinton kept separate accounts for the wives of cottagers. He did so, for example, for Caety Robeson, the wife of one of his workers. In 1790 Caety worked the entire year for Brinton. She received 3s. 6d. for a six-day week of work in the house and 1s. 9d. per week when she was also "working for herself" (probably spinning and putting-out flax to other women on the farm). In 1792 she gave up her job in the household but continued to work for Brinton by the day or task as needed, spinning, weaving, reaping, and pulling flax.

Caety's case was not unusual. In October 1799, when Brinton hired William Taylor for the winter season at £2 17s. 6d. ($5.00) a month, he agreed to pay Taylor's wife half that amount. The account of Benjamin Jones's wife shows payments for spinning and hackling as well as washing at 18d. per day. From 1802 through 1804, Brinton hired David and Sarah Thomson and James and Margaret Moore. The couples were given a single account, but each individual was credited separately, the wives for spinning and their husbands for weaving.

Clearly, distinctions were made in women's work, as in men's, by task and skill. In 1799 Susannah Keech was paid 5s. per week for work in the house but only 4s. for spinning. Brinton agreed with Leah Logan's parents, in March 1800, that he would pay Leah 4s. 6d. per week "to do housework and anything else there was to do." While the rate was less than that for male laborers, employment was continuous; Leah could expect to earn £11 14s. a year as well as her room and board.

Another characteristic of the way Brinton managed the Beehive and the Old Thornbury Place was his employment of black laborers. Slavery was exceptional (but not unknown) in Chester County (see table 3). Late-eighteenth-century Quaker opposition to the institution and the egalitarian ideals of the American Revolution led, in 1780, to a gradual emancipation law, but not to the immediate end of slavery. In 1760 there were 293 taxable slaves in Chester; in 1774 there were 208. By 1783 there were 255, and, in 1789, there were still 144 enslaved blacks over the age of eleven (and the slave population was, of course, larger than the number of taxable slaves). A detailed 1780 slave register (listed by owner) shows some 496 slaves in the county (two were Indians), approximately three-fifths of whom were taxable and two-fifths younger children. Before 1820, another eighty-five children would be born to slave families, registered as slaves, and, under the 1780 law, be the servants of their owners until they reached the age of twenty-eight. As the slave population shrank, the free black population grew from perhaps 400 in 1783 to some 1,600 by 1800. Virtually all of them were dependent laborers (or the children of such laborers) rather than householders.[20]

Brinton found workers among the descendants of slaves freed by his family and other local landowners; he also bought slaves, who then entered indentures to work off the purchase price and obtain their freedom. In all, the account book records dealings with some twenty-eight blacks (eight cottagers and their families, fifteen male laborers, and five women), and several more are mentioned in the Brinton family papers. For example, Caesar Evans, who was hired in 1791 (and whose work was discussed above), was probably a free black; Benjamin Jones, a black cottager in 1811, was probably the same Benjamin Jones who was not identified by race when he was a cottager from 1798 to 1802. Dimbo Talley, who hired on in March 1806 at 3s. per day (and rented a cottage at £6), was black. In May, his wife and two children began drawing wages as well, and, in August, a formal agreement stipulated that Dimbo Talley was hired "for 1 month his time to begin on 5th Day morning of the week for 8 Dollars [£3] for the month and he is to find his own washing and mending during the whole time and the money to be paid when the time is fully expired." In September, another contract followed, this

---

20. On slavery, see Lemon, *Best Poor Man's Country*, 234; Soderlund, *Quakers and Slavery*, 153; Futhey and Cope, *History of Chester County*, I, 423–424; and Isaac Gilpin's Chester County Register of Slaves and Servants, 1780, Historical Society of Pennsylvania, Philadelphia. For an estimate of the free black population in 1783, see the 1783 State Return with Census, S-12a, CCA. Additional figures come from the U.S. Bureau of the Census, *Return of the Number of Persons within the Several Districts of the United States, according to "An Act Providing for the Second Census or Enumeration of the Inhabitants of the United States"* (Washington, D.C., 1802 [orig. publ. 1801]); *Census for 1820* (Washington, D.C., 1821); *Heads of Families at the First Census of the United States Taken in the Year 1790: Pennsylvania* (Washington, D.C., 1908), 9; and *Aggregate Amount of Each Description of Persons within the United States of America, and the Territories Thereof, Agreeably to Actual Enumeration Made according to Law, in the Year 1810* (Washington, D.C., 1811), 36–37. On the black poor in Chester County, see Carl D. Oblinger, "Alms for Oblivion: The Making of a Black Underclass in Southeastern Pennsylvania, 1780–1860," in John E. Bodnar, ed., *The Ethnic Experience in Pennsylvania* (Lewisburg, Pa., 1973), 94–119. We are grateful to Jean Soderlund for sharing her data on the slave population with us.

one for $7 (£2 12s. 6d.), and, in December, the monthly wage was lowered to $6 (£2 5s.), his wife receiving 2s. per day for washing. Brinton offered Talley no less than he offered whites for the same work (and charged him no more for rent).[21]

A reward poster circulated in 1804 points to the more coercive aspects of black-white labor relations. Jacob Bolland had been a slave in Delaware. As the poster noted, he had run away from his owner, Ebenezar Rothwell, in about 1800, and fled to Montgomery County, Pennsylvania. After Bolland was apprehended, Brinton "purchased him from his former master at the high rate of two hundred dollars principally through the persuasion of said Negro, and partly through a motive to relieve him from slavery, and to give him an opportunity of seeing his wife" and two children. Bolland and Brinton had agreed to an indenture to return the cost of the purchase, and then Bolland and his family fled. If he was ever caught, there is no record of it. In 1793 Brinton had turned to three referees to recommend a reasonable extension on the time of Charles Berry, a mulatto servant, who had run away several times. In 1799 Brinton paid John Frazier of Maryland one hundred dollars for the release of George Brown, who had been working for Brinton since November 1797; Brown then had to work additional time for Brinton to pay off this expense. In 1801 Brinton purchased a black man, Joseph Sollus, from Jacob Biddle for twenty-five pounds, and, the next year, gave him a pass to seek a new master who would assume his freedom bond and who was better suited to his needs.[22]

Brinton's method of paying his workers was another significant characteristic of how he ran his farm. If he kept a meticulous day-to-day record of work done, he kept an equally careful record of payments made, services rendered, and goods purchased (see table 7). Waggoner's remuneration supported him and his family in a cottage on the Old Thornbury Place shared with Black Tom, who also worked for Brinton. Talley's earnings had to cover the expenses of a family of four. Both families depended on their employer for shelter, fuel, and some of their food. When purchasing food, Waggoner and Talley were charged either a price that changed annually (for example, in the case of corn) or, when the goods were in strong demand, a price set by current market conditions (as in the case of wheat, cheese, pork, and meat). Cash payments seem to have been made in several varieties of both paper and hard money, with accounting done at a

21. Jacob Cuff, son of James, began working for Brinton in 1791; his father had been Joseph Brinton's slave in 1751.
22. The reward poster is in the Murtagh Collection, CCHS.

TABLE 7
George Brinton's Payments to George Waggoner (1799) and Dimbo Talley (1807)

	George Waggoner			Dimbo Talley			
	£ s. d. (% of outlay)				£ s. d. (% of outlay)		
RENTS							
Old Thornbury house	4[a]			Cottage	6		
Cow pasture (30 weeks)	1	10					
Cow fodder (22 weeks)	2	4					
Running sow (3 months)		3	9				
Total	7	17	9		6		
	(22.1)				(21.1)		
SERVICES							
Drawing wood (1¼ days)		10		Drawing wood, sowing			
Drawing wood (7¼ days)	1	1	7	1 pk. flaxseed	2	7	6
Drawing wood (½ day)		3					
Sowing 1 pk. flaxseed		5					
Total	1	19	7		2	7	6
	(5.5)				(8.4)		
PURCHASES OF STOCK AND GOODS							
2 sheep	1	4		Tobacco			3
1 calf		10		Onion seed			9
Flax, wool		3	3				
2 hats		7					
Total	2	5	3			1	
	(6.3)				(0.2)		
FOOD							
15 bus. corn (@ 4s.)	3			12 bus. corn (@ 5s.)	3		
11 bus. potatoes (@ 2s.)	1	2		1½ bus. potatoes			
5 bus. buckwheat (@ 4s.)	1			(@ 4s. 6d.)		6	4
2 bbls. cider	1	6	6	75 gals. cider (@ 9d.)	2	16	10
2 lbs. butter (@ 1s.)		2		3 lbs. butter (@ 1s. 6d.)		4	6
22¼ lbs. cheese		11	11[b]	17¼ lbs. cheese		13	11[b]
Salt			10	Salt		5	4
9½ lbs. beef		2	4	22½ lbs. pork		18	1[b]
6 qts. vinegar (@ 3d.)		1	6	Vinegar			5
1½ bus. barley (@ 6s.)		9		3½ bus. wheat	1	15	6[b]
½ bu. oats		1	3	2 lbs. lard (@ 1s.)		2	
43 lbs. rye meal (@ 2s.)		5	2	2 bus. apples		2	

Table 7. Continued

	George Waggoner				Dimbo Talley		
	£ s. d. (% of outlay)					£ s. d. (% of outlay)	
Calf meat		2	6	5 qts. whiskey (@ 1s. 6d.)		7	6
½ bu. turnips		1					
Total	8	6			10	12	5
	(23.2)					(37.4)	
			CASH				
38 payments	14	1	2[c]	25 payments	6	10	8
3 debts paid	1	4	10	3 debts paid	2	16	8
Total	15	6			9	7	4
	(42.8)				(33.0)		
Grand total	35	14	7		28	8	3
	(99.9)				(100.1)[d]		

Source: George Brinton Account Book, CCHS.
Notes: [a]All amounts are rounded off to eliminate fractional pennies.   [b]Prices varied depending on the market.   [c]Includes four payments made "to wife."   [d]Deviations in totaling from 100.0% are due to rounding.

fixed (rather than a market) rate of exchange. In sum, the pattern of payments reflected both the dependence and the independence of Brinton's workers. Although they relied on customary services to deal with the exigencies of daily life and bought some part of their foodstuffs on the farm, they also received enough cash to make their own market choices.

Brinton's dealings with landless wage workers provide some sense of how much leverage laborers had in bargaining for material security. In some ways, the labor market was extraordinarily fluid: most workers had short-term arrangements; wages were paid by the day, week, month, or year; pay could be negotiated on the basis of days worked or by subtracting days lost from a fixed sum; and women, blacks, and, occasionally, children were employed as well as white male field hands. Both Brinton and those who periodically worked for him continually renegotiated the terms of employment. For Brinton, this meant a continuous effort to find suitable help; for the laborers, this meant moving from farm to farm to find agreeable rents and acceptable wages. In other ways, there was a considerable amount of stability in the labor market; as transient as the labor force was, most laborers recirculated back to Brinton's farm at one time or another. When they returned, they could expect to be offered roughly the same terms as they had worked for before, for the changes in rents and wages were, however important, certainly not dramatically different from those set by other farmers. Moreover, the yearly circulation of the laboring population from farm to farm meant that both workers and landowners shared an assessment of the risks and benefits of particular arrangements with particular people, an assessment reinforced as the years passed.

GEORGE BRINTON'S relationship with George Waggoner, William and Elizabeth Smedley's with John Greentree, and Samuel Swayne's with Daniel Burk provide three overlapping perspectives on the place of wage labor in the Chester County economy. Viewed collectively, these work arrangements suggest that, although most householders made occasional use of wage labor, there were three chief sources of demand for hired workers. First, there were young families, like the Swaynes, for whom wage labor was a temporary substitute for family labor, and who hired field hands and domestics for two or three months each year until their children reached an age at which they were able to help with planting, harvesting, and housework. Second, there were farmer-artisans, like the Smedleys, who needed and could afford more help than this. At first, such a family might, of necessity, rely on apprentices and part-time wage labor. But, as their ability to provide housing and customary services increased along with their need for additional and more consistent labor, they took on cottagers in addition to an assortment of temporary workers. Finally, there were the large farmers and entrepreneurs, like the Brintons, who, by the very nature and size of their operations and market involvement, required a dependable, year-round labor force. They contracted not only with a number of cottagers but regularly hired several male and female workers for specific tasks. The lines between these groups are, admittedly, vague, but it seems clear that, in an expanding economy (given the seasonal nature of agricultural work and the fluctuations in market demand), a large, though probably underemployed, labor force was required if the needs of the householding population were to be met without substantial partition of landholdings. In Chester County (where there were extensive rural industry, a significant number of large landowners, and a consistent effort to avoid division of farm holdings), it is not surprising then that, by 1774, the ratio of householders to landless wage laborers (inmates and freemen) was two to one (see tables 2 and 3). As neither domestic workers nor poorer male laborers were listed in the tax records, the actual ratio of householders to workers was probably one to one.[23]

Viewed chronologically, the three account books tell a somewhat different story. They suggest (without proving) that there was movement, in the mid-eighteenth century, from the occasional employment of dependent laborers for harvest work to, by the end of the century, a more systematic and pervasive utilization of wage workers. At any point in time, to be sure, the export economy and the mix of industry and agriculture in the county created a demand for skilled labor, but the impression the account books leave is that, between 1760 and 1820, this demand intensified (see table 3). In a few instances, such as in Haverford Township, this intensification was associated with the introduction of small factories, but the more general pattern was the use of laborers to facilitate household market production.

The economic balance sheet for individual cottagers and day laborers is much more difficult to determine than the mere presence of these workers in the economy. Rather than speculate on what is a matter for future inquiry, two observations are in order. First, the payment schedule for Brinton's cottagers reflects a not atypical (and a reasonably comfortable) material standard of living (table 7). The record does not, however, answer the question of whether most cottagers were able to accumulate enough to acquire their own smallholding, but it does suggest that, in the post-Revolutionary era, they were not. Although data on real income have not yet been compiled, it seems probable that, given the increase in days worked, the average cottager was no worse off in 1820 than in 1760. The situation facing day laborers (chiefly freemen) was more problematic; while healthy adults clearly had little trouble finding work at harvest-time, it is not clear what unskilled workers did the rest of the year to make a living. Some freemen, of course, were older children living in the homes of their parents, and a few were simply lodgers, but a majority were neither. For these workers, residence in Chester County probably represented a predicament more than an opportunity.

More important, perhaps, than changing wage rates in determining the economic circumstances of the work force was the fact that, between 1760 and 1820, the wage structure in Chester County in-

23. The ratio of one to one is also supported by comparing the number of taxable and not-taxed workers listed in the account books.

creasingly came to incorporate distinctions based on skill and market demand. Initially, the term "common work" covered all farm tasks except reaping. Splitting rails, fencing, spreading dung, mowing, and plowing (for example) were all classified as common work. Wages for such work were customarily 18d.–2s. The lower wage (18d.) was generally paid in the off-season (the winter months), and the higher wage (2s.) during the spring, summer, and fall. Reaping was restricted because of the critical time constraints: grains had to be cut within a few days of ripening if the farmer hoped to realize the full value of the crop. Reapers' wages, locally known as "harvest wages," were 2s. 3d. from 1730 to 1760.

Between 1730 and 1760, wages for mowing (and later wages for plowing) increased to the equivalent of reaping wages; the increase marked a significant change in agricultural methods and productivity. Mowing, like reaping, had to be done when the crop was ready. As livestock herds increased in size and the market price of meat went up, mowing hay to feed cattle during the winter took on new importance. Subsequently, plowing followed mowing into the higher wage bracket as farmers brought more land under cultivation in response to spiraling grain prices. As the change in neither mowing nor plowing wages affected the basic wage scale (18d., 2s., or 2s. 3d.), the new structure of wages that emerged in the mid-eighteenth century is not easily detected, but for field hands it meant considerably better pay and reflected an improvement in their bargaining position.[24]

Was Chester County's labor arrangement typical of late colonial America? At one level of analysis, the prevalence of wage laborers and cottager-landlord agreements set off Chester and the Middle Atlantic region from both New England (where age separated the dependent, unmarried, and nonlanded from the secure and independent) and the Chesapeake (where race defined dependency more rigidly than class). There is, however, a substantial risk in concluding at this level of generalization. For one thing, it can well be argued that, by the middle of the eighteenth century, the elaboration of the Anglo-American market, the growth of population, the establishment of multigenerational communities, and the continuing penetration of the imperial bureaucracy into everyday life all assured certain commonalities in the patterns of development along the Atlantic seaboard. Even more critically, as work on both the Chesapeake and

24. The authors are conducting a study of wages, prices, and rents in Chester County based on land records, inventories, and account books. This paragraph is meant only as a preliminary reflection on that work.

New England has emphasized, differences within regions—from township to township or from county to county—were often as striking as distinctions between regions. Seen in this light, Chester County's labor system was a product of a particular location and relationship to the market.[25]

At the end of the eighteenth century, when John Beale Bordley, a noted agricultural writer, drafted his *Essays and Notes on Husbandry and Rural Affairs*, he paused briefly to consider labor practices in his lengthy prescription for agricultural improvement. Bordley knew well both his native Maryland and the middle colonies, he had seen the gradual shift from tobacco planting to wheat farming in the northern Chesapeake, and he could speculate on the future of slavery as Chesapeake farmers replaced their traditional staple with grain crops. Looking to Europe, Bordley argued the advantage to farmers of having not only servants residing in the family but also rent-paying wage laborers "in a small very confined house called a *cottage*," with enough land so that they could contribute to their own support, but not enough to tempt them to farm. In America, Bordley noted, the English model of cottage labor had taken hold west of Philadelphia, for "there are farmers, particularly in Chester county, Pennsylvania, and as I am informed, in some of the Eastern states, whose [agricultural] practices are very superior, and nearly altogether by the aid of labourers or servants [as in England]." Bordley, of course, did not fully sense how apt his analogy was. For in England, as in Chester County, the development of the cottager class went hand in hand with the commercialization of agriculture and the intensification of rural manufacturing, both helping pave the way, as the future would show, for urban industrialization.[26]

25. Among recent works that deal with the role of the market and regional patterns of development, see, in particular, Stephen Innes, *Labor in a New Land: Economy and Society in Seventeenth-Century Springfield* (Princeton, N.J., 1983); Christine Leigh Heyrman, *Commerce and Culture: The Maritime Communities of Colonial Massachusetts, 1690–1750* (New York, 1984); Winifred B. Rothenberg, "The Market and Massachusetts Farmers, 1750–1855," *Journal of Economic History*, XLI (1981), 283–314; Bettye Hobbs Pruitt, "Self-Sufficiency and the Agricultural Economy of Eighteenth-Century Massachusetts," *WMQ*, 3d Ser., XLI (1984), 333–364; Paul G. E. Clemens, *The Atlantic Economy and Colonial Maryland's Eastern Shore: From Tobacco to Grain* (Ithaca, N.Y., 1980); and Allan Kulikoff, *Tobacco and Slaves: The Development of Southern Cultures in the Chesapeake, 1680–1800* (Chapel Hill, N.C., 1986).

26. J. B. Bordley, *Essays and Notes on Husbandry and Rural Affairs*, 2d ed. (Philadelphia, 1801), 389. On cottagers, see such English studies as J. D. Chambers and G. E. Mingay, *The Agricultural Revolution, 1750–1880* (London, 1966), 18–19, 96–103, 133–147; and H. J. Habakkuk, *Population Growth and Economic Development since 1750* (Leicester, 1972), 40–42.

Lois Green Carr and Lorena S. Walsh

Economic Diversification and Labor Organization in the Chesapeake, 1650–1820

THE PERIOD 1650–1820 saw a major transformation in the work performed on the farm and in the home throughout the Chesapeake. Seventeenth-century Chesapeake planters focused on producing tobacco and marketing it across three thousand miles of ocean. By the early nineteenth century, tobacco was only one of a variety of income-producing activities in a complex network of interlocking economic relationships. Over the same period, short-term servitude of white British immigrants, the seventeenth-century solution to the labor-intensive needs of tobacco, gave way to black slavery, which was, in turn, affected by diversification. These changes had profound effects upon the lives of all Chesapeake inhabitants, black and white, bound and free. Work opportunities both expanded and specialized, work routines changed, and work relationships altered. This essay will examine these changes and assess the consequences for men and women of varying statuses in Chesapeake society.

Seventeenth-century settlers put all their energies into two activities: building family farms and raising and marketing tobacco.[1]

Research for this essay has been funded in part by grants from the National Science Foundation (GS32272) and the National Endowment for the Humanities (RO62218-72-468; RO10585-74-267; RS236-76-431), all made to the St. Mary's City Commission; and RS20199-81-1955, made to the St. Mary's City Commission and Historic Annapolis, Inc. The authors would like to thank Paul Clemens, Gregory Stiverson, Russell Menard, Stanley Engerman, and members of the Washington Area Seminar in Early American History for helpful comments on all or parts of earlier drafts; and Stephen Innes and Philip Morgan for editorial effort far beyond the call of duty in reducing the essay to manageable size.

The second and fourth sections, which deal primarily with slaves, are the work of Lorena S. Walsh.

1. For a good general discussion, see Gloria L. Main, *Tobacco Colony: Life in Early Maryland, 1650–1720* (Princeton, N.J., 1982), chaps. 1 and 2.

Farm building—clearing land, building barns and homes, putting up fences, planting food crops (especially Indian corn), and establishing livestock herds—provided subsistence. Raising and selling tobacco for the European market provided a cash crop to pay for European goods. Because tobacco was a highly labor-intensive crop, until late in the seventeenth century most Chesapeake planters found it cost-effective to import everything except food and timber rather than put time into making cloth or metal or leather products. The only craftsmen common to the early Chesapeake were the carpenters or coopers who were needed to build housing and to provide containers for shipping tobacco.

Several changes began a redirection of labor productivity that started slowly but was visible by the early eighteenth century and pronounced after another fifty years.[2] First, a thirty-year stagnation in the tobacco industry—stagnation that began about 1680—created conditions that encouraged import-replacement activities, especially making cloth and shoes. Low tobacco prices and wars in Europe that interrupted trade provided the necessary incentives. Second, as farms became well established, men and women had more time to devote to additional activities. Some planters began to raise a little wheat, rye, or beans and peas for variety in their diets. When stumps on cleared land had rotted away, or planters had taken time to remove them, men could begin to plow land to facilitate sowing these crops. More women could make time to tend vegetable gardens, transform milk into butter and cheese, spin yarn, salt down meat, brew a little beer, or press fruit to make cider or perry. Furthermore, more women were on hand to perform such work as the population became native-born late in the century and sex ratios, consequently, became more even.[3] By the early 1700s, all these changes were evident throughout the early-settled areas.

This diversification of economic activities did not imply greatly increased self-sufficiency on plantations; rather, diversification encouraged local exchange and created a more complex network of local

2. Except as noted, the rest of this section is based on Lois Green Carr, "Diversification in the Colonial Chesapeake: Somerset County, Maryland, in Comparative Perspective," in Carr, Philip D. Morgan, and Jean B. Russo, eds., *Colonial Chesapeake Society* (Chapel Hill, N.C., 1988). The counties covered in this study are St. Mary's, Prince George's, Anne Arundel, Talbot, and Somerset in Maryland, and York in Virginia.

3. On this transition, see Russell R. Menard, "Immigrants and Their Increase: The Process of Population Growth in Early Colonial Maryland," in Aubrey C. Land, Lois Green Carr, and Edward C. Papenfuse, eds., *Law, Society, and Politics in Early Maryland* (Baltimore, 1977), 88–110.

interdependence. Many women spun yarn, for example, but far fewer households had looms; hence, spinners took their yarn to weavers and either paid them for weaving or took a portion of the cloth as pay for the yarn. Planters who produced surpluses of grains, butter, or cider sold them to neighbors for tobacco or for products such as shoes, cloth, or yarn that they might happen to need. The capacity to make such exchanges was important as a hedge against low prices for export crops. When all manufactures were purchased from Europe in exchange for tobacco, planters suffered severely during the inevitable slumps in the price of the staple. They could purchase little clothing and few tools with the only product they had to sell to an English merchant. Once local manufactures began to appear, these provided an alternative source both of income and of needed goods otherwise not easy to obtain when tobacco prices were low. During the early decades of the tobacco industry, profits were high enough in years of good prices to discourage development of local manufactures. But the long periods of very low prices that characterized the years from 1680 to about 1710 gave import replacement the push it needed to become a permanent element in the economy.

The rich, with their greater resources in bound labor, moved earliest into diversification, but these changes eventually reached all levels of wealth. By the 1760s and 1770s, women in the great majority of farm families spun yarn. Households too poor to own bound labor, far more often than earlier, had tools for carpentry and coopering, equipment for shoemaking, sometimes even looms for weaving. Richer households had more investment than poorer ones in such activities and were more likely to enter those that required substantial capital, like smithing or tanning. Nevertheless, the change had penetrated to some degree at every social level.

Simple woodworking, shoemaking, and yarn making were the crafts for which poor planters most often had equipment, and account books, beginning as early as the 1720s, show that some very wealthy planters turned to poor white families for these services rather than putting their slaves to work at such tasks. A small planter-shoemaker might make shoes for the slaves of a rich neighbor, using leather supplied by the purchaser. The wife of a small planter—perhaps the rich man's tenant or the overseer of his slaves —might spin from the rich man's wool or flax and be paid by the pound for the yarn or thread produced. A weaver in the neighborhood might accept pay by the yard for weaving the spinner's product into cloth for the rich man's slaves.[4] However, probate inventories

4. See, for example, Robert Gouldsborough Memorandum Book, 1696–1771;

indicate that most such small planter householders also worked for themselves, producing shoes or yarn or cloth from their own materials for their own use or to sell to a neighbor.[5] Such activities in poor households were usually by-employments; the main business still was farming. Nevertheless, the more families that participated in by-employment activities, the denser the network of local exchange became and the more protection there was from the vicissitudes of the tobacco market.

Toward the middle of the eighteenth century, the production of corn and wheat for export also began to divert labor from the production of tobacco. The growing market for provisions in the West Indies had led to increased corn production in some Chesapeake areas by the 1730s. Crop failures in southern Europe produced a great increase in demand for wheat beginning in mid-century. As in diversification into import replacement, this move toward new export products began earliest in the richest households and gradually moved down the social scale, but it appeared much more vigorously in some areas than in others, depending on soil resources and the organization of markets. St. Mary's County, Maryland, showed the fewest effects of any area so far studied. But even there, by the late 1750s, merchants recorded sales of European goods in corn and wheat as well as in tobacco. What they collected in these crop payments they undoubtedly exported or sold to someone who did.[6]

This expansion of crop diversification had other ramifications. It

---

and the Robert Goldsborough Ledger, 1687–1719, 1751–1755, both in private hands (microfilm copy available at the Maryland Hall of Records); Tilghman Family Papers, 1712–1843, Ledger A, 1718–1741; and the James Carroll Day Book, 1714–1721, both in Georgetown University Library, Washington, D.C.

5. The nature of these probate records, and how we have used them, is described in Lois Green Carr and Lorena S. Walsh, "Inventories and the Analysis of Wealth and Consumption Patterns in St. Mary's County, Maryland, 1658–1777," *Historical Methods*, XIII (1980), 81–104. Other literature on the uses of inventories is cited there. Further citations to the data base and analysis will be to St. Mary's City Commission Inventory Files (hereafter cited as SMCC Inventory Files). All values have been transformed into constant pounds via a commodity price index. For data on home production for the market, see Lois Green Carr and Lorena S. Walsh, "The Transformation of Production on the Farm and in the Household in the Chesapeake, 1658–1820," *Working Papers in Social History, Department of History, University of Minnesota*, 1988, no. 3.

6. Paul G. E. Clemens, *The Atlantic Economy and Colonial Maryland's Eastern Shore: From Tobacco to Grain* (Ithaca, N.Y., 1980), 174–179; Peter Victor Bergstrom, "Markets and Merchants: Economic Diversification in Colonial Virginia, 1700–1775" (Ph.D. diss., University of New Hampshire, 1980); David Klingaman, "The Significance of Grain in the Development of the Tobacco Colonies," *Journal of Economic History*, XXIX (1969), 268–278; Gaspare J. Saladino, "The Maryland and

provided additional encouragement for the development of craft activities. English grains needed more regular plowing of land and required carts and wagons to carry crops from field to barn and then to market. Unlike tobacco or corn, these crops needed milling before they could be exported. Blacksmiths, millwrights, and woodworkers were necessary to keep all the equipment functioning. Millers were needed for grinding wheat into flour.[7] The great majority of people engaged in these activities were also planters or worked for men who were. But such investment increased most wherever these new export crops had importance.

By the mid-eighteenth century, the composition of the labor force that carried out the increasingly varied tasks had also greatly changed. In the seventeenth century, white servants were the fundamental component of bound labor; by 1750, black slaves had almost entirely replaced them. This shift, which had begun over the last quarter of the seventeenth century, was related, not to diversification, but to the failure of white servant immigration to supply the labor needs of a growing population.[8] The shift to slaves at first concentrated labor into the hands of the rich—those with movable property worth £226 or more. Men of this wealth turned quickly to slaves. After the 1680s, poor planters—those worth less than £50—never again had much chance of acquiring bound labor. Servants were increasingly unavailable, and slaves were too expensive. Planters in the middle (those with movables worth £50 to £225) took longer to move toward slavery, and fewer, proportionately, used bound laborers early in the eighteenth century. But, gradually, slaves began to appear in such

Virginia Wheat Trade from Its Beginnings to the American Revolution" (master's thesis, University of Wisconsin, 1960). On St. Mary's County, see below.

7. This idea is developed in Carville Earle and Ronald Hoffman, "Staple Crops and Urban Development in the Eighteenth-Century South," *Perspectives in American History*, X (1976), 7–78. Our findings give corroboration. However, for Robert "King" Carter's use of hoes for raising wheat, see Jack P. Greene, ed., *The Diary of Colonel Landon Carter of Sabine Hall, 1752–1778*, 2 vols. (Charlottesville, Va., 1965) II, 1038–1039.

8. Russell R. Menard, "From Servants to Slaves: The Transformation of the Chesapeake Labor System," *Southern Studies*, XVI (1977), 355–390; and "Five Maryland Censuses, 1700 to 1712: A Note on the Quality of the Quantities," *William and Mary Quarterly*, 3d Ser., XXXVII (1980), 616–626; *Gentleman's Magazine, and Historical Chronicle*, XXXIV (1764), 261; Allan Kulikoff, *Tobacco and Slaves: The Development of Southern Cultures in the Chesapeake, 1680–1800* (Chapel Hill, N.C., 1986), 54–76; Darrett B. Rutman and Anita H. Rutman, *A Place in Time: Middlesex County, Virginia, 1650–1750* (New York, 1984), chap. 6; and Edmund S. Morgan, *American Slavery, American Freedom: The Ordeal of Colonial Virginia* (New York, 1975), chap. 15.

estates, and, by the 1750s, in some counties, any planter with movables worth £50 or more was more likely than not to own a slave.[9]

WHAT THESE CHANGES in the labor force and the activities it pursued meant to the lives of the inhabitants, bound and free, can be better understood by looking at working plantations. The operation of the Cole Plantation in St. Mary's County, Maryland, is a good example for the 1660s.[10] In 1652 Robert Cole, a Catholic yeoman from Heston in Middlesex, had settled with his wife and children on a three-hundred-acre freehold in St. Clement's Manor. Ten years later, he died on a visit to England, leaving five motherless children and a stepchild on his Maryland plantation. For the next eleven years, Cole's friend and neighbor, Luke Gardiner, watched over plantation activities and saw to it that the children were cared for and educated. When Cole's oldest child, Robert, became twenty-one, Gardiner's guardianship ended. In 1673 he submitted an account to the judge of probate, a document that offers a fascinating glimpse of how a seventeenth-century yeoman planter operated.

9. For tables to document these assertions, see Carr and Walsh, "Transformation of Production," *Working Papers*. We have found wealth divisions of £50 and £226 useful in defining social groups. Planters worth less than £50 in movable property included most tenants as well as many small landowners. In the 17th century, such men occasionally had servants; after 1700, almost never. Planters with £50–£225 in movables were usually landowners and much more likely than poorer men to have bound labor. Planters with £226 or more in movables not only had both land and labor but lived much more comfortably and fashionably than those below them. In the 17th century, inventoried estates worth less than £50 were, depending on the county, 40%–60% of the total. Those worth more than £225 were 8%–15%. Over the 18th century, the proportion of the bottom group decreased, and that of the top group increased, but we are not certain that this change does not, in part, represent a decline in the proportion of poor men who went through probate. In any case, since inventories are biased toward wealth (see Carr and Walsh, "Inventories and Analysis," *Hist. Meth.*, XIII [1980], 81–104), over the whole colonial period the proportion of the poor was much larger in the living population than among the inventoried, and the proportion of the top group was much smaller.

10. The following section is based on Robert Cole's will, an inventory he took himself of his movable assets, and a 10-year guardian account, 1662–1673, recorded in Wills 1, pp. 182–186, MS; and in Testamentary Proceedings 6, pp. 118–147, MS, both in Maryland State Archives, Annapolis. More detailed discussions of these records appear in Russell R. Menard, Lois Green Carr, and Lorena S. Walsh, "A Small Planter's Profits: The Cole Estate and the Growth of the Early Chesapeake Economy," *WMQ*, 3d Ser., XL (1983), 171–196; in Lorena Seebach Walsh, "Charles County, Maryland, 1658–1705: A Study of Chesapeake Social and Political Structure" (Ph.D. diss., Michigan State University, 1977), 262–305;

The amount of labor available was the key to land use in a newly settled region where land was cheap and the export crop, tobacco, was labor-intensive. Over the years of Gardiner's guardianship, 1662–1673, there were usually the equivalent of about four working male hands on the plantation. Two or three, at times four, were servants. As some became free, Gardiner purchased others. Cole's stepson and three sons were also sources of labor, part-time at first, but full hands once they reached age sixteen. This labor force kept about twenty-three acres of land in cultivation each year. About eleven acres were in corn, enough to feed the family and servants and pay three barrels rent due the lord of the manor. Tobacco, the cash crop, required about three acres per full-time hand. Consequently, about twelve acres per year, on the average, were in tobacco.[11]

Cultivation of these crops took all the time from mid-February, when special beds were prepared and planted with tobacco seed, through late September to mid-October, when the tobacco crop was fully housed. Cole had no plow, and all preparation of the ground was done with hoes. Corn fitted well into the schedule for tobacco. It was planted in April or May—before tobacco seedlings were ready to be transplanted—grew rapidly, and needed no weeding after late June to mid-July. At this time, worming and suckering, in addition to weeding, were essential for the tobacco. All male hands were needed for cutting tobacco, beginning late in August or early in September, since the crop had to be hung for curing in the tobacco houses before the first frost. The processes of stripping and packing cured tobacco might last into December, depending upon how weather affected curing, but time was also available for other work, including gathering and storing the ears of corn. This was also the convenient season for slaughtering hogs and cattle and salting them down for meat.[12]

Clearing the ground for planting food and export crops was just

---

and in Lois Green Carr, Russell R. Menard, and Lorena S. Walsh, "Robert Cole's World: Agriculture and Society in Early Maryland," MS, in preparation.

11. Carr, Menard, and Walsh, "Robert Cole's World," chap. 2.

12. For an excellent description of tobacco culture, see Main, *Tobacco Colony*, 31–35. An illuminating portrayal of corn culture, based on 18th-century sources but applicable to the mid-17th century, is offered in David O. Percy, "Agricultural Labor on an Eighteenth-Century Chesapeake Plantation" (paper presented to the 45th Conference in Early American History, Baltimore, Sept. 13, 1984), 13–20. See also Harold B. Gill, Jr., "Tobacco Culture in Colonial Virginia" (1972) and "Cereal Grains in Colonial Virginia" (1974) (unpublished reports prepared for the Colonial Williamsburg Foundation). For the timing of curing tobacco and gathering corn, see also Greene, ed., *Diary of Carter*, I, 133, 162, 189, 196, 510, 525, 532.

as important as cultivating and harvesting them. Tobacco could be grown in one spot for only four years, followed by a year (or possibly two) of corn. Thereafter, the ground had to lie fallow for twenty years to regain its fertility. In consequence, new land was required nearly every year. For the amount of land the Cole Plantation kept in production, probably each male adult hand cleared an acre or two most years, taking three or four weeks per acre in late fall and winter to do it.[13]

At first, Gardiner kept a hired housekeeper and an indentured woman servant on the plantation to tend the children and to cook and wash. In so large a household, the women had no time for field work, nor were they needed. Only about 110 acres of Cole's land was first-class soil, and the number of male hands available represented the most that could be used for tobacco and corn if the necessary rotation of crops and fallow were practiced. Many Chesapeake women were not so fortunate. In households too poor to purchase male servants sufficient to work the available land, what time women could spare from essential household duties was required in the fields to maximize production.

Gardiner retained the women only until the youngest child, Betty, was age seven. Betty was then boarded where she could attend school, and seven men and boys fended for themselves. It is likely that they lived far less comfortably than before—that less washing was done, for example, and more vermin abounded. The family probably also ate less well. Any vegetable growing, the province of women, was doubtless cut back or abandoned, and it may well be that no one milked, although the two youngest boys may have been assigned the task. Processing milk was entirely women's work. What milk was not drunk or used in cooking must have gone to the hogs, and surely no efforts were made to keep cows producing. They dried up when calves stopped sucking. Matters may have improved on Betty's return at age nine. Even so young a child could milk, wash,

13. On crop rotations, see Lewis Cecil Gray, *History of Agriculture in the Southern United States to 1860* (Gloucester, Mass., 1958 [orig. publ. Washington, D.C., 1932]), I, 215–216; Carville V. Earle, *The Evolution of a Tidewater Settlement System: All Hallows Parish, Maryland, 1650–1783*, University of Chicago Department of Geography Research Paper no. 170 (Chicago, 1975), 28–30. We have found no estimates of how long a single hand would take to clear an acre in the 17th century. Martin L. Primack has estimated that, in forest areas in the midwest in the 1850s, the median number of man-days to clear an acre was 33. However, girdling cut down on the time. "Land Clearing under Nineteenth-Century Techniques: Some Preliminary Calculations," *Jour. Econ. Hist.*, XXII (1962), 484.

and cook, although she must have required assistance, especially with the eighteen-gallon copper pot. However, little Betty died the following year, and the household was womanless once more.[14]

Although tobacco was the main cash crop, Gardiner's accounts show that, under his management, the plantation produced salable surpluses of livestock, hides, meat, tallow, butter (while the women were present), and cider. The chief income from these sources came from the sale of cattle, probably mostly pregnant cows, and salted or smoked beef and pork. Toward the end of his guardianship, income also derived from the sale of horses. Cole had owned none, but, in 1663, Gardiner had purchased a mare for the estate, and the investment was a spectacular success. By 1673, several mares had been sold, and there were thirty-odd horses to be divided among the heirs. There was a local market for such items, because new households were continually appearing in the area. In 1662 there were only twenty-five families within the five or six miles of the Cole Plantation (the maximum distance that made easy communication possible), but, by 1673, there were sixty households within this distance. New households needed pregnant cows and mares to start their own herds and might purchase meat, butter, or cider until their own supplies were adequate. The income from these surpluses was an important supplement to the Cole Plantation. Over the years of the Cole account, such income averaged more than a fifth of the total earned beyond the value of a comfortable subsistence.[15]

For planters starting out, of course, such supplement was not so available. Their livestock herds were not yet well established, their orchards hardly started. Their time was absorbed, instead, in clearing land and constructing housing and fencing. The majority of new planters, furthermore, were much poorer than Cole had been at his beginnings and took longer to acquire (or died before acquiring) the bound labor that helped to produce such surpluses. Nevertheless, those who did not die prematurely—as many did—could aspire to the comforts and opportunities that the Cole Plantation's operation represented.

What the labor force on the plantation did not do is as interesting as what it did. Gardiner hired a carpenter to build a new tobacco

14. On women's work, see Lois Green Carr and Lorena S. Walsh, "The Planter's Wife: The Experience of White Women in Seventeenth-Century Maryland," *WMQ*, 3d Ser., XXXIV (1977), 561; Main, *Tobacco Colony*, 175–177, 264.

15. Lorena S. Walsh, "Community Networks in the Colonial Chesapeake," in Carr, Morgan, and Russo, eds., *Chesapeake Society*; Menard, Carr, and Walsh, "A Small Planter's Profits," *WMQ*, 3d Ser., XL (1983), 183.

house and paid Cole's stepson to build a henhouse. A cooper regularly made casks for tobacco and other uses. Woodworking by the servants probably was confined to repair and to fencing. No one in the household made clothes, even when the women were on hand. A tailor came to the house each year to make and mend clothing for children and servants. Gardiner purchased tanned hides for mending shoes, but no one made shoes from scratch. New shoes for everyone were a regular item among purchases and probably were imports. Nor did anyone spin yarn or weave cloth. No equipment for the purpose was present. Similarly, no one made or repaired metal tools or pots and pans, nor was anyone in the neighborhood paid for such work. As hoes and axes wore out, Gardiner purchased new ones, and the supply of metal equipment for cooking dwindled with wear and tear. There is no sign that any of these products, with the possible exception of shoes, were purchased locally. This was a household entirely dependent upon imports for cloth, tools, and other manufactured equipment.

Cole's contemporaries had similar operations. Of the estates of householders in St. Mary's County inventoried through 1665, all had some livestock, nearly always including a cow. Milk and meat were available everywhere. On the other hand, none had plows or the equipment for yarn making or weaving or tools for blacksmith's work. Most tools, apart from hoes and axes necessary for clearing ground and planting corn and tobacco, were those needed for simple carpentry or coopering. The majority of households (57 percent) lacked even these.[16] Generally, labor time went into raising food for subsistence and growing tobacco for export.

Gardiner's accounts do not reveal much about working conditions for the Cole servants, except that suits and shoes to clothe them were regular expenditures. Cole had no separate building to house his laborers. Family and servants lived together in the dwelling house. Probably, the servants slept in the loft, along with some of the children, and shared meals and work with the family. On some plantations with work forces as large or larger, planters had separate quarters for servants. But, in the 1660s, the great majority of servant-owning households were organized like Cole's, and such planters owned the majority of servants.[17]

These facts indicate that, over the third quarter of the seventeenth century, most masters and servants shared work routines.[18] Small

16. SMCC Inventory File, St. Mary's County.
17. *Ibid.*
18. Lorena S. Walsh, "Servitude and Opportunity in Charles County, Mary-

and middling planters, the great majority of householders, worked with their hands and joined their servants in tasks about the farm. Their wives necessarily worked side by side with any woman servant they were lucky enough to own. Planters who had arrived with or acquired enough wealth to merit the title of gentleman might employ overseers—usually newly freed servants—to monitor their laborers and might confine participation in farm work to general supervision. But, otherwise, everyone shared in labor. Work routines were similar in servantless households, except that wives and children shared more of the field work.

Although work was hard on a New World tobacco plantation, even unfree laborers could usually command a certain amount of leisure time. In contrast to the apparently more industrious Puritan colonies, English work customs tended to prevail in the seventeenth-century Chesapeake, reinforced by the effects of a climate in which summers were hotter and winters colder than in Britain. The working day ran from sunrise to sunset, but John Hammond observed in 1656 that, even during the growing season, field laborers were permitted five hours rest in the heat of the day, Saturday afternoon off, and the "old Holidayes . . . observed." He also asserted that no work was done in winter except dressing victuals and making fires.[19] Sir John Colleton noted that laborers in Barbados worked the year round, but that Virginians worked diligently "but half the year." George Alsop, himself a former servant, stated that servants in Maryland worked only five and a half days a week, with three hours rest in the summer heat. During the three winter months, they generally did little but cut firewood and hunt. Although such promotional literature may well be suspect, other supporting evidence can

land, 1658–1705," in Land, Carr, and Papenfuse, eds., *Law, Society, and Politics*, 118–120; Lois Green Carr and Russell R. Menard, "Immigration and Opportunity: The Freedman in Early Colonial Maryland," in Thad W. Tate and David L. Ammerman, eds., *The Chesapeake in the Seventeenth Century: Essays on Anglo-American Society* (Chapel Hill, N.C., 1979), 228–229.

19. John Hammond, "Leah and Rachel; or, The Two Fruitful Sisters, Virginia and Mary-land," in *Narratives of Early Maryland, 1633–1684*, ed. Clayton Colman Hall, Original Narratives of Early American History (New York, 1925), 290. Hammond was apparently referring to pre-Reformation holidays. It would not be surprising if Maryland Catholics chose to observe holidays that Protestant reformers in England had worked hard to abolish. It seems doubtful that this practice would have been officially sanctioned in Virginia, where the Anglican church was legally established. In 1638 Maryland's assembly declared that "no such customs" of "resting of servants on Satterdaies in the afternoon" was to be enacted. William Hand Browne et al., eds., *Archives of Maryland*, 72 vols. to date (Baltimore, 1883–), I, 21.

be found. In 1657, for example, Maryland's provincial court ruled that a master could not keep his servants in the fields so long that they must beat corn for their victuals at night, except "in case of necessity." In Lancaster County, Virginia, in 1661, the court enjoined a servant owner from asking his laborers to "doe any kind of Labour after day light shutt in." In England itself, as E. P. Thompson has pointed out, the custom of free Saturday afternoons for agricultural laborers continued at least into the eighteenth century. One writer declared that, in country places on Saturday afternoons, "the Labours of the Plough Ceast, and Refreshment and Ease are over all the Village."[20]

Custom ruled not only work hours but other conditions of servants' lives. Maryland and Virginia law required only that masters provide "sufficient" food, clothing, and shelter; a Sunday free of hard labor; and moderation in correction.[21] In practice, masters varied, and it was up to the courts, to which servants could and did turn, to define what provision was adequate and to determine when correction became mistreatment. In making these decisions, the judges considered, foremost, what was customary. In this immigrant society, customs of the mother country might be modified in the light of New World conditions, usually to the detriment of the laborer, but they could not be entirely eradicated and had the concurrence of most of the local community. Servants might be forced to eat unfamiliar food, but they could not go unfed; they might be worked to exhaustion five or six days a week, but, on Sunday, they could rest.[22]

20. Sir John Colleton to Peter Carteret, Sept. 9, 1665, in William S. Powell, ed., *Ye Countie of Albemarle in Carolina: A Collection of Documents, 1664–1675* (Raleigh, N.C., 1958), 8; George Alsop, "A Character of the Province of Mary-land [1666]," in Hall, ed., *Narratives of Maryland*, 357. Cf. Morgan, *American Slavery*, chaps. 3 and 4; Browne *et al.*, eds., *Archives*, X, 521; and Rutman and Rutman, *A Place in Time*, 133; H. Bourne, *Antiquitates Vulgares* (Newcastle, 1725), quoted in E. P. Thompson, "Time, Work-Discipline, and Industrial Capitalism," *Past and Present*, no. 38 (Dec. 1967), 72 n. 57.

21. Browne *et al.*, eds., *Archives*, VII, 51, XIII, 426, 457; William Waller Hening, ed., *The Statues at Large, Being a Collection of All the Laws of Virginia . . .* , 13 vols. (Richmond, Va., 1819–1823), I, 440, II, 48, 117–118.

22. Raw and unsettled conditions in the very early years of Virginia enabled some labor owners to exploit their servants brutally, but it is our opinion that, once settlements were more firmly established and local governments were functioning, such severe exploitation was kept in check. The importance of both English custom and local opinion is suggested by the nature of servants' complaints, their attempts to secure free members of the local community to testify in their behalf, and the willingness of neighbors to inform the court of abuses of indentured orphans. The case for continued exploitation is presented in Morgan, *American Slavery*, chaps. 1–6; T. H. Breen, *Puritans and Adventurers: Change and*

Chesapeake servants had protections; nevertheless, they had given up some freedoms possessed by servants in England. In England, servants in husbandry contracted for work by the year, and their labor could not be bought or sold without their consent.[23] But the Chesapeake servant owed for transportation across an ocean. His labor was the property of another for a four- or five-year term and was salable like any other form of property. Furthermore, penalties for running away or for costing a master time by bearing a child were severe and could lead to months or years of additional service. There was probably also greater tolerance in the Chesapeake than in England for abuse of servants, especially those too sick or too unhappy to work diligently. Planter-judges had heavy investments in their servants and could sympathize with masters whose bound laborers could not or would not work. On the other hand, there was a recompense for the servants, once free, if they did not die too soon: the opportunity to become planters and even masters and mistresses themselves.[24]

Servants on the Cole Plantation seem to have been treated well, although one ran away and was eventually sold and replaced by another more amenable. Gardiner recorded no costs for time spent at court in connection with servants' complaints. Calculations made

---

Persistence in Early America (New York, 1980), chap. 6; and Breen and Stephen Innes, *"Myne Owne Ground": Race and Freedom on Virginia's Eastern Shore, 1640–1676* (New York, 1980). See also Joseph Douglas Deal III, "Race and Class in Colonial Virginia: Indians, Englishmen, and Africans on the Eastern Shore during the Seventeenth Century" (Ph.D. diss., University of Rochester, 1981). For countering arguments, see Russell R. Menard, "From Servant to Freeholder: Status Mobility and Property Accumulation in Seventeenth-Century Maryland," *WMQ*, 3d Ser., XXX (1973), 37–64; Carr and Menard, "Immigration and Opportunity," in Tate and Ammerman, eds., *The Chesapeake in the Seventeenth Century*, 206–242; Walsh, "Servitude and Opportunity," in Land, Carr, and Papenfuse, eds., *Law, Society, and Politics*, chap. 4; and Lois Green Carr, "Sources of Political Stability and Upheaval in Seventeenth-Century Maryland," *Maryland Historical Magazine*, LXXIX (1984), 46.

23. For working conditions of agricultural servants in England, see Ann Kussmaul, *Servants in Husbandry in Early Modern England* (Cambridge, 1981). Kussmaul concludes that service in husbandry was "for the most part . . . a private institution, practised within the farmer's family, defined not by law but by custom" (31).

24. Carr, "Sources of Political Stability," *Md. Hist. Mag.*, LXXIX (1984), 52. This is not to deny that some labor owners had ample scope and opportunity to abuse their unfree workers. The wheels of justice ground slowly, then as now. However, more responsible county benches, at least, would eventually give aggrieved servants the benefit of the doubt, even to the point of disciplining one of their own members who had established a record for abusing his servants.

from the account of meat slaughtered but not sold suggest plenty of protein in everyone's diet; otherwise, food would have gone to waste, a very unlikely event. Clothing made for servants was similar to that supplied the children. Freedom dues were regularly paid as the servants left the household. It is unlikely that these servants had much occasion to complain.

The Cole Plantation shows the seventeenth-century Chesapeake labor system at its best, both in productivity and in working conditions. How exceptional the plantation may have been is another question. Certainly not every planter had servants who worked as successfully or suffered as little, and contemporary opinion was divided as to the humanity of indentured servitude. What is certain is that, until close to the end of the century, former servants must have constituted the majority of planters. Many freemen did not enjoy this kind of success, especially those who died early or who became free after the 1670s and faced a stagnating economy. But those who did succeed were the backbone of seventeenth-century Chesapeake society.[25]

THE SHIFT from servants to slaves changed much of the character of the Chesapeake work system. Slaves were in evidence in Cole's day, although he had none, and slavery was well established on Maryland's lower western shore by the turn of the century. In the 1660s, fewer than a fifth of all bound laborers were slaves, but, shortly after 1700, two-thirds were slaves. Servants still dominated some parts of the Chesapeake, such as the Eastern Shore of Maryland, but the future lay with slavery.[26]

So long as slaves were few and intermingled with servants, work rules for whites probably also applied to blacks. But, once slaves became dominant in the bound labor force, late in the seventeenth century, the experiences of slaves and servants began to diverge. Slaves had no claim to English workers' customary rights to food of reasonable quantity and quality, adequate clothing and shelter, and a certain amount of rest and leisure. And, across the last half of the century, laws stripped the slaves of any significant freedom for themselves or their children and denied them any security for their

25. Carr and Menard, "Immigration and Opportunity," in Tate and Ammerman, eds., *The Chesapeake in the Seventeenth Century*, 232–235; Main, *Tobacco Colony*, 113–115, 118–123.

26. Proportions are calculated from Russell Menard, "From Servants to Slaves: The Transformation of the Chesapeake Labor System," *Southern Studies*, XVI (1977), 369, table 5.

persons against whatever brutality any white chose to inflict, much less any right to hold property. After slaves had become a majority, their working conditions began to deteriorate and ultimately affected conditions provided for all bound laborers.[27]

Planters began by imposing new, more stringent work routines.[28] First, the number of workdays was increased. For servants as well as slaves, holidays were reduced to three events a year—Christmas (the duration of the holiday was a matter for the discretion of the master) and the Monday and Tuesday following Easter and Whitsuntide. In addition, for slaves on almost all plantations, Saturday became a full workday, and the same rule began to be applied to servants. By the 1730s, in Virginia, only skilled servants who arrived under indenture could claim the customary Saturday afternoon. In Maryland, by the 1760s, free laborers also worked all day on Saturday. When aggregating daily wages for hired labor into monthly payments, Dr. Charles Carroll of Annapolis, for example, figured twenty-six working days to the month.[29]

An especially revealing example of this new, stricter labor regime for white servants is found in a letter John, Robert, Charles, and Colonel Robert Carter wrote to London merchant Edward Athawes, in 1732, attempting to ascertain the prevailing work customs for English miners. The Carters had acquired some Falmouth miners and other indentured servants to work in a copper mine that they owned jointly. They wrote that the miners, unhappy with the longer working hours in Virginia, "plead as the customs of miners that every red letter day are holy days to them and that Saturdays in the afternoon are their own. . . . Upon this pretense they have made so many holy days which we never heard of before." The miners, therefore, not

27. For the development of slave codes, see Morgan, *American Slavery*; and Breen and Innes, *"Myne Owne Ground,"* and sources cited therein. Morgan (126–130) discusses the refusal of white Virginians to extend the rights of Englishmen to blacks with respect to law. He does not take up the more ambiguous issue of customary rights.

28. The parts of this essay that deal with slave work roles are an outgrowth of Walsh's work in progress on plantation management in the Chesapeake, 1620–1820, conducted for the Colonial Williamsburg Foundation.

29. Dr. Charles Carroll of Annapolis, Account Book, 1754–1784, MS 211, pp. 25, 28, Maryland Historical Society, Baltimore; Robert Carter Letterbooks, 1731–1732, Alderman Library, University of Virginia. It is, of course, possible that working conditions for English laborers were also deteriorating in this period and that what we are seeing is part of a general trend throughout the North Atlantic economy. Thompson, in "Time, Work-Discipline, and Capitalism," *Past and Present*, no. 38 (Dec. 1967), 56–97, suggests that this may have been the case, as employees shifted from task orientation to timed labor.

only wanted the customary Saturday afternoons off, but they also wanted to observe the Catholic calendar with its some 130 feast days. They protested the New World of unrelenting work by slowdowns and shoddy workmanship.[30]

For slaves, the work regimen was stricter still; even Sundays were far from inviolable. The house servants were the worst off, for they were expected to prepare meals for and to serve numerous guests. Field laborers were less likely to be forced to work on the Lord's Day, but they too had to respond to situations the master declared to be an emergency—everything from housing tobacco in danger of being damaged by rain, to a wheat harvest behind schedule, to a maple sugar run. The slaves' workday, furthermore, more often was extended into the night. Night work probably originated with the need to beat corn into meal with mortars and pestles daily. In 1679 Jaspar Dankers, traveling on Maryland's upper Eastern Shore, observed, "The servants and negroes after they have worn themselves down the whole day, and come home to rest, have yet to grind and pound the grain, which is generally maize, for their masters and all their families as well as themselves, and all the negroes, to eat." Beginning in the 1690s, the construction of gristmills, at least in some older-settled areas, substantially reduced or entirely eliminated this task.

However, as growers of sweet-scented tobacco in Virginia commenced further processing of their crops by stripping the tobacco leaves from their stems, a new evening chore was created, and, eventually, oronoco growers also began to strike tobacco after dark. By the 1770s, for example, Landon Carter was requiring his slaves to tie up ninety tobacco plants into hands each night. In addition, once planters began to grow corn for export as well as for home use, there was more shucking and shelling to do. All these added tasks could be done by firelight, and increasing numbers of masters required such work regularly. By 1789, Thomas Anburey stated that, after dusk, "each has a task of stripping allotted which takes them up some hours, or else they have such a quantity of Indian corn to husk, and if they neglect it, are tied up in the morning, and receive a number of lashes." In 1808 tobacco grower Leonard Covington of Calvert County, Maryland, was contemplating a move to the Mississippi territory to become a cotton planter. He planned to send his slaves west ahead of the family and to rent them out for the first year to an already established planter. He also wanted to ensure that they would not be used too rigorously. He considered it necessary to inquire from a relative there whether night work was expected, as it

30. Carter Letterbooks.

had come to be in the Chesapeake, or whether, by custom in cotton country, slaves were "only compelled to work from 'sun to sun.' "³¹

Finally, both summer and winter work intensified. Most whites believed that blacks were better able to work in intense heat than they, and, whatever the truth, the slaves had little choice in the matter. Apparently, only on the most sultry days were work routines relaxed. In addition, midday breaks were kept to a minimum. If planters of the 1650s and 1660s found little to do in December, January, and February, a century later there was plenty of work to fill all but the most inclement winter days as well. As markets for timber and casks in the West Indies and the Wine Islands expanded, and localized urban demand for firewood and lumber developed, more timber was cut and carted in winter. Small grains, threshed out, if possible, immediately after harvest, remained to be winnowed and the seed picked over in the off-season. Planters who wished to improve their lands found this an optimal period for grubbing swamps and cleaning pastures. The agricultural year was filled.³²

31. Published sources that document weekly work routines, including demands for labor on Sundays, include Louis B. Wright and Marion Tinling, eds., *The Secret Diary of William Byrd of Westover, 1709–1712* (Richmond, Va., 1941); and Greene, ed., *Diary of Carter*. An entry in the *Journal of Jaspar Danckaerts, 1679–1680*, ed. Bartlett Burleigh James and J. Franklin Jameson, Original Narratives of Early American History (New York, 1913), 133 (quotation), suggests a clear link between tobacco, slaves, and a diminution of the customary privileges of white laborers. The following document night work: *Diary of Carter*, I, 357, 492, 495, 519, 616; Thomas Anburey, *Travels through the Interior Parts of America* (Boston, 1923 [orig. publ. 1789]), 192–193; and Leonard Covington, Aquasco, Maryland, to Alexander Covington in Mississippi, in Ulrich B. Phillips, ed., *Plantation and Frontier: Documents: 1649–1863*, 2 vols. (Cleveland, Ohio, 1909), II, 201–203. By the end of the 19th century, English servants in husbandry were also expected to do odd jobs in the evening, such as mending shoes and tools, beating hemp, stamping apples, grinding malt, and threshing grain. See Kussmaul, *Servants in Husbandry*, chap. 3. For a discussion of the effects of seasonal variation, specific crop requirements, and local custom on the length of the slaves' workday in another area, see B. W. Higman, *Slave Populations of the British Caribbean, 1807–1834* (Baltimore, 1984), 182–188.

32. For seasonal routines, see the published diaries of William Byrd and Landon Carter; Donald Jackson and Dorothy Twohig, eds., *The Diaries of George Washington*, 6 vols. (Charlottesville, Va., 1976–1979); Ralph Emmett Fall, ed., *The Diary of Robert Rose: A View of Virginia by a Scottish Colonial Parson, 1746–1751* (Verona, Va., 1977); "Journal of Col. James Gordon, of Lancaster County, Va.," *WMQ*, 1st Ser., XI (1902–1903), 98–112, 195–205, 217–236, XII (1903–1904), 1–12; Robert Carter Diary, MS, Alderman Library; and especially the Journal of Work on Plantations, [1786]–1787, MS, Additional Washington Family Papers, series 9, container 26, Library of Congress. Ralph V. Anderson, "Labor Utilization and Productivity, Diversification and Self Sufficiency, Southern Plantations, 1800–

Slave women shared plantation tasks with slave men. Initially, Englishmen, newly introduced to slave labor, were uncertain how to employ female slaves in plantation agriculture. In the early 1630s, Captain Roger Wood, writing from Bermuda, asked Bermuda Company officials for instructions about three slave women and their ten children belonging to the company, for "they doe little else than to looke to theire children for no man wilbe troubled with them." By the 1650s, however, Chesapeake planters had no doubts that slave women should perform field labor. Labor-short planters were even putting some white servant women to work at the hoe, although with a certain ambivalence about the types of work proper for female servants. A promotional tract of the 1650s asserted that only a few "nasty" wenches not fit for anything else performed field labor, but evidence from seventeenth-century court records suggests that some female servants always did field work, while early acts defining taxable laborers periodically recognized a class of servant women who worked primarily in tobacco.[33] However, once slaves predominated in the labor force, references to white women servants working in the fields all but disappear. Eighteenth-century plantation accounts show almost every able-bodied slave woman, and most slave girls aged twelve or above, assigned to regular field labor.

The size of work units undoubtedly affected the work experience of laborers. The larger the unit, the more likely that they worked in gangs—"a number of Negroes [or servants] follow[ing] each other's tail the day long," as an observer of the 1770s described it. Gang labor in the tobacco and cornfields, under supervision of an overseer, must have been the most monotonous and least satisfying kind of work for those condemned to do it daily.[34]

1840" (Ph.D. diss., University of North Carolina at Chapel Hill, 1974), found that, by the early 19th century, in North and South Carolina, Georgia, Alabama, and Mississippi, slaves were employed almost to capacity year-round—an average of 290 days a year with 75 days off (52 Sundays and 20 days lost to holidays, illness, or bad weather). The more diversified the plantation, the more fully was all labor time employed.

33. J. H. Lefroy, ed., *Memorials of the Discovery and Early Settlement of the Bermudas or Somers Islands, 1515–1685*, 2 vols. (Bermuda, 1932 [orig. publ. 1876], I, 539 n. 1 (quotation); Hammond, "Leah and Rachel," in Hall, ed., *Narratives of Maryland*, 290–291; Morgan, *American Slavery*, 400–401 (on 17th-century Virginia tithable legislation); John A. Kinnaman, "The Public Levy in Colonial Maryland to 1689," *Md. Hist. Mag.*, LIII (1958), 253–274.

34. [Janet Schaw], *Journal of a Lady of Quality: Being the Narrative of a Journey from Scotland to the West Indies, North Carolina, and Portugal, in the Years 1774 to 1776*, ed. Evangeline Walker Andrews and Charles McLean Andrews (New Haven, Conn., 1923), 163 (quotation); cf. Isaac Weld, Jr., *Travels through the States of North America*

There were upper and lower bounds to the sizes of gangs. Large slaveowners found it most efficient to divide their slaves into work groups of from six to seventeen working hands; nine to twelve workers were the most common. While the majority of slaveowners did not own so many workers, gang labor did appear on smaller plantations. We have made two assumptions about gang labor. First, there must be a minimum of three laborers working side by side to have a gang. Second, even on the least diversified plantation there were enough needful tasks aside from cultivation (cutting, hauling, and chopping firewood; fetching water; mending or constructing fences; tending livestock; and the like) to occupy at least one laborer most of the time. Therefore, we have assumed that gang work was probably not a regular experience on quarters with fewer than four bound laborers.[35]

Given these limitations, what proportion of all workers suffered the experience of working in gangs? In Anne Arundel County, Maryland, gang work affected the majority of laborers and increased over the colonial period, although it never appeared on the majority of plantations (see table 1). In the seventeenth century, despite the fact that two-thirds of inventoried planters had work units of fewer than four laborers, fewer than one-third of the total number of laborers worked in these small units, and, beginning early in the eighteenth century, labor became even more concentrated. By the mid-eighteenth century, only about a fifth to a quarter of all inventoried laborers—by then, nearly all slaves—worked in units of one to three. Over the whole colonial period, another quarter to one-third worked in groups of four to six, where there was probably some mixture of group labor and individual assignments, depending upon the task and the season. Before the 1680s, when servants still dominated the

. . . (New York, 1968 [orig. publ. 1807]), 133. Usually, slave work systems are classified as either gang or task labor. The first implies regimented work in closely supervised groups throughout the customary working day, and the second involves less supervision, with slaves assigned a certain amount of work for the day, after which they might use any time remaining as they pleased. See Gray, *History of Agriculture*, I, 550–551; and Philip D. Morgan, "Work and Culture: The Task System and the World of Lowcountry Blacks, 1700 to 1880," *WMQ*, 3d Ser., XXXIX (1982), 563–599, as well as Morgan's essay in this volume. Walsh's evidence from account books suggests that, in the Chesapeake, fewer slaves than historians once thought normally worked in groups.

35. The word "quarter" was used both to denote slave cottages and to indicate a plantation at a distance from the home farm. In Anne Arundel County, work units can be studied, because probate inventories usually list slaves and equipment by quarters. In most counties, inventories do not usually locate slaves by quarters but list them together, making a study of work units impossible.

labor force, work units of seven or more contained 30 percent of all bound laborers, but, thereafter, the proportion ranged from 40 to 50 percent until the American Revolution. In these work units, gang labor was a regular experience for most participants.

Still, growing diversification had a mitigating effect, but, at first, more for whites than for blacks. As many planters began to cultivate new crops, use plows and carts, produce a greater variety of foods, and engage in more import-replacement activities, the variety of tasks increased. Early on, white male servants or free laborers performed almost all the artisanal work. The planter's wife, along with white female servants, did most of the domestic work and dairying. What little plowing was done was probably most often assigned to English servants already familiar with this method of cultivation. The slaves, by contrast, continued to grow corn and tobacco with hoes and axes in ones and twos (or in larger mixed gangs), depending on the size of the holding. Even when planters added wheat to their market crop mix, there was often no change. Robert "King" Carter, for example, grew sizable wheat crops on fields prepared only with hoes, the seed scratched in with brush, and the grain carried to the barns on the heads or backs of the slaves. The brunt of land clearing also fell on the slaves. When quarters were set up on new tracts or additional working units added to the home plantation, a group of slaves was sent out to make the new farm.[36]

Indeed, by 1724, work roles for whites and blacks apparently had diverged sufficiently that Hugh Jones could speculate on the possibilities for two sorts of agriculture in the region, their nature determined entirely by race. More poor Englishmen, he thought, ought to be imported to pursue crafts while in service and then to take up "English husbandry" in the backcountry. "They need not be employed about Tobacco and Corn," he added, "for that might be compleatly managed by the *Negroes*." In fact, the market for servants was already reflecting this appraisal. Over the years 1718–1759, servants who came from London to the Chesapeake with indentures were much more likely to have skills than had been their seventeenth-century counterparts.[37]

36. Greene, ed., *Diary of Carter*, II, 1038–1039; Hugh Jones, *The Present State of Virginia* (London, 1724), 137–138; Gregory A. Stiverson and Patrick H. Butler III, "Virginia in 1732: The Travel Journal of William Hugh Grove," *Virginia Magazine of History and Biography*, LXXXV (1977), 44. For a good description of the process of settling a frontier quarter in the early 18th century, see the letter of Robert Carter to Robert Jones, Oct. 10, 1727, Carter Letterbooks, 1727–1728, Alderman Library.

37. Jones, *State of Virginia*, 136; David W. Galenson, *White Servitude in Colonial America: An Economic Analysis* (Cambridge, 1981), 51–64.

TABLE 1

Division of Laborers into Work Units, Anne Arundel County

Size of Work Unit[a]	Units (N)	Laborers (N)	All Units (%)	All Laborers (%)
		1658–1677		
1–3	41	80	67	41
4–6	13	57	21	29
7–9	6	36	10	23
10+	1	13	2	7
Total	61	186	100	100
		1678–1687		
1–3	32	59	65	31
4–6	8	39	16	21
7–9	5	39	10	21
10+	4	52	8	28
Total	49	189	99[b]	101
		1688–1699		
1–3	50	77	67	31
4–6	15	74	20	30
7–9	5	38	7	15
10+	5	59	7	24
Total	75	248	101	100
		1700–1709		
1–3	49	86	67	32
4–6	15	71	21	27
7–9	5	62	7	23
10+	4	46	5	17
Total	73	265	100	99
		1710–1722		
1–3	38	71	56	28
4–6	19	85	28	33
7–9	7	54	10	21
10+	4	47	6	18
Total	68	257	100	100

Table 1. Continued

Size of Work Unit[a]	Units (N)	Laborers (N)	All Units (%)	All Laborers (%)
		1723–1732		
1–3	30	59	48	20
4–6	17	84	27	28
7–9	10	80	16	27
10+	6	75	10	25
Total	63	298	101	100
		1733–1744		
1–3	68	204	54	34
4–6	41	210	32	35
7–9	10	81	8	14
10+	8	98	6	17
Total	127	593	100	100
		1745–1754		
1–3	56	97	51	21
4–6	32	156	29	34
7–9	13	101	12	22
10+	9	106	8	23
Total	110	460	100	100
		1755–1767		
1–3	84	140	55	21
4–6	36	175	24	26
7–9	18	132	12	20
10+	14	219	9	33
Total	152	666	100	100
		1768–1777		
1–3	58	112	51	23
4–6	31	150	27	30
7–9	14	110	12	22
10+	10	122	9	23
Total	113	494	99	98

Source: Anne Arundel County Inventories.
Notes: [a]Quarters with servants only, slaves only, and both servants and slaves were first tabulated separately. As there were no differences in size distributions, they are combined in this table.   [b]Deviations in totaling from 100% are due to rounding.

Diversification, nevertheless, ultimately reached the work of slaves and helped effect a shift for some from gang to task labor. Plantation accounts from a variety of areas show that, as time went on, and particularly after mid-century, more slaves than earlier were assigned to different individual tasks. With the increasing variety of activities undertaken throughout all seasons, the chance that gang labor prevailed in units of fewer than seven workers must have diminished considerably. In Anne Arundel County, the proportion of slaves normally working in gangs very probably declined from about three-quarters early in the century to about half by the time of the American Revolution. A somewhat similar change, with probable variations in timing, was occurring throughout the Chesapeake.

THE EFFECTS of these shifts, both in economic activity and in the organization of labor to carry it out, can be seen in a study of the Town Land of St. Mary's County in the mid-eighteenth century. The Town Land, located about twenty miles south of St. Clement's Manor, was some eighteen hundred acres along the St. Mary's River and included the site of Maryland's first settlement. After 1660, a village had developed in one corner to service growing government functions, but it disappeared quickly after the capital was moved to Annapolis in 1695. By the 1740s, the "metropolis of Maryland"—in fact, probably never more than a few dozen or so structures—was only a memory, kept alive by scattered signs of ruins and by the statehouse built in 1676. This large brick building still stood and served as a Church of England chapel. But, otherwise, the Town Land was an agricultural settlement like any other in the county.[38]

Town Land inhabitants represented a wide range of social levels in Maryland society at mid-century.[39] At the top was William Deacon,

38. Lois Green Carr, "'The Metropolis of Maryland': A Comment on Town Development along the Tobacco Coast," *Md. Hist. Mag.*, LXIX (1974), 124–145; and "Ceramics from the John Hicks Site, 1723–1743: The St. Mary's Town Land Community," in Ian M. G. Quimby, ed., *Ceramics in America* (Charlottesville, Va., 1973), 75–102.

39. Except as noted, the following analysis is based on Carr, "Town Land," in Quimby, ed., *Ceramics*, 75–102; and on the following MS documents, except as noted. For William Deacon: Wills 30, pp. 819–820; Inventories 70, pp. 72–82; Accounts 47, pp. 227–228; and Accounts 61, pp. 115–116. For John Hicks: Wills 28, pp. 517–518; Inventories 55, pp. 27–30; and Inventories 57, p. 59. For William Hicks: Wills 30, pp. 497–498 (William Hebb); Chancery Papers, Nos. 5783 and 5668; Summaries of William Hicks Factorage Accounts, Cumbria County Record Office, Carlisle (Xerox at Historic St. Mary's City History Office at the Maryland State Archives). For Daniel Clocker III: Wills 25, pp. 94–95. For Daniel Clocker IV: Wills 34, p. 97; Inventories 91, pp. 89–90; Accounts 62, pp. 401–402. For Joseph

Esq., royal collector of customs for the North Potomac District, a justice of the peace, and one of the few very wealthy men in the county. At his death, in 1759, he had about 350 acres of generally first-rate land—for many years he owned much more—and £1,307 in movable property and credits. Deacon's neighbor, John Hicks (at various times a county justice, the county sheriff, and a justice of the provincial court) was a retired sea captain and probably a merchant as well as a planter. He was also well off, perhaps in the top 8–10 percent of St. Mary's County planters whose estates were inventoried over those years, but not nearly so wealthy as Deacon. At his death, Hicks had about 350 acres of some of the best Town Land and £427 in movables. Other households fell much further down on the social scale. All family members worked with their hands, and no one had more than 200 acres. Among the landowners, Thomas Ingalls was a joiner; the Daniel Clockers, father and son (third and fourth generation of that name on their land), were small planters; and Mary Taylor, widow, was a weaver. Her deceased husband, Joseph, had been a blacksmith. Only Ingalls possessed bound labor, one servant, whereas Deacon and Hicks were well supplied with slaves, and only the Taylors had genuinely excellent land. The tenant farmers, whoever they were, were the poorest householders, with movables probably worth less than £50.[40] By contrast, Ingalls, at his death, had £141 in movables; Taylor had £72; and Daniel Clocker, the younger, had only £44, but he also owned his land.

Procedures for the cultivation of tobacco and corn differed little from those of the seventeenth century (except that plows were now often used), but the introduction of other grains added new work routines. Deacon and Ingalls grew wheat, and Ingalls had a bit of rye. By the mid-eighteenth century, it was the practice to sow wheat or rye in between corn hills or on old cornfields, which, for a year or two, might produce six bushels of grain to the acre. The productivity was low, but the land was already cleared, and the labor time required was small and usually not competitive with the needs of tobacco. Once the ground was plowed and sowed in the fall—after the tobacco was housed—the crop needed no attention until spring. Some weeding might then be desirable but could be forgone if necessary. Harvesting would take inconvenient time in mid-summer, but,

Taylor: Wills 20, pp. 657–658; Inventories 17, pp. 166–167; Accounts 12, p. 510; Accounts 16, pp. 87–88. For Thomas Ingalls: Wills 28, p. 307; Inventories 51, pp. 67–71; Accounts 34, pp. 159–161. All values have been transformed into constant pounds.

40. Among identified tenants inventoried in St. Mary's County, the majority had movables worth less than £50 (St. Mary's County Inventory Files).

here, young children could be of major assistance. While threshing the grain for next year's seed needed to be done quickly to ensure high quality, other threshing and winnowing could be a fall and winter activity, after the demands of tobacco had diminished. By one estimate of the required time, the wheat that one full-time male hand could raise took about 22 ten-hour days, as opposed to 113 days for tobacco and 27 days for corn. With the help of his family, even a small planter could add small grains to his diet and to his marketable crops.[41]

Nevertheless, in this part of Maryland, tobacco was still the major cash crop.[42] Maximum tobacco production per hand at mid-century on the Town Land can be estimated only from Hicks's estate and only on the supposition that the nineteen hogsheads his son, William, shipped to England in 1753 and 1754 represented the crops made on the plantation in 1752 and 1753. At the prevailing weight of hogsheads, this came to about 18,800 pounds of tobacco.[43] To raise these crops, the plantation had four male and four female adult slaves. Since a female slave produced only three-quarters of what a male could raise, each male slave must have produced close to 1,350 pounds. This estimate of the yield omits trash tobacco but probably includes what the tobacco inspectors termed seconds. The total of 1,350 pounds was less than the yields of the early eighteenth century, but whether because the land was less productive, or because Hicks was raising some corn or rye, is not clear.[44]

Deacon's operation was the most heavily diversified. He certainly raised tobacco, but much labor time clearly went into other activities.[45] One of his slaves was a blacksmith worth forty-five pounds (in

41. These estimates are developed from Percy, "Agricultural Labor."

42. Carr, "Diversification in the Colonial Chesapeake," in Carr, Morgan, and Russo, eds., *Chesapeake Society.*

43. Hicks Factorage Accounts, Schedule D. The figure used for hogshead weights is a mean of the weights found throughout the accounts.

44. Walsh's recent work with planter account books indicates that usually only trash tobacco was burned and that this was a small fraction of the crop. By law, overseers had to make their employers' satisfaction out of their share of the crop for any tobacco burned. Where this is mentioned in the accounts of planters with their overseers, the amount burned was no more than 5% of the crop. When tobacco inspection acts were first debated, some planters feared that inferior grades of tobacco, as well as pure trash, would be destroyed; however, there is no evidence that this, in fact, became standard practice in either colony. Using Anne Arundel County inventories, Earle estimated a higher proportion of trash, 20%. If this estimate is closer to the true loss, Hicks's male slaves produced 1,620 pounds per hand. Earle, *Evolution of a Tidewater Settlement,* 26.

45. Tobacco is missing from Deacon's inventory accounts, but the Hicks Factor-

constant pounds), as opposed to the thirty-four pounds for a prime-age field hand, and Deacon owned a substantial amount of smithing equipment. Another slave must have made and repaired shoes, although probably not as a full-time occupation. No slave is valued as a shoemaker. Deacon also had an investment in equipment for building and repairing boats. For this activity, he may have hired free labor, since no slave is valued as a carpenter, but at least one of the male hands probably worked in the boatyard. At one time, Deacon had also operated a gristmill on a small but unreliable stream that bounded his land, and he had invested in a larger mill near the head of the St. Mary's River.

Deacon's field hands produced more than tobacco for market; they also raised surpluses of corn. His inventory shows much more corn on hand than would be needed before the next crop was in, and it may be that all ninety barrels appraised were intended for sale.[46] The slaves also raised wheat, but, if they produced a surplus, this, like the tobacco, must have been sold before Deacon's death. In addition, cypress logs and forty thousand shingles were on hand. Making shingles was a wintertime occupation for slaves, and shingles could be either marketed locally or exported.

Although gang labor seems likely on Deacon's plantations, his operations offered a variety of activities in addition to work in the fields. Four blacks—two prime male hands, a young woman, and a boy—were listed as "at the House." One is tempted to believe that Deacon, with candelabra on his walls or ceilings ("six Brass Condors fast to the freehold") and an extraordinary 70 pounds worth of clothing, was enough of a grandee to employ all four slaves in the household. With no children to provide for, he could afford such conspicuous consumption. On the other hand, Deacon's house, while large and comfortable (forty-eight by thirty feet with four rooms on each floor and a separate kitchen), was not a great Chesapeake mansion. One can imagine liveried footmen in Governor Horatio Sharpe's pleasure dome at Whitehall, near Annapolis, but not in Deacon's small corner of St. Mary's.[47] Doubtless, Priscilla and the boy, Ben,

---

age Accounts, Schedule B, show two sales of tobacco, between 2,000 and 3,000 pounds each, by Deacon to Hicks, sometime between 1757 and 1760. Unfortunately, it is possible that a man in Deacon's position sold his tobacco to more than one merchant or that he also consigned directly. His crops may have been much larger.

46. We do not know whether corn for the family was systematically excluded from inventories. It must have been, in many cases, since many inventories contain no corn.

47. For a discussion of Sharpe's Whitehall, see Charles Scarlett, Jr., "Governor

assisted Deacon's housekeeper full-time, but James and Ignatius probably varied work in the boatyard or on the farm with service in the house.

How Deacon's slave work force was otherwise divided in its labors is impossible to prove, because we do not know the size of his field crops and hence the labor time they would require. Speculation, however, is possible. Toney presumably worked full-time in his smithy—located at the mill near the head of the river—and performed no field labor at all; his skills likely served all the neighborhood. The shoemaker probably worked at his craft primarily in winter and was in the fields during the growing season. If no slaves worked in the boatyard—or, say, only James and Ignatius did—then four males and three females in their twenties and thirties and a nearly grown boy spent all their time at plantation tasks: raising tobacco, corn, and wheat; keeping track of livestock; caring for vegetables and orchards; maintaining buildings and fences; and cutting firewood. They had assistance from fifty-year-old Ned (unless he was the shoemaker) and two old women, both valued at less than half a hand. Four children, aged seven to nine, also provided some labor, although they were too young to perform major field work. Six children under six and three blacks too decrepit to work (one was valued at only a shilling) made no discernible contribution.

Given the varied signs of diversification, Deacon may have been investing less in tobacco and more in grain than were most of his neighbors. Perhaps he even followed the example of Nicholas Lewis Sewall, a wealthy planter who left plantation accounts, beginning in the 1760s, that show less crop value in tobacco than in corn, wheat, and meat.[48] However, like most planters in the county, Deacon may not have moved so decisively away from tobacco. Estates inventoried from 1755 through 1776 show mean values of tobacco three to four times that of all grains combined except among the very rich, and, even in these estates, tobacco was the dominant crop.[49]

Whatever Deacon's crop mix, plantation work, in his time, offered much more variety of tasks than it had in the seventeenth century.

Horatio Sharpe's Whitehall," *Md. Hist. Mag.*, XLVI (1951), 8–26. A description of Deacon's house is recorded in the 1798 Federal Tax Assessment, Lower St. Mary's Hundred, MS (microfilm), Hall of Records, Annapolis, under the name Deborah Wolstenholme. Daniel Wolstenholme replaced Deacon as royal customs collector and purchased the property. See Carr, "Town Land," in Quimby, ed., *Ceramics*, 75–102.

48. For Sewall, see Jesuit Provincial Archives, 161A, 161B, 161C, MSS, Georgetown University Library.

49. Carr and Walsh, "Transformation of Production," *Working Papers*, table 4.

His slaves had the use of plows; they did not do all preparation of land with the hoe. They had the use of carts for hauling. They gave livestock more care than had been the practice a century earlier. Cattle and horses did not range in virgin forest. Indeed, the law now required that, during the growing season, horses had to be fenced in; and, in the winter, it was standard practice to provide livestock with more feed as well. Oxen and horses, furthermore, needed to be broken to the plow or cart. Sheep, rare in the seventeenth century because it was difficult to protect them from wolves, were increasingly abundant; they required shearing and special care at lambing. Manure from penned livestock was spread in the cornfields and sometimes where tobacco was grown. In addition, if Deacon resembled other gentlemen of wealth, more time than earlier went into raising a greater variety of vegetables such as broccoli and asparagus in addition to the standard cabbages and root crops of the seventeenth century.[50] Finally, Deacon had more buildings and fences to maintain than were usual except on a handful of plantations a century earlier.[51]

One activity Deacon did not undertake, although by this time the great majority of households did, was the spinning of fibers—wool, flax, hemp, or cotton. Deacon had a huge flock of sheep and 184 pounds of wool on hand, with eight pairs of wool cards for preparing it for spinning. Carding wool probably occupied the time of the two old women and possibly some of the children, but he had no

50. For fencing, see Thomas Bacon, ed., *The Laws of Maryland* . . . (Annapolis, Md., 1765), Acts 1715, chap. 31. Inventories of the 17th century regularly refer to hogs running in the woods. By the mid-18th century, such references have disappeared. After 1700, inventories occasionally show fodder, an item that never appeared in the 17th century. On the use of manure, see Gray, *History of Agriculture*, I, 198, 217; and Greene, ed., *Diary of Carter*, I, 157, 570. William Tatham, who visited Virginia in the 1770s, asserted that it was still conventional wisdom not to manure tobacco (G. Melvin Herndon, *William Tatham and the Culture of Tobacco* [Coral Gables, Fla., 1969]). Nevertheless, Walsh has found 18th-century Virginia correspondence and diaries abounding with evidence that planters relied on manure. On vegetables, see *Diary of Carter*, I, 293, 567; Edwin Morris Betts, ed., *Thomas Jefferson's Garden Book, 1766–1824, with Relevant Extracts from His Other Writings* (Philadelphia, 1974 [orig. publ. 1944]).

51. Deacon's property was advertised as having all necessary outbuildings, *Maryland Gazette* (Annapolis), Oct. 8, 1761. A comparison of 17th-century room-by-room inventories with 18th-century orphan's court valuations makes differences clear. For examples of valuations, see Queen Anne's County Deeds RT No. G, pp. 165, 304, 341; and RT No. H, pp. 40, 42, 83, 206, 216. In all the counties that we have studied, only one inventory for the period 1658–1673, that of Robert Slye of St. Clement's Manor, suggests so many buildings, and few for the 17th century show such variety. SMCC Inventory Files.

equipment for spinning or weaving. Nor did he grow or process flax or hemp or cotton, although others in the neighborhood did.

Deacon's smaller planter neighbors, such as the Taylors and the Clockers, also carried on a variety of activities, including the processing of fibers that was missing from Deacon's operation. Mary Taylor had looms as well as wheels, and one of her sons may have continued his father's craft as a blacksmith.[52] The Clockers raised tobacco, but at the death of the fourth Daniel in 1766, his crop weighed only 750 pounds. While he had no bound labor, he did have a nineteen-year-old son and five younger children. Clearly, much time went toward producing income in other ways. Clocker's carpenter's tools were worth, in constant pounds, three times what had appeared in Hicks's estate, and Clocker probably had carpentry skills. Perhaps he worked in Deacon's boatyard. His wife and daughters spun yarn—wool, cotton, and flax. He had sheep, and he either grew a little cotton and flax or he bought the raw fibers from a neighbor who did.

Another family, the Ingallses, offered other specialized skills. Thomas Ingalls was a joiner and furniture maker. He may have been the only Town Land resident not to raise tobacco. Besides corn, he grew wheat and rye, which took far less labor time than did tobacco, and his wheat and rye crop of 1752 had more value, in constant pounds, than had Clocker's tobacco crop of 1766. Nevertheless, raising crops for the market was not his primary activity. At his death, he left behind chests, desks, and "fiddils" in the making and quantities of walnut, pine, and cherry wood. Leather and cloth for upholstery and fastenings and fittings of many kinds were also part of his equipment. His servant probably did most of the field work, while Ingalls himself pursued his craft. Unfortunately for Ingalls, he evidently had the least to offer that a country neighborhood, in fact, really wanted. He was the only Town Land landowner inventoried whose movable property could not pay his debts. His chief creditor, a nearby planter-tailor, paid what was owed and took over Ingalls's land. Luckily, Ingalls, originally from New England, had property there that he could leave to his motherless children.

Clearly, these families depended heavily upon local exchange both to supply their needs and to utilize available resources. No plantation was self-sufficient, and the area provided a variety of skills. Dea-

52. Weaving was a man's skill, and men are occasionally identified in the records as weavers, but it is clear from account books that women also did weaving. Joseph Taylor could have been both a weaver and a smith, but it is likely that his wife at least assisted with the weaving and continued the work after his death.

con offered his neighbors the most and needed the least, but even he relied on others for processing leather and wool and for providing needed skills in his boatyard. The Clocker and Taylor women must have spun for the Hickses and Deacon, and the wife of a tenant-farmer neighbor may have done the same. By mid-century, in this county, nearly 90 percent of married, inventoried tenants with property worth less than fifty pounds had spinning wheels.[53] Opportunities for such income were not being overlooked.

The exchanges of William Hicks, who ran a store from about 1756 to 1759, and of his father-in-law and neighbor, merchant William Hebb, reflect the diversity of economic activities found in the Town Land. Some area residents paid Hicks for goods from surpluses of corn and wheat as well as tobacco.[54] Hebb, who died in 1758, left 395 debts receivable, of which 164—or 42 percent—were payable in grains. Hicks's personal expenditures reflect other diversified local activities. He made purchases from local planters of butter, pork and beef, feathers by the pound, beeswax, myrtle wax, tallow, plank, staves, barrels, tar, and pitch. He bought live cattle, hogs, and turkeys. He paid for coopering and tailoring, and one John Cole built him a pigeon house. He outfitted a ship, *Betsy*, with sails, masts, and other fittings he obtained from local residents (although not from Deacon, by that time deceased). And he purchased some locally made walnut tables, although not from Ingalls, who, likewise, had been dead for several years.[55]

While some of these sales to Hicks are similar to sales and purchases made from the Cole Plantation a century earlier, the variety of products exchanged was far greater and the activities represented far more diverse. Particularly important was the work of women in spinning yarn and weaving it into cloth. These were home industries entirely absent in the mid-seventeenth century, and they greatly enlarged women's contributions to the household economy. By the

53. SMCC Inventory Files.
54. The Hicks Factorage Accounts contain references to his "corn book" and his "wheat book." Hicks, who inherited property in Whitehaven and returned there in 1759, ran a factorage business with his Whitehaven uncle. Later, the heir of his uncle's widow sued Hicks for sums he believed due to the uncle's estate, hence the account summaries.
55. Hicks Factorage Accounts, Schedules B, E, D; Inventories 67, pp. 67–90 (William Hebb). The South Potomac Naval Office records for Oct. 13, 1760, show *Betsy* as a ship built in Annapolis in 1759, but it hardly seems that she could have reached St. Mary's City without the spar and sails mentioned. Perhaps she was really built in Deacon's boatyard. Annapolis may have been a surrogate for any Maryland location (CO 5/1448, 47 [microfilm, Colonial Williamsburg Foundation]).

mid-eighteenth century, furthermore, all income supplements were probably much less tied than earlier to the fortunes of tobacco. On the Cole Plantation, sales of products diminished when tobacco prices were low; the purchasing power of neighbors was also low at such times.[56] In the 1750s, planters whose incomes depended less completely on tobacco suffered less from fluctuations in the price of the staple. The far denser network of local exchange must have enabled planters both to earn income and spend it, even when profits from tobacco fell.

Although the Town Land neighborhood could supply many needs locally, it was by no means independent of imports. Hicks's store, supplied by an uncle in Whitehaven, brought in shiploads each year. From April 1756 through January 1759, Hicks received seven cargoes valued overall (in sterling) at nearly £4,722. Whatever local wares were available, planters clearly were spending their income for great quantities of imported goods.[57]

A century earlier, planters had been even more dependent on imports, but, by Hicks's day, the variety and character of the goods had undergone a striking change. In the 1660s and 1670s, both merchants' stocks and household furnishings were confined mostly to what was necessary and durable, even in well-to-do households. People ate with spoons from a common dish or off wooden or pewter plates and drank from common cups or flagons. Ceramics consisted mostly of equipment for the dairy. Glassware of any kind had been rare. An increasing tendency to purchase nonessentials, and a gradual redefinition of what essentials were, had begun early in the eighteenth century. As with the movement toward diversification, the acquisition of household amenities started with the rich, those with estates worth more than £225. But, by Hicks's time, even households with movable property worth less than £50 had items that had once been luxuries, such as tea and the equipment to drink it. On the Town Land, Daniel Clocker owned glassware and case knives and forks. Earthenware for household uses of all kinds was ubiquitous; it was not confined primarily to the dairy. A rising standard of consumption had reached well down the social scale.[58]

56. Menard, Carr, and Walsh, "A Small Planter's Profits," *WMQ*, 3d Ser., XL (1983), 182.

57. Hicks Factorage Accounts, Schedule F; Daniel Hay, *Whitehaven: A Short History* (Whitehaven, Eng., 1968), 118; Exports, Port of Carlisle, Whitehaven Creek, customer entries for Feb. 22, Mar. 16, and Dec. 9, 1739, E190, 1460/4, MS, Public Record Office, London; Leonardtown Ledger, Glassford Papers, 1759, MS, Library of Congress.

58. Lois Green Carr and Lorena S. Walsh, "Changing Lifestyles in Colonial St.

Economic diversification improved the ability of planters to obtain these consumer goods, although it did not bring about the shifts in cultural attitudes that in part underlay these changes. Other work has demonstrated that the extent of diversified activity is directly related to the rise in the standard of consumption in every Chesapeake county so far examined. The reasons are complex.[59] But the processes seen here in St. Mary's County were all at work. Diversification and local exchange contributed to more stable income, and household production could free some of that income for purchases of extras.

Between the death of Cole and the death of Deacon, then, a redirection of labor productivity transformed the area economy and the daily lives of its inhabitants in some basic ways despite continued dependence on tobacco. Internal economic development made employments possible for free white men and women that were not open to their seventeenth-century predecessors at the same time that it promoted economic stability. Overall, these changes contributed to an improved standard of living for most white households. Diversification also provided a greater variety of tasks for bound laborers, although they did not otherwise share in the benefits of the transformation. Indeed, as we shall see, some laborers—namely female slaves—became even more tied to drudgery as time passed.

THE PERIOD 1760–1820 saw the complexity of work routines increase. Home industry increased markedly, in part triggered by the Revolution, which, for a while, cut off imports from England. Much of this work—hackling flax, carding wool, spinning, weaving, knitting, sewing, candle molding, butter making, cidering, and salting down meat—was undertaken, as before, by the planter's wife and his daughters. Increasingly, furthermore, the wives and daughters of tenant farmers and other landless laborers took in piecework for slaveowners, processing the slaveowners' fibers, weaving them into cloth, and making clothing for slaves. Growing agricultural diversification, both between various regions and on individual farms, even-

Mary's County," *Working Papers from the Regional Economic History Research Center,* I, no. 3 (1978), 72–118; Lorena S. Walsh, "Urban Amenities and Rural Sufficiency: Living Standards and Consumer Behavior in the Colonial Chesapeake, 1643–1777," *Jour. Econ. Hist.,* XLIII (1983), 109–117; Barbara Carson and Cary Carson, "Styles and Standards of Living in Southern Maryland, 1670–1752" (paper presented to the Southern Historical Association, Atlanta, Ga., November 1976).

59. Lois Green Carr and Lorena S. Walsh, "Consumer Behavior in the Colonial Chesapeake," in Cary Carson *et al.,* eds., *Of Consuming Interests: The Style of Life in the Eighteenth Century* (Charlottesville, Va., forthcoming).

tually changed work outside the home still more. In parts of Maryland and Virginia, tobacco was abandoned for wheat, and grains and livestock became more important as significant sources of farm income everywhere. The agricultural routine changed markedly, with more extensive plowing (instead of preparing cropland by hand), penning and winterfeeding of livestock, cultivation of fodder crops, and the wider use of manure for fertilizer.[60] With these changes, increasing numbers of workers were exposed to a greater variety of tasks, and with this variety came some shifts in the division of labor, especially slave labor.

The result, for slaves, of increased complexity of work tasks was a marked increase in the sexual division of labor. So long as tobacco and corn were the chief crops—cultivated largely with hoes, harvested and stored without the aid of carts and draft animals, and prepared for consumption or packed for market with the most primitive equipment—work routines probably varied little for men and women. But the new crops and routines often involved some degree of skill—sowing and mowing grains, plowing, harrowing, carting, ditching, lumbering, fishing, and milling, for examples.[61] These new jobs fell primarily to men. Slave women, on the other hand, probably lost considerably from agricultural change. A few became more

60. Carr, "Diversification in the Colonial Chesapeake" in Carr, Morgan, and Russo, eds., *Chesapeake Society*; Cary Carson and Lorena S. Walsh, "The Material Life of the Early American Housewife," *Winterthur Portfolio* (forthcoming); Clemens, *Atlantic Economy*, 168–206; and the unpublished research of Lorena S. Walsh.

61. Gerald W. Mullin, *Flight and Rebellion: Slave Resistance in Eighteenth-Century Virginia* (New York, 1972); and, more recently, Kulikoff, *Tobacco and Slaves*, argue that there was a close association between the appearance of a majority of well-acculturated, native-born adult slaves in the labor force and extensive diversification. There is considerable evidence to back the argument that slaveowners were more likely to train creole slaves as artisans than the African-born. On the other hand, the argument that slaveowners trusted only creole slaves to use plows and carts (*Tobacco and Slaves*, chap. 10) seems to rise from an unexamined assumption that because two things—the more frequent appearance of plows and carts in inventories and the emergence of a majority of creoles among slaves—happened about the same time, there was some necessary connection between the two. An increasingly robust market for grains would seem a much more cogent explanation for greater use of plows, harrows, and carts. Indeed, a breakdown of plow ownership in inventories by region shows a much closer relationship between extensive wheat cultivation and an increase in these devices than between the appearance of many plows and a largely creole slave force. In older tidewater counties, a black creole labor force emerged well before a widespread plow culture, while in newer piedmont counties well suited to the marketing of wheat, plows became common even in counties where much of the labor force consisted of recently imported Africans.

involved in textile production and house service than in earlier years. However, free white women filled most of the slots created by expanded home industry. The great majority of black women continued to perform unskilled manual field labor, such as hand hoeing and weeding, and now more often without the help of their menfolk. The new jobs assigned to slave women (or the old jobs formerly shared with men) included many of the least desirable chores: building fences, grubbing swamps in the dead of winter, cleaning winnowed grain of weed seed, breaking up new ground too rough or weedy to plow, cleaning stables, and loading and spreading manure. While a sexual division of labor between field and home had always characterized most of the white society, a similar split occurred among slaves only with widespread agricultural diversification at the end of the eighteenth century. For blacks, however, the division was not between field and domestic production, but between semiskilled and unskilled agricultural tasks.[62]

These transformations in work routines are illustrated by Landon Carter's farm diary for the 1770s. Despite his diary-keeping habit, Carter was much more of a traditional planter and less of an innovative farmer than has sometimes been supposed. Still, some departures from the work routines of his father's time are clearly evident in his diary entries. On his Richmond County, Virginia, plantations, Carter grew a triad of cash crops—corn, wheat, and tobacco. A few of the slave women did not work in the fields. Carter mentioned that some adult females spun, cooked, washed, made candles, and waited on the family. One was a midwife, and others minded poultry, hogs, and cattle. Young girls were noted spinning, tending sheep, and picking cotton. But, otherwise, women were mentioned only as performing the routine manual farm chores that had always characterized Chesapeake agriculture: weeding, planting, and thinning corn; worming tobacco; cutting corn tops; carrying corn to the barn on their heads; and shelling corn. Carter continued to cultivate most of his crops with hoes, for he did not grow enough fodder or maintain enough pasture to feed draft animals adequately. Consequently, male as well as female slaves spent much of their time at the hoe. Still, the men were performing a greater variety of tasks than

62. Jacqueline Jones, *Labor of Love, Labor of Sorrow: Black Women, Work, and the Family from Slavery to the Present* (New York, 1985), chap. 1, comes to similar conclusions about slave women's work in the antebellum period. Work was similarly divided by gender in the Caribbean. See the discussion in Barry W. Higman, *Slave Populations of the Caribbean*, chap. 6 and statistical supplement, sect. 7 (tables 5–14).

were the women. Most of the artisans were men, including a gardener, sawyer, tailor, weaver, waiting- and coachman, and numerous carpenters. Male slaves did the plowing, all the sowing and mowing of grain or hay, sheepshearing, ditching, and carting. When most of the men were occupied with these chores, gangs of women went out to do the hoeing, usually under the direction either of a white overseer or of a male slave supervisor. However, at least one woman, Grace, sometimes worked as supervisor of a hoe gang.

In contrast, in George Washington's diary for 1786 and 1787 (Washington was, without question, a true agricultural innovator), one finds a much greater division of labor based on gender. This change can be attributed, in great measure, to shifts in crop base and cultivation techniques. Washington had, by then, abandoned tobacco culture and was growing corn, wheat, oats, and rye. He had also completed the transition to a much more mechanized agriculture. On the Mount Vernon complex, there were sufficient meadowland, straw, fodder, and other forage crops to feed as many draft animals as could be utilized. Where, in the 1770s, Landon Carter had difficulty keeping two plows in operation, Washington seldom used fewer than nine and, at peak periods, could keep as many as twenty-seven plows going simultaneously as well as several harrows, carts, and wagons.[63]

The sexual division of labor on Washington's farms appeared most graphically in the wheat harvest, with slave men and some hired free whites doing the mowing, while the women and adolescents raked, gathered, bound, and carried the harvested grain.[64] Haymaking followed a similar division of labor. Division did not end there, however, for Washington regularly put the field hands on each plantation into two work groups—one composed almost exclusively of men and another of women and adolescent boys and girls. The men's gangs cut and shaped timber and fence rails, carted goods, made ditches and roads, plowed, harrowed, and sowed. Often the men worked by

63. Jackson and Twohig, eds., *Diaries of Washington*, IV and V. Washington's diary entries were apparently taken from a much more complete Journal of Work on Plantations, [1786]–1787, prepared by the farm manager (Washington Family Papers, Library of Congress). This document provides much greater detail than do his *Diaries*.

64. At Monticello, Thomas Jefferson used a somewhat different division of labor at wheat harvest. The cradlers were all men; the binders, women and abler boys; the gatherers, small boys; the loaders, stackers, and carters, men; the cooks, women; and the water carriers, probably boys. Edwin Morris Betts, ed., *Thomas Jefferson's Farm Book, with Commentary and Relevant Extracts from Other Writings* (1953; Charlottesville, Va., 1976), 45–47, 54, 58.

themselves at individual tasks, and, even when they worked in groups, in any given week, they usually worked at two or more different chores. The women's gangs, usually working directly under the supervision of an overseer, grubbed swamps and meadows, weeded corn and vegetables, hoed ground the plows could not adequately break up, erected fences, cleaned the stables, heaped the dung, spread the manure, harvested the corn, and, at the end of the year, threshed and cleaned grain and husked the corn. The women, unlike the men, almost always worked in groups, and there was much less variation in their weekly assignments (see appendix 1).

A list of slaves, which includes their occupation and residence in 1786, further clarifies the reasons for a particular division of labor in the fields. Washington kept twenty-eight of his adult male slaves at the home house, where most of them performed craftwork and domestic service. The males included waiting men, cooks, stablemen, stockkeepers, carpenters, smiths, a gardener, a carter, and a wagoner. In addition, a male miller and three coopers occupied and ran a nearby gristmill. There were only thirteen adult women at the home house, who were assigned to washing, spinning, sewing, and house service. On the four outlying quarters, all adults were agricultural laborers except for three male overseers. (The wives of two of the three foremen were apparently exempted from field labor.) On each farm, women outnumbered men. A total of thirty-one male slaves worked the outlying farms, but forty-six "laboring women" carried out a substantial proportion of the agricultural tasks.[65]

A similar pattern of diversification and labor division is revealed by the daily work record of Joseph Hornsby in Missouri in 1803. Hornsby was a former tidewater Virginia resident who moved to Missouri with Virginia slaves and who grew typical Virginia backcountry crops with techniques and even seed borrowed from piedmont Virginia planters. Consequently, his plantation can be considered reasonably representative of newer, backcountry Virginia farms. Hornsby grew corn, wheat, oats, cotton, flax, hemp, and hay; kept an orchard and a large "truck patch"; and raised hogs, cattle, and horses. As much of his farm was new ground, there was a great deal of clearing and breaking that had to be done with hoes and axes. Where possible, however, he employed plows, harrows, and carts. Hornsby's working slaves consisted of three men, one boy, and eight women and older girls. He employed no overseer and directed the work of the slaves himself. However, aside from working in the gar-

65. Jackson and Twohig, eds., *Diaries of Washington*, IV, 277–283.

den, as much a hobby as a necessity, Hornsby did not engage in field labor.[66]

Here, too, there was a fairly marked division of labor between men and women. In January and February, men and women often worked together, clearing and burning off new fields and shucking corn when the weather was too bad to work outside. The men ventured out on better days to run errands, to take grain to the mill, and to cut timber and firewood (one of them made shoes), and the women hauled manure out of the stable or made maple sugar. Once the fields became fit to plow in the spring, men and women worked together less often. The men prepared ground for the garden and plowed the fields, subsequently doing whatever weeding could be accomplished with a plow, and sowed the oats. The women hoed the ground the plows could not handle, planted and weeded the corn, weeded the wheat, and tended the garden. The men cut timber for fences, and then both men and women put them up. Whenever a slave man worked along with the women, Hornsby listed him as in charge of the group. However, the women very often worked alone. Then, one woman, Dicey, was listed as in charge. When she was sick, another woman, Delphia, took her place as leader.

In June, the slaves joined forces to harvest the hay and, in July, the wheat and oats; they trod out the grain in August. Again, the men cut, and the women did the gathering and binding. Also, at the end of the summer, the slaves all worked together for a few days getting in the hemp and then turned to a second cutting of hay. Once the small grains were housed, the entire labor force worked in late August and early September at picking corn and at getting in the flax and hemp. Whenever the women were not busy with these jobs, they grubbed and hoed incompletely plowed fields and tended the garden, while the men sowed the wheat.

In October, November, and December, all worked at housing and shelling the corn and slaughtering hogs. Men helped in inclement weather with cleaning the wheat, but the women did more than the men. The women also harvested and stored the vegetables and began to spin cotton and flax. Otherwise, the men were busy cutting firewood, running errands, making shoes, and going to the mill.

How the household itself functioned is something of a mystery. Hornsby never mentioned his wife (who may very well have been dead), and a single daughter, Peggy, who was living at home, ran the household. Except at Christmas, the women seldom were listed as

66. Joseph Hornsby, Diary of Planting and Gardening, MS, Missouri Historical Society, St. Louis.

working in the kitchen, and only once was one noted as doing washing. The only slave known to be available to help with daily cooking, cleaning, washing, milking, fire building, and water fetching was a superannuated woman, Old Hannah, whom Hornsby mentioned only once, as knitting stockings. Very probably, the older children helped with these chores, and they, together with Old Hannah, must have looked after the youngest black children.

This difficulty underscores a problem that most of the farm records pose—the ranks of domestic servants were almost invariably understaffed. Carole Shammas, from an examination of slave lists that included notations of occupation, concluded: "Plantation societies such as the one founded in Colonial Virginia were largely the creation of white men and reflected their priorities. . . . The 18th century planter had climbed aboard a tobacco treadmill, featuring uncertain prices, uncooperative soil, and from his perspective, a slave population destined to have too many young and old. The 'Great House' economized by using the too young, the too old, and the unspecialized worker for domestic and housewifery chores."[67] The analysis of farm diaries here confirms her argument.

Aside from the few adult slave women who did cooking and washing for large planter families (and the few younger girls who served as personal attendants, scullery maids, or looked after white children), most female slaves were virtually excluded from the domestic sphere of their white mistresses, or so the records left by white male planters would lead us to believe. Where families were too large or the wife was dead, planters employed white women to serve as housekeepers and, often as not, nurses. On big operations, housekeepers or the wives of overseers did the dairying.[68]

This leaves only textile production and clothing construction as a growing source of nonagricultural work for female slaves. That this was a matter of much import seems very much more fiction than fact. True, large planters, the owners of bound laborers, were the first to introduce carding and spinning around the beginning of the eighteenth century. However, surviving records show spinning and knitting as the tasks only of old or disabled slaves. Except in marginal tobacco areas, most cloth continued to be imported, and, through the 1730s, white male tailors, both servant and free, made most slave clothing, and poor white women often did the knitting.

67. Carole Shammas, "Black Women's Work and the Evolution of Plantation Society in Virginia," *Labor History*, XXVI (1985), 25.
68. *Ibid*. Again, Walsh's research in other sources serves only to reinforce Shammas's conclusions.

By mid-century, when spinning, weaving, knitting, and sewing had become common activities in poor white families, individual plantation accounts indicate that the various stages in producing slave clothing were increasingly put out to poor white widows and to the wives and daughters of overseers and tenant farmers.

During the decade preceding the Revolution, nonimportation agreements spurred more domestic industry, and, during the war itself, supplies of cloth were so short that many planters either could not find fabric or could not afford to buy enough to clothe their slaves. Consequently, some slave women and girls were shifted from tobacco (which often could not be marketed) into spinning and weaving. However, once the war ended, the market for agricultural products rose, and the great majority of slave women went back to the fields. Planters resumed putting out their wool and flax to poor white women to spin and knit, and the finished yarn went to local weavers. Those slave women who continued to spend much time making yarn or clothing belonged to masters who were deeply in debt or who lived in newly settled, isolated areas.[69]

What are the implications of these changes in work roles? Deborah White, in a study of sex roles and status on antebellum plantations, concluded that, to the extent that slave women did the same work as men, "parity in the field may have encouraged equalitarianism in the slave quarters" and that "where widespread private property is not a factor, participation in production gives women freedom and independence." To the extent that work roles were gender-stratified, women workers were better able to form strong bonds among themselves. A separate "female slave world allowed women the opportunity to rank and order themselves and obtain a sense of self which was quite apart from the men of their race and even the men of the master class."[70]

Conversely, Ester Boserup concluded that "in the regions of plough cultivation, agricultural work is distributed between the two sexes in a very different way." Wherever the plow displaced the hoe, men, equipped with superior strength, took over the job of plowing, even where hoeing had formerly been women's work. Consequently, a

69. This argument, so far, has generated considerable controversy. We have no doubt about its general soundness, and Walsh plans soon, in another publication, to provide substantial documentation. Cf. Mary Beth Norton, " 'What an Alarming Crisis Is This': Southern Women in the American Revolution," in Jeffrey J. Crow and Larry E. Tise, eds., *The Southern Experience in the American Revolution* (Chapel Hill, N.C., 1978), 203–234.

70. Deborah G. White, "Female Slaves: Sex Roles and Status in the Antebellum Plantation South," *Journal of Family History*, VIII (1983), 251, 254.

conversion to extensive plowing brings about a change in the economic and social relationships between the sexes—never to women's advantage.[71]

On the basis of the evidence so far found, Boserup's analysis seems closest to the truth. Changes in the agriculture and economy of the eighteenth- and early nineteenth-century Chesapeake brought the work roles of adult male slaves more closely into alignment with the work roles of the dominant Anglo-American male-oriented society. These changes had the practical advantage of removing more slave men more often from the minute supervision of master or overseer.[72] More intangibly, and to the extent that slaves had accepted the value systems of their white male masters, there were many more opportunities for taking satisfaction from specialized work well done in fields, shops, and in service.

Most slave women, on the other hand, participated infrequently, if at all, in the domestic sphere of their white mistresses; at the same time, they were allowed very little time to care for their own families. A certain amount of parity in the fields may have encouraged greater egalitarianism among slaves. At the same time, a more complete separation of men's and women's work may well have strengthened bonds between black women and contributed to the formation of an independent sense of identity. On the other hand, the increasing tendency among whites to equate the most inglorious and monotonous of manual agricultural labor with slave women's work must have made the twin burdens of race and gender doubly galling.

OVER THE SPAN of 170 years, a great transformation had taken place in the tidewater Chesapeake. In 1660 it consisted of immigrant outposts with a labor system based on white indentured servitude,

71. Ester Boserup, *Woman's Role in Economic Development* (New York, 1970), chap. 1 (quotation on 24). With respect to women's work roles, we believe that this technological change had a major impact. This is not to imply that black women's status was not also affected by many other aspects of gender and race relationships.

72. Stefano Fenoaltea, in "Slavery and Supervision in Comparative Perspective: A Model," *Jour. Econ. Hist.*, XLIV (1984), 635–668, uses a transaction costs model to argue that slave laborers performing unskilled manual tasks are usually subjected to close supervision and "pain incentives"—the continual and immediate threat of the lash—because the greatest quantity of work can be extracted from them by this method. On the other hand, when slaves are assigned skilled jobs that require considerable care, supervision is relaxed, since careful work is incompatible with a high level of anxiety, and some positive rewards (a share of the profits earned, for example, and perhaps, ultimately, an option of self-purchase) are substituted for the threat of pain.

organized primarily around the production and marketing of tobacco to exchange for European goods. In 1820 tobacco was still a primary crop in many areas, although black slaves, not white servants, produced the bulk of it, and it helped to pay for continued imports. However, internal economic development—promoted, in part, by the introduction of new export crops—had created a much larger variety of occupations, especially for whites. Accompanying this economic diversity was a rising standard of consumption for whites that was beginning to affect even families quite low on the economic scale. These gains, of course, did not reach a major portion of the population, the slaves, with one exception: male slaves benefited, to some degree, from the increased variety of tasks available.

Many questions about the causes and effects of these changes await further investigation. Who benefited, who suffered, and how from by-employments and new occupations? For example, were opportunities for white women to spin, knit, or weave for piecework wages improving, or depressing the condition of the very poor? Did the prospects of such employment encourage marriage and household formation without ensuring a sufficiency based on the produce of land? Alternatively, was the standard of living in poor households raised through the additional income? If inventories are correctly informing us, then, before the Revolution, improvement was probably the rule, but, over a longer run, the question is still unsettled. Similarly, we need much more information on how new employments and their social consequences relate to other social and economic processes: filling up of the land, productivity changes, inheritance practices, urbanization (or its absence), migration out, and shifts in the fortunes of the export sector of the economy. Only as we learn more about all these processes and how they relate to one another will we understand better the meaning of changing work roles and their effects on economic opportunity and social relations across all social groups.

APPENDIX 1

Tasks on George Washington's Plantations,
by Age, Sex, and Season, 1786–1787

MEN

Skills

overseer
sawyer
carpenter
miller
cooper
blacksmith

shoemaker
house servant
ferryman
carter / wagoner
brickmaker / bricklayer
gardener

Winter

work on millrace
dig ditches
plow
cut rails, posts, and timber
cut firewood
haul timber and grain
kill hogs
help fill icehouse
maul rails
make fences and livestock pens
saw timber
build roads

work in new ground
frame barn
make fagots
shell corn
cut straw
thresh wheat and rye
strip tobacco
make baskets and horse collars
beat out hominy
tend stable
tan leather
do odd jobs

Spring / Summer

plow
harrow
roll grain fields
seine fish
sow carrots, cabbage, flax,
   barley, oats, wheat, and
   clover
weed peas
cut straw
cut brush and burn logs
tie and heap hemp

cradle at harvest of wheat and
   rye
bind at harvest
shock wheat and oats
gather basket splits and tan
   bark
cut and maul fence rails and
   posts
clean swamp
fill gullies
grub fields

thresh wheat and clover seed
plant potatoes and jerusalem
   artichokes
make corn hills and weed corn
plant corn, pumpkins, and peas
   and replant these

dig ditches
make baskets and horse collars
cut hay and clover
cut corn stalks
cut firewood
shell corn

Fall

harvest corn and peas
plow
sow winter grain
harrow

thresh peas
make livestock pens and feed
   racks

WOMEN

Skills

milking
spinning
weaving
washing

ironing
cooking
doing scullery
being house servant

Winter

help at icehouse
cut and gather cornstalks
beat out hominy
hoe new ground
thin trees in swamp
clean out stable
heap dung
carry fence rails
grub swamp, woods, and
   meadow
husk and shell corn

burn brush
fill gullies
plow
kill and salt hogs
thresh wheat, rye, and clover
   seed
strip tobacco
pack fish
strip basket splits
make baskets

Spring / Summer

dig post holes
make fences
heap and burn trash
chop plowed ground
harrow
plow
grub meadow
clear new grounds
load dung in carts
gather and spread fish offal
make holes for corn
make pumpkin hills
plant and replant melons
sow carrots
hoe corn ground
bind oats at harvest
stack wheat and rye at harvest
thresh wheat and clover seed
cut sprouts from tree stumps in
    fields
pile grass tussocks hoed out of
    weedy ground
hoe rough or wet ground plows
    can't touch

prepare meadow for oats and
    timothy
make hills for sweet potatoes
    and plant them
weed pumpkins (old women
    and those with young
    children)
care for cattle
pick up apples
level ditches
chop after harrows
grub after plows
clean hedgerows
clean fields
fill gullies in fields
spread dung
hill for peas
plant corn
weed peas
plant cabbages
cut up cornstalks
shell corn

Fall

break and swingle flax
chop in flax
make livestock pens
cut down cornstalks
harvest corn

thresh rye, clover seed, peas,
    wheat, oats
dig carrots
clean oat and wheat seed
pile cornstalks

BOYS

weed peas
clear trash from fields
carry wheat at harvest
thresh wheat

hoe around stumps
burn brush
help with carting
work on road

assist tanners
help in stable
fence (with women's gang)
grub meadow (with women's
    gang)
fill gullies (with women's gang)

gather cornstalks
do odd jobs
make corn hills (with women's
    gang)
plant corn (with women's gang)

GIRLS

make hay
beat out hominy
burn brush
help with carting
make fences
bake bread
plow (age 14)
shell corn

secure grain at harvest
    (ages 16, 13, and 12)
thresh wheat
work on road
help in stable
get water for washing
tend sick children

CHILDREN

gather at harvest that included
    children not taken out before

carry at harvest

Sources: Donald Jackson and Dorothy Twohig, eds., *The Diaries of George Washington*, 6 vols. (Charlottesville, Va., 1976–1979), V, 1–259; Journal of Work on Plantations, [1786]–1787, Washington Family Papers, Library of Congress.

Philip D. Morgan

Task and Gang Systems

The Organization of Labor

on New World Plantations

TO THINK OF slaves and of plantation labor is invariably to envision gangs of laborers toiling from sunup to sundown, working in unison, under direct and close supervision. To picture the gang at work is to visualize them ranged in a line, proceeding in regular rows, the pace being set by one or two key laborers, urged on by a driver or foreman. It is to see, through Janet Schaw's eyes, "a number of Negroes follow[ing] each other's tail the day long"; it is to see, as one southern cotton planter described it, slaves "all keeping up with their leader"; and it is to see, in Henry Harcourt's words, slaves "drawn out in a line, like troops on a parade, with their driver and his whip close at hand . . . all work[ing] or paus[ing] together." This gang system, according to U. B. Phillips, was employed on "virtually all of the tobacco, short staple cotton and sugar plantations" of the New World.[1]

The author wishes to thank many friends for their comments and advice on earlier drafts of this paper. Michael Craton, Barry Higman, Stephen Innes, Sidney Mintz, and Marcus Rediker made particularly valuable suggestions. Stanley Engerman, always the model of generosity and intelligence, raised so many penetrating questions that it will require another essay to answer all of them. Naturally, therefore, the author takes full responsibility for the remaining inadequacies of this version. A condensed version of this essay appeared in Élise Marienstras and Barbara Karsky, eds., *Autre temps, autre espace / An Other Time, an Other Space: Études sur l'Amérique pré-industrielle* (Nancy, 1986), 147–162.

1. [Janet Schaw], *Journal of a Lady of Quality, Being the Narrative of a Journey from Scotland to the West Indies, North Carolina, and Portugal, in the Years 1774 to 1776*, ed. Evangeline Walker Andrews and Charles McLean Andrews (New Haven, Conn., 1923), 163; James Townes, "Farm Management," *Southern Cultivator*, V (Apr. 1847), 26; Henry Harcourt, *The Adventures of a Sugar-Plantation* (London, 1836), 90–92; Ulrich Bonnell Phillips, *American Negro Slavery: A Survey of the Supply, Employment, and Control of Negro Labor as Determined by the Plantation Regime* (Baton Rouge, La., 1966 [orig. publ. New York, 1918]), 247.

As we will discern, however, Phillips oversimplified matters even with respect to these three staples. More important, there was a variety of other New World products—arrowroot, cocoa, coffee, long-staple cotton, hemp, naval stores, pimento, rice, and timber—for which another system, that of tasking, was generally employed. So prevalent did tasking seem to a Jamaican writing in the early nineteenth century that he thought it "practised among the American planters in Louisiana, and in some parts of Virginia and North-Carolina, and perhaps, also in Maryland, as well as in South-Carolina and Georgia." He also believed that "the Spaniards task their negroes in gathering gold dust."[2] For this Caribbean planter, it was the sugar producer who was out of step with his contemporaries, not vice versa. And when we think of the form of labor organization known as tasking, we envisage slaves working neither in unison nor under close supervision; rather, we should picture them being assigned a certain amount of work for the day or perhaps week, upon the completion of which they were free to use their time as they pleased.[3]

This essay will outline some of the features of these two systems, investigate their origins, and suggest some of their consequences. The consequences, the implications of these different labor systems for those who were involved in them, constitute my ultimate quarry. Of particular concern are the domestic economies of the slaves—their attitudes toward resource allocation, their attempts to acquire property, and their patterns of consumption—which were related, in some cases very closely, to different modes of labor organization. The broader context for this essay, then, is an investigation into the relationship between the work styles of slaves (of which only one component would be the labor system) and their cultures (within which their domestic economy is my primary focus) in a number of different societies up to and immediately beyond emancipation.[4]

T A S K I N G   A N D   G A N G I N G were not hermetically sealed systems. Rather, we should think of them as two extremes in a range of labor

2. *An Essay on Task-Work: Its Practicability and the Modes to Be Adopted for Its Application to Different Kinds of Agricultural Labour* (Spanish Town, Jamaica, ca. 1809), i, 8. This pamphlet is extremely informative. The only copy that I have managed to locate is in the Houghton Library, Harvard University.

3. The best study of task and gang systems, upon which this essay attempts to build, is Lewis Cecil Gray, *History of Agriculture in the Southern United States to 1860*, 2 vols. (Gloucester, Mass., 1958 [orig. publ. Washington, D.C., 1933]), I, 550–556.

4. I hope to write a book on this subject, the prolegomenon of which is this essay.

systems, represented by individual tasking at one pole and large-scale, regimented ganging at the other. In between these two ideal types were various hybrids, most notably a system of collective tasking on the one hand and small, relatively unsupervised gangs or squads on the other. If we take these two ideal types and the two most distinctive hybrids, and if we remember that in any place and at any time more than one would likely be present (perhaps even in the cultivation of the same staple), can we identify particular plantation staples and societies with each one?

Individual tasking arrangements were associated with many more slave societies than the stereotypical picture of slave labor allows. Rice and Sea Island cotton production in the lowcountry of South Carolina and Georgia generated an extensive and deeply rooted task system. According to the anonymous Jamaican writing in the early nineteenth century, "In South Carolina and Georgia, it appears that task-work is the mode in which all their negroes are put to labour, and that it is reduced to a complete system; our mode of working them in a row being altogether unknown, or at least never practised."[5] The basic task unit, the quarter-acre, became so ingrained in lowcountry life that ex-slaves in the twentieth century still thought in terms of it.[6]

Long-staple cotton production in various Caribbean societies, like that of the lowcountry, also generated a task system. In Bahamian cotton planting, work was, according to one visitor to the islands at the beginning of the nineteenth century, "allotted to [the slaves] . . . daily and individually, according to their strength; and if they are so diligent as to have finished it at an early hour, the rest of the day is allowed to them."[7] In 1823 Bahamian slaveowners claimed that task-work had been universal in the islands " 'within the memory of the oldest of us,' for all slaves except those employed as domestics, sailors, or tradespeople." In Grenada, taskwork was first introduced by the planters of Carriacou, who were cotton planters.[8]

Timber or naval stores production—as the Bahamian case also il-

---

5. *Essay on Task-Work*, 8.

6. Philip D. Morgan, "Work and Culture: The Task System and the World of Lowcountry Blacks, 1700 to 1880," *William and Mary Quarterly*, 3d Ser., XXXIX (1982), 566.

7. Daniel McKinnen, *A Tour through the British West Indies, in the Years 1802 and 1803: Giving a Particular Account of the Bahama Islands* (London, 1804), 172.

8. *An Official Letter from the Commissioners of Correspondence of the Bahama Islands* (Nassau, 1823), 41; *St. George's Chronicle and Grenada Gazette*, Aug. 24, 1833. Both these references are from B. W. Higman, *Slave Populations of the British Caribbean, 1807–1834* (Baltimore, 1984), 179.

lustrates—was associated with tasking. In places as remote from one another as the forests of British Honduras, North Carolina, and Surinam, taskwork was the norm for slave workers. The work of mahogany cutters in British Honduras was said to be almost entirely by task.[9] Each operation in the North Carolina turpentine work cycle had its own quota: an axman ought to be able to "box" 125 trees daily, "chip" about 12,000 trees a week, and "dip" at least four barrels daily. Each slave was allocated what one early nineteenth-century observer referred to as a "district" of some 3,000–5,000 trees, which formed the slave's stint. Many slaves calculated their task by the week and had completed it by midafternoon on Friday. As a result of such a system in Surinam, slaves on timber estates enjoyed a significant "measure of freedom" and thereby "developed a strong feeling of independence."[10]

In the Caribbean, coffee and tasking generally went hand in hand. James Kelly, a bookkeeper on a Jamaican coffee plantation, noted that almost all the work was "by task." The slaves, he continued, "weed the coffee-field, picked the coffee from the trees, billed the savannah or pastures, and built stone walls, by task." According to a Jamaican, writing in the early nineteenth century, "task-work had been practised for many years" on the island's coffee plantations. According to him, coffee fields were "laid off so as to form square acres or half acres" by means of stakes, known appropriately as "task-sticks." In fact, land in Jamaican coffee plantations (like that in lowcountry rice and Sea Island cotton estates) "was laid off by what they call the task acre, which is somewhat larger than the statute-acre," so that more regular divisions—of 105 square feet for a quarter-acre and of 150 square feet for a half-acre—could be employed. This Jamaican specified quotas for a whole host of operations from pruning the trees to picking the berries.[11] Henry de La Beche

9. See, once again, Higman, *Slave Populations*, 179.

10. Thomas Gamble, comp., *Naval Stores: History, Production, Distribution, and Consumption* (Savannah, Ga., 1921), 11, 26–27; Percival Perry, "The Naval Stores Industry in the Ante-Bellum South, 1789–1861" (Ph.D. diss., Duke University, 1947), 22–26, 30–33, 40, 74; Luigi Castiglioni, *Luigi Castiglioni's Viaggio: Travels in the United States of North America, 1785–1787*, trans. and ed. Antonio Pace (Syracuse, N.Y., 1983), 181; Adam Hodgson, *Letters from North America, Written during a Tour in the United States and Canada* (London, 1824), I, 39; Herbert A. Kellar, ed., *Solon Robinson, Pioneer and Agriculturalist: Selected Writings* (Indianapolis, 1936), II, 222. For tasking in the late-19th-century lowcountry turpentine industry, see Thomas F. Armstrong, "The Transformation of Work: Turpentine Workers in Coastal Georgia, 1865–1901," *Labor History*, XXV (1984), 526–528. R.A.J. van Lier, *Frontier Society: A Social Analysis of the History of Surinam* (The Hague, 1971), 152.

11. James Kelly, *Voyage to Jamaica; Being a Narrative of Seventeen Years' Residence in*

thought that industrious Jamaican slaves could complete their assignment of picking coffeeberries by one or two in the afternoon. Apparently, other slaves on coffee estates also found their tasks relatively congenial. In early nineteenth-century Berbice, ten slave women reported that their master gave them as "a task one hundred [coffee] trees to be weeded and cleansed." They noted that "with this [task] we were satisfied."[12]

The planting of many lesser crops, as well as a number of ancillary plantation activities, was accomplished by slaves organized into tasks. Pimento, hemp, and arrowroot production was generally typified by task systems. Even on sugar estates, ancillary operations, like the cutting of copper wood or the building of stone walls, were completed by task.[13] Moreover, artisans in many slave societies were tasked in their work. Coopers in societies as distant as Jamaica and Louisiana were set quotas of so many barrels a day. Slave women were tasked in spinning and weaving. Slave woodworkers in the island of Mauritius, noted Charles Telfair, could finish their task of sawing planks in "little more than a half a day's labour."[14]

The archetypal form of gang labor was associated with sugar production. There was no better-brigaded, better-supervised form of labor. In cutting cane, for example, William Beckford marveled at the "regular discipline in the work." Dividing the labor force into two, perhaps three gangs (common for most of the seventeenth and eighteenth centuries), the West Indian sugar planter placed great empha-

That Island . . . (Belfast, 1838), 18; *Essay on Task-Work*, 10, 14, 21–24. See also B. W. Higman, *Slave Population and Economy in Jamaica, 1807–1834* (Cambridge, 1976), 21–24. For the lowcountry task acre, see my "Work and Culture," *WMQ*, 3d Ser., XXXIX (1982), 581–583.

12. H. T. de La Beche, *Notes on the Present Condition of the Negroes in Jamaica* (London, 1825), 19; Zachary Macauley, *The Slave Colonies of Great Britain; or, A Picture of Negro Slavery Drawn by the Colonists Themselves; Being an Abstract of the Various Papers Recently Laid before Parliament on That Subject* (London, 1825), 154.

13. Higman, *Slave Population and Economy*, 24–25; Gray, *History of Agriculture*, I, 552; J. S. Handler, "The History of Arrowroot and the Origin of Peasantries in the British West Indies," *Journal of Caribbean History*, II (1971), 76; *Essay on Task-Work*, 2.

14. Joseph Carlyle Sitterson, *Sugar Country: The Cane Sugar Industry in the South, 1753–1950* (Louisville, Ky., 1953), 112; interview with Catherine Cornelius, Federal Writers' Project Archives, MS Dept., Earl K. Long Library, University of New Orleans, cited in Roderick Alexander McDonald, " 'Goods and Chattels': The Economy of Slaves on Sugar Plantations in Jamaica and Louisiana" (Ph.D. diss., University of Kansas, 1981), 117; J. B. Moreton, *Manners and Customs in the West India Islands* (London, 1790), 148. Perry, "Naval Stores Industry," 76, 78; Gray, *History of Agriculture*, I, 552; Charles Telfair, *Some Account of the State of Slavery at Mauritius, since the British Occupation in 1810* . . . (Port Louis, Mauritius, 1830), 46.

sis on the abilities of his "first row" men to set the pace for the workers and on his superintendents to monitor their progress.[15] The regimentation of sugar planting was legendary or infamous, depending on the observer's point of view. In digging cane holes, for instance, critics likened the slaves to "a regiment drawn out and exercised on parade," with the driver at one end to "keep them in a regular string." Others described the experience more positively: the slaves, "accompanied by rhythmic song, were said to have raised their gleaming hoes all together, and in as exact a time as the performance of a well-conducted orchestra." Thomas Roughley recommended that the "entire gang . . . be spread" out; in that way, they "have a more sightly and better marshalled appearance." But, whatever the perspective, there was no gainsaying that, in James Stephen's words, "the whole line of holers advance together [and that] it is necessary that every hole or section of the trench should be finished in equal time with the rest."[16]

Where the nature of the work did not permit the slaves to be drawn up in a line abreast, as in carrying canes or grass from the fields, they were, instead, "marched in files, each with a bundle on his head, and with the driver in the rear." This led Richard Ligon to

15. William Beckford, *A Descriptive Account of the Island of Jamaica* . . . (London, 1790), II, 47–48; Woodville K. Marshall, ed., *The Colthurst Journal: Journal of a Special Magistrate in the Islands of Barbados and St. Vincent, July 1835–September 1838* (Millwood, N.Y., 1977), 143. The literature on the 17th- and 18th-century sugar gang system is immense. For some of the more important works, see Bryan Edwards, *The History, Civil and Commercial, of the British Colonies in the West Indies*, 2 vols. (London, 1794), II, 132–135; J. Harry Bennett, *Bondsmen and Bishops: Slavery and Apprenticeship on the Codrington Plantations of Barbados, 1710–1838*, University of California Publications in History, LXII (Berkeley, 1958), 11–15; Elsa V. Goveia, *Slave Society in the British Leeward Islands at the End of the Eighteenth Century* (New Haven, Conn., 1965), 129–151; Michael Craton and James Walvin, *A Jamaican Plantation: The History of Worthy Park, 1670–1970* (London, 1970), 95–154; Richard S. Dunn, *Sugar and Slaves: The Rise of the Planter Class in the English West Indies, 1624–1713* (Chapel Hill, N.C., 1972), 188–222; Higman, *Slave Population and Economy*, 188–189; Jerome S. Handler and Frederick W. Lange, *Plantation Slavery in Barbados: An Archaeological and Historical Investigation* (Cambridge, Mass., 1978), 33–34, 72–83.

16. James Stephen, *The Slavery of the British West India Island Colonies* . . . , 2 vols. (London, 1824), I, 54; Richard B. Sheridan, *Sugar and Slavery: An Economic History of the British West Indies, 1623–1775* (Baltimore, 1974), 258; Thomas Roughley, *The Jamaica Planter's Guide; or, A System for Planting and Managing a Sugar Estate, or Other Plantations* . . . (London, 1823), 276. See also William Dickson, *Letters on Slavery* (London, 1789), 23; James Grainger, *The Sugar-Cane: A Poem* (London, 1766), 22; James Stephen, *The Crisis of the Sugar Colonies* . . . (London, 1802), 10 (quotation).

marvel at "the lovely sight [of] . . . a hundred handsome *Negroes*, men and women, with every one a grasse-green bunch . . . on their heads . . . all coming in a train one after another."[17] So pervasive was ganging in Caribbean sugar societies that even mulemen were organized into such groups under the supervision of a "headman," as were various "trade gangs" of carpenters, masons, smiths, and the like. West Indians even thought in terms of gang labor where it did not, in fact, exist. In an agreement drawn up in 1835 between the proprietor and newly emancipated slaves of the small island of Barbuda, a graduated wage scale was established. It specified payments according to the freedmen's capabilities as members of the "first class gang," "weeding gang," and "grass gang." Barbuda, however, contained no sugar estates, and Barbudan slaves had engaged in a wide variety of occupations, none of which were characterized by gang labor.[18]

If the association of sugar and gangs was almost axiomatic, the relationship was not a static, unchanging one. The more progressive planters conceded that an inability or unwillingness to grade the members of a gang carefully could impair efficiency and create hardships for less able slaves. The most obvious remedy—one certainly emphasized by late-eighteenth- and early nineteenth-century treatises on plantation husbandry—was to increase the number of gangs. Consequently, some planters in those years experimented with as many as four to six gangs.[19] Improvements were particularly sought in the arduous operation of cane holing. Proslavery advocate Alexander Barclay claimed that individual slaves were generally given distinct sections of land to hole and were not always constrained to keep in line; others had their slaves work in pairs of one stronger and one weaker laborer, thereby equalizing their efforts. However,

17. Stephen, *Crisis of the Sugar Colonies*, 11; Richard Ligon, *A True and Exact History of the Island of Barbadoes* (London, 1673), 43.

18. Roughley, *Jamaica Planter's Guide*, 110–112; *Marly; or, The Life of a Planter in Jamaica* . . . (Glasgow, 1828), 93–94; Bennett, *Bondsmen and Bishops*, 11; Michael Craton, *Searching for the Invisible Man: Slaves and Plantation Life in Jamaica* (Cambridge, Mass., 1978), 208. The agreement is enclosed with MacGregor's Dispatch to Aberdeen, May 16, 1835, CO 7/41, Public Record Office, London, as cited in Douglas Hall, *Five of the Leewards, 1834–1870: The Major Problems of the Postemancipation Period in Antigua, Barbuda, Montserrat, Nevis, and St. Kitts* (Barbados, 1971), 66.

19. Dr. Collins, *Practical Rules for the Management and Medical Treatment of Negro Slaves in the Sugar Colonies* (Freeport, N.Y., 1971 [orig. publ. London, 1803]), 151; William Dickson, *Mitigation of Slavery* . . . (Miami, Fla., 1969 [orig. publ. London, 1814]), 13–14; Craton, *Searching for the Invisible Man*, 139–140.

the gang generally still began and ended work together and was just as much subject to constant surveillance.[20]

But some Caribbean sugar planters went further, for, in the late eighteenth and early nineteenth century, some introduced individual tasking to at least the cane-holing operation. In the late eighteenth century, Bryan Edwards advocated individual tasking but also noted that "this is not always practicable." John Baillie, testifying in the early nineteenth century, described how a Jamaican slave digging cane holes "does his day's work [by about two or three in the afternoon] . . . and is at liberty to go where he pleases afterwards." On the other hand, he added that they "can scarcely give task-work" in other areas of the sugar cycle.[21] Clement Caines indicates the limits to which progressive minds generally extended. In 1800 he advocated dispensing with the whole process of "lining" in cane-hole digging but acknowledged that this was only feasible with a small row of slaves "on account of the difficulty of preserving a considerable and lengthened row of people in regular order, without a surer guide than their own attention." For the most part, rows and regularity were not to be sacrificed to the new "improving" spirit.[22]

Bahian sugar planters do not appear to have followed the example of their Caribbean counterparts by introducing tasking into cane holing. Indeed, as Stuart Schwartz has emphasized, "field labor in Brazil was essentially gang labor." However, as early as the seventeenth century, this region's sugar planters introduced piecework into cane cutting as one way of stimulating labor productivity. According to Schwartz: "Slaves were assigned a certain number of 'hands' of cane to be cut as their tarefa or daily task. . . . At the completion of the tarefa de corte (daily cane-cutting quota), the slave was free to spend time as he or she liked. Much of the labor on Bahian plantations was assigned by tarefa, not only in the cutting of cane but in the mill, at the pottery, and elsewhere." Important as this development was, it

20. Alexander Barclay, A Practical View of the Present State of Slavery in the West Indies . . . (London, 1826), 310; Edwards, History of British Colonies, II, 210; Marly, 165.

21. Edwards, History of British Colonies, II, 151; Great Britain, Parliamentary Papers, Minutes of Evidence Taken before the Select Committee of the House of Lords Appointed to Inquire into the Laws and Usages of the Several West India Colonies in Relation to the Slave Population, no. 127 (1831–1832), 47. See also Josiah Condor, Wages or the Whip: An Essay on the Comparative Cost and Productiveness of Free and Slave Labour (London, 1833), 75–81.

22. Clement Caines, Letters on the Cultivation of the Otaheite Cane . . . (London, 1801), 51.

was not individual tasking. Teams or pairs of slaves, rather than individuals, formed the basic production unit in cane cutting.[23]

During the early nineteenth century and in colonies where the British government could exert pressure—as in the crown colonies of Trinidad, Demerara-Essequibo, Berbice, and Mauritius—tasking was introduced more widely as part of a broader amelioration campaign to reduce the hours worked by slaves. Advocates of tasking argued that its introduction would increase profitability and reduce the costs of supervision. By the mid-1820s, the system had been adopted on many sugar estates in Trinidad and was widespread in Berbice. By the late 1820s, it was "becoming pretty general" in Demerara. James Alexander, who visited Essequibo in the early 1830s, saw slaves weeding a cane plot by tasks, which were "frequently completed at three in the afternoon."[24] Similarly, in Mauritius, occupied by the British from 1810 onward, "the adoption of tasks, whenever practicable," noted Charles Telfair, "augmented the amount of work performed, . . . simplified the duties of the overseer, [and allowed] . . . many of the more handy negroes . . . to perform their portions before four o'clock, and some even before two o'clock p.m." According to Mr. H. Hunter, testifying before the House of Commons in the mid-nineteenth century, tasks were well established for most operations on Mauritian sugar estates: the "daily tasks of a slave in digging 100 holes; in cutting cane, two to three cart-loads, cut and cleaned; and in cleaning 800 feet by four or five feet of ground."[25] In short, there was a perceptible movement, more prevalent in some of the newer British slave societies, from gang to task, even in the sugar regions.

Plantations in North and South America that grew tobacco, short-staple cotton, and coffee shared many of the same features of the archetypal Caribbean gang system. During the planting season, for example, planters in the cotton South generally divided their slaves into two gangs of plow and hoe hands, respectively.[26] The role of

23. Stuart B. Schwartz, *Sugar Plantations in the Formation of Brazilian Society: Bahia, 1550–1835* (New York, 1985), 109, 139–145, 154–155.

24. Higman, *Slave Populations*, 179; Sir James Edward Alexander, *Transatlantic Sketches, Comprising Visits to the Most Interesting Scenes in North and South America, and the West Indies* . . . (London, 1833), I, 98.

25. Telfair, *Some Account of Slavery at Mauritius*, 33; Great Britain, House of Commons, *Reports from the Select Committee on Sugar and Coffee Planting* (1848), I, 215. See also Moses D. E. Nwulia, *The History of Slavery in Mauritius and the Seychelles, 1810–1875* (Rutherford, N.J., 1981).

26. Phillips, *American Negro Slavery*, 237, 240, 268; Gray, *History of Agriculture*, I,

leaders (or headmen) was as critical in cotton as in sugar cultivation. As one Mississippi planter exhorted:

Have a headman among your plowers; hold him responsible for the quantity of work, at least, and you might for the quality too. . . . Make one of your best hands leader of the hoe hands, and class your hands, so that all may keep up with the leader. Three women will carry two rows, and if first rate women, four will carry three rows. . . . When your rows are of different lengths, make the leader take alternately the longest and shortest rows—this will enable them to keep together.[27]

The same imperatives were at work in Chesapeake tobacco cultivation. When a line of female laborers was found to be weeding too few rows, their Virginia master, Landon Carter, promised the foreman "a sound correction" unless he "mended his pace." Under a gang arrangement, an individual's place in the line determined the speed at which he worked. Thus, when this same Chesapeake planter wished to demonstrate to his disgraced gardener that "the hoe [was not] to be his field of diversion," he gave him "the place of my fourth man and have ordered my overseers to keep him to that." He smugly observed that this "made him quicken the motion of his arm."[28]

Coffee planters in nineteenth-century Brazil also organized their slave complements into gangs. During the twice-annual weedings, the four best hands acted as lead-row men, working as pacesetters for those slower workers sandwiched in between. Each gang moved in line from the bottom to the top of hillsides on which coffee trees were always planted. As Warren Dean describes coffee production in the Rio Claro region of Brazil: "This was gang labor, supervised by *feitores* who were sometimes slaves themselves, who maintained discipline mainly with insults and threats, with the whip as a last

548–549. The best way to explore upland cotton ganging is through plantation diaries: see, for example, Franklin L. Riley, "Diary of a Mississippi Planter," *Publications of the Mississippi Historical Quarterly*, X (1909), 305–481; Ulrich Bonnell Phillips and James D. Glunt, eds., *Florida Plantation Records from the Papers of George Noble Jones* (St. Louis, Mo., 1927); Edwin Adams Davis, *Plantation Life in the Florida Parishes of Louisiana, 1836–1846, as Reflected in the Diary of Bennet H. Barrow* (New York, 1967 [orig. publ. 1943]).

27. Townes, "Farm Management," *Southern Cultivator*, V (Feb. 1847), 61 (quotation); see also V (Apr. 1847), 26.

28. Jack P. Greene, ed., *The Diary of Colonel Landon Carter of Sabine Hall, 1752–1778*, 2 vols. (Charlottesville, Va., 1965), I, 397, 430.

resort. . . . The work day was sun to sun, and after dark during harvest."[29]

As in the case of the sugar regime, planters of tobacco, short-staple cotton, and coffee tended either to introduce elements of individual tasking into their operations or, in some cases, to adopt the system wholesale. This tendency became more widespread as time wore on and was particularly noticeable in the nineteenth century. Picking short-staple cotton, collecting coffeeberries, husking corn, and stripping and prizing tobacco were operations that lent themselves to individual tasking, even when most of the other work with these staples was effected by slaves organized into gangs.[30] But, by the early nineteenth century, some upland cotton planters had established individual tasks for virtually all of their operations—from plowing through hoeing to picking the cotton. It would be surprising if some coffee and tobacco planters were not experimenting along similar lines.[31]

Although gang systems, then, had a tendency to employ tasking in some operations and even, in some cases, to evolve into full-scale task systems, there were still two identifiable intermediate stages. The first remained a gang system, but one where the gangs were small and relatively unsupervised. To some extent, this pattern could be found on many tobacco quarters, for the size of their laboring units, generally, was small, but it was most typically found on those plantations engaged in a truly diversified farm routine. Such plantations were most common in the temperate Chesapeake region, particularly in the late eighteenth and nineteenth centuries, when tobacco no longer reigned supreme, at least in the tidewater.[32] Since

29. Stanley J. Stein, *Vassouras: A Brazilian Coffee County, 1850–1900* (New York, 1976 [orig. publ. Cambridge, Mass., 1957]), 34, 163; Warren Dean, *Rio Claro: A Brazilian Plantation System, 1820–1920* (Stanford, Calif., 1976), 64. The careful reader will have noted that coffee and cotton seem to have given rise both to task and gang systems. I will attempt to explain this in the following section.

30. This assessment is based on my incomplete analysis of 19th-century southern agricultural periodicals. For a small sample, see James O. Breeden, ed., *Advice among Masters: The Ideal in Slave Management in the Old South* (Westport, Conn., 1980).

31. Gray, *History of Agriculture*, I, 551–554.

32. The literature on Chesapeake diversification is large. Some of the best works include Paul G. E. Clemens, *The Atlantic Economy and Colonial Maryland's Eastern Shore: From Tobacco to Grain* (Ithaca, N.Y., 1980); Carville V. Earle, *The Evolution of a Tidewater Settlement System: All Hallow's Parish, Maryland, 1650–1783*, University of Chicago Department of Geography Research Paper, no. 170 (Chicago, 1975); David Klingaman, "The Significance of Grain in the Development of

the labor force on such plantations could be divided into as many as six or more units, each composed of about one to five slaves, routinization of labor or the formation of permanent hoe or plow gangs was impossible. Squads of slaves performed a variety of functions, and, although there might have been one slave setting the tempo of the work, there were so few slaves in a group that the notion of their being driven is probably inappropriate. In practice, such an arrangement might closely approximate individual tasking, for many a slave would work alone, completing several jobs during the day. The widespread practice of hiring slaves reinforced the trend toward individual autonomy.[33]

Despite the tendencies toward individual work, however, the small gang was still the most common work unit on diversified plantations of any size. In the early nineteenth century, James Madison noted that "slaves [were] seldom employed in regular task work" in his part of Virginia. During the pea harvest, Landon Carter placed two overseers at each end of a row so that his gang's productivity could be closely monitored. The wheat harvest, which became the central event of the agricultural year in many parts of the Chesapeake by the late eighteenth century, led planters to investigate closely how to make their harvesting gang—this "whole machine," as Thomas Jefferson termed it—move more expeditiously. George Washington, for instance, hoped to produce "more ease, regularity and dispatch" among his harvesters by a careful allocation of roles and division into gangs. For every two cradlers whom Washington and Jefferson employed, seven and five gatherers, respectively, were allocated. This gang system was indeed closely monitored.[34] Chesapeake planters generally organized their children into "small gangs," having them perform simple tasks like shelling corn and sowing grass seed, activi-

---

the Tobacco Colonies," *Journal of Economic History*, XXIX (1969), 268–278; and the essay by Lois Green Carr and Lorena Walsh in this volume.

33. Gray, *History of Agriculture*, I, 554–555; John T. Schlotterbeck, "The 'Social Economy' of an Upper South Community: Orange and Greene Counties, Virginia, 1815–1860," in Orville Vernon Burton and Robert C. McMath, Jr., eds., *Class, Conflict, and Consensus: Antebellum Southern Community Studies* (Westport, Conn., 1982), 11–12; Sarah S. Hughes, "Slaves for Hire: The Allocation of Black Labor in Elizabeth City County, Virginia, 1782 to 1810," *WMQ*, 3d Ser., XXXV (1978), 260–286.

34. "James Madison's Attitude toward the Negro," *Journal of Negro History*, VI (1921), 89; Greene, ed., *Diary of Carter*, I, 497; Edwin M. Betts, ed., *Thomas Jefferson's Garden Book, 1766–1824, with Relevant Extracts from His Other Writings* (Philadelphia, 1944), 228, 230; Donald Jackson and Dorothy Twohig, eds., *The Diaries of George Washington*, 6 vols. (Charlottesville, Va., 1976–1979), II, 172, V, 9–10.

ties not too far removed from the experiences of Caribbean "grass gangs." Such arrangements resemble the small gangs assembled in such diverse work situations as mining, quarrying, or shipbuilding throughout the Western world. All shared at least one feature: teamwork was valued, but the scattered nature of the work made external monitoring of effort difficult and expensive.[35]

A second intermediate stage between tasking and ganging was a combination of both systems—an arrangement best termed collective tasking. The jobbing or task gangs that were hired out to Caribbean planters represent one variant of this form. Henry Bolingbroke provides an admirable definition: "A Task Gang . . . is so called from its undertaking to do a specific quantity of work, such as clearing and preparing so many acres of land, draining and planting the same; which they are paid for by the acre." Such groups were the hardest-worked of any West Indian slaves. According to Benjamin M'Mahon, jobbing gangs "were tasked to perform each a certain amount of work, without any deduction for weather; the consequence was that they had to be at it from day-light till dark, without even stopping for meals."[36] Certainly, jobbing gangs might wreak some form of revenge for their harsh treatment. In 1811 Barbadian planters complained that their hired gangs employed by the task often dug shallow cane holes. But the planters could usually counter the task gangs' stratagems. In this case, they simply ordered the hired gangs to begin work earlier than usual.[37]

Collective tasking was not confined to hired gangs. When a gang lagged behind in its work, an owner might task its members to make up for lost time. An upland cotton planter from South Carolina declared that he did "not believe in tasking Negroes all the time, but I believe in tasking them when it is necessary, in case of a push, when the crop is suffering." A Jamaican planter, who was forced to resort to this strategy, observed that the slaves "became very much dissatisfied, at being put off their ordinary routine of working." Jonathan Steele's experiments in late-eighteenth-century Barbados in-

35. Schlotterbeck, "Social Economy," in Burton and McMath, eds., *Class, Consensus, and Conflict*, 11. For references, see Ralph Schlomowitz, "Melanesian Labor and the Development of the Queensland Sugar Industry, 1863–1906," *Research in Economic History*, VII (1982), 335.

36. Henry Bolingbroke, *A Voyage to Demerary, Account of the Settlements There, and of Those on the Essequibo and Berbice, 1799–1806* (London, 1807), 215; Benjamin M'Mahon, *Jamaica Plantership* (London, 1839), 86.

37. Minute Book of the Barbados Agricultural Society, 30, as cited in Higman, *Slave Populations*, 164.

volved collective tasking. Groups of slaves were given financial inducements to hole, weed, and hoe an acre of canes per day.[38] One of the most progressive of early nineteenth-century treatises on plantation husbandry—by Dr. Collins—advocated tasking, but only in holing (the preserve of the task or jobbing gangs). As James Stephens later pointed out, "Dr. Collins had in view, when he recommended taskwork, the assessment of a daily portion of the work required, not *on each individual slave*, but on the *collective gang.*"[39]

But, if individual tasking was not generally countenanced on Jamaican sugar plantations or those of other long-established Anglo-American sugar societies, it was surprisingly widespread in other areas and on other kinds of estates. Not only was the task system associated with a whole range of staple crops and secondary plantation activities, it also became more widely adopted over time. By the early nineteenth century, it was even invading the sugar regimes of newly acquired Anglo-American slave societies. By the third decade of the nineteenth century, perhaps a majority of slaves in the Anglo-American world were working by task rather than in gangs.

HOW DO WE account for the original association of task and gang systems with particular crops, and how do we explain the tendency for gang systems to evolve into task systems? Certainly, staple-crop requirements explain much about the original choice of labor arrangement. In particular, the degree to which direct supervision (or, to put it more technically, external monitoring of input) was required by various crop cycles or by pivotal operations within crop cycles lies at the heart of the association between crops and labor systems. Some staples required close surveillance, either because their production schedule involved a careful synchronization of operations (as with sugar) or because they were delicate plants that were difficult to grow successfully (as with tobacco).[40] Wherever supervision

38. *Farmer and Planter*, V, 229, as cited in Gray, *History of Agriculture*, I, 552; *Marly*, 153; Dickson, *Mitigation of Slavery*, 119–120, 123–133. See also *Slavery in British Guiana* in *Negro Slavery* (London, 1823–1826), 2–4. Task gangs were introduced into royal shipyards in Britain and were opposed by the workers for much the same reasons that jobbing gangs were hated by West Indian slaves. See James M. Haas, "The Introduction of Task Work into the Royal Dockyards, 1775," *Journal of British Studies*, VIII, no. 2 (May 1969), 44–68; and *Essay on Task-Work*, 8.

39. Dr. Collins, *Practical Rules*, 152–154; Stephen, *Slavery of British West India*, I, 57, II, 232–235. The debate between Collins and Stephen is crucial to an understanding of what tasking usually meant in the context of Caribbean sugar production.

40. For the careful synchronization in sugar production, see Ward Barrett, "Caribbean Sugar-Production Standards in the Seventeenth and Eighteenth Centu-

was at a premium, gang systems seem to have arisen. Such associations were not confined only to the New World. In early seventeenth-century England, the commercial growth of special crops like woad gave rise to daily gang labor during the weeding and picking parts of the cycle. Both the laborers' unfamiliarity with the crop and the need for careful timing in the cycle seem to have accounted for this arrangement. In the case of sugar cultivation, where the two most critical features were the careful timing of operations and the assumed benefits of teamwork, gangs were large.[41] Tobacco cultivation, on the other hand, laid the most emphasis on the careful husbandry of a delicate plant. Only a tobacco planter could claim, as one Virginian did, that his crop had been "under my own eye, and [I] may say I saw almost every plant from the planting to the prizing." Such detailed attention was only practicable where gangs were, as one contemporary put it, "generally made into small parcells, not above eight or ten hands at a place."[42]

Conversely, where a crop was relatively hardy (as with rice) or where there was no particular urgency in the production schedule

ries," in John Parker, ed., *Merchants and Scholars: Essays in the History of Exploration and Trade* (Minneapolis, Minn., 1965), 145–170; Richard Pares, *Merchants and Planters*, Economic History Review Supplement no. 4 (Cambridge, 1960), 21; Fernando Ortiz, *Cuban Counterpoint: Tobacco and Sugar*, trans. Harriet de Onís (New York, 1947), 6, 26–27. For one of many descriptions of tobacco, see Joseph M. Hernandez, "On the Cultivation of the Cuban Tobacco Plant," *Southern Agriculturalist*, III (1830), 463.

41. Joan Thirsk, *Economic Policy and Projects: The Development of a Consumer Society in Early Modern England* (Oxford, 1978), 4–5. The best information on this subject comes from the example of sugar production in the postslavery era: teamwork was still seen as valuable, particularly in cane cutting, in spite of the negative connotations associated with gang work. See Jerome Handler, "Some Aspects of Work Organization on Sugar Plantations in Barbados," *Ethnology*, IV (1965), 16–38; Ralph Schlomowitz, "Team Work and Incentives: The Origins and Development of the Butty Gang System in Queenland's Sugar Industry, 1891–1913," *Journal of Comparative Economics*, III (1979), 41–55; and Schlomowitz, "Melanesian Labor," *Res. Econ. Hist.*, VII (1982), 327–361.

42. John Custis to Robert Cary, [1729], John Custis Letterbook, typescript, Research Library, Colonial Williamsburg Foundation; Sir Dalby Thomas, *An Historical Account of the Rise and Growth of the West-India Collonies . . .* (London, 1690), in Jerome E. Brooks, comp., *Tobacco: Its History Illustrated by the Books, Manuscripts, and Engravings in the Library of George Arents, Jr.*, 5 vols. (New York, 1937–1952), II, 531. One June day in 1770, Landon Carter visited one of his gangs three times and, on each occasion, spent two hours monitoring their progress in turning tobacco hills (Greene, ed., *Diary of Carter*, I, 422). More generally, see T. H. Breen, "The Culture of Agriculture: The Symbolic World of the Tidewater Planter, 1760–1790," in David D. Hall, John M. Murrin, and Thad W. Tate, eds., *Saints and Revolutionaries: Essays on Early American History* (New York, 1984), 247–284.

(as with tending pimento or drawing off turpentine), a more relaxed attitude could be taken to the external monitoring of input, and individual tasking arrangements usually evolved.[43] Here again, such associations were not confined to the New World. The great expansion of rice culture in seventeenth-century Lombardy, for instance, was predicated, not on a stable, sophisticated, and well-supervised labor force, but on a pool of transient labor drawn from far afield. Even New World crops produced largely by means of task labor can point up the association between gang labor and intensive supervision. Lowcountry rice was cultivated and processed by an elaborate schedule of tasks, but special work, like the combating of floodwaters, had to be closely supervised and seems to have been accomplished by organizing slaves into gangs. A Jamaican bookkeeper reported that the only work on a coffee plantation *not* carried out by tasks was the drying of the berries, because, in this operation, "constant attention was proper."[44]

Practicability and the costs of supervision, likewise, were vital considerations in the choice between task and gang systems. In the case of rice, naval stores, and, to a lesser extent, coffee and cocoa, a slave could tend a considerable acreage. As a result, the labor force was inevitably scattered, and close supervision of its input would have proved laborious and costly. An eighteenth-century lowcountry slave, for example, was expected to cultivate between three and four acres of rice; by the early nineteenth century, five acres were the norm.[45] A thousand cocoa trees formed the standard employment for an adult West Indian slave, whereas, as we have already noted, three to four times this number of trees constituted the turpentine worker's district. Even in sugar areas, there was some work, such as grass picking, that could, in James Stephen's words, "only be done

43. Arrowroot, like rice, was a hardy plant, which might explain its susceptibility to tasking (Handler, "History of Arrowroot," *Jour. Carib. Hist.*, II [1971], 50). Other staples that, like pimento and naval stores, were produced without hard driving or regimentation include coffee and cocoa: see Augustin Cochin, *The Results of Emancipation*, trans. Mary L. Booth (Boston, 1863), 200–201; and Benjamin Moseley, *A Treatise concerning the Properties and Effects of Coffee* (London, 1792), v.

44. Domenico Sella, *Crisis and Continuity: The Economy of Spanish Lombardy in the Seventeenth Century* (Cambridge, Mass., 1979), 121–122; Phillips, *American Negro Slavery*, 259; Kelly, *Voyage to Jamaica*, 19.

45. These ratios are based on the observations of 25 different 18th-century commentators and about 20 plantation-sale advertisements in South Carolina newspapers, where the number of field hands and amount of cleared rice land are given. See also James M. Clifton, "The Rice Industry in Colonial America," *Agricultural History*, LV (1981), 275.

by the slaves in a state of dispersion"; recourse was, therefore, "to the mode of individual task-work."[46]

Other staples, however, brought workers much closer together and made direct supervision more feasible. The density of laborers engaged in Caribbean sugar cultivation was unparalleled among New World staples. A general rule of thumb dictated one slave for every acre of cane land, although a ratio of three slaves to every two acres was not unusual. One to two acres per slave constituted the norm for tobacco cultivation.[47] The two crops that gave rise to both tasking and ganging in different parts of the New World—cotton and coffee—were characterized by land and labor ratios somewhere in between that of rice, on the one hand, and sugar, on the other.[48]

In addition to the degree of direct supervision required by a staple and the sheer practicability of monitoring input, the facility with which the laborers' output could be measured also shaped different forms of labor organization. For example, the productivity of a single pimento worker could be measured accurately and cheaply, particularly in the harvesting cycle. In Jamaica, Henry Whiteley observed a head bookkeeper examining the baskets of pimento collected by young slaves in order to "ascertain that *each* slave had duly performed the task allotted" (my emphasis). An anonymous Jamaican noted that the task in pimento harvesting was to "pick half a barrel of the pimento berries daily."[49] It was easy, in other words, to weigh an individual's baskets of pimento berries, and tasking may have developed in this stage of the crop cycle before being extended to other operations.

In the case of rice, it was less the harvesting and more the planting of the crop that lent itself to inexpensive and efficient measurement. The ubiquity and long-standing history of the quarter-acre task suggest that the planting and weeding stages of the rice cycle provided the initial rationale for the task system; once tasking became firmly established, it was extended to a whole host of plantation opera-

46. Cochin, *Results of Emancipation*, trans. Booth, 200–201 (see n. 10); Stephen, *Crisis of Sugar Colonies*, 12.

47. Goveia, *Slave Society*, 121; Dunn, *Sugar and Slaves*, 198. The tobacco acreage per hand ratio is based on observations of 10 different 18th- and early 19th-century Chesapeake commentators.

48. Alexander, *Transatlantic Sketches*, I, 24; George Pinckard, *Notes on the West Indies . . .* , 3 vols. (London, 1806), III, 404.

49. Henry Whiteley, *Three Months in Jamaica, in 1832: Comprising a Residence of Seven Weeks on a Sugar Plantation* (London, 1833); William Naish, *The Advantages of Free Labour over the Labour of Slaves, Elucidated in the Cultivation of Pimento, Ginger, and Sugar* (London, [ca. 1825]), 2. Barry Higman first suggested the importance of this factor in a personal communication to me.

tions. Before long, everything in rice cultivation was measured by neatly demarcated, universal standards, and an individual could largely be left to make his share of the crop in his own time with no detriment to the final product.[50]

Monitoring an individual's output was much more problematic in sugar and tobacco production. The large volumes involved in the sugarcane harvest made it impracticable to measure output by the individual task. Moreover, cane, once cut, had to be hurried to the grinders. With such a premium on haste, teamwork was believed to yield a joint output sufficiently larger than the sum of the outputs of laborers working independently.[51] In the case of tobacco, an individual laborer did not produce large volumes; seemingly, there was no apparent prohibition against measuring an individual's product by the task. However, the quality of any tobacco crop was so variable that there could not be, in Fernando Ortiz's words, "an exact unit of measurement for leaf tobacco."[52] One might count hogsheads, it is true, but the quality of the leaf, just as much as the number of hogsheads, determined the crop's worth. Moreover, tasking a single tobacco laborer made little sense when so much depended on the collective care expended on any one crop. For largely different reasons, then, sugar and tobacco production lent themselves to the measurement of collective, rather than individual, output.

Cotton and coffee, once again, were in something of an intermediate position, primarily because these two crops combined qualities that encouraged both tasking and ganging. On the one hand, both crops needed continual care in the planting and weeding parts of their cycles and, thus, proved excellent candidates for a gang system. On the other hand, harvesting of both crops was most efficiently carried out by the task. Thus, in Brazil, where most operations on coffee estates were reserved for slave gangs, the laborers were tasked during the harvest.[53] Similarly, in the upland cotton South, where again the gang system was widespread, the crop was often picked by task. As one upcountry Georgia planter explained: "The usual custom of planters is to work without tasks during the cultivation of their crop; but in gathering cotton tasks are common, and experience

50. Morgan, "Work and Culture," WMQ, 3d Ser., XXXIX (1982), 566.

51. See nn. 15 and 40 above for descriptions of the sugar cycle that stress these points. Bahian sugar plantations seem to be an exception. Slaves were assigned a daily task in cane cutting. However, teamwork was still primary. See Schwartz, Sugar Plantations, 140–141.

52. Ortiz, Cuban Counterpoint, trans. Onís, 36.

53. Stein, Vassouras, 36.

has proven that whenever work is of that kind of character that it can be properly parceled out into tasks, it is much better to do so . . . [because] the overseer . . . will get more work, and the negro will be better satisfied . . . [by] gain[ing] time to devote to his own jobs or pleasure."[54]

A social, rather than an economic, consideration may also have contributed to the adoption of the gang system, in particular. If social control was a pressing imperative, it made sense to gang. As Henry Drax observed as early as the seventeenth century, "The best Way that I know of to prevent Idleness, and to make the Negroes do their Work properly, will be upon the change of Work, constantly to Gang all the Negroes in the Plantations in the Time of Planting." Or, as William Dickson put it, writing from the vantage point of the more civilized nineteenth century, ganging was a "vulgar system (which, perhaps, was the only one that was practicable 150 years ago, with *an untamed set of savages*)."[55] On the other hand, if social control was of overriding, rather than just of contributory, importance, it seems surprising that the rice regime, where plantations were large and social control a concern, did not employ a gang system.

While a variety of staple-crop requirements, rather than concerns about social control, help explain the adoption of one labor arrangement over another, those choices were certainly not fixed or impervious to changing circumstances. The most obvious example is the transformation that began to take place on many sugar estates from gang to task labor toward the end of the slave era. The origins of this transformation can be traced, in part, to progressive metropolitan opinion opposed to slavery. In 1789, for instance, Benjamin Frossard, an antislavery French Protestant, urged planters to "fix up each slave with a task per week, and to allow him to use the time he earns in his own business, or to work on a small uncultivated plot that his master grants him, or to complete another task for a reasonable wage." It was incontestable, argued Frossard, that a slave "would work the

54. Robert Collins, "Essay on the Treatment and Management of Slaves," *Southern Cultivator*, XII (1854), 205–206. However, Stanley Engerman has suggested to me that the cotton harvest was not true tasking in the sense of a measure of labor input. Each worker's output was measured, it is true, but it was work done in a group, supervised closely and done in unison, with no apparent difference in rewards. This seems to me further confirmation that cotton was an intermediate crop, veering more toward a gang, than task, system.

55. Henry Drax, "Instructions for the Management of Drax-Hall and the Irish-Hope Plantation . . . ," in William Belgrove, *A Treatise upon Husbandry or Planting* (Boston, 1755), 64; Dickson, *Mitigation of Slavery*, 121.

whole week with unimaginable zeal, if he was sure that, after finishing on Friday, Saturday belonged to him."[56] According to the author of *An Essay on Task-Work*, "Mr. Wilberforce observed some years ago in the House of Commons, that the planters in the West-Indies ought to work their negroes in tasks, as the planters did in the southern states of America." This author's main argument in support of Wilberforce was that "the negroes, having an expectation of being able to finish their work in good time in the afternoon, which would be a real premium to them, would exert themselves with spirit and alacrity, and work very differently from the drawling manner they generally do, when they have no expectation of getting away while there is any day-light remaining." One author explicitly proposed "task-work" as the "means of paving the way for the introduction of voluntary labour on the part of the negroes."[57]

The other source of change came from below—from the slaves themselves. Naturally, this impetus is less easily documented. However, a study by Mary Turner, which explores a rich set of estate papers for the parish of Saint Thomas-in-the-East, one of the most important sugar-producing areas of Jamaica, is highly suggestive of broader processes. She finds evidence, which can be replicated for other plantations, of a constant struggle between slaves and their managers over the labor process. Through a perpetual testing of wills, a complex process of negotiation and renegotiation, work norms were eventually hammered out which, in turn, created opportunities for the slaves to demand taskwork in the form of food or cash payments for work beyond the agreed-upon norms. According to her account, "No later than the 1820's the slaves were pressing for task work in sugar production."[58] Perhaps the battle can be traced to earlier times, but the broader significance of this development is not in doubt.

56. Benjamin Sigismond Frossard, *La cause des esclaves nègres et des habitans de la Guinée* . . . (Lyon, 1789), II, 269.

57. *Essay on Task-Work*, ii, 6; review ["Condition of the Negroes in Our Colonies"], *Quarterly Review*, XXIX (1823), 500. See also *Plan for the Safe and Profitable Conversion of the Colonial Slaves into Free Labourers* (London, [1833?]); and Reverend George F. W. Mortimer, *The Immediate Abolition of Slavery, Compatible with the Safety and Prosperity of the Colonies* . . . (Newcastle-upon-Tyne, 1833).

58. Mary Turner, "Chattel Slaves into Wage Slaves: A Jamaican Case Study," in Malcolm Cross and Gad Heuman, eds., *Labour in the Caribbean: From Emancipation to Independence*, Warwick Caribbean Series (London, forthcoming). We very much need similar work from other plantations. I attempt to explore the struggle over the labor process in my forthcoming book, *Slave Counterpoint: Black Culture in the Eighteenth-Century Chesapeake and Lowcountry*.

That slaves were important in the shift to taskwork is most graphically displayed in the immediate responses of recently freed bondmen. Operations that previously had been unthinkable without gang labor swiftly became the preserve of task laborers. Much of the responsibility for effecting this transformation lay with the workers themselves. The importance of their preferences can be detected both within and between individual Caribbean islands. Within certain islands—Antigua and Saint Kitts, for instance—those laborers, who lived in independent villages and who therefore enjoyed more room to bargain over their terms of employment than resident estate workers, were in the vanguard of those seeking task or job work over daywork.[59]

Whole islands, not just a few villages, experienced the immediate postslavery years in widely contrasting ways. A society like Montserrat—which contained particularly independent laborers, deriving their autonomy from the use of extensive provision lands allotted to them as slaves and confirmed to them as freedmen—witnessed a more rapid turn from daywork to taskwork than any of her sister Leeward Islands. Similarly, in a society like British Guiana or Trinidad (where the land-labor ratio gave the freedmen greater comparative advantages than, say, freedmen in Barbados), task gangs, less than a fortnight after the proclamation of freedom, everywhere began combining for higher wages or for working only half a day. As Donald Wood has pointed out: "To an observer from Barbados, where daily work was the custom, operations in a Trinidad cane field looked ragged and ill-disciplined; the labourers started their task where they pleased and worked away on their own. In Barbados the labourers worked in line across the field."[60] In 1841 William Whitehouse unfavorably contrasted the rapid emergence and uniform system of tasking in British Guiana with the situation he found in Jamaica.[61] Wherever the freedmen held a modicum of bargaining power, taskwork prevailed.

59. Hall, *Five of the Leewards*, 44–45.

60. *Ibid.*, 50–51; Alan H. Adamson, *Sugar without Slaves: The Political Economy of British Guiana, 1838–1904* (New Haven, Conn., 1972), 34; Donald Wood, *Trinidad in Transition: The Years after Slavery* (London, 1968), 52. See also Claude Levy, *Emancipation, Sugar, and Federalism: Barbados and the West Indies, 1833–1876* (Gainesville, Fla., 1980), 78; W. Emanuel Riviere, "Labour Shortage in the British West Indies after Emancipation," *Jour. Carib. Hist.*, IV (1972), 17.

61. W. F. Whitehouse, *Agricola's Letters and Essays on Sugar Farming in Jamaica* (London, 1845), 17. By contrast, it is interesting that some upland cotton planters in the southern United States employed a modified gang arrangement, known as

The slaves' and ex-slaves' preference for tasking does not mean that its introduction proved an unqualified benefit to them. In Demerara, for instance, many planters in the 1820s inflated tasks beyond a normal day's labor to ensure that the slaves would have no free time. As Alan Adamson has pointed out for postemancipation British Guiana: "The definition of conventional field tasks was prepared by a committee of planters immediately following the abolition of slavery and was still used in the 1850s and 1860s. It is difficult to believe that this committee, nurtured in the climate of slavery, would not have set levels of performance at a relatively high level." In fact, the standard daily task for digging a trench in mid-nineteenth-century British Guiana would have taken the best English laborer between two and three days to complete.[62] Moreover, as Walter Rodney has argued, Guyanese "workers of all categories were subjected to increased rates of exploitation by the simple device of increasing the size of the tasks." Tasking proved most iniquitous for newly arrived Asian labor. According to Hugh Tinker, a task might require a working day of fifteen hours or more for "weaker or less experienced coolies." He quotes Governor Wodehouse of British Guiana, an early critic of the application of tasking to Indians, as saying that task work "is payment . . . of work done without any necessary reference to the time expended. . . . What is this . . . but a device for obtaining a certain amount of work without any trouble of superintendence?"[63]

Still, despite the potential for abuse, absence of supervision was only one of the benefits tasking offered freedmen. Closely related was the opportunity it gave laborers to gain time for their own affairs. More mundanely, an industrious laborer could earn more by the job or task than by daywork. These advantages were particularly

---

the squad system, in the immediate postwar years. See Ralph Schlomowitz, "The Squad System on Postbellum Cotton Plantations," in Orville Vernon Burton and Robert C. McMath, eds., *Toward a New South? Studies in Post–Civil War Southern Communities* (Westport, Conn., 1982), 265–280.

62. Higman, *Slave Populations*, 179; Adamson, *Sugar without Slaves*, 111–112.

63. Walter Rodney, *A History of the Guyanese Working People, 1881–1905* (Baltimore, 1981), 58; Hugh Tinker, *A New System of Slavery: The Export of Indian Labour Overseas, 1830–1920* (London, 1974), 183. The continuance of gangs and forms of collective tasking into the postemancipation era also proved onerous to the freedmen. See John Davy, *The West Indies, before and since Slave Emancipation, Comprising the Windward and Leeward Islands' Military Command* (London, 1854), 134; Adamson, *Sugar without Slaves*, 154; Great Britain, House of Commons, *Reports from the Select Committee on Sugar and Coffee Planting* (1848), III, 3–4. Tasking scales drawn up at emancipation by planters reveal a mixture of individual and collective tasks: see, for example, Marshall, *Colthurst Journal*, 246–254; and Craton and Walvin, *Jamaican Plantation*, 328–331.

valued by a people whose "natural love of independence" drew contemporary comment. This was as true of freedmen on the Eastern Shore of Virginia in the middle of the seventeenth century as of those living in Jamaica two centuries later. Thus, "Anthony the Negro," a resident of Northampton County, Virginia, was reported to have said, after dividing a cornfield in which he and a white farmer had an interest, "I am very glad of [the division, for] now I know myne owne, hee [the white farmer] finds fault with mee that I doe not worke, but now I know myne owne ground and I will worke when I please and play when I please." According to a visitor to Jamaica in 1840, the freedman's overriding priority was not much different. It was to avoid being "tied down to give so many days' labor continuously and continually," and it was a desire "to be at liberty to do anything else that he might want for himself."[64]

THE ADVANTAGES OF tasking, as perceived by freedmen in the Caribbean sugar colonies and elsewhere, bring me, finally, to a consideration of some of the implications of the task and gang systems under slavery. Provided that there were equal commercial opportunities (in terms of available land, the marketing structure, and the like) from one slave society to another, it seems logical to suppose that taskworkers would be better able to exploit these opportunities than gang workers. However onerous tasking could become for some slaves, the system at least allowed them a certain latitude to apportion their day, to work intensively in their task, and then have the balance of their time. Perhaps the best, backhanded testament to this advantage comes from Thomas Cooper, who resided in Jamaica from 1817 to 1820. The reason taskwork was so "very uncommon" on that

64. T. H. Breen and Stephen Innes, *"Myne Owne Ground": Race and Freedom on Virginia's Eastern Shore, 1640–1676* (New York, 1980), 6; Great Britain, House of Commons, *Report from the Select Committee on the West India Colonies* (1842), 6845, as cited in Douglas Hall, "The Flight from the Estates Reconsidered: The British West Indies, 1838–42," *Jour. Carib. Hist.*, X–XI (1978), 19. For other sources which point to the advantages of tasking, see Davy, *West Indies*, 91, 121, 313, 362, 501; Adamson, *Sugar without Slaves*, 165; Douglas Hall, *Free Jamaica, 1838–1865: An Economic History* (New Haven, Conn., 1959), 44–45; Great Britain, House of Commons, *Reports from the Select Committee on Sugar and Coffee Planting* (1848), I, 15, 215–216, II, 17, III, 3–4, 60, 75, 102, 162, 185, 255, 347, 408; James McNeill and Chimman Lal, *Report to the Government of India on the Conditions of Indian Immigrants in Four British Colonies and Surinam* (1915), Cd. 7744, 16–17, 65, Cd. 7745, 206. For an important general survey of the ex-slaves' responses and adjustments to freedom, see Stanley L. Engerman, "Economic Adjustments to Emancipation in the United States and British West Indies," *Journal of Interdisciplinary History*, XIII (1982–1983), 191–220.

island, he maintained, was that it was "held to be dangerous to allow the slave much spare time."[65]

The advantage of having spare time was readily recalled by ex-slaves in the lowcountry. One freedman, for instance, reported that "a good active industrious man would finish his task sometimes at 12, sometimes at 1 and 2 o'clock and the rest of the time was his own to use as he pleased." Lowcountry masters were careful not to encroach upon their slaves' "own time" unless by offering payment. According to a Jamaican, South Carolina and Georgia planters were "very particular in never employing a negro, without his consent, after his task is finished, and agreeing with him for the payment which he is to receive."[66] Many lowcountry slaves put these opportunities to good effect. As one ex-slave explained, "They all worked by tasks, and had a plenty of time to work for themselves and in that way all slaves who were industrious could get around them considerable property in a short-time." This is exactly what happened in the eighteenth- and nineteenth-century lowcountry. By the end of slavery, there was a significant internal slave economy. Some slaves were raising stock, many slave families were growing their own crops on four to five acres apiece, and slave property was being not only produced and exchanged but also inherited.[67]

If the task system in the lowcountry represented one pole in terms of the slaves' domestic economy, the gang system practiced in an area like the Chesapeake represented another. Chesapeake slaves worked, in William Tatham's words, "from daylight until the dusk of the evening, and some part of the night, by moon or candlelight, during the winter."[68] As a result, Chesapeake slaves generally had no time of their own during the week, apart from a rare holiday, and were, therefore, only able to work on their own account on Sundays.

65. Thomas Cooper, *Facts Illustrative of the Condition of the Negro Slaves in Jamaica* (London, 1824), 27.

66. Morgan, "Work and Culture," *WMQ*, 3d Ser., XXXIX (1982), 586; *Essay on Task-Work*, 9.

67. Morgan, "Work and Culture," *WMQ*, 3d Ser., XXXIX (1982), 590; and "The Ownership of Property by Slaves in the Mid-Nineteenth-Century Low Country," *Journal of Southern History*, XLIX (1983), 399–420.

68. G. Melvin Herndon, *William Tatham and the Culture of Tobacco* (Miami, Fla., 1969), 102. The same would apply to the upland cotton South. Interestingly, one traveler who went from lowcountry South Carolina (where he noted the shorter workday associated with the task system) to Mississippi remarked upon the difference. In 1820, while in the Deep South, he observed that the slaves "here . . . seem to work many hours longer than in Carolina" (Adam Hodgson, *Remarks during a Journey through North America in the Years 1819, 1820, and 1821 . . .* [New York, 1823], 174).

Moreover, as Chesapeake planters accorded a much higher priority to foodstuffs production than did their lowcountry counterparts, Chesapeake slaves were much less encouraged to engage in part-time, private subsistence activities. Field hands in eighteenth-century tidewater Virginia produced twice or even three times as much corn per head as did those in the eighteenth-century lowcountry.[69]

These differences, in both available time and white encouragement were, in turn, translated into sharply contrasting domestic economies. The domestic plots cultivated by lowcountry slaves merited the term "little plantations," or "private fields," whereas, in the Chesapeake, they were never more than garden plots. This is not to say that Chesapeake slaves were reluctant, domestic cultivators. William Tatham noted in 1800 that there were crops which were *"permitted* (and greatly *confirmed* by custom) to slaves," namely, "potatoes, garden-stuff, pumpkins, melons, a few particular fruit-trees, peas, hops, flax, and cotton."[70] However, the very diversity of the crops grown by Chesapeake slaves is revealing of their gardening orientation, a reflection of the attenuated time and land allowed them. Furthermore, those account books of nineteenth-century Chesapeake planters that recorded purchases from their slaves reveal only minor subsistence activities by the bondmen. Finally, although slaves in the Chesapeake gained a deserved reputation as the "Chicken Merchants" of the region, this virtually represented the extent of their stock-raising.[71]

69. This is explored at greater length in my *Slave Counterpoint*.

70. For the lowcountry, see "A Curious New Description," *Universal Museum*, I (1762), 477; and Adele Stanton Edwards, ed., *Journals of the Privy Council, 1783–1789*, State Records of South Carolina (Columbia, S.C., 1971), 132. Mere garden plots continued to be reserved to Chesapeake blacks when free: typical labor contracts in the immediate postemancipation era granted freedmen the use of "garden spots" or truck patches. See, for example, Report on the Condition of Bureau Affairs in the Sub-District of Amelia and Powhatan Counties of Virginia, by Lieut. J. B. Clinton, Jan. 31, 1867 (A7829), Freedmen and Southern Society, files of documents in the National Archives, University of Maryland, College Park (hereafter references to documents read at the society will be given in parentheses). William Tatham, *Communications concerning the Agriculture and Commerce of the United States of America* . . . (London, 1800), 55.

71. Account Book, ca. 1845, Bruce of Berry Hill Plantation Volumes, box 5; Plantation Record Book, 1848–1853, and Farm Register, 1850s, Richard Irby Papers; John Tucker Ledger, 1833–1835, Tucker Family Account Books; John Washington Account Book, 1848, Washington Family Papers of Caroline County; Manuscript Volume of William B. Irby, 1862, Neblett and Irby Family Papers, all in Alderman Library, University of Virginia, Charlottesville. James Mercer to B. Muse, Jan. 6, 1782, Battaille Muse Papers, Duke University, Durham, N.C. Labor contracts in the postemancipation Chesapeake, unlike those in the lowcountry,

On some of the smaller, flat or gently sloping Caribbean islands (such as Barbados or Antigua), the situation facing slaves was not too far removed from that encountered by Chesapeake bondmen. Working sunup to sundown, six days a week, under the gang system formed the pervasive reality for most field hands on these islands. Moreover, the planters' agricultural priorities—primarily a function of high prices for sugar and restricted land supplies—demanded that slaves confine their subsistence activities to garden patches. Certainly, Barbadian slaves were renowned for the intensive cultivation of their house plots. In 1824 J. W. Jordan observed that many slaves on one Barbadian estate "reap annually 1000 lbs of yambs each, besides Guinea and Indian corn, eddoes, potatoes, cassava, ginger, and the more industrious plant arrowroot, which they prepare and sell for a good price." Eight years later, Henry Coleridge noticed that "yams, Indian corn, plantains, or even canes, are to be seen growing round every hut." But extensive provision grounds were largely denied these slaves.[72]

A similar reality faced Antiguan slaves. In 1788, when John Luffman visited the island, he observed that adult slaves were allocated patches of ground no more than "twenty five to thirty feet square." A few years later, another visitor pointed out the disadvantages that flowed from a system of subsistence dependent on planter allocations as opposed to slave provision grounds. The quantity and quality of the food supply were inferior, he noted, but also "the negro suffers too in his poultry and little stock, which are his wealth . . . [and] a negro without stock, and means to purchase tobacco and other little conveniences, and some finery too for his wife, is

---

often delimited the stock-raising activities of the freedmen. It is highly likely, as with much else in these contracts, that this was meant to continue the practices of slavery, therefore telling us as much about life under slavery as under freedom. A typical agreement specified that the freedmen "can raise and keep chickens and no other fowls—six to eight hens to each man and when they have a family may raise a hog but no sows or pigs or other kind of stock" (Agreement between E. W. Hubbard, Agent for Miss E. W. Eppes, and 8 Freedmen, Dec. 2, 1865 [A8140]).

72. Joseph William Jordan, *An Account of the Management of Certain Estates in the Island of Barbados* (London, 1826), 4; Henry Nelson Coleridge, *Six Months in the West Indies, in 1825* (London, 1832), 125–126. See also Handler, "History of Arrowroot," *Jour. Carib. Hist.*, XI (1971), 79; Sidney W. Mintz and Douglas Hall, *The Origins of the Jamaican Internal Marketing System*, Yale University Publications in Anthropology no. 57 (New Haven, Conn., 1960), 4, 10; Marshall, *Colthurst Journal*, 140; Dickson, *Letters on Slavery*, 11; Davy, *West Indies*, 16; Stephen, *Slavery of British West India*, II, 261; Pinckard, *Notes on the West Indies*, I, 368; Thomas Rolph, *A Brief Account Together with Observations Made during a Visit in the West Indies . . .* (Dundas, 1836), 52.

miserable."[73] The notion of slaves as gardeners rather than as proto-peasants applies in large measure to the dependent populations of both the smaller Caribbean islands and areas of North America like the Chesapeake.

What clearly demarcated all Caribbean slaves (even those of the smaller islands) from their North American counterparts (the Chesapeake more so than the lowcountry) were radically different marketing opportunities. Even if some Caribbean slaves were more gardeners than large-scale cultivators, great numbers of them were soon producing a surplus that they could sell to their masters, to other slaves, or to other freemen. Once these surpluses were regularly taken to local markets and exchanged for other commodities, or sold for cash, market day became an important social and economic institution. As early as the 1740s, the manager of the Codrington plantations on Barbados remarked that nothing could keep his slaves from the markets short of "locking them up." By the early nineteenth century, George Pinckard declared that Barbadian markets "depend almost wholly" on the slaves' private endeavors. J. B. Moreton, when writing of Jamaica in the late eighteenth century, observed that "Sunday is the greatest market day; the negroes from all parts of the country flock to town, hundreds of them in a gang, carrying with them the product of their grounds." Similarly, John Luffman noted that the small patches allotted Antiguan slaves proved "to be of material benefit to the country, their produce principally supplying the 'Sunday market' . . . with vegetables." By this means, Antiguan whites were "prevented from starving."[74]

In the larger, mountainous Caribbean islands (most notably, Jamaica and Saint Domingue), the slaves' access to extensive provision grounds as well as garden plots provided for even more intensive marketing. On Jamaica, the largest of the British islands, most planters owned land that they would rarely consider using for cane. Over time, these backlands became the preserve of slaves; by the late eighteenth century, slaves were even permitted, in Bryan Edwards's words, "to bequeath their grounds or gardens to such of their fellow-slaves as they think proper." Moreover, the planters so fully recognized the slaves' rights to these grounds that they offered compen-

73. John Luffman, *A Brief Account of the Island of Antigua* . . . (London, 1788), 94–95; Sir William Young, *A Tour through the Several Islands of Barbadoes, St. Vincent, Antigua, Tobago, and Grenada, in the Years 1791 and 1792,* in Bryan Edwards, *History of the British Colonies* . . . (Philadelphia, 1806), IV, 266. See also Goveia, *Slave Society,* 135–139; and Hall, *Five of the Leewards,* 29–30.

74. Bennett, *Bondsmen and Bishops,* 24; Pinckard, *Notes on the West Indies,* I, 369–370; J. B. Moreton, *Manners and Customs,* 36; Luffman, *Brief Account,* 94–95.

sation wherever it became necessary to convert an area of slave cultivation to estate use. As Sidney W. Mintz and Douglas Hall have
emphasized, "It is upon the polinks that the foundations of the free
peasantry were established."[75] By the late eighteenth century, slaves
had become the most important suppliers of foodstuffs to all Ja-
maicans. Many of the island's minor exports—everything from gums
to arrowroot, from oil nuts to goatskins—were produced on their
grounds, and Edward Long could estimate that one-fifth of the currency circulating on the island was in their hands.[76] In the case of
islands like Jamaica, Saint Vincent, and Saint Domingue, the favorable commercial opportunities brought about by a conjunction of
planter preferences, soil, topography, and climate, not to mention
the abilities of slaves, outweighed many of the disadvantages inherent in a gang system. Indeed, on these islands, the extensive provision ground system may be said to have arisen *in spite of* the gang
system, although, in fact, the grounds offered the same sort of psychological and economic benefits of freedom from supervision and
opportunities for choice which were elsewhere offered directly by
the task system.

STILL, it is worth speculating whether taskworkers in the larger
islands were not the best equipped to take advantage of these favorable commercial opportunities. This can only be conjecture at present, because little of the detailed research that would be necessary
to test this hypothesis has been undertaken. But perhaps the gradual introduction of taskwork into some parts of the sugar cycle
around the turn of the nineteenth century helps explain the simulta-
neous burgeoning of the provision ground economy. The development of the provision grounds undoubtedly was encouraged by
what Edward Brathwaite has termed the "Humanitarian Revolution,"
of which one important, and neglected, component was the introduction of tasking.[77] What remains is to discover the precise dimen-
sions of its role. We also will need studies of the provision ground
economies in the crown colonies, where tasking was more fully introduced. We also will need to bear in mind comparative remarks

75. Edwards, *History of British Colonies*, II, 137; Mintz and Hall, *Origins of Jamaican Internal Marketing*, 3–26 (quotation on 9). See also McDonald, "Goods and
Chattels." For the situation in Cuba, see Rebecca J. Scott, *Slave Emancipation in
Cuba: The Transition to Free Labor, 1860–1899* (Princeton, N.J., 1985), 15–16, 50, 149–
150, 183, 244–245.
76. Mintz and Hall, *Origins of Jamaican Internal Marketing*, 3–26.
77. Edward Brathwaite, *The Development of Creole Society in Jamaica, 1770–1820*
(Oxford, 1971), xiv.

like that of Daniel McKinnen, who attributed his observation that "negroes in the Bahama Islands discover, in general, more spirit and exertion than in the southern parts of the West Indies" to the daily and individual allocation of labor to which they were subject.[78]

The situation on Bahian sugar plantations is also instructive. There, it is clear that organizing cane cutting by quota and allowing field hands to use their time freely once tasks had been completed were closely linked to the slaves' own provision grounds. The link is most compellingly drawn in a list of demands submitted by a group of rebellious slaves to their owner. High on their agenda were improvements in the conditions of labor. Reductions in work quotas, for instance, constituted one major claim. But these slaves did not just aim for less taxing work; they sought to control their own work pace. They demanded the right to choose their own overseers and to "play, relax, and sing any time we wish." Leisure was not, however, their primary goal. Rather, as Schwartz observes: "Above all, the slaves' concern [was] to have their own land, grow their own food, and market the surplus. The slaves of Santana requested Friday and Saturday of each week for their own endeavors, the right to plant rice and cut wood wherever they wished, and to be provided with fishing nets and canoes." A search for more such documents, in which slaves lay bare heartfelt grievances and deep aspirations, would advance immeasurably our understanding of the connections between work and culture in their world.[79]

Another avenue of research would be to make comparisons between coffee and sugar workers. Certainly, the question of timing complicates the comparison, as the Jamaican case reveals. Coffee production became important in Jamaica only in the late eighteenth century, so it cannot be expected that the provision grounds and internal markets of the coffee regions would rival those of the long-established sugar areas. On the other hand, the general conditions of coffee estates were far more conducive to the workers' well-being than those of sugar plantations: labor demands were lower, and slave populations were healthier. Added to this, however, was the significant advantage of being able, on occasion, to finish work by late afternoon. A Jamaican bookkeeper recalled that the slaves on his coffee plantation "quit the field, their task satisfactorily done, an hour before the usual time of field-work in the ordinary method." Not surprisingly then, a study of missionaries in late-eighteenth- and early nineteenth-century Jamaica concludes that the missions in the

78. McKinnen, *Tour through West Indies*, 172.
79. Schwartz, *Sugar Plantations*, 156–159.

mountain districts of Saint Mary, Saint Andrew, and Saint Elizabeth benefited immeasurably from the coffee workers' comparative freedom. Weekday visits to stimulate attendance on Sundays gained a more favorable reception on coffee, as opposed to sugar, estates. Similarly, John Stewart noted that coffee workers possessed more livestock than sugar workers, in part a reflection of the greater time on their hands.[80]

One aspect of the slaves' well-being that has been intensively studied in the antebellum South, namely the susceptibility of slave children to sudden infant death syndrome, reveals a marked contrast between areas of gang and of task labor. The smothering of slave infants, as contemporaries termed this phenomenon, is now thought to be closely related to the harshness of physical labor required of pregnant slave women. Death rates for smothered slave infants were much higher in areas where gang labor prevailed. In Georgia's cotton counties, the smothering death rate was more than four times greater than that of the same state's rice counties. Since the coastal counties were generally more unhealthy than the interior, this might seem a surprising finding. Moreover, a similar contrast can be detected in Virginia between those areas still committed to tobacco production and gang labor as against those areas that had converted to wheat production and individual or small gang labor. The author of this study concludes, "This is a pattern one would expect to find if the hard work that masters assigned to pregnant slave women were the major cause of slave smothering deaths."[81]

Finally, there are even tantalizing suggestions that taskwork and property owning might even have had a bearing on slave psychology, perhaps even their propensity to rebel. One historian of slavery in Saint Domingue has noted that "the *caféterie* left more room for the expression of the slave's individuality" than sugar, and a late-eighteenth-century account of coffee planting in Saint Domingue even

80. Kelly, *Voyage to Jamaica*, 19; Mary Turner, *Slaves and Missionaries: The Disintegration of Jamaican Slave Society, 1787–1834* (Urbana, Ill., 1982), 41; John Stewart, *A View of the Past and Present State of the Island of Jamaica* . . . (New York, 1969 [orig. publ. Edinburgh, 1823]), 267–268. Because of their greater free time, slaves on a coffee estate, one contemporary explained, "therefore . . . have good provision grounds . . . [and] are much more comfortable, and less harassed than on a sugar estate" (R. Bickell, *The West Indies as They Are; or, A Real Picture of Slavery* . . . [London, 1825], 23).

81. Michael P. Johnson, "Smothered Slave Infants: Were Slave Mothers at Fault?" *Journal of Southern History*, XLVII (1981), 493–520 (see especially 515–519; quotation on p. 518).

attributed the slave revolt of that island to the common "foolish fancy of enriching negroes," presumably a direct outgrowth of the time available for independent production and acquisition by slaves on coffee estates.[82] Similarly, Barry Higman has argued that the 1831 slave rebellion in Jamaica, while it was concentrated in the mono-cultural sugar areas, was, nevertheless, led by slaves "who had achieved some degree of status within slave society." Higman quotes John Baillie, who had a slave executed for his part in the insurrec-tion: this bondman was said to be "worth six, seven, or eight hun-dred pounds; he had cattle running upon my estate, and other prop-erty. . . . He was originally a mason, and made a great deal of money in that way."[83] Property owning did not necessarily defuse a slave's revolutionary ardor.

On the other hand, the connection between rebelliousness and tasking or marketing or property owning was never straightforward. Tasking was preferred by slaves because, at bottom, it involved their participation, since it called upon them to share in production deci-sions. As soon as masters recognized their slaves' wills in this way, they were, in some senses, acknowledging the humanity of their bondmen. Eliciting this acknowledgment marked a victory for the slaves, however small. Indeed, extracting this admission was in itself a form of resistance, for slaves were now learning valuable skills and resisting the dehumanization inherent in their status. At the same time, however, it is not difficult to see how tasking (or marketing, subsistence cultivation, property owning, or any other independent activity by slaves) could be said to reduce their ability to resist, since it made the state of slavery more tolerable. A slave who had more time for his own affairs might well be a less-discontented slave. Eas-ing the torments of slavery and yet preparing bondmen for freedom, offering a welcome respite from the rigors of hard driving and yet

82. Michel-Rolph Trouillot, "Motion in the System: Coffee, Color, and Slavery in Eighteenth-Century Saint-Domingue," *Review*, V (1981–1982), 376; P. J. Laborie, *The Coffee Planter of Saint Domingo* . . . (London, 1798), 179–180. See also Gabriel Debien, *Les esclaves aux Antilles françaises, XVIIe–XVIIIe siecles* (Basse-Terre, 1974), 144. Incidentally, it is now thought that Toussaint L'Ouverture was not a privi-leged slave living on his master's plantation, but rather was a freeman who owned both land and slaves (G. Debien et al., "Toussaint Louverture avant 1789: Légendes et realités," *Conjonction* [1977], 67–80).

83. Higman, *Slave Population and Economy*, 227–228. There are other associations too, of course. Sidney W. Mintz has explored the connections between slave domestic economies and the rise of postslavery peasantries in his important "Slavery and the Rise of Peasantries," in Michael Craton, ed., *Roots and Branches: Current Directions in Slave Studies* (Toronto, 1979), 213–242.

encouraging slaves to become self-reliant: these were the implications of tasking. And, ultimately, they were profoundly ambiguous.[84]

The prevailing stereotype of plantation labor, with which this essay began, not only never applied to a large range of New World staples but also became increasingly inappropriate for those crops (most notably, sugar) with which it was, at one time, closely associated. The significance of this development for the laborers has been suggested. But an even wider importance might be claimed. The introduction of piecework or taskwork into a whole range of industries employing free labor raised explosive issues. Many saw the development as a new and more subtle instrument of subordination. Karl Marx, for instance, saw piecework as the form of wage payment most suited to capitalism, because it ensured a maximum intensity of labor and stimulated competitive bidding between laborers. Caribbean task gangs, while not at first operating within a wage system, would have provided Marx with proof for his contentions. However, what Marx did not foresee, and the wider history of task labor in the plantation setting would have provided him with vital clues, was the ability of workers to regulate piecework and turn it to their own ends. The inherent ambiguity of piecework—its potential for either subordination or resistance—was well expressed by a prominent British trade union leader in 1967, when he remarked that, "although all the ills of engineering could be blamed on piece-work, engineers fight to retain it because 'you have the man on the floor determining how much effort he will give for a given amount of money.' "[85] Making allowances for a different context, a slave taskworker could easily have echoed the same sentiment.

---

84. Sidney W. Mintz has been my mentor on these matters, both formally and informally. See his "Slavery and the Slaves," *Caribbean Studies*, VIII (June 1969), 69–70; and "Labor Exaction and Cultural Retention in the Antillean Region," in James Schofield Saeger, ed., *Essays on Eighteenth-Century Race Relations in the Americas* (Bethlehem, Pa., 1987), 31–52.

85. Quoted in Richard Price, "Rethinking Labour History: The Importance of Work," in James E. Cronin and Jonathan Schneer, eds., *Social Conflict and the Political Order in Modern Britain* (New Brunswick, N.J., 1982), 201; Price, "The Labour Process and Labour History," *Social History*, VIII (1983), 63.

Billy G. Smith

The Vicissitudes of Fortune
The Careers of Laboring Men in Philadelphia,
1750–1800

MAGNUS MILLER, a young Philadelphia seaman, sailed on the three voyages of the snow *Mary* to Antigua in 1755. He earned £9 per cruise and an additional 3s. 6d. per day for unloading and stowing the cargo, for a total income of about £30 that year. His promotion to ship's mate the following year increased his income by a third. Taking advantage of his greater wealth, Miller married and started a family; William was born in 1761 and James four years later. Miller's career proceeded apace: by the late 1760s, he became a ship's captain, purchased an indentured servant, and paid enough taxes to place him just below the median among taxpayers. During the next few years, he secured more labor—a slave and another servant— and moved into the richest third of the city's inhabitants, a position which he never relinquished. Miller emerged from the Revolution as a merchant rather than as a sea captain. In the following decade, he invested in a house and several stores on the dock, a wagon and horses to haul goods, another slave, gold plate, a rental dwelling valued at more than £1,000, and two thousand acres of land in Pennsylvania's backcountry. In the early 1790s, Miller assumed the title of gentleman. Miller established both of his sons as merchants in the family business, enabling the elder one to acquire a horse, riding chair, and slave driver, all symbols of a genteel style of life. In 1795 Miller moved into an expensive house in an exclusive neighborhood several blocks away from the noise and congestion of his waterfront stores. His appointment as a warden of the city's port at the end of the century represented the apex of his career. When Miller died

I would like to thank Stephen Innes, Lois Green Carr, Philip Morgan, and the members of the seminar sponsored by the Philadelphia Center for Early American Studies for their comments on this essay.

several years later, his sons and grandchildren successfully carried on the family enterprise.[1]

The career of Andrew Dam took a different course. In 1769, at the age of forty-one, he migrated from Sweden to America. After brief stays with several of his kin in the Pennsylvania countryside, Dam moved, along with his brother, Peter, into Philadelphia. Peter died within several years, but Andrew continued to live in the city, working as both a mariner and a gardener. He took extended voyages to Sweden and China during the Revolution, returning to the Quaker City in the late 1780s. Although hardworking, Dam lived the rest of his life in modest circumstances, never acquiring any property. In the words of his minister, "Being an industrious, complaisant man, and of good moral conduct, he was well esteemed and [had] employment sufficient for a pretty comfortable living, till the infirmities of old age obliged him to seek a retreat in the Bettering House for the last." Dam entered the almshouse in 1802; four years later, he was buried in his brother's grave, because he left no money for a plot of his own.[2]

These vignettes provide glimpses of the careers of two men who began their lives in an eighteenth-century American city as members of the laboring classes. While Magnus Miller realized substantial material and occupational advancement for himself and his family, Andrew Dam maintained only a decent competency at best, ending his days in the almshouse. Which man, if either, best typifies the life

1. This vignette is constructed from information contained in the following records: Business Papers of Samuel Coates and John Reynell, 1755–1767, Coates and Reynell Papers, Historical Society of Pennsylvania, Philadelphia; 1767 Tax Assessors' Reports, transcripts, Van Pelt Library, University of Pennsylvania, Philadelphia; the 1772, 1780, 1789, 1791, 1797, 1798, and 1800 Provincial Tax Lists, and the Philadelphia City Constables' Returns, 1775, Philadelphia City Archives, City Hall Annex (hereafter PCA); *Warrantees of Land in the Several Counties of the State of Pennsylvania, 1730–1898*, Pennsylvania Archives, 3d Ser., XXV (1898), 236, 245, 246, 735, 736, 738; U.S. Bureau of the Census, *Heads of Families at the First Census of the United States Taken in the Year 1790: Pennsylvania* (Washington, D.C., 1908), 236; U.S. Census for 1800, microfilm, reel no. 0363346, Mormon Genealogical Society, Salt Lake City, Utah. See also the following city directories: Francis White, *The Philadelphia Directory* (Philadelphia, 1785), 49; Clement Biddle, *The Philadelphia Directory* (Philadelphia, 1791), 89; Edmund Hogan, *The Prospect of Philadelphia* (Philadelphia, 1795), 116, 119; Cornelius William Stafford, *The Philadelphia Directory of 1797* . . . (Philadelphia, 1797), 128; Stafford, *The Philadelphia Directory of 1801* . . . (Philadelphia, 1801), 29, 51, 56; and Jane Aitken, *Census Directory for 1811* . . . (Philadelphia, 1811), 225.

2. The account of Dam's life is drawn from the Burial Records, Old Swedes Church: Gloria Dei, Oct. 21, 1806, Pennsylvania Genealogical Society, Philadelphia; and Admissions and Discharges, 1785–1827, Guardians of the Poor, PCA.

experiences of the urban lower classes during the second half of the eighteenth century?

Several decades ago, most historians, impressed by Benjamin Franklin's rags-to-riches success, the general scarcity of labor, and the lack of restrictions on individual initiative in the colonies, believed that opportunities abounded for urban laboring people to improve their position. David Montgomery asserted that "vertical mobility was . . . remarkable" in preindustrial cities. In Philadelphia itself, Sam Bass Warner, Jr., discovered "abundant opportunity" for advancement. Carl and Jessica Bridenbaugh characterized the city's social structure as "fluid," arguing that "it offered to individualism a degree of fair play seldom exceeded," where "men of ability and ambition could rise and flourish," and "a clever youngster, no matter what his breeding and antecedents, had a good chance to succeed." Charles Olton stated more guardedly that "the city's class barriers were not so high that there was no hope of hurdling them," and he claimed that "being born a mechanic could not be regarded as socially restrictive." Jackson Turner Main concurred that, in Philadelphia, "the poor laborer could normally expect to become a small property owner" and the "chance to rise was indeed a good one." Main concluded that conditions in Revolutionary America generally were so favorable that "immigrants and native-born alike had reason to be confident about their future, and the few whites who failed were defeated not because of any external circumstance but because they lacked some essential quality."[3]

Successors to those historians contradicted their glowing evaluations of the opportunities open to the urban laboring classes. Raymond A. Mohl, John K. Alexander, and Gary B. Nash demonstrated that poverty was more pervasive in American cities than scholars previously had believed. And Nash extended the analysis, painting a dark tableau of the economic conditions of many working people after mid-century.[4] This more pessimistic view, though hardly un-

3. David Montgomery, "The Working Classes of the Pre-Industrial American City, 1780–1830," *Labor History*, IX (1968), 5, 7; Sam Bass Warner, Jr., *The Private City: Philadelphia in Three Periods of Its Growth* (Philadelphia, 1968), 9; Carl Bridenbaugh and Jessica Bridenbaugh, *Rebels and Gentlemen: Philadelphia in the Age of Franklin* (New York, 1942), 13–14, 26; Charles Olton, "Philadelphia's Mechanics in the First Decade of Revolution, 1765–1775," *Journal of American History*, LIX (1972–1973), 313–314; Jackson Turner Main, *The Social Structure of Revolutionary America* (Princeton, N.J., 1965), 194–195, 271–272.

4. Raymond A. Mohl, *Poverty in New York, 1783–1825* (New York, 1971); and "Poverty in Early America, a Reappraisal: The Case of Eighteenth-Century New York City," *New York History*, L (1969), 5–27; John K. Alexander, *Render Them*

questioned, became widely accepted.[5] Yet, lacking a systematic study of the careers of urban laboring people, we still know relatively little about their chances to improve their lot. The subject remains elusive in part because of the limited data: substantially more evidence is available to support an analysis of either the wealthy or the institutional poor for whom government records exist.

This essay examines the economic and occupational experiences and mobility patterns of two groups of Philadelphia's artisans (shoemakers and tailors) and manual workers (laborers and merchant seamen) during the second half of the eighteenth century. Three reasons explain this focus.[6] First, as four of the largest occupational groups, they composed a substantial portion of the working population, accounting for at least one-third, and sometimes as many as one-half, of the city's free males during this period.[7] Second, like

---

Submissive: Responses to Poverty in Philadelphia, 1760–1800 (Amherst, Mass., 1980). Gary B. Nash, "Poverty and Poor Relief in Pre-Revolutionary Philadelphia," *William and Mary Quarterly,* 3d Ser., XXXIII (1976), 3–30; "Urban Wealth and Poverty in Pre-Revolutionary America," *Journal of Interdisciplinary History,* VI (1975–1976), 545–584; "Up from the Bottom in Franklin's Philadelphia," *Past and Present,* no. 77 (Nov. 1977), 57–83; and *The Urban Crucible: Social Change, Political Consciousness, and the Origins of the American Revolution* (Cambridge, Mass., 1979). Billy G. Smith, "The Material Lives of Laboring Philadelphians, 1750 to 1800," *WMQ,* 3d Ser., XXXVIII (1981), 163–202. On the material plight of laboring people in two smaller towns, see Lynne Withey, *Urban Growth in Colonial Rhode Island: Newport and Providence in the Eighteenth Century* (Albany, N.Y., 1984), 51–76, 123–136.

5. Richard S. Dunn discusses this interpretation, in "Servants and Slaves: The Recruitment and Employment of Labor," in Jack P. Greene and J. R. Pole, eds., *Colonial British America: Essays in the New History of the Early Modern Era* (Baltimore, 1984), 180–183. Hermann Wellenreuther challenges the view forwarded by these historians, in "Labor in the Era of the American Revolution: A Discussion of Recent Concepts and Theories," *Labor Hist.,* XXII (1981), 573–600. James A. Henretta raises questions about the approach adopted by these historians, in "The Study of Social Mobility: Ideological Assumptions and Conceptual Bias," *Labor Hist.,* XVIII (1977), 165–178; and "Wealth and Social Structure," in Greene and Pole, eds., *Colonial British America,* 262–289.

6. A considerable range of property, wealth, and economic interests distinguished urban mechanics, and the failure of historians to specify clearly the people being examined has created some confusion in the literature on preindustrial labor. For a discussion of this problem, see Gary B. Nash, Billy G. Smith, and Dirk Hoerder, "Laboring Americans and the American Revolution," *Labor Hist.,* XXIV (1983), 415–417.

7. These four groups composed about one-third of the city's taxables on seven tax lists between 1756 and 1798. This represents a minimum figure of their proportion of the city's free working males, since many poorer men, because of their mobility and poverty, were missed or excused by the assessors and thus did not appear on the rolls. The extraordinary underrepresentation of mariners on the tax lists is discussed in Smith, "Material Lives," *WMQ,* 3d Ser., XXXVIII (1981),

most of the city's laboring people, they clustered near the bottom of the economic hierarchy of taxpayers. But they generally enjoyed better material circumstances than the considerable number of destitute individuals who continually relied on relief or were regularly excused from paying taxes because of their predicament. Thus, these four groups usually lived an independent economic existence which differentiated them from the city's most marginal freemen, the dependent poor. Third, the wide spectrum of jobs which these men performed should make their experiences representative of a great many working Philadelphians.

WORKING Philadelphians were taxed according to the "value" of their occupations as well as the value of their taxable goods and earnings. Three categories of taxpayers can be derived from these assessments. The first category, "propertyless taxpayers," is composed exclusively of men who owned no taxable property and were assessed the minimum rate on their income. Single males without taxable property are included in this group, even though they paid a higher minimum tax as a penalty for their unmarried status. The second category, taxpayers of "minimum property or well-being," consists primarily of propertyless people who, in the judgment of assessors, fared better than those at the minimum tax rate. Propertyless men with moderate occupational valuations composed the bulk of this group, although 20 percent of them also owned a small taxable item such as a very cheap dwelling place or shop, a tiny, undeveloped piece of land, a cow, or a small amount of silver or gold plate. The third category, men of "moderate property," included all other members of the four occupational groups. These individuals possessed more substantial property—usually a house, indentured servant, slave, or some land on which they collected a sizable rent. In addition, their occupational valuations nearly always exceeded the minimum. While property assessment among them varied considerably, their wealth was capped; few of these men ranked among the top 20 percent of taxpayers.[8]

---

190. The 1767, 1772, 1780, 1789, and 1798 Provincial Tax Lists are in the PCA. The 1756 Tax List is in Hannah Benner Roach, comp., "Taxables in the City of Philadelphia, 1756," *Pennsylvania Genealogical Magazine*, XXII (1961), 3–41. Figures for the 1774 Tax List are based on the analysis by Jacob M. Price, "Economic Function and the Growth of American Port Towns in the Eighteenth Century," *Perspectives in American History*, VIII (1974), 123–186.

8. The tax laws directed assessors to evaluate the occupations of taxpayers according to the incomes derived from those occupations. James T. Mitchell and Henry Flanders, comps., *The Statutes at Large of Pennsylvania from 1682 to 1801*, 18

The majority of laborers, mariners, cordwainers, and tailors did not own taxable property, nor did they earn more than minimal incomes in the judgment of assessors (see table 1). One-quarter of the taxpayers either possessed a small quantity of property or paid slightly more than the lowest occupational tax. One of every five owned enough to qualify for the moderate property group. The propertyless proportion was smallest at mid-century (partly because single men were not taxed), expanded rapidly during the final decade of the colonial period, declined during the Revolutionary war, peaked again in 1789, then shrank during the 1790s.[9]

Stability of status was the most common characteristic of the four occupational groups; slightly more than half of the men remained in the same assessment category during any period (see tables 2 and 3). The majority of those who were propertyless and assessed the minimum occupational valuation were unable to improve their position from one tax list to the next. One of every four managed to move into the minimum property group, and one in five acquired moderate property. The fate of those who began with minimum property was mixed: roughly a third remained in their original position, a third lost ground, and the remaining third improved their circumstances. Four of every five taxpayers with moderate property maintained their status.

That the wealth of these workers usually did not increase as they grew older further indicates their limited opportunities. There was a very weak connection between social age (defined by the age of the oldest child living at home) and taxable wealth, and the chances that laboring Philadelphians would acquire a moderate amount of property or earn enough to move into a higher occupational tax bracket

---

vols. (Harrisburg, Pa., 1896–1911), IV, 10–26, V, 207–212, VI, 344–360, VIII, 96–116, 378–382, IX, 443–448, X, 205–214, XI, 454–486, XV, 322–330. To evaluate the careers of the four occupational groups, I traced hundreds of men among tax lists spread through the second half of the eighteenth century. Rather than measure their economic mobility in relative terms, a technique commonly employed by social scientists, I established an absolute standard to assess the economic circumstances of laboring Philadelphians across their life cycle. To belong to a particular category or to move from one level to another during the years between tax lists meant that the individuals experienced a certain set of material attributes. This formulation permits a view of the economic advance, stagnation, or decline which laboring Philadelphians underwent.

9. The 1756 Tax List is biased toward those who owned property, since unmarried men, the majority of whom were propertyless, were not included. However, the effect on the tax assessments should be small because the occupation of most single men rarely was identified on any tax list and, therefore, few unmarried men are included among the four occupational groups under study.

TABLE 1
Tax Assessments, Four Occupational Groups

		Assessment Categories		
Tax List	N	Propertyless (%)	Minimum Property (%)	Moderate Property (%)
1756[a]	424	19	58	22
1767	413	38	40	22
1772	722	69	19	12
1780[b]	345	58	17	25
1789[c]	565	75	9	16
1798[b]	389	51	28	22
Overall	2,858	52	28	20

Sources: The 1767, 1772, 1780, and 1798 Provincial Tax Lists, PCA. The 1756 Tax List is in Hannah Benner Roach, comp., "Taxables in the City of Philadelphia, 1756," *Pennsylvania Genealogical Magazine*, XXII (1961), 3–41.
Notes: Deviations from 100% are due to rounding. [a]Unmarried men are not included. [b]Based on a sample of 60% of all taxpayers. [c]Based on a sample of 80% of all taxpayers.

did not improve significantly as they aged (see table 4). Families in which the eldest child was older than ten (suggesting an age range of the mid-thirties or early forties for their fathers) were the most likely to own property. Yet nearly two-thirds of these adult males, presumably in their economically most productive years, remained without assets. Statistically, age accounted for less than 6 percent of the variation in taxable wealth among laborers, mariners, cordwainers, and tailors.[10] For most laboring Philadelphians, then, growing older did not mean growing wealthier.

10. The 1775 Constables' Returns, which report the name of a householder and the age of his eldest child, permit the head of a family to be categorized by his social age. Social age should serve as an adequate proxy for actual age; the former reflects the latter. Most importantly, social age specifies the stage in the life cycle of taxpayers. The most serious potential problem is that economic necessity probably forced poorer Philadelphians to apprentice their children out of their households at a younger age (see Smith, "Material Lives," *WMQ*, 3d Ser.,

TABLE 2

Short-Term Economic Mobility, Four Occupational Groups

Initial Status	N	Assessment Categories		
		Propertyless (%)	Minimum Property (%)	Moderate Property (%)
1756	87	1767		
Propertyless		40	40	20
Minimum property		25	38	37
Moderate property		16	16	68
1767	248	1772		
Propertyless		69	23	9
Minimum property		29	40	30
Moderate property		7	12	82
1772	125	1780		
Propertyless		57	21	22
Minimum property		32	36	32
Moderate property		3	0	97
1780	84	1789		
Propertyless		73	9	18
Minimum property		62	8	29
Moderate property		4	4	93
1789	129	1798		
Propertyless		41	30	28
Minimum property		25	25	50
Moderate property		12	24	64
1756–1789	673	Aggregate, 1767–1798		
Propertyless		55	24	21
Minimum property		35	31	34
Moderate property		7	10	82

Sources: Cited in table 1.

TABLE 3

Short-Term Mobility between Assessment Categories,
Four Occupational Groups

Time Span	Stable (%)	Up 1 Category (%)	Up 2 Categories (%)	Down 1 Category (%)	Down 2 Categories (%)
1756–1767	47	26	2	20	5
1767–1772	62	20	4	12	2
1772–1780	62	18	11	8	1
1780–1789	61	12	7	19	1
1789–1798	44	26	20	7	2
Aggregate, 1756–1798	56	20	10	12	2

Sources: Cited in table 1.

TABLE 4

1772 Tax Assessment Categories by 1775 Social Age Groups

Age of Eldest Child	N	Assessment Categories		
		Propertyless (%)	Minimum Property (%)	Moderate Property (%)
0– 5	103	85	11	4
6–10	116	69	21	10
11–15	90	68	13	19
16–24	61	61	21	18

Sources: 1772 Provincial Tax List and 1775 Constables' Returns, PCA.

Some men, however, followed Franklin's way to wealth, although their successes were more limited. Peter Dicks was a young, married tailor without taxable assets in 1756. During the next decade, he acquired an indentured servant, one of the most valuable houses owned by anyone in his profession, and a high occupational assessment, all of which placed him among the city's wealthiest tailors. Purchasing another indentured servant, Dicks continued to enjoy his comparatively comfortable position with his wife and three children until the Revolution. Peter January was propertyless himself in 1767, although his status as a master cordwainer warranted a higher than average occupational valuation. Within the next eight years, January obtained the services of at least seven servants and two apprentices, rented a building sufficient to house them all, and organized a virtual shoe manufactory. Consequently, he was among the handful of artisans who changed their status to merchant on the 1780 tax roll.

But contrast their careers with those of Hugh Nelson, John Burns, Martin Shire, and George Bicherton. Assessors levied a higher than minimum tax on Hugh Nelson in 1767, because, even though propertyless, he earned more than most tailors. Within five years he lost his advantage, however, and paid the least possible tax. John Burns did not improve his taxable position during sixteen years' toil as a laborer; he and his family were still without property in 1772. Martin Shire, a married laborer in his early thirties, paid the minimum rate in 1767 and for the next thirteen years as well. George Bicherton was propertyless, earning a minimal income for a journeyman cordwainer in 1789. Nine years later, his condition had not changed.

The vast majority of Philadelphia's laboring people were without property at any given point during the late eighteenth century. A few who resided in the city for a decade could expect to enjoy the same material success as Dicks or January, although generally on a more modest scale. Most, however, fared like Burns, Shire, and Bicherton—they were unable to acquire property or improve their economic status. The experiences of men who possessed little or no property or were assessed slightly above minimal occupational valuations varied widely during the years between tax lists, with their

XXXVIII [1981], 188–189). If so, then older, poorer householders were categorized in a younger social age bracket than is appropriate. This would artificially magnify the correlation between age and taxable wealth. Social age (and any connection between it and taxable wealth) was determined by matching a 50% sample of the 1775 Constables' Returns against the 1772 Provincial Tax List, both in the PCA. The coefficient which measures the correlation between social age and taxable wealth is the $r = .235$ and the $r^2 = .055$ at a significance level of .00001.

fortunes about evenly distributed among three groups: the economically successful men, such as Dicks and January; those whose slight
edge slipped away, such as Nelson; and those who maintained their
identical position.

Affluent members of the four occupational groups generally maintained their status, although not all were so fortunate. John Stille, a
master tailor, ranked among the wealthiest 10 percent of his profession in 1789, a position he preserved throughout the 1790s. Even
though he lost some property (a riding chair and a slave) during that
decade, Stille lived in relatively comfortable conditions. William Bell's
experience was more unusual. As a twenty-eight-year-old tailor, he
took up residence in Philadelphia after the British evacuated the city.
By 1789, he had gained sufficient property to place him near the top
of his profession, where he continued until the century's end. But his
good fortune quickly evaporated. When his eyesight failed in 1801,
Bell applied for admission to the almshouse as a pauper.[11]

But, despite the experience of Bell, stability of condition was still
an important characteristic of economic mobility (see tables 5 and 6).
At least 48 percent of laboring men remained at their initial economic
level over the long term (only 8 percent shy of that for short-term
mobility). The mobility profile of the propertyless improved from the
short term to the long term: one-third of those who were propertyless remained so, one-fifth acquired minimum property, and two-
fifths acquired moderate property (table 5). Workers who began with
either minimum or moderate property had similar experiences over
both the short and long term.

To summarize the major findings of this section on economic mobility, the majority, and frequently a substantial majority, of members
of the four occupational groups were propertyless during the last
half of the eighteenth century. Most such men failed to acquire any
taxable property within a decade, and, while their chances of improving their economic position increased marginally with the length
of their stay in the city, the odds were still against their obtaining
property even after a decade and a half. One of every five individuals possessed moderate assets—likely a house, lot, indentured servant, or slave. While this measure of economic security, once attained, was seldom relinquished, very rarely did any of these men
amass true riches as defined by contemporary standards. Laboring
men generally fared best during the late 1750s, early 1760s, and

11. The vignettes in this and the preceding paragraphs are drawn from the tax
lists cited in n. 7 and the Daily Occurrences, May 30, 1801, Guardians of the
Poor, PCA.

TABLE 5
Long-Term Economic Mobility, Four Occupational Groups

Initial Status	N	Assessment Categories		
		Propertyless (%)	Minimum Property (%)	Moderate Property (%)
1756	53		1772	
Propertyless		100	0	0
Minimum property		21	45	33
Moderate property		12	24	65
1767	55		1780	
Propertyless		39	39	22
Minimum property		33	11	56
Moderate property	0		5	95
1772	28		1789	
Propertyless		38	12	50
Minimum property		50	17	33
Moderate property		0	0	100
1780	18		1798	
Propertyless		17	0	83
Minimum property		33	50	17
Moderate property		17	17	67
1756–1780	154	Aggregate, 1772–1798		
Propertyless		36	21	43
Minimum property		33	29	38
Moderate property		7	12	82

Sources: Cited in table 1.

TABLE 6

Long-Term Mobility between Assessment Categories,
Four Occupational Groups

Time Span	Stable (%)	Up 1 Category (%)	Up 2 Categories (%)	Down 1 Category (%)	Down 2 Categories (%)
1756–1772	55	21	0	21	4
1767–1780	50	31	7	13	0
1772–1789	46	18	14	21	0
1780–1798	44	6	28	17	6
Aggregate, 1756–1798	48	21	11	17	2

Sources: Cited in table 1.

1790s, when the smallest proportion of them were propertyless and the greatest advancement opportunities existed. Their chances for material improvement were most restricted (and the propertyless proportion the largest) from the mid-1760s until 1790.[12] That the economic prospects of workers did not significantly increase as they grew older reflects the limited ability of many laboring people to improve their economic condition.

12. The economic experiences of members of the four occupational groups were most favorable during the two end decades 1756–1767 and 1789–1798 and most restricted during the period 1767–1789. One possible demographic explanation of these variations in mobility rates requires brief consideration. Differences in the age structure of the various cohorts could have created spurious changes in their career patterns. The apparent openness of the 1790s, compared to the more restricted opportunity of the 1780s, for example, might be illusory if the cohort in 1789 was significantly younger than the one in 1780. However, the weak correlation between age and wealth discussed previously makes it highly unlikely that alterations in the age structure significantly affected mobility. And when the rates of economic mobility are controlled by the social age of taxpayers for the 1767–1772, 1772–1780, and 1780–1789 periods, the patterns are similar to those which emerge when mobility is not controlled by age. Following the methodology explained above, I used the social age of men on the 1775 Constables' Returns as a control of their economic mobility during the periods indicated.

THIS PICTURE of the economic mobility of the "lower sort," as contemporaries called them, has three shortcomings. First, it includes only those people who resided in the city long enough to be recorded on at least two of the six selected tax lists. But how did the careers of the men who stayed in the city differ from those who left? This question cannot be answered with certainty, but the attributes of the migrants and persisters provide clues. Approximately one-third of the laborers, mariners, cordwainers, and tailors who appeared on a tax list remained in the city a decade later. Even when adjusted for mortality, this persistence rate falls markedly below that of many American contemporary small towns and rural areas.[13] The greater inclination of citizens to leave the Quaker City strongly suggests that many of them found that the prospects there compared unfavorably with those available in agricultural regions. Moreover, the rate of emigration of Philadelphia's taxpayers related inversely to their position on the tax list: poorer men moved more frequently than did wealthier ones.[14] The previous analysis of the career patterns of the less itinerant portion of the population is, thus, very likely skewed in favor of the *most* successful men.

Although it is impossible to ascertain the fate of all the migrants, it is unlikely that they would have been better prepared to achieve material success than those who stayed behind. In one respect, their success or failure is not essential to an assessment of conditions within the city itself, for those who remained were unable to or chose not to seize the opportunities available elsewhere. After all, the residents most resistant to the pressures to migrate were those who had attained at least a modicum of economic success.[15] But those who were the most inclined to leave—the poor, the journey-

13. Even if such a high proportion as 20% of adult males died each decade, Philadelphia's persistence rate of approximately 53% would still have been less than the 66%–93% rates which characterized many colonial American areas. Persistence rates in other areas are presented in Douglas Lamar Jones, *Village and Seaport: Migration and Society in Eighteenth-Century Massachusetts* (Hanover, N.H., 1981), 111–113.

14. Allan Kulikoff discovered a similar relationship between economic status and emigration in Boston, in "The Progress of Inequality in Revolutionary Boston," *WMQ*, 3d Ser., XXVIII (1971), 402. See also Jones, *Village and Seaport*, 47–54; and Nash, *Urban Crucible*, 185–186. This contradicts speculation by Jeffrey G. Williamson and Peter H. Lindert that "those who migrated *from* the cities had, in all likelihood, more middling wealth and age than those who migrated *to* the cities. Emigrants to the hinterland presumably had enough wealth to start a farm." *American Inequality: A Macroeconomic History* (New York, 1980), 29–30.

15. These statements are based on the persistence patterns of taxpayers among the tax lists cited in n. 7 (except 1774).

men, and the unskilled—generally earned incomes far too low to permit the accumulation of savings for their own farm, particularly during the late-colonial period when land prices outside the city rose rapidly. The objection raised against the safety-valve theory of the frontier applies here: transients rarely would have possessed either the capital or skills necessary to take full advantage of the available land and opportunities which may have existed in the hinterland.[16]

Evidence about the experiences of a handful of migrants from Philadelphia supports this argument. Forty-eight men in the four occupational groups who left the city during the late 1760s and 1770s were traced into eight of the surrounding counties.[17] Slightly more than 50 percent of these people remained propertyless, assessed at the lowest tax rate. Nearly 40 percent paid slightly above the minimum rate because of the cow, sheep, or horse which they owned. Five of the forty-eight were taxed a higher amount, three of them having acquired small parcels of land. The sample, although regrettably small, represents one of the only pieces of hard evidence about the fortunes of migrants. And it does not indicate any greater, and perhaps indicates even a lesser, rate of material success for men who emigrated from the city.

A second problem with this picture of economic mobility is that it is linear, showing the career patterns of laboring Philadelphians as either rising or not rising during a specific period. While this reveals the structure of opportunity, it obscures the cyclical reality of the lives of many eighteenth-century urban laboring people. Some bettered their position during favorable periods, then fell upon hard times that eradicated their previous gains. Such a pattern is nearly impossible to measure, but it is evident in the experiences of men such as Cadwalader Dickinson, Charles Jenkins, and John Campbell. A propertyless master cordwainer in 1767, Dickinson acquired a house and indentured servant during the next five years but then lost it all during the economic dislocation of the Revolutionary war. Jenkins, a ship's mate, possessed a moderate amount of property in

16. Smith, "Material Lives," *WMQ*, 3d Ser., XXXVIII (1981). On the rising price of land, see James T. Lemon, *The Best Poor Man's Country: A Geographical Study of Early Southeastern Pennsylvania* (Baltimore, 1972), 67–69; and Arthur L. Jensen, *The Maritime Commerce of Colonial Philadelphia* (Madison, Wis., 1963), 126–127. See also Carter Goodrich and Sol Davison, "The Wage Earner in the Westward Movement," *Political Science Quarterly*, L (1935), 161–185, and LI (1936), 61–110; and Fred A. Shannon, "A Post Mortem on the Labor-Safety-Valve Theory," *Agricultural History*, XIX (1945), 31–37.

17. These men were traced using the index and tax lists published in *Warrantees of Land, Pennsylvania Archives*, 3d Ser., XI–XXIX (1898–1899).

1756. The economic setback at the end of the Seven Years' War hit him hard, for, when the tax collectors made their rounds in 1767, he owned hardly any assets. Jenkins recouped much of his losses, however, during the following five years. John Campbell led a still more dramatic rags-to-riches-to-rags career. Hobbled by a sore leg and too poor to maintain himself, Campbell languished in the almshouse in 1796. Within two years of his recovery, he bought a house and earned a relatively high income. But, several years later, injured and penniless once again, he returned to the almshouse.[18]

A third problem is that a great many of the most marginal men were, because of their poverty or mobility, excused or missed by tax assessors. In Philadelphia, their numbers ranged as high as 20 percent of the tax-inscribed population, with most of the "missing" men belonging to the laboring classes.[19] The economic experiences of this portion of the lower sort cannot be calculated with precision, but they are, nonetheless, important to our understanding of the opportunities available to laboring men. A considerable number of tailors and cordwainers, and even more laborers and merchant seamen, not only failed to improve their material conditions, but they led extremely precarious material lives which, in times of distress, forced them to rely on public and private assistance. Thus, many less-skilled workers and artisans were heavily represented in the population of the city's almshouse. The reasons for their institutionalization were many and varied. Unemployment posed a major problem. In 1789 laborer James Thompson "for want of work is now sent in as a Pauper," according to the almshouse clerk. John Machman, a sailor, applied for admission because he was "out of Employment and cannot get a Birth to go to sea—or any thing to do on Shore." The institution released other inmates when they found jobs; the managers discharged William Cox with the note that he had "got a birth and gone to Sea." Some unemployed men managed to avoid the almshouse, but they still required assistance to meet their normal financial obligations. When their infants died, neither mariner John Ward, tailor William Dunwick, nor laborer Peter Carle could afford to

18. Daily Occurrences, Apr. 6, 1796, PCA.

19. For example, while nearly 4,000 Philadelphians paid taxes in 1772, assessors missed as many as 1,000 mariners who resided in the city (see Smith, "Material Lives," WMQ, 3d Ser., XXXVIII [1981], 190). Nash found that 471 adult males were excused from taxation that year because of their poverty ("Poverty and Poor Relief," WMQ, 3d Ser., XXXIII [1976], 22–23). See also Sharon V. Salinger and Charles Wetherell, "A Note on the Population of Pre-Revolutionary Philadelphia," Pennsylvania Magazine of History and Biography, CIX (1985), 372–373.

pay the full funeral costs because they were out of work. To assist them, the rector of their church agreed to abate his fee.[20]

Illness and disease likewise pushed many laboring men below subsistence. Smallpox, yellow fever, venereal disease, asthma, alcoholism, and tuberculosis numbered among the afflictions that regularly sent laboring men and their families in search of aid. Venereal disease plagued mariners in particular. After two years' suffering from the "large pox" in the Pennsylvania Hospital, sailor John Rigg was released even "tho He seems yet to be ill, perhaps of the Cure." At age thirty-five, Mathew King, "much afflicted with the Asthma and . . . far advanced in a Consumption," applied for admission to the almshouse. George Lowerman drew the following description from the clerk: "Formerly a reputable industrious Taylor, but having of late years given himself up to hard drinking, is reduced to that situation which totally renders him unable of taking care, and providing for a livelihood, and is come here in a naked and perishing condition." When the father in a laboring-class household grew ill, his family's financial situation often became desperate. Dennis McElwell, his wife, and two children entered the almshouse in 1793. "Formerely a very striveing industerous Man," noted the clerk, McElwell was "now, from long Sickness, Much Reduced." Andrew and Mary Gibb were admitted in 1801, "formerely in good circumstances . . . but now reduced by misfortunes of [his] sickness."[21]

Laboring Philadelphians were continually exposed to job-related risks which could impair their ability to earn a living, leaving them dependent on friends, neighbors, and the community for their welfare. After sailing from the city's port for five years, Jonas Kellman was admitted to the almshouse in 1800. "On his last vessel," wrote the clerk, "he had the misfortune of breaking one of his thigh bones on board said ship; as they [were] weighing the Anchor, the Pall of the Windless not catching, the handspike struck his thigh and broke

20. These stories are drawn from the Daily Occurrences, PCA: Thompson was admitted on Jan. 20, 1789; Machman on Feb. 6, 1790; and Cox on Mar. 10, 1796. The accounts of the funerals are in the Burial Records, 1799, Penn. Gen. Soc.: Ward on Mar. 4; Dunwick on Aug. 28; and Carle on Nov. 12. The clerk's descriptions of the circumstances of many of the new admittees to the almshouse are available in Billy G. Smith and Cynthia Shelton, eds., "The Daily Occurrence Docket of the Philadelphia Almshouse, 1800," *Pennsylvania History*, LII (1985), 86–116.

21. These vignettes are contained in the Daily Occurrences, PCA: Rigg was admitted on December 24, 1789; King on Jan. 29, 1801; Lowerman on Dec. 30, 1800; McElwell on Dec. 26, 1793; and the Gibbs on June 10 and 26, 1801, respectively.

it. This accident happened thirteen months ago and it has never been set—there being no Doctor on board the vessel." Eneos Lyon landed in the almshouse in the same year because while "assisting in sinking a pump he unfortunately fell in the Well, which has bruised and lamed him so as to render him incapable of labouring for a livelyhood." Not only were the lower sort vulnerable to injury, but their occupations exposed mariners and laborers to a variety of ailments. Laborer William Weyford and seaman James Lloyd were both rheumatic; Henry Digle's frostbitten feet forced him to seek public aid several times; and mariner James Unions contracted a fever in the West Indies that sent him initially to the almshouse and then to his grave. On the admission of Thomas Loudon, an "old Sea-faring man," the clerk cited the physical toll of his occupation, observing that Loudon suffered from the "casualties, and accidents in his Way of life, and the vicissitudes of fortune to which such men are liable seems now to manifest itself."[22]

Many of the men who never appeared on a tax list lived in perpetual poverty, keeping afloat by working periodically, utilizing various welfare strategies, and engaging in an underground economy. John Barret, a baker, frequently depended on the almshouse, being "in and out as often as the number of his fingers and toes." Others drew on poor relief seasonally. Usually applying to the almshouse in November or December, Robert and Rebecca McBean were "frequent autumnal Customers, who like many others, make a Practice of Comeing in at this Season, in very Distress'd and Necessitous circumstances, and when fed up cured and well Cloathed, by Spring become Insolent and then go off and wear out or make way with their Cloaths—and return again the next Fall naked."[23]

Occupational mobility (measured by the transition from journeyman to master, the propensity of lesser artisans and unskilled workers to change jobs, and the transition from common seaman to ship's officer) was, for the lower sort, little better than economic mobility. Some members of the four occupational groups, however, did enjoy some upward mobility. For artisans, the transition from journeyman to master represented the most significant change in their work life. Craft guilds of a European type to control that transition did not exist

22. These stories are reconstructed from *ibid.*: Kellman entered the almshouse on Nov. 11, 1800; Lyon on Nov. 17, 1800; Weyford on Aug. 11, 1796; Lloyd on Aug. 22, 1796; Unions on Nov. 18, 1793; and Loudon on Apr. 29, 1800. Digle appears in the Admissions and Discharges, Dec. 6, 1800, and May 1801, PCA.
23. Daily Occurrences, PCA: entry on Barret, Dec. 12, 1800; entry on the McBeans on Dec. 9, 1789.

(as such) in America, although the Cordwainers' Fire Company and the Taylors' Company in Philadelphia assumed many of the functions of such organizations. Nevertheless, few legal or social impediments restricted a journeyman from becoming a master by setting up an independent business and selling directly to customers. Before opening a shop, a cordwainer or tailor had to be skilled in making shoes or clothes, although these lesser crafts—when compared to goldsmiths or clockmakers—were considered relatively easy to master. The capital available to support such a venture may have been more significant in determining the ability of many journeymen to move to a position of independence. The tools necessary for shoemakers and tailors cost relatively little, but the initial investment required to establish a shop, purchase raw materials, obtain a clientele, wait for weeks or months for customers' payments, and simultaneously support a family would have been substantial, far beyond the savings of most journeymen.

Benjamin Franklin's struggle to raise money for his own printing house is instructive. He entered into partnership with Hugh Meredith, an alcoholic with few printing skills, solely because Meredith's father agreed to finance the business. Subsequently, Franklin borrowed from his friends and even bargained for a marriage, providing the dowry was large enough to pay off his debt and fully establish him as a master. Recognizing the problems journeymen faced, Franklin provided two thousand pounds sterling in his will to be lent to young, married artisans in Boston and Philadelphia to enable them to set up their own shops.[24] Philadelphia's journeymen printers were acutely aware of these difficulties during the 1790s. An apprentice to Franklin's grandson reported their advice: "All the . . . Journay men tell that I had not better learn the printing. . . . They say if they had money to set up independently they could make a fortune but without it, it is but a poor business."[25]

This complaint seems to apply to journeymen cordwainers and tailors (as well as printers) because of a lack of occupational mobility. Approximately one-third of cordwainers and tailors could be identified as journeymen and another third as masters, with the status of the remainder unclear. Maintenance of the same status was the most

24. Benjamin Franklin, *The Autobiography and Other Writings*, ed. L. Jesse Lemisch (New York, 1961), 63–68, 80; "Encouragement for Apprentices to be Sober . . ." (1800), Broadside Collection, Historical Society of Pennsylvania; and Accounts Ledger, 1791–1868, Franklin Legacy, Record Series 95.56, PCA.

25. As quoted in W. J. Rorabaugh, *The Craft Apprentice: From Franklin to the Machine Age in America* (New York, 1986), 29.

pervasive experience for these artisans over any given period (see table 7).[26] At least 42 percent of journeymen remained employees, and 25 percent of them became masters during the years between tax lists. Assuming that the men of unknown status divided in a pattern identical to that of men with known status, the best estimate is that 61 percent of journeymen continued in their initial situation and 39 percent set up as masters during any eight-year time period. Journeymen were most restricted in their mobility from the late 1760s through the Revolution but often achieved independence during the late 1780s and 1790s. The position of master craftsman, once achieved, was relatively permanent. At least 75 percent, and likely closer to 85 percent, of masters retained their position between tax lists. The few who lost their status probably went broke and were forced, once again, to hire out to another craftsman.

Journeymen cordwainers and tailors may have fared somewhat better over the long term. Although the sample numbers are small, at least two-fifths of them became masters during any sixteen-year period, and one-fifth definitely remained in their dependent status (see table 8). Masters rarely relinquished their position. That so few cordwainers and tailors remained in the city for sixteen years, however, may indicate that many were discouraged by the prospects for further advancement.

Another characteristic of occupational mobility for lesser artisans

26. Historians have rarely examined the transition from journeyman to master, since records distinguishing between masters and journeymen in any trade usually are nonexistent. But the status of most Philadelphia cordwainers and tailors can be determined from certain of their distinguishing traits. A number of masters and journeymen, for example, were identified from the Taylors' Company, the Cordwainers' Fire Company, bills submitted for work, and newspaper advertisements. (The minutes of the two companies, bills, and issues of the *Pennsylvania Gazette* are at the Historical Society of Pennsylvania.) Matching the men of known status to the tax rolls and Constables' Returns isolated the particular attributes of journeymen and masters. The principal trait separating masters and journeymen was their tax assessment, since it was based not only on the taxable property owned but also on the value of the taxpayer's occupation. The occupation of a master was nearly always assessed at a substantially higher rate than that of a journeyman. Other qualities—such as the ownership of indentured servants, slaves, rental property, a house, the presence of a hired servant, the amount of house rent paid, and the status of the taxpayer as an inmate or household head—made it possible to distinguish between many masters and journeymen with some assurance. For a detailed explanation of this methodology, see Thomas Smith, "Reconstructing Occupational Structures: The Case of the Ambiguous Artisans," *Historical Methods Newsletter*, VIII (1975), 134–146. Again, for reasons discussed above, the data are biased, indicating greater opportunity than most laboring men actually enjoyed.

TABLE 7
Short-Term Occupational Mobility of Artisans

Initial Status	N	Journeyman (%)	Master (%)	Unknown (%)
			Status over Time	
1756	32		1767	
Journeyman		23	38	38
Master		11	84	5
1767	116		1772	
Journeyman		61	3	36
Master		14	69	17
1772	65		1780	
Journeyman		43	22	35
Master		7	86	7
1780	41		1789	
Journeyman		31	46	23
Master		4	89	7
1789	54		1798	
Journeyman		26	53	21
Master		26	66	9
1756–1789	308		Aggregate, 1767–1798	
Journeyman		42	27	32
Master		13	76	11

Sources: Cited in table 1.

was their propensity to change jobs. Most cordwainers and tailors continued in the same line of employment; only 9 percent assumed a new occupation each decade. The few masters who changed their occupational title followed the prevailing trend in many crafts, becoming merchants, shopkeepers, and grocers and thereby focusing on the distribution rather than the production of goods. Journeymen sometimes floated among a variety of less-skilled jobs when in need of employment, but they seldom moved permanently into other skilled occupations. After investing a substantial number of years in learning their craft, most artisans had few options but to continue in their line of work. Since most men in the lesser crafts never achieved the success enjoyed by many merchants, goldsmiths, carpenters, and the like, the trades to which boys initially were apprenticed dictated the limits of their future advancement.

Most unskilled workers functioned in that capacity throughout their lives. Even though 25 percent of laborers changed their occupational designation each decade, few of them developed new marketable skills. Instead, they worked as bricklayers, soldiers, draymen, painters, whitewashers, potato diggers, and bartenders. Their highest rate of occupational mobility occurred during the 1790s, when 20 percent of laborers obtained skilled positions as mast makers, coopers, and carpenters. Those able to learn a skill usually fared better materially. As is often the case, the higher rate of success may well have come to those men who were in the right place at the right time.

Occupational mobility among mariners was no better than it was among journeymen cordwainers and tailors. The promotion of a common sailor to a ship's officer was extremely rare. Among the 128 mariners examined, only George Craig successfully climbed the entire ladder from seaman to mate to captain, while Thomas Carew and Jacques LeBon were able to step one rung up to become mates. Many common seamen continued in their status for considerable periods of time. John Smith sailed as a ship's hand for at least twenty-three years and Thomas Loudon and Lawrence Mahon for more than four decades.[27] That the age structures among common seamen and

27. Tax lists do not reveal much about the careers of mariners, since most of them were at sea when assessors made their rounds; only 1 of 10 mariners appears on the tax rolls. However, a sample of 128 mariners, randomly drawn from the crew lists of vessels clearing port, shows the low occupational mobility of sailors. These lists are part of the Maritime Records of the Port of Philadelphia, 1789–1860, Library of Congress. All crew members on ships clearing the port during this period are listed in separate volumes for each year. For Craig, see 1799 (54), 1800 (59, 112), and 1804 (272); for Carew, see 1798 (6), 1799 (36), 1800

TABLE 8

Long-Term Occupational Mobility of Artisans

		Status over Time		
Initial Status	N	Journeyman (%)	Master (%)	Unknown (%)
1756	20		1772	
Journeyman		29	42	29
Master		0	92	8
1767	29		1780	
Journeyman		25	25	50
Master		5	86	10
1772	21		1789	
Journeyman		14	57	29
Master		0	91	7
1780	5		1798	
Journeyman		0	100	0
Master		0	75	25
1756–1780	75	Aggregate, 1772–1798		
Journeyman		22	43	35
Master		2	88	10

Sources: Cited in table 1.

mates were virtually identical further supports this view of limited occupational mobility; if mariners generally won promotions after working a number of years as common seamen, then officers should have been older than sailors.[28]

Since ship captains seldom came from the ranks of common seamen, what was their origin? Most served as mates before assuming command. John Gantlet sailed to the West Indies as a mate on board the brigantine *Augustus*; the following year, at age twenty-one, he became master of that vessel. Twenty-one-year-old Samual Loweth, formerly mate on the ship *Active*, became master of the brigantine *Favourite*. Mate Thomas Brown, twenty-four years old, left the brigantine *Tryphena* to take charge of the schooner *Sally* when its captain died.[29] The notable characteristics of these and other new masters were their youth and their failure to appear in the records as common seamen. Most likely, they had been apprenticed or sent as supercargos by their fathers, often merchants or captains themselves, to learn the art and mystery, not of a common seaman, but of the commander of a vessel. Such was the case for Silas Foster, Jr., who, beginning at age thirteen, served his apprenticeship on vessels which his father commanded and eventually became a captain himself. Laurence Anderson was another shipmaster who brought his son up to the same profession.[30] As ship captains, both Foster and Anderson were required to know the intricacies of seamanship, to be able to read and write, to solve complex mathematical problems, and to deal with merchants in buying and selling products at various ports of call. Common seamen ordinarily did not learn these skills,

---

(24), and 1802 (30); and for LeBon, see 1803 (143), 1804 (18, 198), and 1805 (19, 325). See also Daily Occurrences, PCA: entry on Smith, Aug. 24, 1801; entry on Loudon, Apr. 29, 1800; and entry on Mahon, Dec. 10, 1800.

28. The mean age of both mates and common seamen on vessels which cleared the port in 1803 was 26 years old. The breakdown of both groups into four age categories was very similar. This is based on an analysis of 304 crew members from a random sample of 37 ships leaving Philadelphia, contained in the Ship's Crew Lists, Records of the Bureau of Customs, Record Group 36, National Archives. That many men served as common seamen for their entire lives is discussed by Marcus Rediker's essay in this volume.

29. Maritime Records, Library of Congress: for Gantlet, see 1803 (35), and 1804 (132); and for Loweth, see 1804 (1, 174, 457), 1805 (244), and 1806 (68, 170). Brown is recorded on the list of crew members of the brigantine *Tryphena*, Crew Lists, Bureau of Customs, National Archives.

30. Foster appears in Maritime Records, Library of Congress, 1804 (29, 433), 1805 (135), and 1810 (44). Anderson is in Will Book K, 291, Bureau of Wills, City Hall Annex, Philadelphia.

several of which were beyond the educational training of most mariners.

The barriers between common seamen and ship's officers rarely were hurdled. Once again, as in the case of lesser artisans and laborers, the skills which boys learned (or did not learn) to a large degree determined their future careers. The sons of fathers who possessed the means to apprentice them to a ship captain, a merchant house, or a master in a highly skilled craft and later to assist them to obtain the capital necessary to establish their independence naturally enjoyed greater chances for material and occupational rewards.

NORTH AMERICA numbered among the richest societies in the Western world, and Philadelphia was America's wealthiest major city during the second half of the eighteenth century. Yet many laboring Philadelphians failed to improve their incomes, acquire property, or escape their dependent position within their crafts. What factors contributed to their difficulties? What created the bursts of mobility in the early 1760s and the 1790s which bracketed decades of more restricted opportunity? Irregular employment, low wages, changing labor relations, the availability of capital, patterns of migration, and business cycles best explain these phenomena.

Like workers in all preindustrial societies, Philadelphia's laborers and artisans endured periodic slack times of unemployment because weather, the length of daylight, vacillating consumer demand, the erratic delivery of raw materials, and the natural rhythm of agriculture all affected their jobs. Freezing temperatures, for example, left mariners without berths when ice clogged the harbors; the cold also forced shoemakers to quit their benches when their waxes hardened and slowed or halted the activity of men who built houses and ships. Philadelphia's laboring people undoubtedly were familiar with "cucumber time," as eighteenth-century English tailors referred to the winter months, when they could afford little other dietary fare. Since the city had "little occasion . . . for the labour of the Poor" during colder periods, as newspaper contributors observed, "collections (time immemorial) have been made *every* winter . . . for the poor."[31] The cyclical nature of employment is evident in the increase of ship arrivals in the city's port each spring and their decline each fall. That the number of applicants for poor relief generally rose during late

---

31. *Pennsylvania Packet, and Daily Advertiser* (Philadelphia), Dec. 31, 1787; and *Independent Gazetteer; or the Chronicle of Freedom* (Philadephia), Dec. 31, 1785 (both cited in Alexander, *Render Them Submissive*, 15–16).

autumn and fell in early spring demonstrates the impact of seasonal economic fluctuations on the material conditions of laboring people.[32] As discussed earlier, illness and injury likewise limited the regularity of work. Even more serious, because individuals could not anticipate the financial crisis, was the scarcity of jobs during business slumps.

Some laboring men simply earned too little to maintain their family, even when fully employed. James Ross's wife and three children entered the almshouse, because, as a "Drummer of Marines . . . his pay and rations are not sufficient to support himself and family, who are in a distressed condition, suffering for want of the necessities of life." As a construction worker at the Schuylkill bridge, Charles Johnson could not "provide and take sufficient care" of his wife and son. Another Philadelphian with a large family complained: "I have strove all in my power and find that I cannot support them . . . I could point out a great number in similar circumstances with myself, and I am sure some of them in a more deplorable condition, if possible."[33]

The slow transformation in working conditions for artisans, involving the gradual erosion of a paternalistic structure and its replacement by a wage labor system during the course of the eighteenth century, shifted many of the risks and some of the rewards from masters to journeymen. Early in the century, masters routinely hired journeymen for long periods, reimbursing them with both a wage and found, the latter consisting of meals and, occasionally, lodging. This guaranteed workers a measure of financial security, since their employment was ensured; their pay was not docked during days of illness, injury, or inactivity; and their cost of living was minimized. But, by the end of the colonial era, employees were increasingly dependent entirely on wages, and they bore the full brunt of the vagaries of the economy and their own personal fortune. Some individuals gained from this arrangement, and others lost. During the boom times of the 1790s, for example, high wages and the ready availability of capital enabled half of the journeymen shoemakers to establish their own shops. However, the general economic problems

32. Billy Gordon Smith, "Struggles of the 'Lower Sort': The Lives of Philadelphia's Laboring People, 1750 to 1800" (Ph.D. diss., University of California, Los Angeles, 1981), 221–222. Seasonal fluctuations in the number of almshouse admittees are evident in the Daily Occurrences, PCA. On the seasonal nature of employment for mariners, see Marcus Rediker's essay in this volume.

33. Daily Occurrences, PCA: entry on Ross, Dec. 21, 1802; entry on Johnson, Mar. 8, 1803. The comment by the third man is from the *Penn. Pack.*, Oct. 20, 1784.

in the decade preceding the Revolution restricted the amount of capital accessible to journeymen. This, combined with the controls exercised by masters in Philadelphia's Cordwainers' Fire Company and Taylors' Company, meant that as few as one of every ten journeymen in those crafts became masters during that decade.[34]

Migration patterns and economic cycles also affected the timing of mobility, making the early 1760s and the 1790s the most favorable years for advancement. Two important determinants of the opportunities for laboring men to better their status were employment opportunities and wage levels. These, in turn, were defined primarily by the *demand* for the services of the lower classes and the *supply* of their labor. Migration affected the size of the labor pool, while cycles in the city's economy influenced the demand side of this economic equation. A brief review of changes in Philadelphia between 1750 and 1800 helps explain fluctuations in the achievements of the city's lower sort.

Maritime commerce, shipbuilding, and construction formed the backbone of Philadelphia's economy. During the third quarter of the eighteenth century, the city's rapidly expanding population, augmented by the arrival of Germans and Scotch-Irishmen, outstripped growth in all three of these economic sectors. During the two decades after 1756, laborers increased from 5 percent to 14 percent of the taxable work force. At the same time, when the volume of these sectors is measured per capita—the best available index of the relative number of jobs in these areas—maritime commerce remained stagnant, shipbuilding declined, and the housing industry increased but little. The general consequence for laboring men was underemployment, declining real wages, and constricting opportunities at the end of the colonial period.[35]

More specifically, a series of economic cycles affected the well-being of laboring citizens between mid-century and the Revolution. Military spending during the Seven Years' War and a large overseas

34. On changing labor relations, see Nash, *Urban Crucible*, 258–261; and Salinger, "Transformation of Labor," *WMQ*, 3d Ser., XL (1983), 62–84.

35. The interpretation here (and in the following pages) of the economic and demographic development of the city and the impact on its laboring men is discussed more fully in Smith, "Philadelphia's Laboring People," 190–251; and "Inequality in Late Colonial Philadelphia: A Note on Its Nature and Growth," *WMQ*, 3d Ser., XLI (1984), 640–644. On migration to Philadelphia, see Marianne Wokeck, "The Flow and the Composition of German Immigration to Philadelphia, 1727–1775," *PMHB*, CV (1981), 249–278; and Smith, "Death and Life in a Colonial Immigrant City: A Demographic Analysis of Philadelphia," *Journal of Economic History*, XXXVII (1977), 863–889.

demand for Pennsylvania's grains stimulated the city's economy during the late 1750s and early 1760s, pulling it out of its slump of the preceding few years. As Philadelphia's merchants developed a brisk trade with the West Indies and imported more merchandise directly from Great Britain, the volume of shipping through the city's port increased. Fueled by this growth, both housing construction and shipbuilding boomed. Mariners, dockworkers, and laborers of all types consequently enjoyed higher wages and a wider range of employment possibilities. Meanwhile, the curtailment of overseas immigration, the vigorous recruitment of Pennsylvanians into the British army and provincial militia, and the stampede of many poorer men to sign aboard privateers limited the number of workers in the city. With a relatively small pool of unskilled laborers available in a booming economy, chances for material and occupational advancement rose.

These favorable conditions ended during the final years of the war. Against the background of the 1762 credit crisis in England, the volume of British imports fell. Simultaneously, most Philadelphians fared poorly. A new influx of Scotch-Irish and German migrants joined war veterans drifting into the city, thereby enlarging the ranks of laboring men. As citizens with few skills scrambled after scarce jobs, city leaders complained about the "want of Employment," which was reducing a large number of residents "to great Straits."[36] Only robust housing construction, major public projects like street paving, and a healthy shipbuilding industry yet to feel the full impact of the slump prevented the condition of unskilled workers from declining still further.

Philadelphia emerged briefly from its difficulties in the mid-1760s as maritime activity revived. However, shipbuilding declined during the late 1760s, housing construction slackened, and the nonimportation agreements of 1769–1770 (in combination with the 1772 English credit crisis) again disrupted the economy. At the same time a labor surplus developed; the proportion of laborers in the taxable work force doubled during the early 1770s, primarily because of heavy European immigration. Employment opportunities and the wages of unskilled workers thus declined, while their chances to acquire property deteriorated at the close of the colonial era.

Economic dislocation and depression characterized the city during much of the 1780s. Philadelphia's overseas commerce boomed briefly

36. *Whereas the Number of Poor in and around the City* . . . (Philadelphia, 1764), copy of broadside at the Library Company of Philadelphia.

at the close of the War for Independence, as Great Britain flooded American markets with manufactured goods. But imports soon slumped, responding to the low overseas demand for Pennsylvania foodstuffs and European restrictions on American commerce. Shipbuilding followed a similar path, declining quickly after an immediate postwar boom, while the housing industry remained dormant throughout the decade. Even though few immigrants settled in the city and many residents left, unskilled laborers continued to account for 7 percent of the tax-inscribed population during the 1780s, approximately the same proportion as the early 1770s. As workers struggled to locate employment, public aid to the poor increased. Benjamin Rush's comment that "beggars were to be seen at the doors of the opulent in every street in our city" may have distorted reality little.[37]

Unskilled workers and lesser artisans alike shared in the general prosperity of the mid-1790s. The city's Atlantic trade began its recovery following ratification of the Constitution, then reached new heights during the middle of the decade. Spurred by the outbreak of hostilities between France and England in 1793, America's carrying and reexport business tripled within three years; these endeavors dominated commerce in the Pennsylvania capital during the final decade of the century. Higher wages and greater career opportunities for laboring men thus characterized the 1790s. The proportional decline of laborers in the city, from 7 percent of the taxable work force in 1789 to 5 percent in 1798, contributed further to improvements in their condition.

WHAT EXPECTATIONS of material achievement could Philadelphia's laboring men realistically entertain? The careers of the four occupational groups analyzed in this essay provide solid, if not conclusive, answers to this question. Mariners, laborers, cordwainers, and tailors composed between a third and a half of the city's free adult males. Most of them were near the bottom of the tax-inscribed population, although they surely enjoyed better material conditions and greater career prospects than the lowest substratum of males, whose impoverishment prevented them even from paying taxes. The experiences of these four groups indicate that they stood virtually no

37. George W. Corner, ed., *The Autobiography of Benjamin Rush: His Travels through Life Together with His Commonplace Book for 1789–1813* (Princeton, N.J., 1948), 160. See also George Winthrop Geib, "A History of Philadelphia, 1776–1789" (Ph.D. diss., University of Wisconsin, 1969), 203–205.

chance of rising from the bottom to the top of the economic and social hierarchy. To become a merchant, a professional, or a ship captain was also very difficult, although within the grasp of a few.

If the virtues of Poor Richard did not guarantee riches to most laboring men, did they at least ensure that these workers could achieve a measure of economic security, acquire a bit of property, improve their minimal incomes, or obtain a skilled position? The findings of this analysis suggest that many of the lower sort encountered serious problems fulfilling these more modest goals. A large number of laborers, mariners, cordwainers, and tailors were not only trapped permanently at the bottom, but, as other studies have demonstrated, they led economically precarious lives which sometimes forced them to seek public and private relief.[38] Most laboring people faced difficulties simply caring for their family's basic needs, much less establishing a position secure from the threat of poverty and deprivation. The majority began and ended their careers in the city as propertyless individuals without, in the eyes of the tax assessors, bettering their physical circumstances. Of the sample studied, one of every five of the propertyless obtained some property within eight or nine years, and the chances of improving their lot increased only slightly if they remained in the city an additional decade. Some families made strides during good times, only to slip backward in periods of hardship. Most unskilled urban workers—who, in Franklin's terms, were "bred to country work" or "brought up to no business"—found themselves unable to learn and practice a marketable skill or trade.[39] While the evidence is limited, migrants from the city may not have fared much better, and perhaps not even as well, as those who remained behind. The weak correlation between wealth and age indicates the restricted nature of both economic and occupational mobility for many among the lower sort.

Still, a considerable number of laboring men enjoyed important financial and occupational gains. At least one of every three of the lower sort improved their income or acquired some property during their stay in the city. And, on average, four of every ten journeymen shoemakers and tailors may have become independent each decade. Meanwhile, master craftsmen and property owners tenaciously held on to their position.

What characteristics distinguished those who advanced from those

---

38. Smith, "Material Lives," *WMQ*, 3d Ser., XXXVIII (1981), 163–202; and "Poverty and Economic Marginality in Eighteenth-Century America," American Philosophical Society, *Proceedings*, CXXXII (1988), 85–117.

39. Franklin, *Autobiography*, ed. Lemisch, 65.

who did not? Franklin's professed values undoubtedly had some importance: hard work and frugality played a role, although perhaps not the dominant one. The development of a marketable skill was a key ingredient to achieving modest success, yet it was beyond the control of many boys who either were apprenticed to masters in lesser skilled occupations or were never put out to learn the mystery of any craft. Laborers and mariners had a difficult time compensating for a handicap which often was not of their own making. Journeymen shoemakers and tailors did not automatically become masters after learning the intricacies of their trade; the availability of capital was essential to their making that transition successfully. Some were able to save the required amount, but most must have depended on borrowing from others to set up their own shops. In all of these calculations, the vicissitudes of fortune were significant. Epidemics, illnesses, injuries, unemployment, political unrest, and fluctuations in the economy numbered among the primary factors which distinguished masters and property owners from almshouse inmates.

The portrait limned by these statistical findings supports the more recent interpretations of the economic conditions of the eighteenth-century urban lower classes. In Philadelphia, among the most prosperous American cities at the time, the material circumstances of the lower sort were considerably worse, their position at the bottom more permanent, and their chances to achieve modest economic goals more limited than many historians traditionally have assumed. The increasing wealth thought to have characterized America in general and Philadelphia in particular during much of this period did not trickle down to many laboring men. Indeed, most struggled not to sail ahead, but to remain afloat.

Marcus Rediker

The Anglo-American Seaman
as Collective Worker, 1700–1750

God damn them that fails each other.
Seaman's Toast, 1721

SEAMEN WERE one of the most militant groups of workers in the eighteenth-century British empire. Their expressions of solidarity, whether uttered over a cool can of punch at sea or amid the hot commotion of a port-side riot against impressment, grew increasingly common through the course of the century. The material origins of such sentiments lay in the collective experience of work at sea.[1]

E. J. Hobsbawm has noted that "the creation of a large and expanding market for goods and a large and available free labour force go together, two aspects of the same process."[2] Hobsbawm calls at-

I would like to thank Cambridge University Press for allowing me to use portions of my *Between the Devil and the Deep Blue Sea: Merchant Seamen, Pirates, and the Anglo-American Maritime World, 1700–1750*, copyright © 1987 Cambridge University Press, reprinted with permission. I wish also to thank Alan V. Briceland, Ken Morgan, Philip D. Morgan, John Rust, Daniel F. Vickers, and Alfred F. Young for their helpful comments on an earlier draft of this essay.

1. C. R. Dobson, *Masters and Journeymen: A Prehistory of Industrial Relations, 1717–1800* (London, 1980), 25; Marcus Rediker, *Between the Devil and the Deep Blue Sea: Merchant Seamen, Pirates, and the Anglo-American Maritime World, 1700–1750* (New York, 1987), chap. 5.

2. E. J. Hobsbawm, "The General Crisis of the European Economy in the Seventeenth Century," *Past and Present*, no. 5 (May 1954), 40. Several studies have been especially useful in the conceptualization of this essay: Ralph Davis, *The Rise of the English Shipping Industry in the Seventeenth and Eighteenth Centuries* (London, 1962); J. H. Parry, *Trade and Dominion: The European Overseas Empires in the Eighteenth Century* (New York, 1971); Christopher Lloyd, *The British Seaman, 1200–1860: A Social Survey* (Rutherford, N.J., 1970); Immanuel Wallerstein, *The Modern World-System, II, Mercantilism and the Consolidation of the European World-Economy, 1600–1750* (New York, 1980). Special mention goes to Peter Linebaugh, "All the Atlantic Mountains Shook," *Labour / Le travailleur*, X (1982), 87–121; and to Jesse

tention to the relationship between the growth of commercial markets and the growth of a working class and implicitly to the ways in which labor processes, markets, and experiences were transformed or created during the drive of early capitalist development. C. L. R. James, Grace C. Lee, and Pierre Chaulieu put the same point in a slightly different way: "Marx discerned in capital accumulation two laws, twin themes of the same movement, the law of the concentration and centralization of capital and the law of the socialization of labor." "The more capital succeeds in organizing itself," they concluded, "the more it is forced to organize for itself the working class."[3]

The seaman occupied a pivotal position in the creation of international markets and a waged working class as well as in the worldwide concentration and organization of capital and labor. During the early modern period, merchant capitalists organized themselves, markets, and a working class in increasingly transatlantic and international ways. As capital came to be concentrated in merchant shipping, masses of workers, numbering twenty-five thousand to forty thousand at any one time between 1700 and 1750, were, in turn, concentrated in this vibrant branch of industry. The huge numbers of workers mobilized for shipboard labor were placed in relatively new relationships to capital—as free and fully waged laborers—and to each other. Seamen were, by their experiences in the maritime labor market and labor process, among the first collective laborers. In historical terms, this new collective worker did not possess traditional craft skills, did not own any means of production such as land or tools (and therefore depended completely upon a wage), and labored among a large number of like-situated people. The collective worker, exemplified by the seaman, was the proletarian of the period of "manufacture" and would, of course, become a dominant formal type of laborer with the advent of industrial capitalism.

Early modern maritime workers, by linking the producers and consumers of the world through their labors in international markets, were thus central to the accumulation of wealth on a scale previously unimagined. At the same time, they were crucial to the emergence of new relations between capital and labor. This essay focuses on the organization of maritime labor and some of the challenges to it. After

---

Lemisch, "Jack Tar in the Streets: Merchant Seamen in the Politics of Revolutionary America," *William and Mary Quarterly*, 3d Ser., XXV (1968), 371–407, the study that cleared the way for this and many other histories of working people in early America.

3. C.L.R. James, Grace C. Lee, and Pierre Chaulieu, *Facing Reality* (Detroit, Mich., 1974), 103, 115.

some opening remarks on the maritime labor market, it investigates the labor process at sea between 1700 and 1750, examining the ship as a work environment with its own complex division and organization of labor and technology. Then it turns to the struggles over the labor process, working conditions, and the control of the workplace, emphasizing the ways in which seamen resisted the capitalist organization of production or deflected it toward other purposes of their own. The study concludes with observations on the relationships among the rise of North Atlantic capitalism, maritime work, and the sailors' efforts not to fail each other.[4]

THE MARITIME labor market took shape within the buzz and the hustle of the seaports that handled the commerce of the North Atlantic. Vessels of all varieties (ships, brigs, schooners, hoys, and many others involved in the coastal and deep-sea trades) clogged English, American, and West Indian harbors. Merchants bustled from ship to ship, pausing to watch with satisfaction as dockworkers and seamen lowered the last bale of cargo into a vessel's full belly or to argue furiously with shipbuilders over the cost of repairs. Captains and customs officials haggled, cursed, and winked at each other. Bloodied butchers and deft-dealing pursers stocked the merchant craft with salt beef and pork, and hawkers and peddlers tendered their wares along the stone-and-log wharves. Slaves, indentured servants, and day laborers toiled under the sharp gaze of overseers, lifting from ship's hold to shore's warehouse the commodities of the world. On the vessels, on the quays, or in the nearby alehouses, seamen in Monmouth caps and tarred breeches quizzed merchant captains about destinations and wages, just as they asked each other about the sturdiness of a particular ship or the character of her captain.

These seamen worked in a labor market that was international in character, a fact of first importance that is shown in the work lives of John Young and Edward Coxere. Young, apparently seized by British authorities from a French privateer during the War of Spanish Succession and quickly charged with treason, tried to explain to the High Court of Admiralty how the vicissitudes of an international work experience had got him into his present predicament. He proceeded to outline where his worldwide labors had taken him. Born in Spitalfields, he went to sea at "14 or 15 years of Age," apprenticed to a Captain John Hunter. During the next twelve years, he traveled

4. The labor process is here defined as the transformation of raw materials, other inputs, and labor into products and services having value. For a sample of the growing literature on the labor process, see below, n. 32.

from London to Barbados and Jamaica, sailed and fought aboard three West Indian privateers, went "sugar droghing" in the Caribbean coastal trade, found his way in a merchant ship back to London, and then, in various voyages, on to Bristol, the African coast, Virginia, Lisbon, Genoa, Leghorn, and Cartagena.[5] Ned Coxere, a late-seventeenth-century merchant seaman and privateersman, summed up his maritime experience this way: "I served the Spaniards against the French, then the Hollanders against the English; then I was taken by the English out of a Dunkirker; and then I served the English against the Hollanders; and last I was taken by the Turks, where I was forced to serve then against English, French, Dutch, and Spaniards, and all Christendom." Not surprisingly, this able sailor spoke English, Spanish, French, Dutch, and the Mediterranean lingua franca.[6] Coxere was truly an international workingman, finally refusing to participate in the nationalistic violence of the era of trade wars and becoming, instead, a pacifist and a Quaker.

Both Young and Coxere worked among men who, it must have seemed, came from almost everywhere: from every corner of England, America, and the Caribbean; from Holland, France, Spain, and all of Europe; from Africa and even parts of Asia. Regional, national, and ethnic identities abounded in the ships of the world, even though the Navigation Acts had required that three of four seamen on English ships be subjects of the crown. Such requirements were rarely enforced, especially in times of war and labor scarcity, when even the British state admitted that half or more of ships' crews might be foreign.[7]

The global deployment of thousands of seamen in the early eighteenth century was predicated upon the broad and uneven process of proletarianization, through which these men or their forebears were torn from the land and made to sell their labor power on an open market to keep body and soul together. The major sources for stocking the labor market with "hands" were dispossession—the displacement or eviction of rural producers, most notably by the enclosure of arable farmland—and population growth, which forced the offspring of agrarian laborers or waged workers themselves to sell their mind and muscle for money. England, of course, was known for its teeming share of these "masterless men and women" in the

5. Examination of John Young, 1710, High Court of Admiralty 1/54, 1–2 (hereafter HCA). All HCA records are in the Public Record Office, London.

6. Edward Coxere, *Adventures by Sea of Edward Coxere*, ed. E.H.W. Meyerstein (New York, 1946), 37, 130–134.

7. Davis, *English Shipping*, 327; Ruth Bourne, *Queen Anne's Navy in the West Indies* (New Haven, Conn., 1939), 220.

early modern period. Population growth and dispossession, each with its own oscillating rhythm, combined to swell the number of those who in some way worked for a wage to some 60 percent of Britain's people by the beginning of the eighteenth century. Between 1700 and 1750, the process of proletarianization seems to have stabilized: population growth reached a certain plateau, showing perhaps a small upturn in the 1740s.[8] The numbers of colonists in North America grew both naturally and by immigration throughout the period, and the population of the British West Indies increased only through the massive importation of Africans.[9] There was, with a few exceptions, a general shortage of maritime labor in both areas between 1700 and 1750. But the dominant, overarching tendency, particularly in Britain and America, was toward ever greater employment of waged labor. Seamen were fitting symbols of the trend.

A labor market is defined as "those institutions which mediate, affect, or determine the purchase and sale of labor power." Here, our understanding of maritime labor is deficient, for the practices of labor market entrepreneurs have not been carefully studied.[10] It is clear that crimps—"agents who traded in recruits when men were in great demand either for the armed forces or to man merchant vessels on the point of sailing"—were crucial to the maritime labor market, certainly in England if not in the New World until the late eighteenth century. An equally important if shadowy figure was the "spirit," described by Edward Barlow as "one of those who used to entice any who they think are country people or strangers and do not know

8. Wallerstein, *Modern World-System*, II, 16, 258; B. A. Holderness, *Pre-Industrial England: Economy and Society, 1500–1750* (London, 1976), 11, 24; D. C. Coleman, *The Economy of England, 1450–1750* (London, 1977), 11; Richard S. Dunn, "Servants and Slaves: The Recruitment and Employment of Labor," in Jack P. Greene and J. R. Pole, eds., *Colonial British America: Essays in the New History of the Early Modern Era* (Baltimore, 1984), 158–164; Peter Clark, "Migration in England during the Late Seventeenth and Early Eighteenth Centuries," *Past and Present*, no. 83 (May 1979), 70; Charles Tilly, "Demographic Origins of the European Proletariat" (paper presented at conference, "Proletarianization: Past and Present," Rutgers University, 1983), 40; Robert W. Malcolmson, *Life and Labour in England, 1700–1780* (New York, 1981), chap. 2; John Rule, *The Experience of Labour in Eighteenth-Century English Industry* (New York, 1981), chap. 1.

9. Robert V. Wells, *The Population of the British Colonies in America before 1776: A Survey of Census Data* (Princeton, N.J., 1975), 259–296.

10. Richard C. Edwards, Michael Reich, and David M. Gordon, eds., *Labor Market Segmentation* (Lexington, Mass., 1975), xi. Daniel F. Vickers has done fine work on the labor markets in fishing and whaling, in "Maritime Labor in Colonial Massachusetts: A Case Study of the Essex County Cod Fishery and the Whaling Industry of Nantucket, 1630–1775" (Ph.D. diss., Princeton University, 1981).

their fashion or custom, or any who think they are out of place and cannot get work, and are walking idly about the streets." Spirits promised great wages and often gave advances in money. Those who accepted their offers often found themselves apprenticed as sailors or sold as indentured servants bound to America. Such recruiters operated from gin shops, alehouses, inns, and taverns, where they often seized indebted sailors and paid off their bills. In exchange, crimps and spirits gained the right to sell the seaman's services to outward-bound vessels, usually sailing to distant parts of the globe, and to receive the sailor's advance pay. Some crimps did not adhere even to these minimal standards of conduct, preferring instead to raid the pubs; handcuff, drag off, and incarcerate drunk sailors; and then sell them to merchant captains in search of labor.[11] Probably most of the contracting of maritime labor was handled in less formal and exploitative ways, especially in the New World, where labor was scarce and wages were higher, through the pubs, inns, or taverns where merchants, ship captains, mates, and seamen gathered and through which information of shipping circulated. Seamen also peddled their own skills in the port cities by going from vessel to vessel, jumping aboard, asking the ship's route, pay, and fare. A man who did not possess adequate skills was hired by a master as a ship's boy or as an apprentice to some member of the crew.

Maritime labor in all English Atlantic ports was seasonal and often casual. The rhythms of climate dictated employment opportunities by icing harbors, by fixing the growing seasons of commodities such as sugar and tobacco, or by making parts of the world dangerous with disease or hurricane. Seafaring jobs were most easily found in late spring, summer, and fall, though the demand for labor in each port varied according to the commodities shipped, their destinations, and the length of the shipping season. Many mariners were unable to find year-round employment.[12] Numerous landed occupations,

11. J. Stevenson, "The London 'Crimp' Riots of 1794," *International Review of Social History*, XVI (1971), 41–42. For a good analysis of crimping in the 19th century, see Judith Fingard, *Jack in Port: Sailortowns of Eastern Canada* (Toronto, 1982), chaps. 1 and 5. Edward Barlow, *Barlow's Journal of a Life at Sea in King's Ships, East and West Indiamen, and Other Merchantmen from 1659 to 1703*, ed. Basil Lubbock (London, 1934). See also " 'Crimp' Riots," 42; and Davis, *English Shipping*, 153.

12. Fingard, *Jack in Port*, is especially sensitive to the differences in regional maritime labor markets. See also Gary B. Nash, *The Urban Crucible: Social Change, Political Consciousness, and the Origins of the American Revolution* (Cambridge, Mass., 1979), 12; and T. S. Ashton, *Economic Fluctuations in England, 1700–1800* (London, 1959), 4.

however, were equally seasonal, and, for some, "sailoring was normally a casual employment, into and out of which they drifted as they found employment harder to come by on sea or on land." Such opportunities were always greater and more lucrative during war years. Employments connected to shipping "were notorious then, as later, as precarious occupations." Yet throughout the eighteenth century, it was increasingly the case for Jack Tar that, "once a sailor, the chances were that he would always be a sailor."[13] By 1750, seafaring had become a lifelong occupation for increasing numbers of waged workers.

Seafaring labor consisted mainly of loading, sailing, and unloading the merchant vessel. The essence of the labor process was, quite simply, the movement of cargo. The ship, in many ways prefiguring the factory, demanded a cooperative labor process. Waged workers, the preponderant majority of whom did not own the instruments of their production, were confined within an enclosed setting to perform, with sophisticated machinery and under intense supervision, a unified and collective set of tasks. Large parts of this labor would be performed at sea in isolation from the rest of the population. The character of seafaring work and its lonely setting contributed to the formation of a strong laboring identity among seamen.[14]

By 1700, seafaring labor had been fully standardized. Sailors circulated from ship to ship, even from merchant vessels to the Royal Navy, into privateering or piracy and back again, and found that the tasks performed and the skills required by each were essentially the same.[15] They encountered a basic division of labor on each merchant ship, consisting of a master, a mate, a carpenter, a boatswain, a gunner, a quartermaster, perhaps a cook, and four or five able or ordinary seamen. A larger or more heavily manned ship included a second mate, a carpenter's mate, and four or five more common tars.[16] This division of labor allocated responsibilities and structured work-

13. Davis, *English Shipping*, 116; Malcolmson, *Life and Labour*, 54; Rule, *Experience of Labour*, 49–73; Charles Wilson, *England's Apprenticeship, 1603–1763* (London, 1965), 344; Peter Kemp, *The British Sailor: A Social History of the Lower Deck* (London, 1970), 92; Lloyd, *British Seaman*, 86.

14. Peter Linebaugh, "The Picaresque Proletarian in Eighteenth-Century London" (paper presented at conference, "Proletarianization: Past and Present"), 27; Vilhelm Aubert, "A Total Institution: The Ship," in Aubert, *The Hidden Society* (Totowa, N.J., 1965), 240, 245, 256, 258.

15. Lloyd, *British Seaman*, 12, 53.

16. Davis, *English Shipping*, 110–113, 119–120; William Falconer, *An Universal Dictionary of the Marine* (New York, 1970 [orig. publ. London, 1769]). Colonial vessels were, on the whole, smaller than those owned and operated out of Great Britain.

ing relations among the crew, forming a hierarchy of laboring roles and a corresponding scale of wages.

The organization of labor on each ship began with the master, the representative of merchant capital, who was hired "to manage the navigation and everything relating to [the ship's] cargo, voyage, sailors, etc." Frequently a small part owner himself, the master was the commanding officer. He possessed near-absolute authority. His ship was "virtually a kingdom on its own," his power "well nigh unlimited," and, all too frequently, to the muttering of his sailors, he ruled it like a despot.[17] His primary tasks were navigation, tending the compasses, steering the vessel, and transacting the business throughout the voyage. He procured the ship's provisions and usually inflicted the punishments. Except on the largest of ships, he ran one of the two watches.[18]

The mate, whose powers were vastly inferior to those of the master, was second in the chain of command. He commanded a watch and oversaw the daily functioning of the ship. He was charged with the internal management of the vessel, setting the men to work, governing the crew, securing the cargo, and directing the ship's course. The mate needed a sure knowledge of navigation, since he was to take charge of the vessel in the event of the master's death, a not uncommon occurrence at any time during the age of sail.[19]

The carpenter, an important specialist in a wooden world, was responsible for the soundness of the ship. He repaired masts, yards, boats, and machinery; he checked the hull regularly, placing oakum between the seams of planks, and used wooden plugs on leaks to keep the vessel tight. His search for a leak often required that he wade through stagnant bilge water with vapors strong enough "to poison the Devil."[20] His was highly skilled work which he had learned through apprenticeship. Often he had a mate whom he in turn trained.[21]

The boatswain, like the mate, functioned as something of a foreman. He summoned the crew to duty, sometimes by piping the call to work that brought the inevitable groans and curses from the off-

17. Falconer, *Universal Dictionary*, 191; Lloyd, *British Seaman*, 230; Davis, *English Shipping*, 127, 131; Barnaby Slush, *The Navy Royal; or, A Sea-Cook Turn'd Projector* (London, 1709), 9.

18. Davis, *English Shipping*, 123.

19. *Ibid.*, 126; Barlow, *Journal*, ed. Lubbock, 327; Falconer, *Universal Dictionary*, 192.

20. Jeremy Roch, "The Fourth Journal," in Bruce S. Ingram, ed., *Three Sea Journals of Stuart Times* (London, 1936), 115; Falconer, *Universal Dictionary*, 78.

21. Davis, *English Shipping*, 119.

duty crew. His specific responsibilities centered on the upkeep of the rigging. He had to be sure that all lines and cables were sound and that sails and anchors were in good condition.[22]

The gunner, sometimes with the help of a boy (or powder monkey), tended the artillery and ammunition. He was crucial in an era when trade itself was regarded by many to be a form of warfare, but between 1700 and 1750 his position declined as the convoy system lessened the need for ordnance and because the removal of cannon and a crewman added to speed while subtracting from the merchant's operating expenses. The gunner needed experience to avert or handle a disaster such as a cannon's bursting, overheating, or recoiling out of control. A knowledgeable gunner was essential to the crew's safety if a ship had any pretense to self-defense.[23]

The quartermaster did not require special training. Rather, he was an experienced, or "smart," seaman who was given an additional shilling or two per month to assist the mates. He provided an extra hand in storage, coiling cables, and steering the vessel.[24] The cook, on the other hand, generally was truly "remarkable for his inability to cook."[25] Often a wounded seaman no longer able to perform heavy labor, his status was rather low. According to the doleful and never-ending complaints of the ship's people, he brought no distinctive talents to his job.

The common seaman, Jack Tar himself, was a "person trained in the exercise of fixing the machinery of a ship, and applying it to the purposes of navigation." He needed to know the rigging and the sails as well as how to steer the ship, to knot and splice the lines, and to read the winds, weather, skies, and the mood of his commander. There were two categories of seamen: the able seaman, who fully knew his trade, and the ordinary seaman, usually a younger and less-experienced man. The latter was still learning the mysteries of tying a clove hitch or going aloft to reef in a sail in a blustery thunderstorm.[26] In sum, a merchant ship, like a man-of-war, required a wide variety of skills; it was "too big and unmanageable a machine" to be run by novices.[27]

Some orbits of trade dictated the need for other crew members.

22. Ibid., 112; Falconer, Universal Dictionary, 41, 100.
23. Falconer, Universal Dictionary, 227.
24. Ibid., 226; Davis, English Shipping, 113.
25. Kemp, British Sailor, 72.
26. Falconer, Universal Dictionary, 259; Davis, English Shipping, 113; Mallis v. Wade, 1736, HCA 24/138.
27. Slush, Navy Royal, 3.

Larger ships, particularly those in the slave trade, carried a surgeon whose difficult job it was to keep the crew and slaves alive from one side of the Atlantic to the other. Larger ships occasionally procured the services of a caulker in addition to the carpenter. And in the tobacco and sugar trades, a cooper often signed on to assist in packing the product in casks and hogsheads. Coastal pilots were hired when the ship had to be maneuvered through particularly deceptive, uncharted, or unknown waters.[28]

There were, of course, many variations of this standard division of labor, depending upon the related factors of trade route, cargo carried, and ship size. The northern European trade (transporting largely corn, coal, salt, or wine) featured small ships that made quick and predictable voyages. Trade to the Mediterranean, to the North American colonies, or to the West Indies (carrying food, sugar, and tobacco) used ships of greater size. Some eleven to fourteen men worked a 150–200-ton vessel on voyages that lasted six to nine months. Ships in the African trade were most heavily manned, for security against slave uprisings and as a safeguard against raging mortality, and often bore twenty to twenty-five men on a 200-ton vessel. Slaving voyages took ten to eleven months. Ships of the East India Company were, by eighteenth-century standards, mammoth, often as large as a man-of-war at 300–500 tons, and manned to survive a voyage enduring two years or more. Although ship size varied with the type of trade, the larger the ship's home port, the larger the ship and its crew were likely to be.[29]

It is difficult to determine whether seamen specialized in particular routes, trades, or types of ships. Ned Coxere, for one, seems to have preferred to sail the Mediterranean. Masters and mates, since they had to develop contacts and learn regionally specific business methods, tended to find employment in trade routes where they had already accumulated some experience.[30] As trade orbits matured and the motions of the market chain became more orderly through the eighteenth century, such specialization increased. Yet many masters, like their men, had varied careers. Nathaniel Uring, taking to sea in 1698, managed over the next twenty-three years to find his way to

28. Falconer, *Universal Dictionary*, 60; Davis, *English Shipping*, 112, 120.

29. Davis, *English Shipping*, 204–293; Jonathan Press, *The Merchant Seamen of Bristol, 1747–1789* (Bristol, 1976), 9; Ian K. Steele, "Harmony and Competition: Aspects of English and Colonial Shipping in the Barbados Trade at the End of the Eighteenth Century," MS (1980), 23.

30. Davis, *English Shipping*, 129, 159–170.

Virginia, the Baltic, Africa, Cádiz, the West Indies, New England, Ireland, Cartagena, Campeche, Tunis, Lisbon, and Florence.[31]

The tendency of masters and mates to specialize in certain voyages indicates another crucial part of the maritime division of labor: the distribution of knowledge on board the ship. Masters and mates, as we have seen, needed to know how to use the principles of navigation, but the rest of the crew did not. Yet this separation of mental and manual labor was never complete—indeed, never could become as complete—as it would in later industrial production.[32] The knowledge of seafaring was still contained largely within a broad system of apprenticeship, but one in which the perils of life at sea placed grave limits upon the advisability of keeping trade secrets. Only later, with the introduction of officers' schools and a growing social distance between the lower deck and the quarterdeck, would a consistent separation of conception from execution emerge. Much could be and was learned about navigation through observation of the daily work routine. Consequently, older and more experienced seamen, whatever their formal position, minimized the differential in knowledge that separated the top of the ship's labor hierarchy from its bottom.

The watch, another decisive element in the social arrangement of each ship, was perhaps the most basic unit for organizing the steady work of sailing the ship. Half of the crew was assigned to the starboard and half to the larboard watch: the captain supervised one, the mate the other. On the largest ships, the first and second mates took responsibility for a watch. Each watch served four hours on duty, then four hours off, alternating in work shifts (also called watches) around the clock. The dogwatch, between 4:00 and 8:00 P.M., was subdivided into two-hour shifts. This produced a total of seven shifts, ensuring that a watch would not work the same hours each day. Each sailor alternately worked a ten- and a fourteen-hour workday. The starboard and larboard watches were the essential cycle groups on each ship; their major responsibility was to guarantee the

31. Nathaniel Uring, *The Voyages and Travels of Captain Nathaniel Uring*, ed. Alfred Dewar (London, 1928 [orig. publ. London, 1726]).

32. Davis, *English Shipping*, 113, 122–123. My thinking on this subject owes much to modern works on the labor process, and especially to Conference on Socialist Economists, *The Labour Process and Class Strategies* (London, 1976). See also Harry Braverman, *Labor and Monopoly Capital: The Degradation of Work in the Twentieth Century* (New York, 1974); Michael Burawoy, "Toward a Marxist Theory of the Labor Process: Braverman and Beyond," *Politics and Society*, VIII (1978), 247–312; Andrew Zimbalist, ed., *Case Studies on the Labor Process* (New York, 1979); and Les Levidow and Bob Young, eds., *Science, Technology, and the Labour Process* (London, 1981).

continuity of keeping the vessel running and true. Everyone made a roughly equivalent contribution by helping to keep the ship on course at the highest possible speed.[33]

Even when off duty, one was never far from work. Anytime, anywhere, one might hear the mate's fearful cry: "Up every soul nimbly, for God's sake, or we all perish." Or, in Edward Barlow's dramatic and evocative words:

> At night when we went to take our rest, we were not to lie still above four hours; and many times when it blew hard were not sure to lie one hour, yea often were called up before we had slept half an hour and forced to go up into the maintop or foretop to take in our topsails, half awake and half asleep, with one shoe on and the other off, not having time to put it on: always sleeping in our clothes for readiness, and in stormy weather, when the ship rolled and tumbled as though some great millstone were rolling up one hill and down another, we had much ado to hold ourselves fast, by the small ropes from falling by the board; and being gotten up into the tops, there we must haul and pull to make fast the sail, seeing nothing but air above us and water beneath us: and many times in nights so dark that we could not see one another, and blowing so hard that we could not hear one another speak, being close to one another; and thundering and lightning as though heaven and earth could come together.[34]

Situations of crisis mobilized both watches in urgent cooperation.

The ship's technical division of labor, while demanding cooperation and interdependence, was also highly graded and specialized relative to the total number of men employed.[35] A crew of twelve usually was divided into five or six different ranks and an equal or greater number of pay stations. Rarely did more than four or five occupy equal positions in the laboring hierarchy. Rank, knowledge, watch, and pay were objective lines of demarcation and division within the ship's crew. The organization of work in the merchant service assembled a complex and collective unit of labor, only to separate that unit into shifting, overlapping, task-oriented components.

33. R. J. Cornewall-Jones, *The British Merchant Service: Being a History of the British Mercantile Marine from the Earliest Times to the Present Day* (London, 1898), 296; Falconer, *Universal Dictionary*, 312.

34. Francis Rogers, "The Journal of Francis Rogers," in Ingram, ed., *Three Sea Journals*, 144; Barlow, *Journal*, ed. Lubbock, 60.

35. Vilhelm Aubert, "On the Social Structure of the Ship," in Aubert, *The Hidden Society*, 260.

Despite the many specialized positions on each ship, there existed a general set of chores that everyone knew and performed. These duties constituted the core of the labor process in the merchant shipping industry. They logically centered on the industry's essential economic role—the movement of commodities—and the imperative to move them quickly. The labor process contained two fundamental kinds of work: handling the cargo and handling the ship.

The first stage of most voyages was loading the ship. Here, seamen, dockworkers, and other laborers collectively handled and hoisted the casks, bales, hogsheads, cases, ballast, provisions, and stores into the vessel's hold. In addition to the human strength involved in lifting, several mechanical devices were used to load the ship. Seamen used a wide array of tackle (an arrangement of ropes, pulleys, slings, and hooks) not only to lift and lower cargo into the ship but also to support the masts, extend the rigging, or expand the sails. The parbuckle, a less elaborate system of leverage, was used when no tackle was available.[36] The heaviest tasks required the use of the capstan or its smaller and, in the merchant service, more popular counterpart, the windlass. These machines consisted of a "strong massy column of holes" into which seamen inserted bars or levers called handspikes. This machine worked on the same principle as a horse mill: seamen walked in a circle, and it required "some dexterity and address to manage the handspec to the greatest advantage; and to perform this the sailors must all rise at once upon the windlass, and, fixing their bars therein, give a sudden jerk at the same instant, in which movement they are regulated by a sort of song or howl pronounced by one of their number." By use of the capstan or windlass and their systems of ropes and pulleys, heavy items such as masts, artillery, or bulky cargo were elevated and placed aboard, and anchor was weighed. In heaving or hoisting, it was necessary that the men work to the chant of "Together!" acting "all in concert, or at the same instant."[37] Seafaring labor, in its work chants and songs, revealed its profoundly collective nature.

Next, the cargo had to be maneuvered carefully into the hold, the belly of the ship, and stored properly. The arrangement of the cargo was important, and stowage had to take account of the weight, form, and type of commodity as well as the overall balance of the ship. The heaviest goods had to be placed nearest the keel on the very bottom

36. Falconer, *Universal Dictionary*, 155–156; David Steel, *The Elements and Practice of Rigging and Seamanship*, 2 vols. (London, 1794), I, 176–177.

37. Steel, *Elements and Practice*, I, 54; Falconer, *Universal Dictionary*, 61, 75, 76, 144, 210–211, 270, 288, 293, 324.

and at the center of gravity of the ship. Other items were stowed according to their packaging: bales, boxes, and cases were stacked; hogsheads and casks were wedged into place with chocks. All goods had to be secured to prevent shifting in rolling seas. Ballast was often added, since a proper amount of tonnage had to be on board so that the ship would sit properly, neither too crank (light) nor too stiff (heavy) in the water.[38] The leakiness of any given ship also determined how goods were to be stowed. Some cargo had to be put away bilge-free to avoid water damage. Each ship was equipped with a pump for the safety of the cargo and the crew. Depending on the size of the ship and the pump, a gang of two to seven men pulled large levers that activated a suction cup or a chain and valves, pushing water out of the hold through a channel.[39] A tight ship demanded little pumping, and sailors adored the skillful carpenter who could keep this dreaded, backbreaking work to a minimum. But frequently a ship decaying with age or damaged in a tempest required its crew to spend long spells at the pump. This "very bad work for the ship's company" usually resulted in deadening fatigue.[40] Lifting, hoisting, heaving, stowing, and pumping were operations in the labor process supervised by the captain and the mate.

Once the cargo had been loaded and secured, work shifted from handling the goods to handling the ship. Three basic chores now confronted the crew: steering the ship, managing the rigging, and working the sails, the skillful performance of which determined the speed and sometimes the profitability of the voyage. Steering the ship, along with the associated duties of keeping lookout and sounding, was a central part of the work effort. The helmsman directed the ship's course with the use of the compass, the sun, the moon, and the stars, according to the officer of the watch. Each sailor took a turn at the helm. The lookout acted as an additional pair of eyes for the helmsman. In shallow water, soundings were taken to determine depth. These, with the aid of charts, helped to establish the vessel's location.[41]

The rate of the ship's progress depended directly on the labors performed on the riggings and the sails. There were two kinds of rigging: the standing rigging (shrouds, stays, forestays, and back-

38. Falconer, Universal Dictionary, 28–29, 81, 262, 281–282; Steel, Elements and Practice, I, 7, 82–151.

39. Falconer, Universal Dictionary, 221–223, 282.

40. John Cremer, Ramblin' Jack: The Journal of Captain John Cremer, 1700–1774, ed. R. Reynall Bellamy (London, 1936), 115.

41. Falconer, Universal Dictionary, 80, 104, 184, 271–272, 277–278.

stays) was the collection of ropes that supported the masts, and the running rigging (braces, sheets, halyards, clew lines, and brails) was used "to extend and reduce the sails, or arrange them to the disposition of the wind." A series of lines running through blocks, or pulleys, were used to manage the sails, and, although much of this work was done from the deck, frequently a sailor had to climb aloft "hand-over-hand," carefully using the "horses" (rigging made expressly for sailors to stand upon or hold) to adjust a sail or a rope.[42] Rigging work also demanded a superior knowledge of tying and connecting ropes, whether by hitches or knots, using lanyards or lashings, or splicing one piece of hemp to another. The strong but nimble fingers of the seaman deftly arranged a cat's-paw, a flemish eye, a sheepshank, a timber hitch, or a diamond knot.[43]

Most deep-sea ships were either two- or three-masted vessels with a complex arrangement of sails, consisting of the course sails, topsails, and gallant sails as well as the smaller staysails, studding sails, and jibs, among many others. Sailors positioned the sails to accelerate or modify the ship's course by backing, balancing, reefing, shortening, furling, or loosing the enormous pieces of canvas. The tars scuttled from the deck to the tops, as high as sixty to seventy-five feet on most merchantmen, expanding this sail or reducing that one, according to the directions and strength of the winds.[44] As in the loading of cargo, work on the helm, the rigging, and the sails required careful coordination.

Once the ship was in port, attention turned back to the cargo. Breaking bulk, or discharging the first part of the cargo, began with the same equipment and labor used in loading. Cargo was lifted, hoisted, or heaved from the hold and transferred with the help of other workers into smaller craft such as hoys, barges, prams, and boats.[45] In the smaller ports, seamen were required to row the cargo ashore. Even here, the work remained collective, as Robert Hansell discovered in 1726. He was given a severe beating by his captain, Joseph Wilkinson, because he was "not rowing regularly with the rest of the Boat's Crew as he ought to have done."[46]

The maritime labor process was extraordinarily dangerous. Rec-

42. Ibid., 27, 37, 42, 56, 143, 244, 267; Steel, Elements and Practice, I, 149–160, 167.

43. Steel, Elements and Practice, I, 181–185; Falconer, Universal Dictionary, 155, 168, 171, 172, 273.

44. Falconer, Universal Dictionary, 27, 28, 135, 157, 184, 186, 239, 252, 286, 293–294, 298; Steel, Elements and Practice, I, 7, 82–151.

45. Falconer, Universal Dictionary, 48, 89, 155, 184.

46. Hansell v. Wilkinson, 1728, HCA 24/136.

ords do not exist that allow the computation of death rates for maritime industries and the comparison of these to rates for other occupations. Yet in the judgment of the late Ralph Davis, one of the finest historians of maritime affairs, "the chances of a seaman ending his life in . . . a catastrophe were high, and many a man fell from the rigging, was washed overboard, or was fatally struck by falling gear."[47] Indeed, a crucial part of the seaman's socialization was to learn to endure physical trial and minimal provisions. As Edward Barlow explained in 1696, those men who "were not used to hardship and had not known the lack of drink" were the first to collapse and die in hard times. Quite apart from the dangers of scurvy, rheumatism, typhus, yellow fever, ulcers, and skin diseases, seamen had to contend with an extensive range of disabilities and afflictions that resulted from their work. Frequently lifting or pulling, seamen were peculiarly susceptible to hernia or the "bursted belly," as they preferred to call it. It was not unusual to lose a finger to a rolling cask, for an arm or leg to be broken by shifting cargo, or for a hand to be burned in tarring ropes. And of course numberless men drowned and "took their habitation among the haddocks."[48]

One of the most hazardous aspects of the labor process was the dispensation of discipline, the necessary and bloody complement of the increasing productivity of seafaring labor in the eighteenth century. This "class discipline at its most personal and sadistic," as Peter Linebaugh has put it, resulted in masters' and mates' inflicting many disabling injuries upon the common men of the deep. Having been beaten nearly senseless with a pitch mop, John Laws cried to George Burrell: "Captain, you have ruined me. I shall never be my own Man again." Such beating often produced what seamen called the "Falling Sickness." John Marchant, caned in 1735 by mate John Yates, was, as he told the High Court of Admiralty, "troubled with a diziness in his Head . . . in so much that he cannot go aloft without danger of falling down." Others considered themselves "incapable of going to sea," since they were, in their words, "damnify'd" like a piece of cargo.[49] Seamen also suffered injury in battle against men-of-war,

---

47. Davis, *English Shipping*, 156. Knut Weibust, in *Deep Sea Sailors: A Study in Maritime Ethnology* (Stockholm, 1976), 435, notes the solidarity occasioned by the dangerous work environment at sea.

48. Barlow, *Journal*, ed. Lubbock, 462; Lloyd, *British Seaman*, 262; Journal of Surgeon Browne, Sloane Manuscript 1689, 23, British Library; Cremer, *Ramblin' Jack*, ed. Bellamy, 73; and Jeremy Roch, "The Third Journal," in Ingram, ed., *Three Sea Journals*, 104.

49. Linebaugh, "Picaresque Proletarian," 27; *Laws* v. *Burrell*, 1735, HCA 24/138; *Marchant* v. *Yates* and *Hance* v. *Jeffrey*, 1736, HCA 24/139; *Macquam* v. *Anstell*, 1744,

privateers, pirates, or coastal raiders. Upon discovering in 1713 that their captain had changed the voyage to a more dangerous destination, William Howell penned a protest for his shipmates, saying "that they did not hire themselves to fight" and properly wondering "In case they should lose a Legg or an Arme who would maintaine them and their Familys." It was a good question, for lucky was the seaman who, after fifteen years of service, could say, "I had my health and was able to seek for more employment."[50]

The deep-sea sailor labored on a frail vessel surrounded by omnipotent forces of nature, and this situation imparted a special urgency to cooperative labor. Upon hitting a rock or being overtaken by a turbulent squall, many crews realized that they had to turn out, all hands high, to "work for our Lives." Ned Coxere and his mates once found themselves surrounded by mountainous waves that soon tossed their vessel on its side, made them think of "their poor wives and children," and look "on [one] another with sorrowful hearts." After the desperate measure of cutting away the mainmast, the seamen took frantically to the pump to save themselves. Eager to know their fate, Coxere took a piece of chalk and marked the dangerously high waterline in the hold. After a strenuous turn at the pump he returned "to see whether the score of the chalk were above the water." If they had "gained with pumping," the verdict would be "life"; if the mark was underwater, then their fate was to be "death." The water had in fact receded by "about an inch," and Coxere and his comrades lived to tell the tale.[51] Their life-and-death example reveals the massive confrontation between the seaman and his work. The labor was physical. It required extraordinary strength, stamina, dexterity, and agility. The labor was also dangerous. It required courage and a continual renewal of initiative and daring.

Many smaller but still crucial chores filled out the shipboard routine of labor. These included shadow work such as overhauling the rigging, coiling ropes, repairing and oiling gear, changing and mending sail canvas, tarring ropes, cleaning the guns, painting, swabbing and holystoning the deck, and checking the cargo.[52] Such maintenance made it possible for seafaring work to be almost perpetual.

HCA 15/43; *Clancy* v. *Bennet*, 1737, Records of the South Carolina Admiralty, 164, Manuscripts Division, Library of Congress; *Phillips* v. *Haskins*, 1722, HCA 24/133; *Macknash* v. *Wood*, 1724, HCA 24/134; *Hamilton* v. *Harris*, 1728, HCA 24/135.

50. *Howell* v. *Rawlins*, 1714, HCA 24/130; Uring, *Voyages*, ed. Dewar, 66; Barlow, *Journal*, ed. Lubbock, 262.

51. William Dampier, *A Collection of Voyages*, 4 vols. (London, 1729), II, pt. 2, 23; Coxere, *Adventures*, ed. Meyerstein, 141–144.

52. Cornewall-Jones, *British Merchant Service*, 299.

Since the forces of nature dictated many of the tasks to be performed at sea, shadow work was used to fill the hours not directly devoted to sailing the ship. These chores made up one of the most contested domains of the labor process. How much and what kinds of work were seamen willing to give for their wages? This question had to be answered through a process of negotiation on every change of crew.

One of the central features of seafaring work was its social visibility. Work was a public activity, and crews were extremely sophisticated in judging the quality of each man's contribution. Everyone knew how to perform the basic tasks, and most men had been on other ships and had seen every chore, from the captain's duties downward, executed by others.[53] Consequently, even the lowest ordinary seaman considered himself a judge of his officers. Further, work was closely scrutinized, since collective well-being depended on it. There was considerable pressure to demonstrate one's skills, and when a man could do a job better than his superior, it was rarely a secret. When a captain was unskillful in his station, a crew might follow his incorrect orders with precision just to expose his ignorance. A drunken captain shouting incoherent orders put the ship's company "in great fear and danger of their Lives."[54] Fortunately, seamen were usually able to counteract such danger through their own knowledge of the labor process. That such knowledge was broadly held was central to the negotiation of labor in the merchant shipping industry.

This extensive knowledge of shipboard affairs frequently translated into severe problems for the captain. He found that some of his men were of an "unruly and Ungovernable Disposition" or a "grumbling unwilling mind." Captains endlessly groused about crew members they described as "self-willed" and "obstinate."[55] Such intransigence usually came from one of two sources: either the seaman was new and unaccustomed to the nature of work and authority on board ship, or, knowing the ways of the merchant service, he objected to the manner in which the ship was being run. This latter attitude was summed up by Ned Ward: "The better sailor he is, he becomes the more lazy, and fancies himself like a sheet-anchor, to be reserved for desperate occasions."[56] Many such seamen had their own ideas

53. *Ibid.*, 195; Kemp, *British Sailor*, 86; Aubert, "Social Structure," in Aubert, *Hidden Society*, 286.

54. Falconer, *Universal Dictionary*, 195; *Brazier* v. *Kennett*, 1730, HCA 24/136.

55. *Carr* v. *Harris*, 1725, HCA 24/135; Barlow, *Journal*, ed. Lubbock, 452; *Knight* v. *Lawson*, 1732, HCA 24/137; Uring, *Voyages*, ed. Dewar, 235.

56. Edward ["Ned"] Ward, *The Wooden World Dissected: In the Characters of a Ship of War* (London, 1708), 67. See also Matthew Bishop, *The Life and Adventures of*

about the social relations of work at sea. The organization, the pace, and the process of work became the focus of an often fierce struggle for control.

One way seamen attempted to expand their control over the labor process was by trying to enforce their own notions of what consti-tuted a proper crew. In 1705 John Tunbridge deserted the *Neptune* because "the Ship had not hands enough on board to work her." Seamen commonly complained that their vessels were "too weakly man'd." In 1722 sailors refused to proceed in a voyage from London to northern Europe because the "Master had not eleven hands on board" as he had promised in his "first Agreement." In Charleston, South Carolina, in 1736, a crew of seamen was brought on board the *Fenton* only to walk out en masse when they discovered how much pumping would be required to control a riverlike leak. A second crew hired by the same master took a similarly quick exit. Captain John Rushton took his crew to court in 1732 for refusing to sail; they too had charged a lack of sufficient men. The judge of the Massachu-setts admiralty sided with the captain, ruling that the seamen were "not proper Judges what hands the Master ought to carry" and or-dered that the ship and crew set sail.[57] This form of protest, some-thing of a preemptive strike, was, from the seaman's point of view, limited in its effectiveness. During times of peace, maritime workers were so abundant that they could not exert much pressure without fear of dismissal. Those who made up the reserve navy of the unem-ployed, those put out of work by the demobilization of the Royal Navy, waited anxiously for any vacant berth. During wartime, with the navy and privateers scouring the seas, labor was so scarce that ships often had no alternative but to sail with smaller crews. Seamen usually took their advantage in the form of higher wages.[58]

Given the limits of this tactic, many mariners resorted to the work stoppage. Some stoppages were primarily defensive, used by sea-men to preserve the privileges that previous generations of seafarers had won. They insisted, for example, that their work regimen was to be relaxed while they were in harbor. The sailors of the *Hind* com-

---

Matthew Bishop of Deddington in Oxfordshire (London, 1744), 79: "There is more Prospect of a good Sailor from a Country-man than from a Waterman, that pre-tends to know more than his Teachers."

57. Examination of John Tunbridge, 1706, HCA 1/53; Cremer, *Ramblin' Jack*, ed. Bellamy, 76; *Thompson v. Curling*, 1735, HCA 24/139; *Hays v. Russell*, 1724, HCA 24/139; *Brown v. Graer*, 1737, HCA 24/139; *Rushton v. Seamen*, 1732, Records of the Court of Admiralty of the Province of Massachusetts Bay, 105, Manuscripts Divi-sion, Library of Congress.

58. Kemp, *British Sailor*, 105.

plained in 1720 that, while lying at anchor, Captain John Hunter "obliged them to work every day and to do more labour and duty than when at Sea." Seamen also insisted that Sundays in port were their own. When Thomas Revit ordered his crew to unload the ship on a Sunday, he was told that "they were Christians and not slaves [and] they would not then work." A significant number of work stoppages resulted from individual acts of defiance. In 1735 Captain Joseph Barnes asked Henry Twine, his carpenter, "what he came to Sea for if he would not do his Business and Duty as Carpenter." Twine "replyed that he came to Sea for his Pleasure and would do what he pleased and nothing more."[59] Actions of this sort in the workplace were highly visible and carried expansive social meanings, affording examples, even encouragement, to others. Occasionally, they precipitated collective actions.[60] Everyone on board breathed (and worked) a bit more easily within the space created by the successful confrontation. When such conflict called the legitimacy of the command into question, seamen dramatically increased their control over the nature and pace of work. As one captain lamented in 1729, those who neglected their duty "did occasion the like neglect in the other Mariners." And as an agricultural-turned-seafaring maxim had it, "One Scaley Sheep spoils a hole Flock."[61]

The most effective work stoppages, of course, were collective. In 1729 the seamen of the *Young Prince*, when ordered to heave anchor, "one and all . . . unanimously agreed to stop and swore Goddamn their Bloods if they would heave the Anchor or go any further with the said Ship but would go on Shore."[62] On other occasions, a core of dissatisfied mariners might attempt "to raise a Mutiny . . . and to prevent the other Mariners from proceeding on the said Voyage."[63]

Many of these themes were sharply illustrated in an abundantly documented case heard in the South Carolina Court of Admiralty in 1719. John Clipperton, master of the slaveship *Hanover Succession*, brought charges of mutiny against Jacob Key, John Swain, Samuel

59. *Crayton* v. *Hunter*, 1721, *Sharpless* v. *Durrell*, 1720, *Wallis* v. *Wills*, 1721, *Dunkin* v. *Revit*, 1721, and *Gouldin* v. *Saunders*, 1721, all HCA 24/133; Information of Thomas Blood, 1715, HCA 1/54; *Twine* v. *Barnes*, 1736, HCA 24/136.

60. I am indebted here to Martin Glaberman, *Wartime Strikes: The Struggle against the No Strike Pledge in the UAW during World War II* (Detroit, Mich., 1980), 31.

61. *Latouche* v. *Roure*, 1729, HCA 24/136; Cremer, *Ramblin' Jack*, ed. Bellamy, 162.

62. *Brazier* v. *Kennet*, 1730, HCA 24/136; *Beck* v. *Seamen*, 1716, South Carolina Admiralty, 33–47; *Moodie* v. *Hogg*, 1726, HCA 24/135; *Mason* v. *Pomeroy*, 1701, HCA 24/137.

63. *Plummer* v. *Burnaby*, 1725, HCA 24/135.

Woodbrey, Alexander Spencer, Joseph Coke, Benjamin Waistcoat, and David Allen—seven of his seamen. Clipperton claimed that Key, his mate, had "behaved himself mighty Ill and after a threatning and insolent manner" in their passages from London to Charleston by way of the African coast. Key "absolutely" refused to do his duty and "incensed" other members of the crew "to fall from their Duty and also to declare that they would not goe the Voyage." When the master asked the seamen why they refused, they "all answered the Vessel was incapable," meaning that it leaked badly. Having left Charleston for London, the crew made Clipperton return to the South Carolina port, "reviling him with hard words" all the way. Key "kept severall Caballs" with the other sailors; soon, according to Clipperton, they were "combining together" in an ominous design.[64]

The effects of this combination were visible when Clipperton ordered his men to weigh anchor. Jacob Key bid him defiance. Samuel Woodbrey "threw away his hand spike saying Damn it He would heave no more." Several seamen then announced that unless Captain Clipperton "would be guided and ordered by them they would take from him his Boats and leave him to the wide ocean to perish together with his Ship." The sailors then "drew up a Paper," and Jacob Key told Clipperton, "Wee'll make a Protest against you and nail it on the Main Mast and you are a Young Rascally Dogg and I'le take Charge of the Vessel for you intend to Destroy it." Key then suggested a deep source of tension by adding, "Damn you I'le make you take a Spell at the Pump as well as the rest." Key was soon obeyed by some as captain, and the command had been fully divided. Some seamen apparently continued to support Clipperton, because the protest was eventually ripped from the mast. But the ship had to return to Charleston. Clipperton cursed his "hard usage" by this "bad Crew." The seamen had their own complaints. They were "weary with pumping," having been called up while off duty, and they had but "little Water and Provisions." Key complained that Clipperton had beaten him "without the least Occasion."[65]

Several themes are vividly illustrated here: the coalescence of support around individual resistance, the struggle over the control of work, the negotiation of authority, the efforts of the crew to set standards of safety, and the omnipresence of danger. Allegations of incompetence were crucial, with Clipperton calling Key "an Old Rogue and Villain," and Key calling Clipperton a "Drunken Fellow," unfit

64. *Clipperton* v. *Seamen*, 1719, South Carolina Admiralty, 493, 494.
65. *Ibid.*, 494, 495, 505, 507.

for command.[66] But so too does this case illustrate one of the limits of work stoppage. It was often simply too dangerous. If the ship had not been near Charleston when the conflict broke out, little could have been done, and the men would have been obliged to "work for their Lives."[67]

The law also placed sharp limits upon the use of work stoppages at sea. As Richard B. Morris has noted, "A strike which might have been treated as an illegal combination at common law would, if committed by mariners, be deemed a mutiny." Most seamen, therefore, resorted to another tactic to influence the conditions and character of their work, a tactic summed up in the lyrics of an old sea song:

> O, the times are hard and the wages low,
> Leave her, John-ny, leave her;
> I'll pack my bag and go be-low;
> It's time for us to leave her.[68]

If seamen were unable to limit hard usage by controlling the labor process, they could at least escape it by using their fast feet.

Desertion was one of the most chronic and dangerous problems faced by the merchant capitalists of the shipping industry.[69] Merchants bought the seaman's labor power in a contractual exchange. Monthly wages were paid for work on a specified voyage. Vast bodies of legislation and legal opinion were produced in an effort to guarantee that exchange. In signing a set of articles, the legal agreement between owner and captain and crew, seamen were usually required to affirm that they would not "go away from, Quit or leave the said Ship . . . in any port abroad, or go on board of any other Ship whatsoever," unless impressed or required to by force. But seamen always reserved to themselves the right to terminate that contract, to take their chances with the law, and to demonstrate that labor power was a commodity unlike any other. What merchant capitalists and their apologists saw as "the natural unsteddiness of seamen" was in fact the use of autonomous mobility to set the conditions of work.[70]

---

66. *Ibid.*, 589.

67. See also *Seamen* v. *Alloyn*, 1730, South Carolina Admiralty, 764–802, in which a work stoppage almost produced a disaster.

68. Richard B. Morris, *Government and Labor in Early America* (New York, 1946), 225, 248 (poem).

69. *Ibid.*, 247.

70. *Linam* v. *Chapman*, 1730, HCA 24/136; Arthur Pierce Middleton, *Tobacco Coast: A Maritime History of Chesapeake Bay in the Colonial Era* (Newport News, Va.,

The tactic of desertion was used in complex and sometimes inge-
nious ways. Seamen resorted to desertion to stay out of areas where
they were likely to be pressed into the Royal Navy. When William
Trewfitt and other mariners, in 1735, found themselves sailing toward a port rumored to contain a hot press, they immediately put
the ship on another course, "hindring any others of the Mariners on
board who attempted . . . to have her keep a proper course." At the
first available moment, Trewfitt and several men ran from the ship.[71]

Desertion was also used to avoid sailing into disease-ridden cli-
mates. When Captain Robert Ranson altered his voyage to go to
Callabar in Africa, some of his men deserted, calling the new destination "a very unhealthful place and for which the said Mar[ine]rs or
several of them would not have shipt themselves." Seafarers also ran
from their ships to escape inadequate rations of food. Richard Young
claimed in 1720 that he and twenty-three others deserted the *Pompey*
"by reason that they could not live upon their Allowance of Provisions." A band of seamen left the *William* in 1729 because they "were
afraid of being pinched in their Provisions."[72]

Perhaps most crucially, desertion was used to escape the grasp of a
brutal master or mate. In 1706, after one of their fellow tars had
jumped overboard and eventually drowned in an attempt to escape
the "severity" of their captain, William Bedford, John Lade, and John
Tunbridge collectively deserted. They "being not able to suffer his
Tirany any longer took the Boate and came on Shore." In 1726 William Hamilton, John Slater, Joseph Pattison, Thomas Trummel, and
Charles Hicks deserted the *Judith* in Maryland, complaining of the
abuses of Captain Joseph Wilkinson. The captain "had beaten some
of them and [they] did not know how soon he might beat the rest."
They swore "they would not go on Board unless they were carried
on mens backs" and that, for all they cared, the captain might be
"cut into half crown pieces." In 1737 four seamen of the *Charming
Anne* ran from their less than charming captain, Henry Curling. The
seamen had apparently heard that Curling was a rough master, and
they signed on for only one part of the voyage to see "if they liked

---

1953), 273–274. See the many plans proposed to guarantee maritime labor power
in J. S. Bromley, ed., *The Manning of the Royal Navy: Selected Public Pamphlets, 1693–
1873*, Navy Records Society, *Publications*, CXIX (London, 1974). William Gordon
to Thomas Corbett, Dec. 30, 1742, ADM 1/1827, PRO.

71. *Trewfitt v. Storm*, 1735, HCA 24/138. It should be noted that desertion from
the Royal Navy, into which so many had been impressed, was a very different
social phenomenon.

72. *Arnold v. Ranson*, 1706, HCA 24/129; Examination of Richard Young, 1720,
HCA 1/54; *Macnamera v. Barry*, 1729, South Carolina Admiralty, 726.

and approved" of the captain's "usage and treatment of them." One of the sailors, Richard Hudschon, claimed that Curling "threatened to Shoot him and to tye him by his private parts and hang him over board." Hudschon and several others deserted, presumably with great determination. Mariners endlessly alleged in court that a captain's cruelty was a primary reason for running from one ship to another.[73]

On many occasions, the mere threat of desertion was enough to wrest an advantage from a captain. Some seamen threatened to desert during harsh weather, and others swore they would leave if a drunken and abusive mate were continued in service.[74] One can imagine the fears of Captain Joseph Chapman in 1725, when two seamen "endeavoured to perswade all the Foremastmen on board to leave and desert the said Ships Service" while the ship was full of slaves. Four men deserted, and if the Africans "had revolted . . . there could not have been sufficient force to suppress them."[75]

Desertion was encouraged by the extraordinary competition waged between the Royal Navy and the merchant service for the sailor's labor power. During war years, the bidding grew especially intense as privateers joined the rivalry, offering Jack Tar the prospects of greater riches for less work. Merchant captains were notorious for spiriting seamen away from the king's ships by offering high wages and generous allotments of rum.[76] The sailor, even during peacetime, could shuttle back and forth between these two enterprises with great profit. As members of the Massachusetts Court of Admiralty heard in 1731:

> One great inducement why Sailors so frequently leave the merchants service in these parts is, the Wages given from hence are greater than out of Great Brittain and they don't value loosing two or three months Wages to get clear of a long and tedious Voyage upon smaller Wages and in order the better to do it Enter themselves on board His Majestys Ships that happen to be here and so soon as a profitable Voyage offers, Desert the Kings Ser-

73. Petition of William Bedford, John Lake, and John Tunbridge, 1706(?), HCA 1/29; *Hamilton v. Wilkinson*, 1728, HCA 24/136; *Hudschon v. Curling*, 1737, *Bennet v. Bride*, 1740, both HCA 24/139.

74. *Young v. Higgins*, 1704, HCA 24/128; *Webber v. Prust*, 1735, HCA 24/138.

75. *Wistridge v. Chapman*, 1727, HCA 24/135.

76. Lloyd, *British Seaman*, 52–57; Kemp, *British Sailor*, 105; *Forest v. Leveron*, 1704, HCA 24/128. See also, for example, William Gordon to Thomas Corbett, Nov. 10, 1742, ADM 1/1827, on the "great number of Gallons of Rum" offered to seamen to desert.

vice by which practices the Voyage they originally contracted to proceed is very much retarded if not quite overset.

At times, seamen could desert to the navy without losing any money. According to the Act for the Better Regulation and Government of Seamen in the Merchants Service passed in Britain in 1729, those mariners who joined a royal ship were entitled to full pay from the ship they left behind.[77] The enforcement of this statute depended very much upon which court and judge heard the seaman's case, but in general it seems that sailors successfully used the admiralty courts to argue their claims throughout the period. In order to escape contracts, mariners libeled incessantly "for wages and liberation."[78]

The sprawling nature of the international labor market and the empire made desertion extremely attractive. Many seamen, like those who congregated in Massachusetts, migrated to the edges of the empire, where seafaring labor was scarce, taking advantage of high wages and better working conditions. Many a tar was willing "to leave the ship . . . if he could better himselfe," and such betterment was not hard to find in the West Indies.[79]

By 1700, the plantation mode of production in the Caribbean had developed to the point that free wage labor there had become something of an anomaly. A crippling mortality affected practically every ship that sailed into West Indian ports, and this, combined with the scarcity of free labor, created a situation in which sailors quickly seized an advantage. Desertion served to destabilize the labor market and drive wages up. As one merchant captain explained in 1717, "It was and is usuall for Marriners of Ships who were and are hired at monthly wages to leave and desert their respective services at Ja-

77. *Guy* v. *Skinner*, 1731, Massachusetts Admiralty, 6; An Act for the Better Regulation and Government of Seamen in the Merchants Service, copy in HCA 30/999; *Robinson* v. *Comyn*, 1736, South Carolina Admiralty, 51; Lords of Admiralty to William Bull, Aug. 14, 1742, 87–89, CO 5/358, PRO.

78. *Roberts* v. *Kipping*, 1726, Massachusetts Admiralty, 6. While many a sailor deserted to a man-of-war to elude the clutches of a violent merchant captain, some merchant captains, in turn, used the king's ships as repositories for mutinous and disobedient seamen. Some captains apparently forced seamen from their ships in order to save labor costs. As Edward Barlow lamented in the late 17th century, conflicts with a captain led to his being turned out "without a penny of what was my due for the time of my service" (*Journal*, ed. Lubbock, 358). See also *Pattison* v. *Beesley*, 1709, HCA 24/129; *Jones* v. *Purnell*, 1715, HCA 24/131; *Vesey* v. *Yoakley*, 1707, HCA 24/129.

79. "Account of the Discovery of an Horrid Plot and Conspiracy on Board the Ship *Antelope*," 1699, CO 323/3.

maica and other parts in the west Indies and to ship and enter themselves into the Service of Ships att much greater wages by the Run." Once free of command, seamen were footloose in the port towns, "rambling to and fro about the Country," as one disapproving captain put it.[80] They looked to sell their dear labor for "the run home" to London. "A Rambler in the West Indies," who made two pounds per month on the voyage to Jamaica, stood to make ten to twenty pounds and ten gallons of rum for the passage back to London.[81] Such bargains drastically reduced the literal exploitation of maritime labor.

As the examples of William Trewfitt, William Bedford, Richard Hudschon, and their comrades in flight indicate, many seamen ran from their ships "in combination," often leaving behind an incapacitated vessel. Captains thus faced difficult choices: they could look for relatively cheap labor, risking a lengthy delay during which time all those sailors who remained in service had to be paid, or they could pay the high wages demanded by the men looking to work their way home to London. Often, the second was the only alternative. But it should be noted that not all seamen saw wisdom in desertion. As one man viewed it, anyone who deserted "would be a fool . . . for it was giving his Wages to another Man."[82] And so it was. But in return, many men received wages two, three, four, or more times as great as those they forfeited. Some sailors were even known as chronic deserters, men who, in the words of a vexed captain, "never went out and returned in the same ship a whole voyage." Some were considered "stragling Fellows that can't leave their old Trade of Deserting."[83] Desertion was not so much a trade as a trademark of a footloose maritime proletariat.

Desertion also served as a firm demarcation of the captain's authority and as an affirmation of the sailor's own power. As Henry Fielding perceptively observed during his voyage to Portugal in 1754, the ship captain found that "it was easier to send his men on shore than to recall them. They acknowledged him to be their master while

---

80. *Mathew v. Lawton*, 1717, HCA 24/131; *Vincent v. Curtis*, 1735, HCA 24/139.

81. R. Pares, "The Manning of the Royal Navy in the West Indies, 1702–63," Royal Historical Society, *Transactions*, 4th Ser., XX (1937), 31–60; Thomas Coale to Josiah Burchett, July 22, 1699, ADM 1/1588. See also *Lone v. Lewis*, 1715, HCA 24/131; and *Deverell v. Pierson*, 1719, HCA 24/129.

82. *Bruce v. Cathcart*, 1734, HCA 24/138; *French v. Meake*, 1729, HCA 24/126.

83. *Wilson v. Parsons*, 1710, HCA 24/129; Woodes Rogers, *A Cruising Voyage round the World*, ed. G. E. Manwaring (London, 1928 [orig. publ. London, 1712]), 299.

they remained on shipboard, but did not allow his power to extend to the shores, where they no sooner set their feet than every man became *sui juris*, and thought himself at full liberty to return when he pleased."[84]

Desertion was, in all, an essential component of seafaring labor: as the seamen who flew from Fielding's ship demonstrated, it affirmed the "free" in free wage labor. In so doing, it went far beyond and frequently contradicted the free wage labor imagined and endorsed by the merchant capitalist who paid for that labor and the merchant captain who supervised it. Merchants, masters, and governmental officials made resolute efforts to control the autonomous mobility of maritime workers. They issued acts and proclamations against straggling seamen in ports, they ran advertisements in newspapers for deserters, they sued incessantly in court, and they tried to implement a seaman's registry and a certificate system to identify sailors and make their labor readily available. The large measure of power held by these figures gave them some success in controlling Jack's mobility, for the seaman was not only free to find a job but also free to starve if he was unable to find one. Yet mobility was an essential component in the seaman's strategy for survival. The mariner had to maintain a continuity of income when often there was no continuity of available work.[85] As Gary Nash has shown, free laborers in the colonial port cities were able to count on little more than 200–250 days of work per year. Jack Tar's rhythm of keeping body and soul together and the merchant's rhythm of capital accumulation did not move in the same motions. As a form of struggle and a means of survival, desertion had a pervasively wide circulation among maritime workers.[86] The seafarer's mobility was a central part of his

84. Henry Fielding, *The Journal of a Voyage to Lisbon* (London, 1976 [orig. publ. London, 1755]), 255.

85. Lloyd, *British Seaman*, 173–191; *Piracy Destroy'd; or, A Short Discourse Shewing the Rise, Growth, and Causes of Piracy of Late; with a Sure Method How to Put a Speedy Stop to That Growing Evil* (London, 1701), 22; John Dennis, *An Essay on the Navy; or, England's Advantage and Safety, Prov'd Dependent on a Formidable and Well-Disciplined Navy; and the Encrease and Encouragement of Seamen* (London, 1702), 36–53; An Act for Punishing Mutinous and Disobedient Seamen and for the More Speedy Determination of Controversies Arising between Masters of Ships and Their Crews, 1772, CO 412/22. This paragraph owes much to Michael Sonenscher, "Work and Wages in Paris in the Eighteenth Century," in Maxine Berg, Pat Hudson, and Sonenscher, eds., *Manufacture in Town and Country before the Factory* (Cambridge, 1983), 147–172.

86. Nash, *Urban Crucible*, 55–57. The complaints and allegations of desertion in the English and colonial admiralty courts are incessant.

strategy to control the means of finding employment. It was a mobility made effective by the amorphous collective network through which rumor, reputation, and information circulated among sailors of the English Atlantic.

The tactic of work stoppage was a form of collective disobedience that often shaded into the more ominous crime of mutiny. Most mutinies between 1700 and 1750 were fleeting affairs, ranging from the downing of tools to the violent, almost always temporary seizure of ships. According to merchant captains, sailors formed "cabals" among themselves, and support usually coalesced around a particularly defiant member of the crew. For example, Captain Thomas King, in 1723, called Peter Lester a "mutineer," a man with whom "most part of the Sailors seemed to be in a cabal." King tried to maneuver Lester out of the ship but had "much difficulty . . . for noe Violence cou'd be us'd where the Major part of the Ships Company were inclin'd to favour him." Off the African coast in 1736, another crew attempted "to raise a mutiny" in response to the harsh punishments administered by their captain for work-related offenses. One of the sailors was placed in irons for his role in the rising. When asked by the captain of another merchant vessel why they were so angry, the seamen said, "By God, they would not be serv'd so, no Man shou'd confine any of them, for they were one and all resolved to stand by one another." In 1721 John Sedgewick and several other mariners designed to desert their ship. On arrival in Saint Kitts, and when ordered by their captain to load some casks of sugar, Sedgewick replied: "God damn you take them on board yourselfe. [H]ere is one Boat on Shore and another at anchor, look after them and be damned." The captain persisted in his order and was told by several men, "God damn y[ou]r Blood carry them on Board your selfe for wee will not sett our feet on Board y[ou]r Ship any more." A band of men deserted, but they were soon captured and taken before a magistrate, who threatened them with jail. Sedgewick then reportedly "damned his Blood and sayd they were one and all." One and all they were, and this was precisely how they went to jail.[87]

In 1714 the crew of the *St. Joseph* "all as one" refused to go any further once their captain had changed the destination from that stipulated in their original agreement. In other disputes, seamen swore "they would stand by one another and stand Knock for Knock . . . meaning they would Resist" their master "by Force." To avert a

---

87. *Lester* v. *King*, 1723, HCA 24/134; *Powell* v. *Hardwicke*, 1738, HCA 24/139; *Sedgewick* v. *Burroughs*, 1723, HCA 24/134.

captain's wrath over some anonymous misdeed, sailors often must have "turned freemasons and kept a secret." Not for nothing did seamen call each other "Brother Tar."[88]

Mutiny sometimes took on a more permanent and material form; that is, it ceased to be a redressive and defensive posture and assumed the aggressive stance of piracy. Sailors then expropriated the workplace and arranged it anew. Since piracy represented a social world constructed apart from the ways of the merchant and the captain—and, hence, apart in significant ways from capital—robbery at sea can illuminate certain aspects of the labor process as seen by those whose lives were shaped by it.[89]

Almost all early eighteenth-century pirates had worked in the merchant shipping industry, and piracy was deeply imbued with the collectivistic tendencies produced by life and labor at sea. Against the omnipotent authority of the merchant shipmaster, pirates elected their captain and other officers. Against the hierarchical pay system of the merchant service, pirates distributed their plunder in markedly egalitarian fashion. Pirates also exhibited a pervasive consciousness of kind.[90]

The nature of the tasks performed by a seaman did not change for the bold tar who exchanged a life of legal trade for one of illegal plunder. In either employ, the same work had to be performed. Yet once among pirates, the intensity of labor decreased dramatically, because pirate ships were hugely overmanned. An average vessel of two hundred tons carried eighty or more men, but a merchant ship of equivalent size contained only thirteen to seventeen hands. These outlaws maintained the maritime division of labor but strictly limited its tendency to function as a hierarchy of status and privilege. They also altered its relation to income. There were, among pirates, only three pay stations for some eighty men, rather than five or six slots for fifteen sailors. Even more revealingly, pirates abolished the wage. They considered themselves risk-sharing partners rather than a collection of "hands" who sold their muscle on an open market.[91]

Some mariners cast their lots with pirates in order to escape hard labor. As pirate Joseph Mansfield said in 1722, "the love of Drink and a Lazy Life" were "Stronger Motives with him than Gold." Admiral

88. *Longust* v. *Youron*, 1714, HCA 24/130; *Parker* v. *Boucher*, 1719, HCA 24/132; Cremer, *Ramblin' Jack*, ed. Bellamy, 86, 117.
89. This section draws from material and conclusions that I presented in " 'Under the Banner of King Death': The Social World of Anglo-American Pirates, 1716 to 1726," *WMQ*, 3d Ser., XXXVIII (1981), 203–227.
90. *Ibid*.
91. *Ibid*.

Edward Vernon, taking sixteen suspected pirates aboard his man-of-war, said that, since he needed "hands for the pump, it might be of service to carry them out of the way of falling into their old Courses, and that it might be a Means to learn them . . . working," which, Vernon noted, "They turned Rogues to avoid."[92] As an officer of an East India Company ship observed of seamen in 1701:

> They run from Ship to Ship, and are encouraged in it by advancing their pay, which makes up what they lost in the other they left, and after they are a little accustomed to this extravagant course of leaving their ships at Pleasure, . . . they seldom care to proceed to their intended Voyage, but getting a custome of Roving, they leave their Commander upon every slight distaste, and at last grow so ungovernable, that nothing will serve them but going where they shall all be equal, or all Masters by turns. This I think is the occasion of such numbers of Pirates.

And as Woodes Rogers, the governor of the Bahama Islands, long-experienced in battles against sea robbers, said of pirates, "For work they mortally hate it." Samuel Buck, a long-time resident of the Bahamas, agreed: "Working does not agree with them."[93]

The social contours of piracy, while fully congruent with the labor process at sea, were often formed in violent antipathy to that world of work from which many seamen gladly escaped. "Lower class utopias," writes Christopher Hill, for centuries aimed "to abolish wage-labour altogether, or drastically to reduce the working day." The social organization of piracy, even though based upon a relatively new form of collectivism, was part of that tenacious tradition that linked medieval peasants, seventeenth-century radicals such as the Diggers and Levellers, and the free wage laborers of the eighteenth century.[94]

Perhaps the most telling evidence, much of it dating from the later eighteenth century, of the increasingly collective consciousness and activity among seamen lay in their resort to the strike. Given, in fact, the logic of collectivism that informed seafaring work, it comes as no

92. "Proceedings of the Court held on the Coast of Africa upon Trying of 100 Pirates taken by his Ma[jes]ties Ship *Swallow*," 1722, MS, HCA 1/99, 116; Edward Vernon to Josiah Burchett, Aug. 12, 1721, Edward Vernon Letterbook, 1720–1721, Add. Ms. 40813, 128, British Library.

93. *Piracy Destroy'd*, 15; Rogers to Council of Trade and Plantations, May 29, 1719, CO 23/11; Memorial of Samuel Buck, 1720, CO 23/1, 103.

94. Christopher Hill, "Pottage for Freeborn Englishmen: Attitudes to Wage Labour," in Hill, *Change and Continuity in Seventeenth-Century England* (Cambridge, Mass., 1975), 235. See Linebaugh, "Atlantic Mountains," *Labour / Le travailleur*, X (1982), 87–121, for a pathbreaking analysis of many of these continuities.

surprise that the very term "strike" evolved from the decision of seamen, in 1768, to strike the sails of their vessels and, thereby, to cripple the commerce of the empire's capital city. The strike may have been born of shipboard cooperation, but, as a concept in language and in practical political and economic activity, it began to circulate with increasing velocity among all of those men and women involved in collective industrial labor.[95]

These are some of the many ways in which the relationships initiated by the concentration of labor on the ship were soon transformed by seamen into a new basis for the organization of community. Sharing almost every aspect of life, separated from family and church, seafarers forged new social relations. Their new solidarity was often undercut by the diversity of the men who made their livings by the sea as well as by the mobility and dispersion that were essential features of their work. Yet for all of these men, self-protection—from harsh conditions, excessive work, and oppressive authority—was necessary to survival. Too often, claimed Edward Barlow, when under command "all the men in the ship except the master" were "little better than slaves."[96] Social bonds among sailors arose from the very conditions and relations of their work. These men possessed a concrete and situational outlook forged within the power relations that guided their lives. Theirs was a collectivism of necessity.

THE COEXISTENCE and integration of diverse types of labor, the coordination of efforts to combat a menacing laboring environment, the clearly demarcated shifts of work as organized by the watch system, and the interdependence of the stages of production combined to produce a new laboring experience. The seaman, in sum, was one of the first collective workers. There were, to be sure, several broad continuities in the nature of work between the early days of sail and the eighteenth century: certain aspects of the division and organization of labor and some of the chores, tasks, and dangers remained essentially the same. Yet there were also decisive changes in the nature, pace, and context of work at sea, both in the labor process and, perhaps even more importantly, in the maritime labor market.

Several technological changes affected the labor process between

95. *Oxford English Dictionary*, s.v. "strike." See Dobson, *Masters and Journeymen*, 154–170, for a partial listing of seamen's strike activity.

96. Aubert, "Total Institution," in Aubert, *Hidden Society*, 257. Jesse Lemisch, in "Listening to the 'Inarticulate': William Widger's Dream and the Loyalties of American Revolutionary Seamen in British Prisons," *Journal of Social History*, III (1969–1970), 1–29, discusses this same collectivistic ethos as it appeared in the Revolutionary era. Barlow, *Journal*, ed. Lubbock, 339.

1700 and 1750. Major alterations were made in rigging, steering, and the complexity of sails. By 1700, vessels were being designed and built for smaller crews, and the production of more manageable, two-masted ships (brigs and scows) increased significantly. Merchants deployed wide-bottom Dutch hull forms in order to ship larger amounts of cargo with fewer workers.[97] Throughout the eighteenth century, crew sizes decreased in relation to tonnage. A typical two-hundred-ton Virginia trader carried twenty or twenty-one crew members in 1700, about sixteen in 1750, and as few as thirteen by 1770. The number of tons of cargo handled per seaman increased from the 1720s to 1770.[98] Some of these declining crew sizes, however, were offset by an increase in the size of the average transatlantic vessel.

What appeared to the merchant capitalist or captain as an increase in productivity often appeared to the seaman as an increase in exploitation. As crew sizes were reduced through the removal of ordnance, the specialization of function, and technological change, more work was required of the seamen who remained on each ship. As Robert K. Schaeffer has written of the seventeenth and eighteenth centuries, "The multiplication of sails and rigging and the use of block and tackle made the work of running the ship much more complex." Mastery of shipboard labor required crews both to learn more and to "work harder."[99] The smaller crews, subjected over time to ever harsher discipline, were forced to take part in a more intensively cooperative labor process. As merchants hired fewer men to do seafaring work, they required greater concert from all aboard ship. A quantitative reduction of the collectivity of the crew led to a qualitative expansion of collective work.[100]

The maritime labor market also witnessed crucial changes. As the luxury trades of the period 1450–1650 gave way to the bulk trades of the late seventeenth and eighteenth centuries, the merchant shipping industry created increasingly stable, lifelong employment for an ever-larger mass of waged workers. Thus the seaman's work was

97. Parry, *Trade and Dominion*, 207–209; Davis, *English Shipping*, 65–66, 72; Abbott Payson Usher, "The Growth of English Shipping, 1572–1922," *Quarterly Journal of Economics*, XLII (1928), 476.

98. James F. Shepherd and Gary M. Walton, *Shipping, Maritime Trade, and the Economic Development of Colonial North America* (Cambridge, 1972), 73–81; Davis, *English Shipping*, 71–78; Parry, *Trade and Dominion*, 214–215.

99. Robert K. Schaeffer, "The Chains of Bondage Broke: The Proletarianization of Seafaring Labor, 1600–1800" (Ph.D. diss., State University of New York, Binghamton, 1983), chap. 3.

100. Davis, *English Shipping*, 154.

collective not only within the technical process and division of labor that existed on each ship but, more broadly, within the social division of labor. Occupying a central position in the international economy, the seaman came into contact with an extraordinary assortment of other laborers, working alongside lightermen, porters, coastal traders, dockworkers, and others in Europe's port cities and with slaves, indentured servants, and day laborers in the colonies. He regularly crossed paths with customs officials, provisioners, merchants, supercargos, coopers, shipbuilders, and ship chandlers, to name but a few who performed dockside labor.[101] The turnover of personnel from ship to ship brought the sailor into association with an exceptionally large number of his fellow tars. The cooperative character of his position owed much to his mobile circulation within an expansive labor market and extended from the technicalities of the workplace to the production and exchange of goods within the empire and beyond, to the international market chain, the global economy increasingly dominated by Europe. The international capitalist economy was emerging as an increasingly cooperative totality, and the strategically situated merchant seaman provided many of the links in the system.

The labor process on the early eighteenth-century deep-sea sailing craft provides a classic example of what Karl Marx called "the formal subsumption of labor under capital." In the age of manufacture, merchant capitalists, such as those in international trade, gradually took over existing labor processes that in many cases had "developed by different and more archaic modes of production." Gradual changes, such as the regularization and intensification of work "under the eye of the interested capitalist," were introduced, but the control of capital remained merely formal: there existed "no fixed political and social relationship of supremacy and subordination." Revolutionary changes and "the real subsumption of labor under capital" came later, wrought by the large-scale introduction of machinery.[102]

Eighteenth-century seafaring work, therefore, even though highly synchronized and continuous, remained distinct in one crucial respect from the machine-dominated factory of the nineteenth century: it depended in the final instance upon nature, upon the movements of wind and water. As Edward Barlow insisted, "A fair wind . . . is a seaman's best friend." Or, in the verse of sailor John Baltharpe:

101. Peter Linebaugh, "Socking: Tobacco Porters, the Hogshead, and Excise," MS (1978), 37, 53.

102. Karl Marx, *Capital: A Critique of Political Economy*, trans. Ben Fowkes (New York, 1977), 1021, 1026, 1019–1038.

> The Merchants Ships did with us Sail
> Bound towards *Legorne*, with merry Gale;
> But four days after we did want
> No wind but fair, one which was scant,
> And ne're unwelcome is to Seamen,
> For by that means he is a Freeman
> From toylsom Labour, and sad Care,
> Which winds contrary bring for fare.[103]

The sailing ship did not rely upon the continuous application of mechanical power for its progress; consequently, the labor process could not be infused with as much continuity, uniformity, regularity, order, or intensity as would characterize later industrial production. The seaman's workday remained "porous," marked by periods of intensity and inactivity that could not easily be filled with steady toil.[104] Labor's subordination to capital remained formal so long as a "merry Gale" made a seaman into a "Freeman."

Yet the experience of the early eighteenth-century seaman illuminates a vital moment in the transition to a free wage labor system.[105] Seamen occupied a pivotal spot in the movement from paternalistic forms of labor control to the contested negotiation of waged work. The completely contractual and waged nature of maritime work represented a capital-labor relation quite distinct from landlord-tenant, master-servant, or master-apprentice relationships. The sailor was both a free wage laborer located in a critical sector of the economy and a collective laborer located among an unprecedented number of men much like himself. Like others, including those waged laborers in agriculture and manufacture who had no alternative incomes from the land, the seaman found that he had only "a pair of good Hands, and a stout Heart to recommend him."[106] Such was the central reality of proletarian life.

The seaman's world of labor was a complex blend of cooperation and confrontation. Within this world, he devised many tactics to break the formal control of capital and to assert his own ends against

---

103. Barlow, *Journal*, ed. Lubbock, 243; John Baltharpe, *The Straights Voyage; or, St. Davids Poem*, ed. J. S. Bromley (Oxford, 1959 [orig. publ. London, 1671]), 38.

104. Marx, *Capital*, trans. Fowkes, 465; Christian Palloix, "The Labour Process: From Fordism to Neo-Fordism," in *Labour Process*, 149.

105. E. P. Thompson, "Patrician Society, Plebeian Culture," *Jour. Soc. Hist.*, VII (1973–1974), 383, 384.

106. Slush, *Navy Royal*, 11. See Malcolmson, *Life and Labour*, 136–159; Rule, *Experience of Labour*, 194–216; and Rediker, *Between the Devil and the Deep Blue Sea*, conclusion.

those mandated from above: he resorted to preemptive strikes, work stoppages, mutinies, and piracies. But his greatest source of power, at least in the early eighteenth century, was his mobility, and desertion was a crucial part of the self-activity of maritime working people. As Barnaby Slush said, early eighteenth-century seamen "will not bellow forth their complaints, like a Mob of Spittle-Fields Weavers, they e'en shrug up their loaded shoulders, and suppress their groans, but yet with an unchangeable Resolution of deserting at the first opportunity."[107] Just as the merchant financed the aggregation of labor for the sake of productivity and the accumulation of capital, seamen, through desertion, asserted their power to disaggregate that labor, to disrupt that productivity and accumulation, and to contest the course of capitalist development.[108]

In the end, we see that the abstract themes with which we began—the labor process, the creation of the free and collective worker, and the concentration of capital and the socialization of labor—were, for the seaman, concretely and densely interrelated. As seamen confronted their lot as collective laborers within the sprawling and thriving capitalist economy of the North Atlantic, they began to see their responsibilities to each other and to see the wisdom of the advice given to Jack Cremer by some Brother Tars: "It is not going voages abroad that makes a Man, but makes Slaves, if we have no Sociaty."[109] Jack Tar and his brothers thus began to discover in the eighteenth century the necessary relationships of collectivism, resistance, and freedom, an early set of lessons that would be studied by working people in the nineteenth century as well as in our own.

107. Slush, *Navy Royal*, 63.
108. See the excellent article by James O'Connor, "Productive and Unproductive Labor," *Politics and Society*, V (1975), 297–336.
109. Cremer, *Ramblin' Jack*, ed. Bellamy, 211.

Index

Notes on Contributors

LOIS GREEN CARR is Historian at Historic St. Mary's City and the author (with David W. Jordan) of *Maryland's Revolution of Government, 1689–1692*.

PAUL G. E. CLEMENS is Associate Professor of History and Vice-Chairperson for Graduate Education at Rutgers University–New Brunswick and the author of *The Atlantic Economy and Colonial Maryland's Eastern Shore: From Tobacco to Grain*.

STEPHEN INNES is Associate Professor of History at the University of Virginia and the author of *Labor in a New Land: Economy and Society in Seventeenth-Century Springfield*.

PHILIP D. MORGAN is Associate Professor of History at Florida State University and the author of *Slave Counterpoint: Black Culture in the Eighteenth-Century Lowcountry and Chesapeake* (forthcoming).

MARCUS REDIKER is Associate Professor of History at Georgetown University and the author of *Between the Devil and the Deep Blue Sea: Merchant Seamen, Pirates, and the Anglo-American Maritime World, 1700–1750*.

LUCY SIMLER is Associate Director of the Center for Early Modern History at the University of Minnesota and is completing a book on the transformation of the rural economy of Pennsylvania from 1700 to 1820.

BILLY G. SMITH is Associate Professor of History at Montana State University and the author of *Blacks Who Stole Themselves: Advertisements for Runaways in the Pennsylvania Gazette, 1728–1790* (forthcoming).

LAUREL THATCHER ULRICH is Associate Professor of History at the University of New Hampshire and the author of *Good Wives: Image and Reality in the Lives of Women in Northern New England, 1650–1750*.

DANIEL VICKERS is Associate Professor of History at the Memorial University of Newfoundland and is completing a book on farming and fishing in Essex County, Massachusetts, from 1630 to 1850.

LORENA S. WALSH is Research Fellow at The Colonial Williamsburg Foundation and the author of *"To Labour for Profit": Plantation Management in the Chesapeake, 1620–1820* (forthcoming).